Probably More Than You Want to Know About the Fishes of the Pacific Coast

by MILTON LOVE

REALLY **BIG**

PRESS

SANTA BARBARA, CA

To Shoshanna, Elan and Larry

*And to James Madison and Thomas Jefferson -
Thanks for the First Amendment, guys*

*And, let us not forget Charles Solomon, ace book reviewer of the
Los Angeles Times, who absolutely despised the humor in the
first edition. Get a life, Chuck.*

*And to Jim Henson. Why is Jim Henson dead and
Saddam Hussein still alive?*

And to Berke Breathed

And to Jane

OTHER BOOKS BY MILTON LOVE
Everyman's Guide to Ecological Living (with G. M. Cailliet and P. Y. Setzer)
Readings in Ichthyology (with G. M. Cailliet)
Fishes: A Field and Laboratory Manual on Their Structure, Identification, and Natural History (with G. M. Cailliet and A. W. Ebeling)

BOOKS MILTON LOVE WISHES HE HAD WRITTEN
The Way of Lao Tzu, by Lao Tzu
Dirk Gently's Holistic Detective Agency, by Douglas Adams
The Princess Bride, by William Goldman
Ender's Game, by Orson Scott Card

BOOKS MILTON LOVE IS GLAD HE DID NOT WRITE
Materialism and Empiro-Criticism, by Vladimir Lenin
The Monuments of Mars, by Richard Hoagland
The Users, by Joyce Haber
Daisy Miller, by Henry James

BOOKS MILTON LOVE WOULD LIKE TO WRITE IN THE FUTURE
The Big Book of Dental Tartar
The Mississippi Chain Gang Diet
Making Friends Through Intimidation
Mucous in the Morning: Everyone's Guide to Slug Raising

MILTON LOVE'S FAVORITE MAXIM
"*We are born. We eat sweet potatoes. We die.*" Attributed to
New Guinean Highlanders

MILTON LOVE'S SECOND FAVORITE MAXIM
"*Once you have their money, you never give it back.*" First Rule of Ferengi Acquisition

PROBABLY MORE THAN YOU WANT TO KNOW
ABOUT THE FISHES OF THE PACIFIC COAST
Copyright 1996

All rights reserved.

Published by Really Big Press, PO Box 60123
Santa Barbara, California 93160

Cover design and interior layout: Cyndi Burt
Front cover photos: Richard Herrmann, Marc Chamberlain
Printed and bound by McNaughton and Gunn Inc.
Library of Congress Catalog Card Number 91-090108

ISBN 0-9628725-5-5

CONTENTS

PREFACE TO THE FIRST EDITION

There is no preface.

PREFACE TO THE SECOND EDITION

There still is no preface.

INTRODUCTION
TO THE FIRST EDITION

I'm going to keep this short.

I hate introductions. They are usually pretty self-serving and, besides, nobody reads them.

I wrote this book for two reasons. First, I want to help you snow your friends with how much you know about the fishes of the Pacific Coast.

Second, I want to make big, big bucks.

INTRODUCTION TO THE
SECOND EDITION

Ditto.

ACKNOWLEDGMENTS

To the people who helped out on this book: Shane Anderson, Pat Bixler, Andy Brooks, Greg Cailliet, Molly Cummings, Al Ebeling, Tina Wyllie Echeverria, William Eschmeyer, Craig Fusaro, Jim Hardwick, Bruce Leaman, Shoshanna Love, Jeffrey Marliave, Richard Martin, Terry Maas, Mike Moser, Ken Nealson, Tory O'Connell, John O'Sullivan, John Richards, Brian Sak, Donna Schroeder, Sue Smith, Rocky Strong, Ramona Swenson, Mark Tognazzini, Patty Wolf and Mary Yoklavich - Thanks a heap, people. Particular thanks go to Elan Love, who thought up some of the best bits.

Paul Nakatsuka checked the first edition, made some solid suggestions, and copy edited the new one.

Most of the fish illustrations in this book were appropriated (totally legally, if not totally ethically) from the first really good field guide to California fishes, Guide to the Coastal Marine Fishes of California, by D. J. Miller and R. N. Lea, available (rather improbably I think) from Publications, Division of Agricultural Sciences, University of California, 6701 San Pablo Ave, Oakland, CA, 94608. These illustrations were prepared by Dan Miller, one of the best fish biologists Fish and Game ever had. The anglerfish drawing comes to us through the courtesy of Bruce Stewart and the elegant drawings of the scalloped hammerhead, Puget Sound rockfish and yellowfin sole were created by the inspired Lynn McMaster.

FISH PARTS

Unfortunately, many of you do not know the names of various parts of fishes. I blame this on the deplorable state of the American educational system, which continues to concentrate on reading and mathematics and refuses to insist that every child under the age of 8 know the difference between pelvic and pectoral fins. To bring you up to speed (so that you will be able to enjoy this book to the fullest possible extent), below you will find a drawing of a typical spiny-rayed fish (in this case a rockfish, genus *Sebastes*) which identifies fins and various body parts. You are, of course, responsible for this material and you cannot read further until you have memorized every detail.

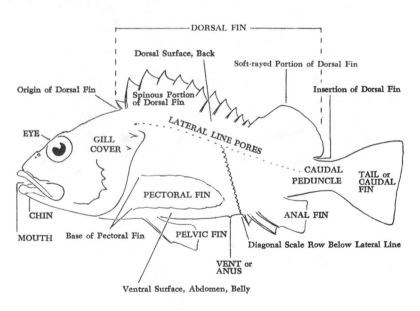

ASSORTED QUESTIONS YOU MIGHT WANT ANSWERED

How did you decide what fish species to include in this book?

That is a very good question and you should be very proud of yourself. In selecting fishes for this book, my goal was to cover those species which you are most likely to see when diving, fishing or hiding in dumpsters behind fish markets. I have also tried to give a nod to some sort of geographic balance and have included representative fishes from throughout most of the Pacific Coast of North America.

Why is my favorite fish not in this book?

Actually, considering the efforts I have gone to, this is a pretty ungrateful question. Here is a sad fact of life: I could not include every species of fish of the Pacific Coast in this work. I am not only the writer and editor, but also publisher of this book, and to include all 900+ species in this tome would have meant a book so large and so expensive that you would not have bought it.

Who is this book for?

It's for Seekers of Truth, Lovers of Wisdom and Those Who Wish to Be One with the Grand Design. It's for men who want more than wealth; it's for women who want more than fame; it's for children who want more than a secure future as middle managers at a mid-sized Ohio steel mill. It's for the girl you left behind, Mom's apple pie, Yankee Stadium on a July afternoon and sitting in front of the radio listening to Jack Benny, The Lone Ranger and I Was A Communist for the FBI.

Of course, if you are an illiterate vacuum-head with enough cash to make the purchase, that's okay too.

Why aren't all the fishes listed in the Table of Contents?

Oh, but you are a sly one, you are! You noticed that didn't you? It must be difficult keeping a secret around your house, what with all your constant snooping and prying. The reason I did not include a listing of all the fishes in the Table of Contents was that it would have eaten up about 4 pages and made for a long, really boring segment right at the beginning of the book. Remember, we aren't here (cosmically speaking, that is) to be bored. We are here to Sample Life's Pleasures to the Fullest, so go out there and boogie. If you want to find your favorite fish, look in the Index. That's what it is for.

What should I do if I have a question about fish?

What you need is a friendly, local marine biologist. Call me up or write me a letter. I am at the Marine Science Institute at UCSB or you can also write to Really Big Press, P. O. Box 60123, Santa Barbara, California, 93106.

What is a fish?

Don't laugh at this question; it isn't as easy as it sounds. "Fish" covers a wide variety of animals, many of which have little in common with each other. Here, try this. Try to think of some characteristic that all fishes have in common. Go on, don't be afraid, no one is reading this. *Scales?* No, lots of fish are scaleless. *Fins?* How about eels. No fins. *Jaws?* Nope, hagfish and lampreys are jawless. *Okay, how about eyes?* Blind cave fish and hagfish don't have them. *Well, they all breathe in water.* Yes and no. All fish are capable of breathing underwater, but many are capable of breathing in the air and a few, such as the mudskipper, may drown if you keep them under water. *What about a well-developed sense of the absurd?* That is only found in fishes living near southern California or Big Sur.

Basically, fish are mostly water-dwelling vertebrates, most have lateral lines (for water motion detection), most breathe at least part time through gills, most are protected by scales and almost all have a simple, one-way heart.

Sorry, it's not easy, but hey, get this straight: biology is not for pencil-necked geeks.

How smart are fish?

Good question. Let's say you've got yourself, oh, 10,000 mice and you run them through all sorts of mouse exams. You put them in mazes, you give them little mouse IQ tests (complete with itsy-bitsy "Number 2 pencils"), you run them through the whole enchilada. And out of those 10,000 mice, you find the most stupid mouse, the one that can barely get out of its own way. That mouse, a mouse which probably still believes we can win a land war in Asia, that mouse is smarter than any fish that ever lived.

I know, I know, you are going to bring up "Old Mossback" or

"Old Snagglejaw" or "Old Duck Slurper," the "smartest durn" cat-fish, kelp bass, steelhead or guppy you've ever heard of. Well, you are wrong. A fish's brain (and we're talking about a really big fish) is not much bigger than a walnut and most of it is used for inter-preting sounds, smells, sights and tastes, not for thinking. What passes for smarts in "Old Squid Snarfer" is really a well-oiled set of instincts. They don't think; they just react in a way that impresses you.

Do fish sleep?

Some do. Along our coast a number of reef fishes, such as sheephead (*Semicossyphus pulcher*), senorita (*Oxyjulis californica*), rock wrasse (*Halichoeres semicinctus*) and blacksmith (*Chromis punc-tipinnis*), certainly appear to conk out for the night. You will find them buried in the sand or passed out in crevices and you can often approach and even pick them up. On the other hand, fishes which must swim continually in order to breathe, such as albacore (*Thunnus alalunga*), Pacific bonito (*Sarda chiliensis*) and yellowtail (*Seriola lalandi*), seem to partially shut down for a time. They keep moving, but they are not operating at peak performance.

There are relatively few nocturnal species; most of the fishes on the Pacific Coast are active during daylight hours. This is in sharp contrast with coral reef communities, where fish are divided into "shifts," some coming out in the light and some active during the dark. No one seems to know why so few fishes along our coast are active at night. Just a friendly warning. If you know the answer and have been keeping this information to yourself, you will sure-ly come back as a hagfish in your next life.

How long do fish live?

Well, it depends on the species. Off of our coast, a few species (such as the bluebanded goby, *Lythrypnus dalli*) live only about one year. Most of the species live from 5 to maybe 20 years, with a few living considerably longer. At the extreme (according to very hot fisheries biologist Bruce Leaman), rougheye rockfish (*Sebastes aleu-tianus*) may live as long as 148 years. I think this last fact deserves a moment's pondering. Fish this old were alive when Lincoln was President, when the Wright brothers were in diapers and when the United States could take over Third World countries without any sense of guilt whatsoever. Fish this old were alive before digital watches, Barbie Dolls, even before printed toilet tissue (I bet you thought that was invented by the Romans). It gives me sort of a queasy sensation to think that 148-year-old fish are being caught, filleted and sold as "Sea Burgers" at Cowboy Slim's fast food restau-rants (the ones where you drive through and talk into the rear end of a buffalo).

What is that strip of red muscle along the sides of the albacore I caught? Is the Federal Government withholding this information as part of the massive conspiracy involving the Trilateral Commission, The Men in Black, The Roswell Incident and putting fluoride in our water supply?

The level of your paranoia is probably the best proof I know that Americans have too much leisure time.

Albacore and many other pelagic (open water) fishes must swim continuously in order to breathe; they can't pump water over their gills, as do such fishes as rockfishes, basses and flatfishes. Basically, they swim with their mouths open, forcing water over the gills. If you hold an albacore motionless under water it will drown. Most pelagic animals have a strip of bright red muscle along their flanks. This muscle is used for continuous swimming. It is loaded with blood vessels, bringing oxygen-carrying molecules to active muscles. The muscles are also kept warm (warm muscles work more efficiently) through an ingenious heat exchange system. In general, among fishes and birds, muscles are red if they are used often. They are white if only used occasionally.

Remember that Thanksgiving in 1958? Sure you do it was the one that your Uncle Zolton and his wife, Aunt Costanza, attended. You remember, as the Masked Kidney Smashers, they were the only male-female tag team on the Ohio-Indiana wrestling circuit in the the late 1950s. They arrived just before dinner, and because they had a match later that evening, they came dressed in their badly-stressed spandex tights and their blood-red kidney masks. And remember how, despite your mom's look of horror, they insisted on demonstrating their famous "Flying Renal Failure" throw, right there in the living room? There was that heart-rending screech of wood pushed beyond its limits, as Uncle Zolton slammed through the floor and fell onto dear Mr. Spalzoni's oak credenza, badly chipping the finish.

So, after the damage was assessed and Mr. Spalzoni was given several fingers of your father's best bourbon, dinner was served. Right away, there was that annual fight over who got the white meat and who ended up with the dark portions. As usual, the first ones to the buffet line sucked up the white, which in practice meant that 82-year-old Great Cousin Elmo and your 4-year-old sister were forced to eat the dark stuff. And while your sister was pretty philosophical about it all, Cousin Elmo was definitely miffed. He spent much of the next 45 minutes, well into the apple, pumpkin and sweet potato pies, either sulking or dwelling on Harold Stassen's chances of grabbing the Republican nomination in 1960.

The dark meat of the turkey, mostly on the legs and wings, is red muscle; the light meat is white muscle.

Why do fish have those unununderstandable scientific names? Is it some sort of Communist plot to undermine our national morale?
    Yes.

Gee, really?
    Okay, no. Here's the real scoop.
    Why do we use scientific names? Well, a major reason is to reduce the confusion that might occur when people worldwide try to discuss an organism. As an example, let us say there is a fish that is green-finned, big-toothed and only eats lobsters. The good citizens of Eastern Zolonia call this fish a "Zaxjoflob," in honor of Latislov Zaxjoflob, the inventor of the national dish of Eastern Zolonia, coal-smoked turkey-lip sausages. Now, the people in neighboring Upper Uremia hate turkey-lip sausages and they don't call the fish a "Zaxjoflob." To them it is a Ulolopumatoklot, which roughly translates to "green-finned fish which can bite you where the sun don't shine if you turn your back on it." Lastly, halfway around the world, in Wretched Harbor, New Hampshire, the locals refer to it as the "red–headed lobster–eater", the name given to it by a fisherman who was, unfortunately, color blind. Imagine the confusion that might occur if scientists, fish buyers or certified public accountants from these various areas tried to communicate with each other about this fish. To help cut down on this confusion, all organisms are given scientific names (usually in Latin or Greek) that by general agreement will be used worldwide. The organisms may still have many common (local) names, but at least a person can fall back on the scientific ones in order to avoid misunderstandings.
    This system was first formalized and followed by Karl von Linne, an 18th Century Swedish botanist. In his research, old Karl called himself Carolus Linnaeus; maybe he thought women would really go for a guy with a Latin name. Linnaeus selected Latin and Greek for several reasons. First, they were languages that were understood by virtually all learned persons of his day, regardless of their mother tongues. Second, Latin in particular was (and is) a dead language and hence did not change. In a really remarkable undertaking, Linnaeus attempted to categorize and describe most of the species of organisms on Earth, falling only several million short. Nevertheless, he really did make a good stab at it, reminding us what could be done when there was no Nintendo and when your name scared women off and you couldn't get dates.

Are there fishes out there with my number?
    I beg your pardon?

You know, what fishes off our coast can harm me?
   Physically or emotionally?

Physically.
   Actually, compared to the animals on your average coral reef, few of the fishes along the Pacific Coast are in any way harmful to humans. Of course, there are a few fishes you should not eat, including the flesh of the swell shark (*Cephaloscyllium ventriosum*), which is reputed to be toxic, and the eggs of both the cabezon (*Scorpaenichthys marmoratus*) and the spotted ratfish (*Hydrolagus colliei*) which definitely are poisonous.
   A number of our fishes carry venomous sharp parts. The stings of stingrays, the spine on the back of the spotted ratfish, the cheek spines on plainfin (*Porichthys notatus*) and specklefin midshipmen (*P. myriaster*), the spine above the pectoral fin on smooth stargazers (*Kathetostoma averruncus*), and sharp spines on the dorsal, anal and pelvic fins of the California scorpionfish (*Scorpaena guttata*) and various rockfishes (*Sebastes* spp.), are all more or less venomous. However, with the exception of 2 fatalities (which I believe were caused by California scorpionfish), I know of no deaths from any of these fishes. In all of these species, the poison is produced in glands at the base of, inside or along the sharp structures. Spiny dogfish have sharp spines in front of their dorsal fins which can give painful, but not envenomed, wounds.
   There are also a few fish around that can eat you. Topping that hit list is, of course, the white shark (*Carcharodon carcharias*), which is common in our range and regularly attempts to snack on divers, surfers, etc. Bonito sharks (*Isurus oxyrinchus*) have also attacked humans, although not along our coast. Blue sharks are another abundant shark off our shore which have been implicated in attacks on humans and are definitely fish to be avoided. However, at least some of these attacks have occurred when the sharks were being intentionally driven into a frenzy by blood or fish poured into the water. My own feeling is that if you insist on playing marbles on a freeway during rush hour, don't be surprised if a milk truck lays tread marks down your back. In addition, a number of sharks which are very rare in our area (they are found here only during warm water periods), such as hammerhead sharks (*Sphyrna* spp.), narrowtooth sharks (*Carcharhinus brachyurus*), oceanic whitetip sharks (*C. longimanus*), dusky sharks (*C. obscurus*) and tiger sharks (*Galeocerdo cuvier*) have attacked humans in other parts of the world.
   A number of other fishes, including California morays (*Gymnothorax mordax*), Pacific angel sharks (*Squatina californica*), California halibut (*Paralichthys californicus*) and California barracu-

da (*Sphyraena argentea*) have sharp teeth and will bite you if they are cornered, harassed, speared or taken out of the water with a hook in their mouths or a net around them. However, ounce for ounce, the most ferocious fish in our area is the sarcastic fringehead (*Neoclinus blanchardi*). This is a little reef fish which lives in crevices and beer bottles and is nearly all head, mouth and teeth. This fish, which on a good day reaches all of 1 foot, will snap at anything (divers included) and if boated will try to bite whatever is near. If sarcastic fringeheads grew to 3 feet long, no one would go in the water.

Probably the hippest way to be injured by a local fish is to be shocked by a Pacific electric ray (*Torpedo californica*), whose disc-shaped head can give you a pretty good wallop.

What is El Niño and is it really responsible for most of the world's ills?

Times change. Twenty years ago, if you had stood on a stool at your local watering hole and yelled "El Niño," you would have been greeted with blank stares, stony silence and the bartender would have asked you to leave. Today, if you yell "El Niño," the bar crowd will scream and duck for cover, and the bartender will ask you to leave.

The reason for this change of heart is shown in Plates 38 and 39. These are two images of the southern California Bight, taken two years apart by the NOAA-7 satellite. This satellite makes a number of passes over this area every day and one of its functions is to determine sea surface temperature. While doing research on fishes of this area, I had the Scripps Institution of Oceanography-Satellite Oceanography Facility pick out images from a non-El Niño and an El Niño year. To highlight water temperature, the Facility made each degree a different color: the reds are hottest and blue or grays are coldest. The top image was taken on July 19, 1982 and shows a "typical" summer day. There is a pool of warm water between about Los Angeles and San Diego, while further north and out to sea the water is cooler. The following year saw the largest El Niño in this century, as a massive pool of warm, equatorial water made its way north; this is shown in the bottom image. You can see that the entire area is immersed in warm water, some of it hotter than the hottest conditions of the previous year.

El Niño is a tongue of warm water that flows north and south from the equatorial Pacific, displacing usual currents. Off the Pacific Coast of North America, El Niños are not particularly rare events; in the recent past we have had them at least in 1926, 1931, 1941, 1957–58, 1972–73, 1976, 1982–83, 1988 and 1992. However, they do vary in size and duration and hence in their effects, and El Niño's effect on fish species in our waters can be dramatic. Numerous warm water or even tropical fishes (e.g.,

25

yellowfin tuna, dolphinfish, skipjack, seahorses, triggerfishes) cruise up the line and invade southern California waters from Baja California. Further north, fishes typical of southern California (such as white seabass, California barracuda or Pacific bonito) become common. For example, during the 1982–83 El Niño, many California halibut appear to have migrated north from southern California to central and northern California. By the same token, fishes that prefer cold water either go deeper or travel north (e. g., chinook and coho salmon catches from California to Washington were way down during this same period). Some species, such as the albacore, may avoid the area altogether. While adult and juvenile fishes may swim north with the warm current, fish larvae are also swept along, leading to small expatriate populations far north of their usual ranges. For instance, during the 1957–58 El Niño, sheephead larvae were carried into Monterey Bay (central California). The waters of the Bay are usually too cool for the larvae of this species, but some managed to survive that year, leading to a small group of similar-sized fish which lived for years in the Bay. An El Niño can also harm fishes. In 1983, zooplankton became less abundant, and some zooplankton eaters (such as Pacific herring, northern anchovy and yellowtail rockfish) suffered; perhaps they grew more slowly than normal or produced fewer eggs.

And what about all the other horror stories attached to El Niños?
  Well, remember that these are large scale, very complex processes, which involve a big chunk of the Pacific Ocean. There is evidence that they often drastically increase coastal rainfall, raise sea levels and help produce stronger storms. Off Ecuador and Peru, recent El Niños have produced red tides (causing mass die-offs of fish), have driven coastal fish populations away (causing seabirds to starve) and have killed off algae (leading to the starvation of marine iguanas). However, during the 1983 El Niño, this poor event was blamed for just about everything, and it seems excessive to blame El Niños for increased divorce rates in Malawi, the poor showing of the Albanian National Lawn Bowling Team or the death of Elvis Presley (assuming he is really dead).

How do fish reproduce?
  That's rather an impertinent question, don't you think?

Well...I hadn't really given it much thought.
  Obviously.

I'm, I'm terribly sorry. I was just curious...
  Sorry, oh, of course you're sorry. But that doesn't cut it; not for

one second. Look, you just can't go about poking your nose into everyone's business without a fairtheewell. I mean, there has to be at least some sense of propriety, some sense of decorum in this book. After all, we have to think of the sensibilities of our readers.

But this is America. Sex always increases sales.
Hmmm. Now that you mention it, what readers' sensibilities?
I'm not going to flog this subject. It is huge and there are positively exhaustive treatises on the subject. However, because I use the terms in the text, I will briefly discuss the three modes of reproduction that seem to cover fishes: oviparity, ovoviviparity and viviparity. Basically, oviparous fishes either emit their eggs unfertilized (to be fertilized in the water) or, if they have internal fertilization, the females retain them for only a short period. Now, some fishes retain their eggs for longer and longer periods and somewhere up this continuum are the ovoviviparous fishes. Ovoviviparous females retain their eggs for a while, at least long enough for the young to develop and be more or less able to fend for themselves. Normally, ovoviviparity means that while in the uterus, the young live off their yolk; they receive no nourishment from mom. However, in some sharks, the term has been broadened to mean sharks that bear live young, may or may not provide some nourishment to the embryos, but have no placental connection to them. And this, as day follows night, pimples follow puberty and Jung follows Freud (at least in his dreams), brings us to viviparity. Viviparous females have internal fertilization and the embryos have some sort of placental connection to the uterine walls; there is some sort of nutrient transport from mom to the kids.

So, what's your favorite fish reproduction story?
As defined by?

Any definition you want.
How about the one I love so much, I got a tattoo honoring it?

Sure.
The most scrumptious story of reproduction among fishes was recounted by Ted Pietsch (Copeia, 1976, p. 781-793) in his paper dealing with deepsea anglerfishes. These are small, big-toothed fishes, often found thousands of feet down. It is a story of travail and triumph, of the loss of innocence, of one male's search for the female of his dreams. And mainly it is the story of a bunch of guys, in the families Ceratiidae, Linophrynidae and perhaps Neoceratiidae, who dearly want to become sexual parasites. What seems to occur is that, when males of these families metamorphose from larvae to

juveniles, they begin to sniff the water, searching for a scent trail laid down by the female. When the male finds a female, he bites her, right near the anus — and never lets go. In some species, the female's circulatory system unites with the male's, and the male becomes little more than a sac of sperm. Males will not mature until they are attached to the female, and females do not produce fertilizable eggs until they sense the male's presence.

As you can imagine, all of this has quite touched me and I was moved to pen the following:

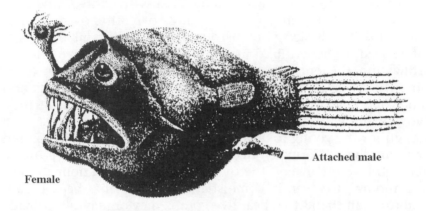

Attached male

Female

WHEN A FELLOW NEEDS A FRIEND

The anglers are fish quite rapacious
With mouths both toothed and capacious
But of far more import
Is the way they disport
For we speak now of matters salacious.

They live in deep waters - *sans* light
Their numbers are really quite slight
Though finding a mate's
In the hands of the Fates
Still the prospects would not seem too bright.

When two meet there's no hesitating -
To increase the chances of mating
Ignoring her flaws
He clamps down his jaws
Ever wedded without even dating.

In quest of the opposite sex
The male angler has reason to vex
In seeking another
He might find his mother
Thus branding him Oedifish Rex.

I don't dive. In fact, I have such an unreasoning fear of water, it's been over 6 years since I bathed.
And I thought a vulture had expired behind the davenport.

And yet, and yet, I love fishes. Where can I see lots of them without actually getting wet?
Do you want to see dead or living fishes?

Your choice.
   Well, let's start with living. The following (listed from south to north) are some of the very nice aquariums on the Pacific Coast: Scripps Institution of Oceanography Aquarium, La Jolla, CA; Cabrillo Beach Museum, San Pedro, CA; Monterey Bay Aquarium, Monterey, CA; Steinhart Aquarium, Golden Gate Park, San Francisco, CA; Humboldt State University Aquarium, Arcata, CA; Oregon Coast Aquarium, Newport, OR; Oregon State University Marine Science Center, Newport, OR; Seattle Aquarium, Seattle, WA; Point Defiance Zoo, Tacoma, WA; Vancouver Aquarium, Vancouver, British Columbia. Hands down, the Monterey Bay Aquarium is the best of the bunch, but the others are quite pleasant.
   And now to the not-alive. Actually, fish markets are some of the most wonderful places to see fishes. Some of them have an absolutely awesome selection of scaly wonders. However, if you want to experience this transcendent realm, forget about going to supermarkets. Fishes in these charnel houses have the dispirited and angst-ridden demeanor of Raskolnikov just before confessing to murder in *Crime and Punishment*. (Actually, even Sonya looked pretty peaked at that point. "There was an expression of pain and exhaustion on her face, something akin to despair." I've seen that look on past-their-prime white croakers at several markets).
   No, what you need is a market that fairly worships at the altar of pisces; an establishment that has sunk it's psychic tendrils deep into the Cosmic Piscine. You need a place where fish fillets and steaks are only for the faint of heart, where the true believer can come and commune with the fish, the whole fish and nothing but the fish.
   Just for the occasion, I've surveyed some markets and here, as of 1995, are some real nice ones. This is not an exhaustive study and it is open to revision. If you know of a very spiff one, drop me a line. Note that markets do change owners, managers and philosophies and what is gold today may be peat moss tomorrow.
   Dragon Market, 1145 Stockton St., San Francisco, CA:
A jewel in the scepter piscatorial. It's not much bigger than your living room, but, oh what a nice selection of fish are piled on ice (there are also several tanks of live ones). And they look so good, too. On my last visit, there was not a dud in the lot. On that typi-

cal summer day, there were 8 species of rockfish, along with white croaker, tilapia, butterfish, lingcod, catfish, smelt, jackmackerel, carp, farmed striped bass, various flatfishes and a few other odds and ends. The fish here fairly sing to you, "It's okay, we love being dead!"

Seafood Center, 831 Clement St., San Francisco, CA:
The Seafood Center is a little more upscale and a little larger than the Dragon Market, but it still has the right ethos. During my visit, along with a nice selection of local species, there were a number of imported ones, including red snapper, milkfish and pompano. Live fish are big here, and these included rockfishes, tilapia, carp, catfish and some husky sturgeon.

Seafood City, 1420 E. Plaza Blvd., National City, CA:
I liked the selection in this one (28 species), one of the largest I saw. On the other hand, some of the fishes looked like they had not been treated too well. Seafood City had a fairly nice bunch of local (southern California) species (such as Pacific barracuda, Pacific bonito, Pacific mackerel, blackgill rockfish, white croaker, California scorpionfish), farmed ones (tilapia, catfish, carp) and an extensive number of imports, including red snapper, fusiliers, several species of groupers and jacks, sierra mackerel, and pompano.

Is every marine biologist as all-knowing as you?
No.

WHAT ABOUT
FISH TATTOOS?

America is going to hell in a hand basket and here is why. Our beautiful country is overrun with people claiming to be marine biologists. It seems that every yahoo who has ever eaten deep-fried monkfish feels that he/she can assume that mantle. So how can you, the befuddled public, separate the real marine biologists from those who are but egregious *poseurs*?

There is, of course, only one sure way.

Check for tattoos.

Really, true biologists will have a tattoo of their favorite organism somewhere on their bodies.

I got my first tattoo in May, 1994.

I decided to get one about a year before, while writing a grant proposal to do research on rockfishes. Sitting in my dreary University garret, the dank walls illuminated only by the cold light of my Mac SE/30, feeling not completely in control of my life, it suddenly struck me that it would be very cool indeed to get a tattoo of a rockfish. I had always loved rockfish; there were so many species, they were really quite spectacular and I had been doing research on them for over 20 years. Cow rockfish, *Sebastes levis*, were my favorites. They are big and spiny, and underwater they really do look sort of bovine, but even slower and more stupid. Yes, I thought, if I get this proposal funded I'm going to get a tattoo of a cow rockfish. I mean, I'm forty-six, what's my mother going to do about it?

Predictably, when I told my kids, they had somewhat mixed feelings. Fifteen-year-old Shoshanna thought it was a wonderful idea, while eleven-year-old Elan said that I could always gnaw my arm off if I ever changed my mind.

Just to make sure the proposal was funded, I decided to hold a little ceremony on the night before the granting agency made their selections. I tried the broad spectrum approach, attempting to appeal to the widest possible range of deities. That night I went to a crossroads at midnight, sat down and chanted, "Please, please, please, make them give me the money. Thank you". Just to be on the safe side, I was going to sacrifice a goat, but instead I purchased a take-out order of curried goat from a Santa Barbara restaurant and ate that while chanting. Admittedly, there was one moment when, with the chanting and goat-eating, I felt mildly foolish. But then I decided it was really Performance Art and if I played my cards right, I could get funding from the National Endowment for the Arts.

Well, I didn't get the grant, but I did decide to go ahead with the tattoo, anyway.

Okay, I had made the decision. Now there was just the minor detail of who was going to do the deed? I don't travel much in tattooing circles and I mentioned my quandary to my friend, Mary. As luck would have it, she knew a graduate student at Moss Landing Marine Laboratory whom, she said, had "an entire kelp bed tattooed on his back". Ooh, that sounded good to me. So I checked with Pat, the student, and he said that the man for the job was James McDermott in Santa Cruz.

I called James up and made an appointment for a consultation. For emotional support, I brought my friends Jane and Mary with me. At the time, James had his shop in the back of a smoke-filled establishment that specialized in heavy metal records, along with comic books and tee shirts that would have made Henry Miller stand up, take notice and order three of each. I noticed a guy about 18 years old behind the counter, whom I believed at the time had a raw hot dog hanging from one ear. "That wasn't a hot dog," Jane said later. "That was his earlobe." Apparently, the gentleman had hung a weight from the lobe, and with time it had reached to his shoulder. I made a mental note to explore that possibility another time.

I loved that place. And James McDermott was all I could have asked for. Cool, calm and collected, with manners befitting a brain surgeon, he was very laid back and had the right answers for everything. I would have followed him into battle.

"I don't want to get AIDS." "The needles are sterilized when I buy them and I only use them once ."

"How do you know what to draw?" "You and I will sit down and make a drawing together. When you are satisfied, I'll reduce it on a copier to the size you want. Then I'll ink it, place it on your skin and use that as a template."

"Should it be in color?" "Blacks and grays give a more three dimensional effect."

"Well, what about...pain?" "If we do it on a fleshy part, like your upper arm, it shouldn't hurt much. It's when I do it on bone, like around ankles, that it hurts. Take some Advil before you come in."

"How much will it cost?" "Oh, about $60."

Sold. I returned about two months later, more-or-less ready for the big event. There was only one really bad moment. I forgot to bring any photographs of a cow rockfish for James to use in his drawing. I had a line drawing, but I thought that wouldn't be enough. I had driven 300 miles for this, and I hated the thought of cancelling. But James overcame that. Mary and I stood by, offering advice as he took a two-dimensional figure and drew it in three dimensions. "No, the lower jaw is slightly longer than the upper one...Can you make the dorsal spines just a little longer...And it has dusky bars on the sides."

Well, actually there was one other bad moment. Just before James put needle to skin, as he was swabbing my upper arm with antiperspirant, he said, "You know, some people get light-headed just after I start. If you feel like you are going to pass out, let me know." "Ah, and why would people feel that way?" "Because their bodies start to secrete endorphins, the natural painkiller."

Yes indeed, I thought. Your body secretes endorphins when your kneecap has been bitten off by a rottweiler or when you slam your ear in a door. This is insane why am I doing this? If I want to be in pain, I could run as a Democrat in the next election. And what if I hate it? What if James has some sort of seizure right now and decides to ignore the template and tattoo the entire Vienna Boys Choir singing the best of Cole Porter? What if he actually tattoos all of the lyrics to *Another Op'nin, Another Show* on my shoulder? Well, actually, I've always kind of liked that one so maybe it wouldn't be that bad. And what if...

And it turned out really neat (see Plate 40). It didn't hurt; at most it felt like a mild sunburn. It looked reasonably accurate and most important, I felt like a real man. I suddenly realized that I could go into any biker bar, order a diet soda, roll up the sleeves of my polo shirt and flex my cow rockfish with the best of them. "Hey buddy, you want to be in the 'break a beer bottle on the fore-head' contest?" Sure, I have a tattoo of a cow rockfish!

Since that time, I've gotten another one, this of an anglerfish. Who knows, someday I may have an entire aquarium for company.

James is still in the business. At this writing, he's at the Staircase Tattoo Palace, 607 Front St., Santa Cruz, CA, (408) 425-7644.

THE FISHES

Hagfishes - Family Myxinidae

PACIFIC HAGFISH (*EPTATRETUS STOUTI*)

NAMES: Slime Eel.  *Eptatretus* is a combination of 2 Greek words, which translate to "7 apertures"; *stouti* honors Dr. A. B. Stout, a secretary of the California Academy of Sciences during the 19th Century.

IDENTIFYING CHARACTERS: Hey, let's face it, hagfish are the most disgusting creatures on earth (with the possible exception of junk bond salesmen and defense attorneys in one particular high profile case). These are blind, eel-shaped fish, with 10–14 round gill openings on each side of their bodies. They have no jaws; a rasp-like structure is thrust out of their permanently open mouths. Pacific hagfish come in a variety of appealing colors, especially brown and gray, and occasionally white or mottled. Probably the best way to tell if your fish is a hagfish is to look at the hand holding the fish. If it is completely covered with thick, ropy slime, that's all the proof you need. While Pacific hagfish may be confused with black hagfish (*Eptatretus deani*), the latter are purplish-black in color.

DISTRIBUTION AND BIOLOGY: Pacific hagfish are found from southeast Alaska to central Baja California, commonly from at least Vancouver Island southward. They live in a variety of habitats, including mud, sand and rock, probably preferring mud. From a submarine, I have seen them over, and in, almost every kind of habitat, lying coiled up on the bottom or with their heads sticking out of burrows or crevices. While they have been caught from 60–3,096 feet, they appear to be most abundant in perhaps 250–1,200 feet.

Hagfish are reported to reach 32 inches in length, but that one must have been a mutant; anything over 25 inches is a large fish. Remarkably little is known about this species' biology. Some males mature at 14 inches, some females at 12 inches. All males are mature by 18 inches, females by 20 inches. No one knows if there is a discrete spawning season or if spawning migrations occur. Females produce 15–30 eggs per spawning period. The eggs resemble little cocktail hot dogs, held together by strands. We don't know how long they live, how fast they grow or how old they are when first mature. These fish are not parasitic as was once thought. However, no one is sure what they do eat. They do burrow into fish which are hooked on set lines, caught in traps or tangled in gillnets. It is likely that they also feed on small invertebrates. Northern elephant seals and harbor seals eat them.

FISHERY: Pacific hagfish are only occasionally taken by sport anglers. There is a relatively new commercial fishery for them, with most of the fish going to Korea, where they are turned into eel skin wallets, etc. When the fishery began a few years back, a Gold Rush fever took hold in some ports and every boat that could float was out there trapping the little goopers. The fishery soon cooled off as fish buyers lowered their prices and currently a medium-sized fishery extends from British Columbia to California.

REMARKS: They are not called slime eels for nothing. Hagfish produce truly gargantuan amounts of slime. We are talking major league quantities here. Your average hagfish can take a bucket full of water and almost solidify it with slime in a few minutes. (I don't know about you, but that makes me proud to be an American.) And this is quality slime too; entirely different from the sad, gooey stuff other fishes produce. It has millions of microscopic threads running through it, giving it a cohesion lacking in other slimes. There is research going on to see whether these threads can be used in microsurgery (for instance in eye operations), to suture openings. While the function of this slime is unclear, it may be used in defense.

Here's a really juicy quote from the 1896 masterpiece by Jordan and Evermann, *The Fishes of North and Middle America*: "The hagfish fastens itself usually on the gills or isthmus of large fishes, sometimes on the eyes, whence it works its way very rapidly into the inside of the body. It then devours all the flesh of the body without breaking the skin, so that the fish is left a living hulk of head, skin, and bones."

I love that.

Lampreys - Family Petromyzontidae

PACIFIC LAMPREY (LAMPETRA TRIDENTATA)

NAMES: Sea Lamprey, Yafutsuyatsume (Japanese), *Lampetra* 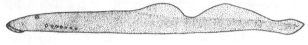 is a combination of 2 Latin words meaning "stone sucker," which probably refers to the lamprey's habit of holding onto rocks while it migrates upstream and/or its ability to move around rocks during nest building by sucking onto them; *tridentata* is Latin for "3 toothed" because the fish has a tooth with 3 points at the top of its mouth.

IDENTIFYING CHARACTERS: Pacific lampreys are eel-shaped fish, with a disc-shaped suckerlike mouth and 7 round gill openings. They usually have brown to almost black backs and pale bellies.

DISTRIBUTION AND BIOLOGY: Pacific lampreys are anadromous fish, born in rivers and streams, living their adult lives in the ocean, then returning to their birth waters to spawn. Pacifics have been taken from Hokkaido, Japan to the Bering Sea and southward to off north-central Baja California, to depths of at least 1,050 feet. They are difficult to catch in the ocean and their true abundance there can only be guessed. Particularly in the ocean, their presence is often inferred from the typically disc-shaped scars and depressed expressions on fishes that have served as temporary hosts. Lampreys spawn in streams and rivers from Alaska to about the Ventura River system in southern California. In the past, spawning occurred at least as far south as the Los Angeles River drainage (such as the Santa Ana River). Since there is essentially no water in this river (one California politician proposed converting the L.A. River to a freeway), it is not surprising that lampreys (which have a distinct preference for water) are locally extinct. Today, it is likely that central California is the furthest south these fish spawn in significant numbers.

Pacific lampreys reach 2.5 feet. As larvae, they may spend as much as 5 years in their birth streams (growing to about 4 inches), and may live another 7 years beyond that (averaging 5 years), spending perhaps 3.5 years at sea. In British Columbia, mature fish (7+ inches) enter streams from April–June, spawning from April–July of the following year. Considering how poorly these fish swim and the current speed in a typical stream, it is amazing they get to where they want to go. Apparently most of the upstream migrations require that the fish make short bursts upsteam, then suck onto rocks with their mouths while they rest and remind themselves that sex is worth it. Pacific lampreys usually spawn in shallow parts of streams (very occasionally in lakes),

37

forming bowl-shaped nests (8.5 inches wide, 2–4 inches deep) in gravel and coarse sand. During mating, a male attaches its mouth to the female's head, twists tightly around her and both undulate violently. (If this description continues much longer, I may have to take a cold shower.) While it has been long supposed that all Pacific lampreys die after spawning, a recent study suggests that some survive to spawn again. Females produce between about 10,000–106,000 eggs and the eggs hatch in 24 weeks. The peppy little larvae move downstream and bury themselves in mud at the bottom of pools. They begin to metamorphose in July and migrate downstream to the ocean, generally entering saltwater from December–June at about 5 inches long. Once at sea, Pacific lampreys rapidly head for deeper water (usually more than 70 feet), down to at least 1,800 feet. Larval fish are not parasitic; they eat diatoms and the like by filtering water through their throats. Juveniles and adults prey on a wide variety of fishes, including salmon, pollock, rockfishes and various flatfishes. They usually glom their jawless mouths in the region just behind the pectoral fin or onto the underside of their prey. In one study, salmon were attacked substantially more often on their right side. Despite the fact that Pacific lampreys suck out blood and muscle from their hosts, many hosts probably survive. Some fish have 3 or 4 disc marks on their bodies, so a single attack need not be fatal. In turn, lampreys are fed on by various fishes as well as marine mammals (i.e., Steller sea lions, northern fur seals, harbor seals, minks, sperm and fin whales).

FISHERY: Even though lampreys are a great delicacy in Europe, there is only a small commercial fishery for them in the North Pacific. Most of the fish are caught by Native Americans in subsistence fisheries.

REMARKS: Recent research indicates that lampreys, like sharks and rays, detect electric fields.

Cow Sharks - Family Hexanchidae

SIXGILL SHARK (HEXANCHUS GRISEUS)

NAMES: Blunt-nose Sixgill Shark, Mud Shark, Requin Griset (French). *Hexanchus* is a combination of 2 Greek words meaning "six bends," referring to the six gill slits; *griseus* is Latin for "gray".

IDENTIFYING CHARACTERS: We don't have to make a big production about this. If it's got six gill slits on each side of the head, you're in business. Most sixgills are brown or blackish-gray on their backs

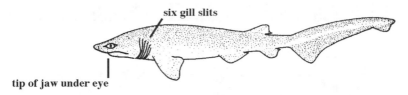

six gill slits

tip of jaw under eye

and white underneath, and they only have one dorsal fin (most other Pacific Coast sharks have two dorsal fins, dontcha know).

DISTRIBUTION AND BIOLOGY: Sixgills are found worldwide in temperate oceans. On the Pacific Coast, you find them from the Aleutian Islands to Bahia Todos Santos, northern Baja California. Adults have been taken down to at least 6,188 feet. Immature, small ones occur in shallow water; the bigger ones stay deeper. Sixgills are found both near the bottom and in the water column.

Richard Martin, of ReefQuest Expeditions in British Columbia, has studied these phlegmatic beauties and much of the following information comes from him. He notes there are two main sixgill concentrations in B. C., one around Tyler Rock, in Barkeley Sound; the other around Hornby Island (also the home of Wayne Ngan, a most excellent ceramicist - stop by and see his exquisite garden), off the east coast of Vancouver Island. In these waters, sixgills move into the shallows (typically 60-90 feet but as shallow as 10) in the summer, retreating into more than 300 feet in late fall. At least some individuals return to the same spots year after year. The animals are also vertical migrators, moving up-slope with dusk and downwards at dawn.

They get big, to 15.5 feet. Males mature at around 11 feet, females at 14 feet. Females are ovoviparous and produce 22-108 young ones. They are about 2 feet at birth. Off British Columbia, pupping probably occurs in shallow waters in the summer. Worldwide, sixgills eat a wide variety of prey, including sharks, herring, cod, hake, flounders and, amazingly enough, dolphinfish and various billfishes. Various invertebrates (squids, crabs, etc.) have also shown up, as well as seals. Off British Columbia, Richard reports they eat spiny dogfish, hagfish, lingcod, cabezon and perhaps octopi. He also notes that he saw one eat a lingcod. It came from deeper water up a rock face, then came down vertically on the ling's back, pinning it to the bottom. The shark then pivoted, turning the prey so that it was head-first, and swallowed it.

FISHERY: There is no directed fishery off the Pacific Coast. Worldwide, they are taken for food, fishmeal and oil.

REMARKS: Aboard the research submarine Delta, I saw one of these (perhaps an 8-footer) in about 600 feet of water in Carmel Submarine Canyon, just south of Monterey. It came right at the sub and seemed pretty interested in us.

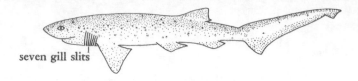

BROADNOSE SEVENGILL SHARK (NOTORYNCHUS CEPIDIANUS)

seven gill slits

NAMES: Sevengill Shark, Pratnez (French), Cañabota Gata (Spanish). *Notorynchus* is formed from 2 Greek words, one meaning "back," the other, "snout"; *cepedianus* honors Mr. Lacepede, an 18th and 19th Century natural historian. Regarding the name *Notorynchus*, no one has any idea what Dr. Ayres was getting at in 1856 when he created this word. How about a seance to find out?

IDENTIFYING CHARACTERS: This is the only shark on our coast with 7 gill slits. Makes it easy, doesn't it? Sevengills seem to vary in color. In Humboldt Bay they are reported to be pale silvery gray to reddish brown, while in San Francisco Bay they come in olive-brown to muddy gray. All sevengills have black spots. A white one with dense dark spotting has been reported.

DISTRIBUTION AND BIOLOGY: Sevengills are found in the temperate waters of the Pacific, Indian and South Atlantic. Off North America, they are found from southeastern Alaska to the Gulf of California, most commonly from about the latitude of San Francisco, Northern California, northward. While relatively little is known about these sharks, they appear to be an inshore species, often taken near the bottom of bays. In Humboldt and San Francisco Bays, where the only studies have been conducted, they are more abundant in spring and summer; most seem to migrate out to deeper water during fall. Sevengills have been taken down to 152 feet.

Sevengills grow to about 10 feet in length. All males are mature by 5+ feet, females by 8-9 feet. Females are ovoviviparous and, in the only study available, females produced 82-95 young. Embryos develop for 1 year before they are released, and newborns are 1.5-2 feet long. Females give birth in shallow, inshore waters. Adults seem to eat whatever is not bolted down. In Humboldt and San Francisco Bays, they feed on such delicacies as spiny dogfish, brown smoothhounds, bat rays, harbor seals and crabs, as well as dead dolphins and rats. Yum, yummy.

FISHERY: While in the past taken incidentally by recreational fishermen in Humboldt and San Francisco Bays, some anglers now target this good-eating, feisty species. A small, but steady, commercial fishery also exists in these bays, primarily during spring and summer. In other regions, such as China, it is also harvested for its skin (used for leather) and the vitamin A in its liver.

REMARKS: This one is suspected of a few unprovoked, but non-fatal, attacks on humans.

Sevengill remains are occasionally found in Native American middens.

Dogfish Sharks - Family Squalidae

SPINY DOGFISH (SQUALUS ACANTHIAS)

NAME: Pinback Shark, Piked Dogfish, Tiburón de Espina (Mexico), Kaad (Tlingit and Haida - North-

no anal fin

western Native American), Aburatsunozame (Japanese), Aiguillat Commun (French). *Squalus* appears to come from a similar Greek word meaning "shark"; *acanthias* is Greek for "spine."

IDENTIFYING CHARACTERS: Dogfish are relatively small sharks, gray or light brown on backs, and usually (but not always) with white spots on backs and sides. There are spines at the front of each dorsal fin (which are occasionally broken off in larger individuals). The spines separate dogs from other sharks in the North Pacific, except for the horn shark, which has black spots and a squared-off head.

DISTRIBUTION AND BIOLOGY: Spiny dogfish are found worldwide in temperate (occasionally subtropical) and subarctic waters. On our coast, they have been taken from the Bering Sea and Alaska southward to central Baja California and possibly from the Gulf of California. They also live off Chile. While dogs are most abundant off British Columbia and Washington, they are still common off southern California, as both sport and commercial fishermen will attest. These are schooling fish, found from the intertidal zone down to at least 4,080 feet. In a survey conducted from California to the Bering Sea, most dogfish were taken in waters less than 1,000 feet deep. An almost nomadic species, they move about in ways and for reasons that are not completely clear. Certainly, food supply is important and when prey is unavailable the fish move on. But water temperature seems to be another major factor. Dogs prefer 45–59° F and appear to move about in an attempt to stay within that range. In some areas, such as off California, the fish seem to move onshore during spring, remain through summer and early fall, then move offshore during winter.

41

However, in southern California I was unable to locate dogfish during winter, even in deep water. Perhaps southern California dogs migrate north into central California, or even further north, during late fall and winter. Tagging experiments have shown some extensive movements; for example, a fish tagged off Washington and another tagged off British Columbia were recovered off Japan. While there appears to be considerable coastal movement along British Columbia, Washington and Oregon, most of the dogfish living in the Strait of Georgia (between the British Columbia mainland and Vancouver Island) seem to stay in that area. Similarly, most Puget Sound dogs seem to remain there.

Dogfish grow to 5.25 feet, but fish over about 4 feet are relatively rare. These are slow-growing, long-lived fish; the oldest one found so far was about 70 years old. A 2-footer is about 10 years old, a 3-footer has stuck around about 30 years. Males grow somewhat more slowly, attain a smaller size and live a shorter time than females. Dogfish take a long time to mature. Females mature at anywhere from 16-35 years (averaging 24 years and 37 inches), while males average 14 years and about 30 inches. Females are oviparous and produce from 1-20 young (off British Columbia, the range was 2-16, averaging 6-7). Dogfish have very long gestation periods, estimated to last from 18-24 months. Dogs seem to spawn year-round, although fall and winter may be peak periods. Off British Columbia, spawning probably occurs in midwater over deep water (around 600-1,200 feet). Young juveniles remain near the surface for some time, eventually settling near the bottom. Dogfish eat just about anything unfortunate enough to be in the way. Bony fishes (such as herring, midshipmen and sardines) make up a major part of their diet, but krill, squid, octopi, crabs, sea cucumbers, jellyfish and the like are all fair game. Although they are basically bottom feeders, dogs commonly rise to the surface to feed. Northern elephant seals, California sea lions, northern fur seals, sevengill sharks, lingcod and sablefish eat them.

FISHERY: Dogfish are taken by party and private vessel, pier and occasionally shore sport anglers. Yet almost no one, neither angler nor fish, is particularly enthusiastic about it. Most dogfish unfortunate enough to be caught are sworn at, killed and tossed back. When caught, the species' unhappy habit of rolling and tangling large amounts of gear particularly endears it to anglers already nonplussed about making their acquaintance.

On the other hand, there have been several periods when dogs were a major commercial species. In the 19th Century, dogfish were taken for their liver oil, which was used in lamps; during the first part of the 20th Century they were ground up for fish meal. These were small fisheries and they had little impact on the dogfish population. In the 1940s, dogfish liver was extremely valuable as a source of vitamin A and the dogfish population was severely reduced from this onslaught. After vitamin A was cheaply synthesized, the fishery collapsed, giving the fish a bit of a breather. Currently, a medium-sized fishery off British Columbia utilizes the fish for meat, and much of it is shipped overseas. (In Germany, smoked dogfish bellies, called *schillerlochen*, are a big hit. Dogfish eggs are also eaten.) However, it is almost certain that the fishery will increase all along the coast. This species is quite edible, and processors will soon pick up on that.

Sharks, and dogfish in particular, are very susceptible to overfishing. If you think about it, here is a fish that takes perhaps 20 years to mature and only produces a few young at a time. It is relatively easy to deplete populations through heavy fishing pressure. REMARKS: The dorsal spines are reported to be mildly venomous. But I've been nailed pretty deeply by them and didn't feel anything unusual.

Dogfish were one of the crest symbols of the Haida, Native Americans of southeastern Alaska and British Columbia. Here, as repeated in M. Boelscher, *The Curtain Within, Haida Social and Mythical Discourse* (University of British Columbia Press, 1988), is the story of how that animal was adopted. "A woman made fun of dogfish. She is taken down under the sea by one of them; there she discovers that they are actually people. She grows fins, but her face is unchanged. After many years her husband finds her. She does not return home, but since that time her lineage use the dogfish crest and their house is called K'aad Naas ('dogfish house')".

Dogfish are often found in single-sex schools, perhaps leading to a lot of grumpy dogfish.

Native Americans, at least in the Puget Sound region, ate a lot of doggies.

Bullhead and Hornsharks – Family Heterodontidae

HORN SHARK (HETERODONTUS FRANCISCI)

NAMES: *Heterodontus* is Greek for "mixed tooth"; *francisci* refers to San Francisco, though ironically the species either does not occur there or is quite rare.

IDENTIFYING CHARACTERS: This is one of the two shark species in our area with spines in front of each dorsal fin (the other is the spiny dogfish). Combine this with brown or gray backs, black spots and ridges along each eye and you can't miss.

HORN SHARK

DISTRIBUTION AND BIOLOGY: Horn sharks are found from central California south to the Gulf of California (and possibly Ecuador and Peru),

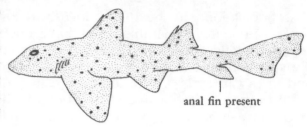

anal fin present

rarely north of Pt. Conception, usually around reefs and large algae. These are bottom-dwelling fish, rarely rising more than about 6 feet above the substrate. Often found as solitary individuals, these small sharks occasionally form aggregations. Juveniles occur in relatively shallow (sometimes intertidal) waters, frequently on sand near reefs, often sitting in the depressions made by bat rays. Adults have been taken from the intertidal zone to 492 feet. Off Catalina, adults seem to make seasonal movements, to shallow water during summer and to water deeper than 120 feet during winter. Again off Catalina, fish between about 1–1.5 feet appear to move out of shallow water and may spend their time farther offshore. Horn sharks are primarily nocturnal animals, seeking shelter in caves, crevices, or algae by day and wandering about at night. Individuals may return to the same daytime shelter day after day. These sharks also have individual shelter preferences. Ones with long spines prefer algae (where spine wear is low); the ones with short spines live in rocky areas (where their spines tend to be rubbed away).

The largest horn shark we know of was 38 inches long. Males and females mature at about 2 feet. Mating occurs in December or January, and females spawn from about February-April. Horn shark eggs are found lodged under rocks or in reef crevices, and it appears that the females push them into these really tight spots. Eggs hatch in 7-9 months and the young ones greet the day at about 6 inches long. These fish are night feeders. Juveniles may feed on worms and have been observed eating club anemones, sometimes in intertidal waters. Adults feed on fishes, squids, crabs, sea urchins, etc. Northern elephant seals prey on them, as do bald eagles at Santa Catalina Island – an event which must make for rather dramatic viewing. Elephant seals also eat their distinctive spiral eggs.

FISHERY: Horn sharks are taken occasionally by anglers and often by commercial fishermen, usually in lobster and crab traps or in gillnets and trawls. However, there is no market for this small species because this fish is a pain to clean and little remains after the process. Reportedly, the dorsal spines are used for jewelry.

REMARKS: Horn sharks are one of the few sharks in our area that lay eggs. Horn shark eggs are spiral-shaped, so laying them might be the kind of experience to share with your next Lamaze class.

Whale Sharks - Family Rhincodontidae

WHALE SHARK (RHINCODON TYPUS)

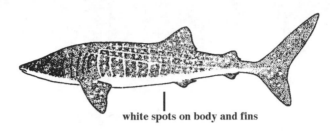

white spots on body and fins

NAMES: Requin Baleine (French). *Rhincodon* is a misspelling of the original name, *Rhiniodon*, which means "file tooth" in Greek, a reference to the small teeth.

IDENTIFYING CHARACTERS: These are very distinctive animals: dark gray or greenish with lots of white or yellow dots and bars. Whale sharks are the largest of the sharks and, in fact, the largest fishes.

DISTRIBUTION AND BIOLOGY: Whale sharks are tropical fishes, found throughout the world in warm seas; they are very occasionally found off southern California. They are usually found near the surface and may occur in either oceanic waters or near shore. On occasion, they will come into coral lagoons. These are migratory animals, probably timing their movements to taken advantage of prey movements and blooms.

The biggest fish in the world, whales sharks have been authenticated to 46 feet; they possibly reach 60 feet. Relatively little is known of their biology. Ovoviviparous or, perhaps oviparous, females are immature until at least 18 feet and probably larger. The smallest known individuals were about 1.8 feet long, so they may be born at about that size. Despite their reputations as a sort of passive vacuum cleaner, swimming with mouth open, lazily engulfing plankton (as does the basking shark), whale sharks are rather active predators. They are suction feeders, likely able to pull in considerable amounts of water rather quickly. This may explain why, along with krill, coral larvae and other planktonic creatures, whale shark guts also regularly contain sardines, mackerels and squids. Whale sharks may feed by swimming vertically with giant mouths wide open. It has been reported that small tunas have actually swum down the mouths during this time.

FISHERY: Worldwide, they are occasionally harpooned and eaten.

REMARKS: One study in a Chinese journal (Journal of Marine Drugs Haiyang Yaowu, 1988, vol. 7, no. 4, p. 3-5) notes that whale shark liver oil showed "very strong activity against" solid tumors in mice.

Thresher Sharks - Family Alopiidae

COMMON THRESHER (ALOPIAS VULPINUS)

NAMES: Fox Shark, Sea Fox, Whiptail Shark, Thintail Shark, Renard (French), Forro (Spanish). *Alopias* is Greek for "fox"; *vulpes* is Latin for "fox." This species was known to the ancient Greeks as "fox-like."

IDENTIFYING CHARACTERS: Threshers are immediately identifiable by the remarkably long upper lobes of their caudal fins. The common thresher comes in a variety of colors, including backs of purple, gray, brown, bluish or almost black; sides of blue, golden or silvery; and white bellies. The bigeye thresher (*A. superciliosis*) is also found off California. It has a relatively large eye and a horizontal groove running from eye to midbody.

DISTRIBUTION AND BIOLOGY: Common threshers are found worldwide in temperate and subtropical waters (but possibly not in equatorial areas), including the Pacific, Atlantic and Indian Oceans, and Mediterranean and Red Seas. In the eastern Pacific, they have been taken from Vancouver Island to Chile, though not near the Equator. Threshers are common off the Pacific Coast northward to at least Oregon, but more often from southern California southward. Both adults and subadults congregate in inshore waters in spring and summer. While they are generally found at or near the surface, common threshers have been taken at depths of at least 1,208 feet. Based on only a few tagging studies, threshers are likely to be highly migratory. Many of those taken off California have Japanese longline hooks in them. Since this fishery is conducted hundreds of miles off California, it is clear that at least some of these fish have travelled substantial distances.

Worldwide, common threshers reach 20 feet in length and 18-footers have been taken off California. Females are ovoviviparous; young threshers are born alive (not as eggs) and at birth the kids are already 4–5 feet long. A 10 footer is 4–5 years old and one 17 footer was about 15 years old. Off southern California, males mature at about 11 feet (3–7 years), and throughout the world females mature at anywhere from 9–14 feet. Spawning (pupping) occurs from March–June and females typically produce only 4 young ones. Threshers eat small fishes and squids. There are numerous reports that they herd and smash their prey with their huge tail fins.

FISHERY: Threshers are excellent to eat and they are a popular shark with southern California sport fishermen. Most of the sport catch comes from anglers on party boats and small vessels, with an occasional one taken from piers and jetties. Worldwide, threshers are an important commercial species, taken by gillnet and long-line. Off the Pacific Coast, they are taken mainly by drift gillnet, mostly within about 50 miles of the coast. Threshers are market-ed both fresh and frozen and some are sold smoked. Fresh fish have a shelf life of 5-7 days at 40° F. Frozen fish are good for 9 months at 0° F.

REMARKS: Juvenile common threshers often leap out of the water, for unknown reasons. A couple of my friends had one leap out of the water right in front of their boat; when it came back down it landed in the boat, a most delicious accident.

Thresher embryos probably practice uterine cannibalism, a behavior also found in some other shark species and in board rooms across the country. In uterine cannibalism, the most devel-oped embryo eats the eggs and/or the other embryos around it. In threshers, the advanced embryo at least eats the eggs. Whether it eats the other embryos is not known.

Fossil thresher teeth have been found in deposits over one mil-lion years old at Playa del Rey, southern California.

Basking Sharks - Family Cetorhinidae

BASKING SHARK (CETORHINUS MAXIMUS)

NAMES: Pélerian (French), Per-egrino (Spanish). *Cetorhinus* is a combination of 2 Greek words meaning "whale"

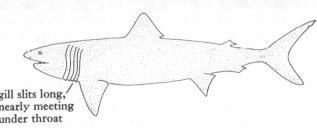

gill slits long, nearly meeting under throat

and "rasp" or "file," the latter referring to the rough skin of the animal; *maximus* is Latin for "greatest."

IDENTIFYING CHARACTERS: If the shark is bigger than your boat, it's probably a basking shark (Plate 1). These are immense animals, routinely 20–25 feet long, usually colored brown, gray or black, often with lighter patches. The caudal fin is crescent shaped, with a distinct notch near the tip. Baskers have huge, white mouths and extremely long gill slits.

DISTRIBUTION AND BIOLOGY: Baskers are found throughout the world in temperate and subtropical seas. Along the Pacific, this species has been reported from the Aleutian Islands and Gulf of Alaska, southeast to the Gulf of California and from Ecuador to Chile. These sharks are often seen at or near the surface, in numbers ranging from one to several hundred. While they usually swim with their dorsal fins upward, there are reports of them swimming belly upward. It is really quite a sight watching these very large animals slowly swimming along with their great mouths open wide. Based on reports from divers, when a few sharks can be seen at the surface, many more are probably swimming below, out of sight. These sharks are common along our coast in spring and summer (one report says that they are also found off Monterey Bay in winter), often appearing in the same general area at about the same time each year. For instance, within the Santa Barbara Channel, they appear in March or April and hang out for a few months. They predictably congregate in several discrete areas, probably sites with heavy plankton concentrations. Baskers tend to surface on calm days and may be nearby during choppy conditions. Where baskers go when they are not along the coast (in fall and winter) is anyone's guess. Some people believe they migrate into deep water, lose their gill rakers and sort of ruminate until spring, but no one knows for sure.

The longest basking shark ever reported was about 45 feet long, probably something of an exaggeration; certainly, fish over 30 feet are unusual. Males mature at about 13-16 feet, females at 25-30 feet. It is assumed these sharks are ovoviviparous, but nothing is known of spawning seasons or the number of young produced. The pups may be about 5.5 feet long at birth. One young one, estimated to be 6 months old, was 7.5 feet long. Baskers feed on plankton, including copepods, invertebrate larvae and fish eggs. There may be 1,000 pounds or more of food material in a typical basking shark stomach. The fish may swim in straight lines for a while, then suddenly veer or circle. During one observation, basking sharks kept their mouths open for 30-60 seconds, then shut them and swallowed the plankton that had accumulated on the gills. In their continual quest for the perfect copepod, baskers filter somewhere in the vicinity of 2,000 tons of water per hour.

FISHERY: Over the years, there have been sporadic commercial fisheries for basking sharks. In the late 1940s, surplus World War II landing craft were used in the fishery off Pismo Beach. Planes spotted the sharks just offshore and radioed their position to landing craft on the beach. Fishermen drove along the coast until they approached the sharks, then entered the water and harpooned the fish. Currently, there is a small, sporadic harpoon fishery for basking sharks off California. The sharks are taken for their livers, which yield a high-grade oil. There are also attempts to market the immense quantity of meat each shark provides. Basking sharks can be a major problem to commercial fishermen, accidentally fouling nets, becoming snagged on trolling lines or even getting caught in trawls. This species is very susceptible to overfishing, and it is likely that strict regulations will be needed on the fishery sometime in the future to prevent overharvesting.

REMARKS: Baskers seem to be fascinated by propeller wash. I have seen these sharks swim full bore at a moving propeller, only to veer off at the last moment.

There has been some research on the possible medical uses of stuff from basking sharks, and both anti-thrombosis and anticoagulant properties have been discovered. Probably the most intriguing results comes from the pages of the Journal of Marine Drugs, Haiyang Yaowu, 1989, vol. 8, no. 1, p. 41-45. In this study, basking shark oil was administered to patients with several kinds of tumors. The study reported that some improvement was noted in these patients, though none were cured.

Why are some of the largest fish in the world (basking sharks), basically plankton eaters? Here's a hint. Why are the largest animals in the world (blue whales) plankton eaters and why are the largest land animals (elephants) plant eaters?

Mostly, it comes down to energy consumption. Let's look at elephants and lions. Now the reality is that an elephant probably could eat lions instead of trees. Given sufficient time, Jumbo could chase down a lion, kick it a good one, then slurp it up. But why bother? A lion would probably have the distressing habit of running away if an elephant tried to kick one and while an elephant would probably eventually catch it, Jumbo would expend an unholy amount of energy doing it. Besides, a lion just might turn around and bite and it's tacky to have the *pate* nip your butt during high tea. In addition, lions just aren't that common out there on the veldt. Trees, on the other hand, are perfect for eating. First, there are lots of them (certainly compared to lions) and second, they don't have that annoying tendency to escape when an elephant approaches. No, trees just sort of stand there and let themselves be ripped apart and devoured, so it takes relatively little energy to eat them. Similarly, while a basking shark probably could run down a tuna, it takes far less energy to just lazily swim along, mouth open, inhaling zillions of abundant planktonic creatures.

Mackerel Sharks - Lamnidae

WHITE SHARK (CARCHARODON CARCHARIAS)

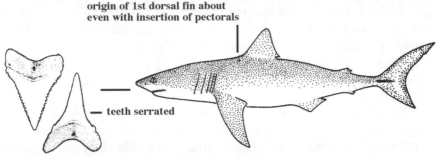

origin of 1st dorsal fin about
even with insertion of pectorals

— teeth serrated

NAMES: Man–eater, Grand Requin Blanc (French), Jaquetón Blanc (Spanish). *Carcharodon* is Greek for "rough tooth," referring to the serrated edges on the teeth; *carcharias* is an old Greek name for a variety of sharks that attack humans.

IDENTIFYING CHARACTERS: White sharks, as you might expect, are not white. You will find them in brown, gray or maybe gray-blue, with a strong keel on their caudal fin. Fish over 9 feet long have very characteristic triangular, serrated teeth. Smaller whites have mostly long teeth without serrations. Bonito sharks are the only fish you may confuse this one with. Bonito sharks are deep blue in color.

DISTRIBUTION AND BIOLOGY: Whites are found worldwide, primarily in temperate and subtropical waters, but occasionally in tropical environments. Off our coast they have been taken from the Gulf of Alaska southward to the Gulf of California, and from Panama to Chile. While whites occur mainly inshore, they have been taken down to 4,200 feet. Off our coast, whites are often found in very shallow water, sometimes just behind the surf line. They seem to be particularly abundant where seals and sea lions haul out, and such sites as the Farallon Islands are particularly attractive. We know little of their movements, although there is some evidence that these fish may sort of hang around an area for extended periods. Often solitary, aggregations of 10 or more have been reported.

Although there have been reports of white sharks 25–30 feet long, the longest authenticated fish was 19'6". Considering that this species elicits more human emotion than any other fish, remarkably little is known about it. However, here is what we have figured out. Whites may live for 40 years or more and males mature at perhaps 8 feet. Pregnant females are rarely captured, but a 15 feet long female taken off Japan carried 7 embryos, while one from the Mediterranean had 9. Embryos *in utero* probably eat the surrounding eggs. The pups are about 4 feet long at birth. Essentially nothing is known of spawning season, spawning grounds or fecundity of females, but it is likely that spawning occurs in temperate waters. White sharks eat a remarkable range of items. Worldwide, along with the usual fish prey, they have been reported to eat dolphins, porpoises, seals, sea lions, turtles, sea birds, squids, abalones, crabs and the list goes on and on. Obviously, we are not dealing with a discriminating palate here. Off our coast, white sharks smaller than about 9 feet feed primarily on fishes, including a wide range of bony fishes, such as salmon, hake, rockfish, lingcod, cabezon (they seem to crave these) and the like, and such cartilaginous species as dogfish and bat rays. Small whites eat only limited amounts of marine mammals. On the other hand, whites over 9 feet seem to switch over to marine mammals, only occasionally nibbling on fishes. On our coast, northern elephant seals are a preferred food, although various other seals and sea lions are also scarfed. A white attacked a pygmy sperm whale in Monterey Bay. Numerous sea otters have been found dead and dying with lacerations and white shark teeth embedded in their bodies. However, no otters have been found inside white shark stomachs—one of those Mysteries of Nature you can thrill your friends with.

FISHERY: Off the Pacific Coast, whites are occasionally taken by sport anglers, but more often by commercial fishermen. There is a good market for the small ones, which are really tasty. While set-lining for a dogfish research project, I caught a 6-footer and it was excellent eating. Even my daughter, who believes fish are to be seen but not eaten, liked it.

However, a recent California law makes it illegal to catch white sharks for either recreational or commercial purposes.

REMARKS: I almost hate to discuss white sharks, because so much has been written about them and so much emotion has been expended on them. I don't know how many poor, harmless shark species have been stabbed to death on piers while 13-year-olds screamed "Jaws, Jaws!"

However, make no mistake: white sharks really are awesome predators. When you have an animal that can munch on bat rays and elephant seals, you aren't talking chicken fat. White sharks are responsible for most of the shark attacks on humans off California (and all of them north of Pt. Conception). Interestingly, most people survive the attacks, as do many of the marine mammals. The reason may have to do with the way these sharks attack their prey. As mentioned earlier, large white sharks seem to prefer marine mammals, particularly seals and sea lions and they probably surprise them from underneath and behind.

51

(Many seals and sea lions have wounds from white sharks, and most of these are on the rear of the animals.) One theory (termed "bite and spit") holds that after attacking and biting a marine mammal, whites let go and back off, waiting for the animal to bleed to death. This allows many of the mammals and nearly all humans to escape. Because a white shark can wait at least one month between large meals and because there is often a lot of potential food in the water, whites can perhaps afford to let some prey escape.

Over 70 shark attacks have been recorded off California, Oregon and Washington. Of these, most were from central California northward and most were by white sharks. Of course, to put this into perspective, the ratio of white sharks killed by humans to humans killed by white sharks is maybe a zillion to one. Until recently, no white shark attack had occurred in southern California (if San Miguel Island is included in central California). The white shark attack off Malibu in 1989 was the first to break this pattern. Why there have been so few white shark attacks in southern California is not known. There are certainly white sharks there and many humans in the water.

A harbor seal, tagged with a radio transmitter off San Nicolas Island, southern California, was eaten by a white (transmitter and all) off Anacapa Island.

White shark vertebrae have been found in one-million-plus year old Pliocene deposits in southern California.

White sharks can keep their stomachs warmer than the surrounding waters, perhaps to increase the digestion rates of the massive meals they ingest.

Author's Note: This next tidbit will come as shocking news to some of you, so take a deep breath before reading on. Are you emotionally prepared? Good. It now appears that everyone's favorite primordial shark, *Carcharodon megalodon*, is no more. Stretching back to Eocene days (over 35 million years ago), this humongous shark, with big nasty teeth as much as 6 inches long, must have been the terror of the deep. And until recently, this species was assumed by most to be a good example of a white shark on steroids. However, a closer look at the structure of their teeth has suggested to a growing number of paleontologists that this shark, now often called *Carcharocles megalodon*, is not a white shark. Modern white sharks may have evolved from mako sharks, possibly from the extinct species *Isurus hastalis*.

There are no childrens' stories about white sharks. Have you ever noticed that? I have two kids, and when they were younger I read literally hundreds of stories to them, but not one was about white sharks. Oh, there were lots of tales about prancing little deer, fluffy little bunnies and bushy-tailed squirrels, but look as I might, there was nary one thin volume about white sharks. And it's not just that white sharks aren't cute, winsome, furry little warmbloods. No, sir, because right next to such justly popular works as *Fawny – The Deer Who Wouldn't Chew, Cottonball – The Bunny Who Wouldn't Hop , Flutter – the Bird Who Wouldn't Regurgitate* and *Nutberg – The Squirrel With Bubonic Plague*, are a host of stories about cute, winsome spiders, worms and snakes.

So, with all these classic tales of various vermin, where, oh where, is that sensitive, magical story called, for instance, *Gnashy, The White Shark Who Was Strictly Kosher?*

SHORTFIN MAKO SHARK (ISURUS OXYRINCHUS)

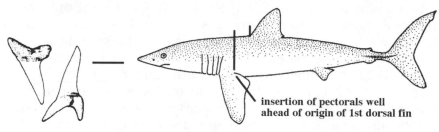

insertion of pectorals well ahead of origin of 1st dorsal fin

NAMES: Mako Shark, Pacific Mako Shark, Blue Pointer, Bonito Shark, Mackerel Shark, Paloma, Taupe Bleu (French), Marrajo Dientuso (Spanish). The Maoris of New Zealand are said to have coined the work "Mako." *Isurus* means "equal tail" in Greek, referring to the nearly equal size of the caudal fin lobes; *oxyrinchus* is Greek for "sharp snout."

IDENTIFYING CHARACTERS: Shortfins are sleek, torpedo-shaped fish, readily identified by their long, pointed snouts and teeth, a large keel on their caudal peduncles and deep blue backs. The only shark you are likely to confuse with this species is the blue shark, and it has a blunter snout, serrated teeth, a much longer upper caudal fin lobe and a small keel on the caudal peduncle.

DISTRIBUTION AND BIOLOGY: Found worldwide in warm and temperate oceans, shortfin makos occur in the eastern Pacific from Washington to Chile. Though primarily a near-surface species, they have been taken down to 500 feet. More fish venture into southern California in warm water years than in cool ones, and juveniles seem to be particularly common in southern California. While these are often pelagic, open water animals, I have seen them within 100 feet of shore near Santa Monica, southern California, happily pulverizing schools of bonito and mackerel.

Shortfin makos reach 12.5 feet in length; in California the

biggest one taken was 11.4 feet long. The oldest one recorded from southern California was 17 years old. A 3-footer is 1-2 years old and a 5-footer is 4-6 years old. These fish mature at anywhere from 6-9 feet (7-8 years). Females are ovoviviparous and the embryos diligently practice uterine cannibalism, busily eating the surrounding eggs. Embryos take about 1 year to develop; females produce 2-16 pups per season and the pups are about 28 inches at birth. The spawning season off California is unknown, but it is believed to be in late spring off the Atlantic coast. Makos eat various fishes, including anchovies, sardines, tunas and swordfish, as well as squids and turtle heads (who eats the rest of the turtle is another Mystery of Nature).

FISHERY: Makos are excellent eating, reminiscent of swordfish, and thrilling to catch. With their power and numerous leaps (perhaps to 20 feet in the air), they are one of the most exciting fish to hook off southern California. Surprisingly, it was not until the 1980s that this species became a popular sport fish. The delay was partly due to the long-standing prejudice against sharks and partly to a lack of knowledge about this fish. Much of that prejudice has disappeared and some party vessels now target these sharks. In line with its rising popularity with recreational anglers, commercial fishermen have also begun to focus on this species. A considerable number are taken by drift gillnet and longline. This species is marketed fresh and frozen, steaked and filleted. Makos have a long shelf life, 7-10 days refrigerated at 40° F. Frozen, they are good for 9-12 months at 0° F.

REMARKS: Worldwide, there are a few reports of shortfin makos attacking humans.

This species was commonly eaten by Native Americans.

SALMON SHARK (LAMNA DITROPIS)

teeth edges smooth

secondary keel on caudal peduncle

NAMES: Nezumizame (Japanese). *Lamna* is the ancient Greek name for a kind of shark. Jordan and Evermann (*The Fishes of North and Middle America*, 1896) report that the Greeks would use the mere mention of that shark as "A bugbear used by the Greeks to frighten refractory children." Obviously, a society that no longer uses the terms "bugbear" or "refractory" has lost something quite wonderful. *Ditropis* is formed from 2 Latin words meaning "two keels."

IDENTIFYING CHARACTERS: This is a pretty stubby shark, short and sort of stout. Their color is variable, ranging from gray or black to dark bluish-gray and often they have blotches or mottling on their lower surfaces. Probably the best diagnostic character is a small keel (raised area) located on the caudal fin, just below the main keel.

DISTRIBUTION AND BIOLOGY: Salmon sharks range from Japan and Korea, northward to the Bering Sea and southward to central Baja California, from the surface to depths of 502 feet. While they are common in offshore waters, they do come in just behind the breakers.

The largest one on record was 11.9 feet. Little is known about their biology. Males mature at 6-8 feet. Females are ovoviviparous and the embryos, bless their little hearts, eat each other in the uterus. The first few to mature chow down on the remaining eggs. As many as 4 little ones survive to birth. As their name implies, these are fish eaters, and salmon are high on their list of favorites. Other fishes on the menu include tomcod, walleye pollock and Atka mackerel.

FISHERY: These are occasionally taken by recreational anglers. Commercial longliners and gillnetters also get them.

Cat Sharks - Family Scyliorhinidae

SWELL SHARK (CEPHALLOSCYLIUM VENTRIOSUM)

NAMES: Balloon Shark, Puffer Shark. *Cephalloscylium* is formed from 2 Greek words meaning "head shark"; *ventriosum* is Latin for "large belly."

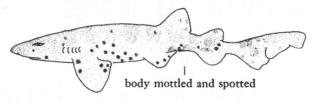

body mottled and spotted

IDENTIFYING CHARACTERS: This is an easily identified shark, usually colored red-brown or yellow- brown, with large dark saddles and blotches and small white or yellow spots. They have a noticeably flat head and small teeth. When excited, swell sharks have the remarkable ability to suck in water or air into their stomachs, making them look rather like balloons with heads and tails. Curiously, small swell sharks, which you would think would benefit from the ability, don't seem to be able to puff up.

DISTRIBUTION AND BIOLOGY: Swell sharks, found from Monterey Bay southward to Acapulco, Mexico, and off Chile, occur occasionally as far north as Morro Bay, central California, and are abundant from about Pt. Conception southward. While often found among rocks and kelp in shallow water, they have been taken down to 1,500 feet, and I have routinely caught them over sandy bottom in 100–200 feet. They are generally solitary bottom fish, spending daylight hours in caves and crevices. Once in a while you will find them grouped up, but this is rare. They are most active at night, swimming 3–6 feet above the bottom.

Swell sharks reach 3.25 feet in length. Very little is known of their life history. They are oviparous, producing brown or black rectangular egg cases, usually with tendrils on the ends that are deposited among rocks and algae. Females lay 2 eggs per clutch. Interestingly, swell sharks living near the mainland produce eggs with long tendrils, while those around Catalina Island do not. Eggs hatch in 7.5 - 10 months, depending on water temperature. The young are about 6 inches long when they hatch. Embryonic sharks leave the egg cases by forcing their way through a small opening at one end, using 2 rows of small, blunt spines on their backs. These spines help insure that the embryo, once it begins to drive its way out of the egg case, does not accidentally slip backward, back into the case. Swell sharks are night feeders, eating small fishes that they catch in two ways: some are sucked in very quickly, while others are captured by what has been called a "yawn." In the "yawn," the immobile shark opens its mouth wider and wider as the unsuspecting prey swims closer and closer. The jaws close when the prey either wanders or is carried in by currents. Swell sharks, like other cartilaginous fishes, locate many of their prey by detecting the weak electric fields generated by the prey's movements and muscle action. Northern elephant seals eat both individuals and eggs.

FISHERY: Swell sharks are taken incidentally by party and private vessel anglers, while fishing for other species in kelp beds and over rocky reefs. They make up a common, though accidental, catch in the commercial fishery, usually taken in lobster and crab traps, gillnets and trawls. Though no scientific studies have been conducted, swell shark meat is reputed to be mildly toxic, causing stomach cramping and diarrhea.

REMARKS: Shane Anderson, at UCSB, reports seeing swell sharks on the Morro Bay mudflats, stranded as the tide went out.

SOUPFIN SHARK (GALEORHINUS GALEUS)

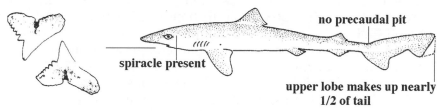

no precaudal pit

spiracle present

upper lobe makes up nearly
1/2 of tail

NAMES: Tope shark. *Galeorhinus* is formed from 2 Greek words, one meaning "a kind of shark like a weasel," the other "shark"; *galeus* means "weasel." It is also called *G. zyopterus*.

IDENTIFYING CHARACTERS: These are elongated, rather pointy-snouted sharks with bluish or gray backs and white bellies. Probably their most distinguishing feature is the large, sharply- defined upper section of the upper lobe of the caudal fin. This deeply-indented lobe is about one-half the length of the upper lobe.

DISTRIBUTION AND BIOLOGY: Soupies are probably found nearly worldwide, from very shallow waters to 1,350 feet. Off the eastern Pacific, they have been taken from British Columbia to central Baja California and off Peru and Chile. You usually find them near the bottom, in bays and off the open coast. Based on commercial catches, soupfins have a most intriguing sexual distribution. Most fish caught north of Pt. Arena, northern California, are males. From Pt. Arena to about Pt. Buchon, central California, the percentage of males to females is about equal; however, many of these females are immature. South of Pt. Buchon, most of the fish taken are females. Most young soupfins are found in the relatively shallow waters of southern California, though Tomales and San Francisco Bays also have them.

Males have been reported to 6.0 feet, females to 6.5 feet. Males mature at 4-5.6 feet, females at 4.3-6.1 feet. Females are ovoviviparous and produce 6-52 young per season; they are about 14 inches at birth. Soupies eat just about any fish that comes within reach. The major study on these sharks was conducted in the early 1940s. It found that they ate lots of sardines, midshipmen, rockfishes and mackerels, as well as a sprinkling of such other fishes as surf perches, barracuda, white seabass, Pacific hake and ratfish, plus some squids.

FISHERY: Soupfins are occasionally taken by recreational boat anglers throughout the species' range.

As far as the commercial fishery is concerned, you were out of luck if you were a soupfin shark in the late 1930s and early 1940s. Before 1937, soupfins were taken in moderate numbers, their fins dried and sent to Asia to be used in, you guessed it, soup. In 1937, it was discovered that soupfin livers contained astronomical

amounts of vitamin A; it was among the richest sources of that vitamin known. Larger sharks had more vitamin A per weight of
liver than did smaller sharks. By 1939, most of the commercial
vessels on the Pacific Coast able to handle gillnets and set lines
were off California, searching for soupies. With the onset of World
War II, other sources of vitamin A dried up and soupie livers
became really valuable. Prices for this shark reached $2,000 per
ton (about $50 per fish), in a time when a house could be bought
for $2,000. Along with spiny dogfish, whose livers also had pret-
ty fair vitamin A levels, soupfin populations promptly took a
header. With the end of the war and the synthesis of vitamin A,
the boom declined and soupie populations have made something
of a recovery. Currently, most are caught by gillnet and marketed
fresh and frozen, as fillets and steaks. Fresh soupfin, refrigerated
at 40° F, remains springtime fresh for 7-10 days. Frozen at 0° F, it
is palatable for 9-12 months.

REMARKS: Fossilized teeth have been found in Pliocene deposits
(one million+ years old) in Long Beach, southern California.

Houndsharks - Family Triakidae

GRAY SMOOTHHOUND (MUSTELUS CALIFORNICUS)

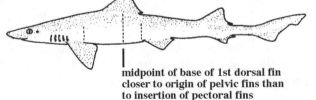

midpoint of base of 1st dorsal fin
closer to origin of pelvic fins than
to insertion of pectoral fins

NAMES: *Mustelus*
means "weasel" in
Latin; *californicus*
denotes where it
was first captured.
IDENTIFYING
CHARACTERS: A
sleek shark, gray or gray-brown on back and white on belly. This
one probably most closely resembles the brown smoothhound,
but three characters differentiate these two species. In grays, the
rear edges of the dorsal fins are smooth (frayed in browns), the
first dorsal fin begins behind the pectoral fin (over the pectorals in
browns) and the teeth are blunt (pointed in browns, with cusps).

DISTRIBUTION AND BIOLOGY: Gray smoothies are found from Cape
Mendocino, northern California to Mazatlan, Mexico. Basically,
this is a schooling, inshore species; while it has been taken down to
150 feet, you can more often find it just behind the surf line. There
is some evidence that these guys migrate into northern California
in the summer, then retreat when the water cools. They are found
from southern California southward throughout the year.

These are medium-sized animals, reaching 5.3 feet. The oldest female yet found was 9 years old; the oldest male was 6 years. Females mature at about 2.3 feet (2-3 years old), males mature between 1.9-2.1 feet (1-2 years). Females are viviparous and produce between 2 and 5 young. Food-wise, crabs are the big items here, along with the inimitable fat innkeepers (*Urechis caupo*), fishes (midshipmen, herring and the like) and shrimps.

FISHERY: Gray smoothhounds are commonly taken by shore and near-shore anglers, from about San Francisco Bay southward, sometimes mixed in with brown smoothies and leopard sharks. Like those two species, there is a fair commercial market for this one.

REMARKS: There are at least three records of albino gray smoothhounds from central California.

BROWN SMOOTHHOUND (MUSTELUS HENLEI)

NAMES: *Mustelus* means weasel in Latin; *henlei* refers to Professor J. Henle, a 19th Century biologist.

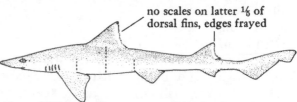

no scales on latter ⅓ of dorsal fins, edges frayed

IDENTIFYING CHARACTERS: This is a bronze or gray shark. The rear part of the dorsal fin is frayed, easily distinguishing this species from other close relatives.

DISTRIBUTION AND BIOLOGY: Brown smoothies are found from Coos Bay, Oregon southward to the Gulf of California and also off Ecuador and Peru. You find a lot of them from northern California southward, usually on sand or mud bottoms, from the intertidal to 1,104 feet. They are particularly abundant in inshore waters, often in bays such as San Francisco and Tomales. I have seen scads of them off southern California, from the surf zone to 200 feet. Smoothies are schooling fish, usually found near the bottom, and schools are often composed of only one sex. Shark expert Leonard Campagro has proposed that brownies move out of San Francisco Bay in winter, as rains decrease the salinity.

Brown smoothies reach 37 inches in length. Females are viviparous and have been aged to 13 years, males to 7. A two-footer is 3 years old, a 3-footer 11+ years. Females grow larger and live longer than males and may have more fun. Males and females mature at around 2 feet. Females produce 1–8 young. The pups when born are about 8 inches. Spawning occurs in spring and summer, probably inshore; very young ones have been taken in San Francisco Bay. Smoothies eat lots of crabs and shrimp and some fish. Northern anchovies, mudsuckers and flatfishes were eaten by individuals taken in San Francisco Bay and Elkhorn Slough. In turn, smoothies are eaten by sevengill and leopard sharks.

FISHERY: Smoothhounds are common catches made by anglers from party and private vessels, and by pier and shore anglers, though they are rarely the target of sport fishermen. They are good to eat and their popularity is slowly increasing. Commercial fishermen catch them incidentally in trawl and gillnets, and there is a small, steady market, particularly in southern California.

LEOPARD SHARK (TRIAKIS SEMIFASCIATA)

NAMES: *Triakis* is Greek for "three pointed," referring to their 3-pointed teeth; *semifasciata* means "half-band-ed" in Latin.

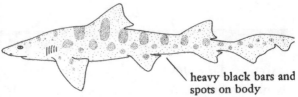

heavy black bars and spots on body

IDENTIFYING CHARACTERS: Leopard sharks are easily identified by their elongate gray bodies with black or dark bars and saddles on backs and sides. Fish larger than 2.5 feet develop additional spots between the saddles. An occasional fish has few or no saddles, but lots of spots. Leopards could possibly be mistaken for swell sharks which, however, are red-brown with flattened heads.

DISTRIBUTION AND BIOLOGY: Leopards are found from Oregon to Baja California and in the northern Gulf of California, and they are particularly abundant in northern California bays. You are most likely to encounter them in northern California, from the intertidal down to 300 feet, usually in 20 feet of water or less. They live over a wide variety of habitats, ranging from the mud-flats in San Francisco Bay to open coast kelp beds and everything in between. These sharks are particularly abundant in northern California bays. Although they usually hang out on or near the bottom, surface gillnets set in kelp beds at night often take sub-stantial numbers. These are schooling critters, sometimes aggre-gating with smoothhounds or dogfish. They are also highly mobile; they'll be in one place for a few hours, then leave, not to be seen again for months or years. I have been told that one of the places they do prefer is the warm water outfall of the Diablo Canyon power plant, near Avila Beach, California. In San Francisco Bay, where most leopard shark research has been con-ducted, the sharks tend to remain in the Bay throughout the year, with some movement out during fall and winter.

Leopards reach 7 feet in length, although fish over 6 feet are unusual. The oldest one on record was a 24-year-old male. Both sexes mature at about 3-3.5 feet, when males are around 7 years old and females are about 10 years. Spawning probably occurs from March-June, with an April-May peak. Females, who are ovoviviparous, produce 4-33 young. Embryos remain in the mother for 10-12 months. The young ones are 8-9 inches at birth. Leopards eat a wide variety of foods, including crabs, clams (they bite off the siphons), fish, fish eggs and shrimp. The fat innkeeper, *Urechis caupo*, are also on the bill of fare, though how leopards get these animals out of their mud burrows is a bit of a mystery. Leopards feed heavily on fish eggs (herring, topsmelt and jacksmelt) attached to plants or rocks. Fishes commonly eaten include midshipmen, sanddabs, shiner perch, bat rays and smoothhounds.

FISHERY: Leopards are good to eat, a fact just recently noted by many sport fishermen. In the past, leopards were taken incidentally, particularly by shore and pier anglers. Now some fishermen, particularly in places like San Francisco Bay, target this species. Commercial fishermen from Eureka southward take substantial numbers with gillnet and longline, and there is a steady market for this species.

REMARKS: There is one report of a leopard jostling a diver with a nosebleed (the diver, not the shark). Fossil leopard sharks have been found in deposits one million plus years old in southern California.

Leopard shark remains have been widely found in Native American middens.

Requiem Sharks - Family Carcharhinidae

TIGER SHARK (GALEOCERDO CUVIER)

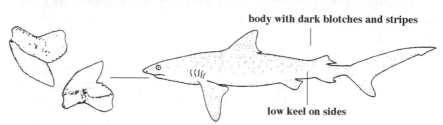

body with dark blotches and stripes

low keel on sides

NAMES: *Galeocerdo* is formed from 2 Greek words, "weasel" and an ancient Greek name for a type of shark; *cuvier* hearkens to Georges Léopold Chrétien Frédéric Dagobert Cuvier (1769-1832), one of the first competent, thoughtful anatomists.

IDENTIFYING CHARACTERS: True to their name, tigers tend to have gray-black or black spots and bars on their backs. However, these

61

start to fade as the fish get older, and large adults may be missing them altogether. So, how do you tell the big ones from anything else? Tigers are relatively compact, blunt-snouted fishes and a very good diagnostic tool is the presence of long grooves at the corners of the mouth. They also have quite wide, heavily-serrated teeth.

DISTRIBUTION AND BIOLOGY: Tiger sharks are basically tropical fish found throughout the world, but they are occasionally found as far north as southern California. There is one possible sighting of a tiger from southeastern Alaska. While most tigers have been seen in surface or near-surface waters, there are reports of individuals down to 462 feet. This is basically an inshore species; only occasionally will you be eaten well offshore.

While tigers reach about 24 feet long, fishes over about 18 feet, are quite rare. Females appear to grow larger than males. Females mature at between 8 and 11.5 feet, males between 7.5 and 9.5 feet, and both are probably around 4-6 years old at that time. Tigers live at least 12 years. Tigers are ovoviviparous and give birth to between 10 and 82 young, measuring 1.6 to 2.5 feet long. Young are produced in spring and early summer (Hawaiian Islands in September-October) and mating may occur in the spring. Females retain embryos for perhaps a bit more than a year.

There are a lot of misconceptions about sharks; one is that they are all scavengers, eating anything that comes their way. In general, this is not true. Actually most species are fairly specific as to their dining habits. However, tigers are the exception, they do appear to be gourmands rather than gourmets. Here is an abbreviated list of what has been found inside of them, gleaned from the pages of L. Compagno's stirring work *Sharks of the World*: Jillions of kinds of fishes, including tarpon, eels, sea catfish, mullet, wrasses, parrotfish, bramble sharks, spiny dogfish, angel sharks, hammerheads, various stingrays, sea turtles, sea snakes, marine iguanas, shearwaters, frigate birds, cormorants, pelicans, sea lions, fur seals, monk seals, dolphins, octopi, squid, cuttlefish, spiny lobsters, crabs, horseshoe crabs, conchs, tunicates, jellyfish, dead chickens, pigs, cattle, sheep, donkeys, dogs, hyenas, monkeys, humans, leather, fabrics, coal, wood, seeds, feathers, plastic bags, burlap bags, small barrels, cans and pieces of metal. To emphasize the point, tigers are one of the few major predators of sea snakes.

FISHERY: Recreational anglers catch fair numbers of these in the tropics. Tigers are often taken in commercial fisheries, primarily by hook and line and gillnets. Like various other shark species, the meat is quite edible. The skin can be used for leather and the liver contains high levels of vitamin A.

REMARKS: This is one of the truly dangerous sharks to humans.

There are more confirmed attacks on people by this species than by any other, except for the great white. The problem is, it's not always clear what measures can be taken to reduce shark attacks. Concerned by a number of shark attacks, primarily by tigers, the state of Hawaii established a shark control program in 1959, followed by a number of other programs in ensuing years, until 1976. Basically, a lot of sharks of various species (both dangerous to humans and innocuous) were taken by hook and line. A recent study evaluated the program's effectiveness in reducing shark attacks (B. M. Wetherbee et al., Pacific Science, 1994, vol. 48, p. 95-115). It concluded that the programs "do not appear to have had measurable effects on the rate of shark attacks in Hawaiian waters," and that "Implementation of large-scale control programs in the future in Hawaii may not be appropriate." Perhaps it would be better to understand the behavior and movements of tiger sharks and learn how to avoid dangerous areas and seasons.

And here, from the closely-guarded files of Rocky Strong, Big Time Shark Biologist, is a rattling good story. Rocky informs me that tiger sharks regularly visit French Frigate Shoals, a little dimple in the Pacific, west of the Hawaiian Islands. The tigers predictably arrive within a day or two of the fledging of albatross young on these islands. They aren't there before and only stay for about a month, as long as there are little albatross trying out their wings. So, do these sharks come to see these impressive birds lift themselves to the heavens in the miracle of flight? Well, no. Actually, tiger sharks clamber into the lagoons to munch on the many clueless juveniles that do not get the hang of it and either fall into the water or just sort of march into the sea. Rocky also notes that when the tigers are about, the normally abundant gray reef sharks are nowhere to be found.

BLUE SHARK (PRIONACE GLAUCA)

NAMES: Requin Bleu (French), Tilmón Azul (Spanish). *Prionace* is Greek for "saw point," probably referring to their serrated teeth; *glauca* is Greek for "blue."

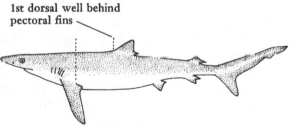

1st dorsal well behind pectoral fins

IDENTIFYING CHARACTERS: Blues are really pretty, dark blue sharks with white bellies (Plate 2). They have long, pointed snouts, a barely noticeable keel on their caudal peduncles and serrated teeth. Bonito sharks resemble blues, but have a more pointed snout, a heavier keel and long, smooth teeth.

DISTRIBUTION AND BIOLOGY: Found worldwide in temperate and subtropical seas, blues in the eastern Pacific are found from the Gulf of Alaska to Chile, from the surface to at least 908 feet. They often swim slightly off the coast, where the water begins to clear. These are the most abundant pelagic sharks off the west coast of North America. Found in water between 52–81°F in the Pacific, blues seem to prefer 52–63 degrees. As coastal ocean waters warm, they move northward and inshore, visiting as far north as the Gulf of Alaska during August and September. While they may be present throughout the year in southern California, their numbers tend to increase in summer. Most blues off California are immature or in the first year or two of reproduction; only occasionally is a large mature individual seen. While you will often see them singly, these sharks sometimes aggregate in particular stretches of water. For instance, on one summer day I saw perhaps 500 small (3–4 feet) blues, spaced 20–30 yards apart strung out just outside a kelp bed north of Santa Barbara. There is evidence that this species also forms single–sex aggregations, where all the fish in an area will be either male or female. Blues migrate widely, though we do not yet know the extent of their migrations in and out of eastern Pacific waters. They seem to be most active at night. Off Santa Catalina Island, blues stay offshore and near the surface by day, then move inshore at night (feeding on such prey as squids), and move offshore again the next morning.

Blues reach lengths of 2.5 feet. No maximum age is known, though they may live to about 20 years. An 8-footer was 9 years old. Your standard 4 foot blue is probably 3-4 years old. Blues mature at about 6-7 feet and at around 7 years of age. Some studies show that mature females may store sperm for many months before fertilizing their eggs. Females are viviparous and produce as many as 135 pups per year. The embryos remain in the mother for 9-12 months and they are about 1.5 feet long at birth. Blues feed on a wide variety of fishes and on such invertebrates as squid. Pelagic red crabs are another hot item. Carrion, in the form of dead whales, sea lions etc., is a perennial favorite. Off Santa Catalina Island blues were found to feed on such items as anchovies, squids, pipefishes and blacksmiths, while in other California studies, they ate dogfish, slender soles, cuskeels, sanddabs and sauries. Bonito sharks eat blues, as do California sea lions and northern elephant seals.

FISHERY: Traditionally, blue sharks have been a nuisance to boat anglers trying to catch other species. In the bad old days, sport fishing vessel skippers would usually shoot any blue that came around. Fortunately, today this practice is less common, but these sharks are still regarded with disdain by many sport anglers. Ironically, certain party vessels have recently begun to run "shark special" trips, targeting blue and bonito sharks.

Over the years, there have been sporadic efforts to generate a commercial fishery for blues off California. A major obstacle is the quick buildup of ammonia–tasting urea, which permeates the shark's meat after death. Unless the fish is very quickly bled and chilled, the meat stands a good chance of becoming inedible. Gill netting, the traditional method of catching large pelagic sharks, easily captures blues, but the long net sets mean the entangled sharks have plenty of time to deteriorate. Experiments in longlining seem to show that this technique is a good one. Blue sharks make excellent jerky. A pamphlet entitled *"Smoked Shark and Shark Jerky"* (J. B. Richards and R. J. Price, 1979, University of California Division of Agricultural Sciences Leaflet 21121) is available through many local Sea Grant marine advisors or through the Food Sciences and Technology Extension, UC Davis, 95616.

REMARKS: If you spend enough time in offshore California waters you will eventually see a group of yellowtail or Pacific mackerel apparently slamming into a blue shark. Although it looks like the fish are trying to kill the shark, the fish are likely rubbing themselves along the rough sides, perhaps to scrape off parasites.

This is a species to be treated with caution, as there have been a few reported attacks on humans. However, at least some of these have been on divers who deliberately jump into the water after luring blues in with chum. Get a life, people. If you insist on playing in traffic, it's not bad karma when you get hit by a milk truck.

Female blue sharks, around 6 feet long, often have bite marks on their backs. These are caused by male blues biting them during mating behavior. The back skins of females are 2-3 times as thick as those of males, and little damage seems to come from the bite.

I know this sounds like something out of a tabloid, but 4 two-headed blues have been reported from waters around Japan.

There is also a report of a shark, likely a blue, leaping over a floating box about 60 miles offshore of the Columbia River. The shark was scraping itself against the box in mid–leap. Gee, it's either *really* boring out there or the animal was scraping off parasites.

Blues were eaten by Native Americans.

Hammerhead Sharks - Family Sphyrnidae

SCALLOPED HAMMERHEAD (SPHYRNA LEWINI)

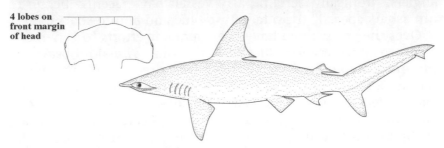

4 lobes on
front margin
of head

NAMES: *Sphyrna* is Greek for "hammer."

IDENTIFYING CHARACTERS: Do we really have to go into any detail here? Okay, their heads look like hammers. There, I've said it. Scalloped hammerheads are gray-brown and have 3 notches on the front of the head, rather than the 2 found in smooth hammerheads (*S. zygaena*). Bonnetheads (*S. tiburo*) have rounded heads, with no large extensions.

DISTRIBUTION AND BIOLOGY: Found worldwide in temperate and warm seas, this hammerhead has been taken as far north as Santa Barbara, southern California and as deep as 908 feet. Scallops are found over a wide range of habitats, from very shallow bays and estuaries to the deep waters adjacent to the continental shelves. Worldwide, these are perhaps the most common of the hammerheads. They occur both as single individuals and in large schools. The juveniles usually hang out in shallow water. In a nursery ground in Kaneohe Bay, Oahu, juveniles spend most of the day in a loose school, leaving during the night, then returning to the same spot the next morning.   A reliable place to find this species is off La Paz, southern Baja California. Peter Klimley, Don Nelson and others have found that large schools of juveniles and adults swarm in these waters over specific seamounts and around several islands. What the fish are doing there is not completely clear. They don't seem to be feeding, and tagging studies show that the fish move off these grounds at dusk, returning at dawn. Females are more common than males at these sites.

This species reaches 12.2 feet long. Males mature at about 4.6-5.4 feet, females at around 7 feet. Around Oahu, adults move into shallow water to mate and drop their young. Females are viviparous and produce between 15 and 31 young, these are 1.3-1.8 feet long at birth. Scalloped hammerheads eat fishes–lots and lots of kinds–as well as squids, octopi, snails, shrimps, crabs and lobsters.

FISHERY: Scalloped hammerheads, and hammerheads in general, are commonly taken by commercial fishermen.   Like many other sharks, hammerheads are widely used for food. Their skins make good leather and the liver is sometimes rendered for the vitamins in its oil.

REMARKS: Do you want to impress your friends? Sure you do; it's one of the few joys you have in a life otherwise devoid of happiness. Well, next time you see a hammerhead, instead of mumbling "Gee, Bertram, that's sure weird looking. Pass the lard-fried pig skins," say "You know, Buffy, 'sphyrnids are unique in having bladelike lateral extensions of the prebranchial head at the level of the horizontal head rim'. And, my love, would you be so kind as to pass the lard-fried pig skins?" Don't thank me–it's a direct quote from Leonard Compagno's moving work *Sharks of the Order Carcharhiniformes* (1988, Princeton University Press), soon to be a major motion picture. On a more somber note, the flattened projections probably serve several functions. One possibility is that it helps give lift to the head region, reducing the amount of energy needed to stay in the water column. Another theory is that the unique shape helps the shark as it twists, elevates or depresses its head.

There have been a few more-or-less authenticated attacks on humans by scalloped hammerheads.

Angel Sharks - Family Squatinidae

PACIFIC ANGEL SHARK (SQUATINA CALIFORNICA)

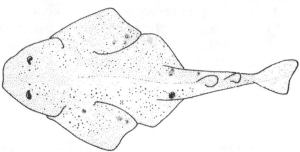

NAMES: *Squatina* is an ancient name, given to a similar species in the Mediterranean; *californica* refers to the locality where the originallydescribed fish was taken.

IDENTIFYING CHARACTERS: Angels (Plate 3) are flattened sharks with large pectoral fins that are not connected to the heads (they are connected, for instance, in guitarfish). Their heads are blunt at the fronts and the mouths are up front (not underneath, as in the guitarfish, rays and skates).

DISTRIBUTION AND BIOLOGY: Angels are found from southern Alaska southward to Baja California and the Gulf of California, as well as off Peru, Chile and (depending on your philosophy) Heaven. They are uncommon north of California. This is a bottom–

dwelling species, found over a wide variety of habitats (near reefs and kelp, over sand and mud) from 10–600 feet, more commonly to 300 feet. They apparently spawn in deep water; I have seen more little ones in 180–300 feet than anywhere else. It is unclear how much these fish move about. In a tagging study in which I participated, a few fish moved extensively, from Santa Barbara to near Pt. Conception or across the Santa Barbara Channel, while others were taken at or near their tagging sites.

Angels reach 5 feet in length. Males and females mature at about 3 feet. Spawning probably occurs from March–June and females produce between 8–13 young. Off southern California, angels eat mainly fishes (including California halibut, queenfish, blacksmith, juvenile white seabass and blackeyed gobies) as well as squids and sea cucumbers. Angels frequently bury themselves in sand (with only eyes and parts of heads exposed) and probably catch at least some of their prey by ambushing them from this retreat. Most activity and probably most feeding occurs at night. During a study off Catalina Island, the fish's swimming activity increased at sundown and peaked around midnight. The fish in this study moved about 1,500 feet per hour and seemed to have fairly large home ranges. They are eaten by northern elephant seals.

FISHERY: Angels are a minor part of the sport fishery, taken primarily from southern California southwards. They are usually caught by party and private vessel anglers and divers, with an occasional one taken from piers and jetties. While in past years this species was discarded by sport fishermen, I have noticed that today the fish are more likely to be kept.

Development of the commercial fishery for this shark makes an interesting story, so put your beer down, tuck in that dirty, gray undershirt and listen up. Until recently, there was essentially no market for this species; when caught, they were killed and thrown back. In 1978, a Santa Barbara fishermen mentioned to Michael Wagner, a fish processor, that a similar fish was commercially valuable in Italy. This prompted Mr. Wagner to purchase small amounts of angel, process it and give it away or sell it at low cost to local markets and restaurants. After some initial resistance, the fish caught on, first in Santa Barbara, then statewide and finally across the nation. The rest, as they say, is history. The angel shark fishery went from 366 pounds in 1977 to over 700,000 pounds in 1984. The fishery is now tightly regulated, with minimum size restrictions. Angels are taken by gillnet and trawl.

REMARKS: You should probably be careful when dealing with angels, as they are usually a mite testy when caught or harassed.

What makes this fish one to avoid is its ability to thrust out its jaws very quickly and remarkably far. More than one fisherman has become an unhappy camper by putting their hands too close to a "dead" angel shark.

Angel remains have been found in Native American middens.

Guitarfishes - Family Rhinobatidae

SHOVELNOSE GUITARFISH (RHINOBATOS PRODUCTUS)

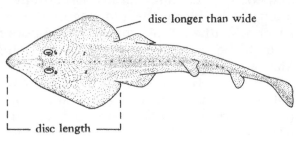

NAMES: Shovelnose Shark. *Rhinobatos* is formed from 2 Greek words meaning "shark skate"; *productus* is Latin for "produced," still another obscure reference from Dr. Ayres, this time in 1854.

IDENTIFYING CHARACTERS: These fish are light brown on top, white on the bottom, have a spadeshaped, flattened head, and a long, thin tail. They also have the most soulful, woebegone eyes you have ever seen (Plate 4).

DISTRIBUTION AND BIOLOGY: Found from San Francisco to the Gulf of California, shovelnoses are common from central California southward. These sandy bottom dwellers inhabit intertidal waters down to 300 feet, most often in bays or along the open coast, but occasionally in estuaries. Most shovelnoses live in 40 feet of water or less, sometimes in very large aggregations. Other researchers and I have noted that they tend to bunch up during the spring (beginning in about March) in shallow water, possible for mating and spawning.

Shovelnoses reach 5.5 feet in length and they live at least 10 years. Some fish mature when between 2 and 3 feet long. Females produce as many as 28 young which are born alive as little 6-inch replicas of the adults. Spawning takes place at least in April and May, in shallow water. Young ones are common in very shallow water, often in protected or semi-protected waters. Crabs, shrimps and fishes form much of the adult diet. I have seen shovelnoses next to the Scripps Institute pier in La Jolla scarf down sand crabs in about 2 inches of water. Apparently, they occasionally strand themselves on beaches and have to flop their way back into the surf, no doubt much embarrassed. In Elkhorn Slough, central

California, shovelnoses eat such fishes as shiner perch, mudsuckers, staghorn sculpins and flatfishes.

FISHERY: Shovelnoses are commonly taken by pier, shore and occasionally vessel sportfishermen from above Morro Bay southward; commonly in southern California. Previously discarded by most anglers, these fish are finally being recognized as the really good - eating species they are. Similarly most guitarfish were discarded from the commercial catch until recently. But today they are usually retained as part of a steady, minor fishery. Most shovelnose are taken in gillnets set for other species. I have seen pretty good numbers of them for sale in Vietnamese markets.

REMARKS: For obscure reasons, large numbers of big shovelnose often reside during the summer in the warm waters of Mugu Lagoon, southern California. They are not reproducing and don't seem to be feeding, so why they are lying around is unclear. Maybe they are just soaking up a few rays.

Mary Ellen Timmons of California State University, Long Beach, tells me she has seen shovelnoses swimming with leopard sharks (the guitarfishes underneath the leopards) at Santa Catalina Island.

Bizarre as it sounds, there is one authenticated report of a shovelnose attacking a human. Apparently, a diver inadvertently interrupted a male guitarfish while it was courting a female. Instead of taking the diver to court and suing him for several million dollars, the fish took the easy, macho way out and rammed into the poor sucker. The diver was probably never in too much danger, as shovelnose have no teeth to speak of and, while they could eat you, it would be a toe at a time. You would have to be real patient—we're talking several months here.

They are abundant in Native American middens.

Thornbacks - Family Platyrhinidae

THORNBACK (PLATYRHINOIDIS TRISERIATA)

NAMES: Banjo Shark. *Platyrhinoidis* comes from a series of Greek words, meaning "broad snout-like"; *triseriata* is Latin for "3 rowed," from the 3 rows of spines on the tail.

IDENTIFYING CHARACTERS: These are flattened fish, composed of a round, flat head and a long tail. The best character (naturally) is the 3 rows of hooked spines on the back and tail.

DISTRIBUTION AND BIOLOGY: Thornbacks are found from Tomales Bay (northern California) to Baja California, commonly from

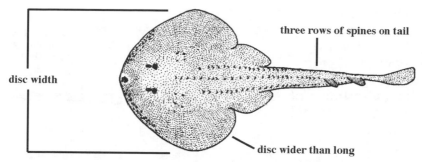

three rows of spines on tail

disc width

disc wider than long

southern California southward. While this fish has been taken from the surf line to 450 feet, it is most abundant in waters shallower than about 20 feet, often in or on sand and mud in shallow, quiet waters.

Thornbacks reach 3 feet in length and fish over 2 feet are unusual. Very little is known about this species. They eat worms, crabs, shrimps and clams. Spawning probably occurs in the summer and they have been found in guts of northern elephant seals...and that's all we know.

FISHERY: These are taken quite frequently by shore and pier fishermen in central and southern California. They are edible, but are so small that there just is not much to nibble on.

REMARKS: For reasons that escape me, this is one of the most maltreated fish caught from piers. These are really inoffensive creatures, usually too small to eat, and certainly not a danger to anything larger that a sand crab. So here's a thought. If you catch one, instead of stomping or stabbing it and letting it die on the deck, why don't you give it a big kiss and release it?

Skates - Family Rajidae

BIG SKATE (RAJA BINOCULATA)

NAMES: Gangiei-rui (Japanese). *Raja* is the Latin word for a skate or ray; *binoculata* is formed from 2 Latin words meaning "two eyed" (referring to this species' large eyespots).

IDENTIFYING CHARACTERS: Skates are notoriously difficult to tell apart. Grown ichthyologists have said bad words, indeed, trying to figure them out. But fortunately for you, this one is pretty easy. Bigs are flat, with long, pointed snouts and (here is the clincher) they *do not* have a prominent notch on the rear edge of their pectoral fins (all other Pacific Coast skates do). They come in a beguiling array of colors, including muddy brown, muddy gray,

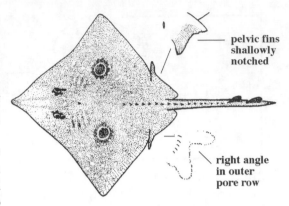

muddy olive and the ever-popular muddy black. Most individuals have two prominent eyespots, along with an assortment of little bright dots and dark mottlings.

DISTRIBUTION AND BIOLOGY: Found from the Bering Sea and southeastern Alaska to central Baja California, these are bottom dwellers, usually found cozying up to soft substrates. They have been taken in depths between 10 and 2,640 feet. Surveys along the Pacific Coast indicate that bigs are most common from shallow waters down to about 1,000 feet.

The largest big on record was 8 feet long, the oldest one about 12 years old. Females mature at around 4.3 feet, 12 years of age, males at 3.3-3.6 feet (10-11 years). Fishes and crustaceans round out their diets. Elephant seals eat their eggs.

FISHERY: They are occasionally taken by recreational anglers. Off California, there is a small commercial trawl fishery for skates, though bigs are not as important as the California skate (*R. inornata*) and longnose skate (*R. rhina*). Regardless of the species, only the pectoral fins, the "wings," are marketed, usually fresh or fresh-frozen.

Electric Rays - Family Torpedinidae

PACIFIC ELECTRIC RAY (TORPEDO CALIFORNICA)

NAME: Torpedo. *Torpedo* is Greek for numbness; *californicas* refers to the location of the first individuals taken by scientists.

IDENTIFYING CHARACTERS: These are unmistakable fish. First, they are flat and gray or bluish-gray with black spots. Second, they are remarkably flabby. Third, if you touch the disk part of their bodies you are likely to get yourself nailed pretty good.

DISTRIBUTION AND BIOLOGY: Electrics are found from northern British Columbia to central Baja California (most frequently south of Pt. Conception) from 10-1,494 feet in depth. During the day you will usually find them sitting in sand or mud, sometimes near a reef and kelp, but often over featureless bottom. On the other hand, I have seen them lying on rocks, in waters as deep as 600 feet.

These big scarfers are more active at night, often swimming 2-3 feet above the bottom onto adjacent reefs.

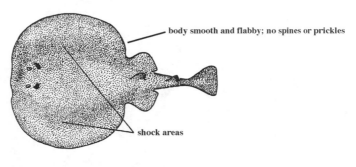

body smooth and flabby; no spines or prickles

shock areas

Electric rays reach 4.5 feet in length. Relatively little is known of their life history. These rays probably detect prey using sight, water motion and the prey's electric field. They hover over the potential tidbits, then stun them with a jolt that can reach at least 45 volts. This is apparently a pretty successful foraging technique because, besides such regular prey as northern anchovies and kelp bass, one 4-footer was found to have eaten a 2-foot-long silver salmon.

FISHERY: There is a small commercial fishery for specimens used in biological research. They are taken by trawl or gillnet.

REMARKS: Electric rays produce so much electricity that handling them can be positively painful. If you must pick them up, lift them by their tails. The juice is produced by kidney-shaped organs in the disk on each side of the fish. These rays are pretty fearless customers. Not surprisingly, considering their weaponry, they do not seem to be intimidated by divers and, in fact, often head straight for them.

Stingrays - Family Dasyatididae

PELAGIC STINGRAY (DASYATIS VIOLACEA)

NAMES: *Dasyatis* comes from 2 Greek words, "shaggy skate"; *violacea* means "purple."

IDENTIFYING CHARACTERS: These are round-headed rays, often dark purplish on backs and purple or gray underneath. Other rays of the northeast Pacific (round - *Urolophis halleri*, diamond - *Dasyatis brevis*, California butterfly - *Gymnura marmorata*) have at least somewhat pointed snouts and they aren't purplish.

DISTRIBUTION AND BIOLOGY: Pelagic stingrays are found throughout much of the world. Off the Pacific Coast, they have been taken from British Columbia to Baja California. Until recently, little was known of their distribution and biology, due to their open ocean habitat and because they are of no commercial or recreational importance. Collections made the Monterey Bay Aquarium and other organ-

izations off
southern
California
show that
these animals
are surpris-
ingly abun-
dant in off-
shore waters.

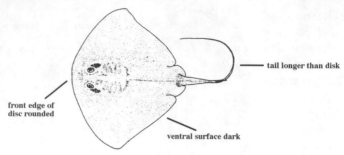

front edge of
disc rounded

tail longer than disk

ventral surface dark

Thanks to Henry Mollet for much of the following information. Pelagics reach 5.3 feet long. Most of the biological literature uses disc width, as opposed to body length, as the primary measurement. Using this measurement, pelagics reach at least 2.6 feet across. Females may grow larger than males. Pelagics may mature at 1-2 years of age. It has been suggested that females mature at disc widths of 16-20 inches. The smallest mature male ever noted had a disc width of 14 inches. Off southern California, pelagics may mate in the fall, with females storing sperm until their eggs are ovulated in June and July. From the time of fertilization, the embryos seem to take about 2 months to fully develop and be extruded. Females may produce between 2-13 young per year. A full-term embryo is about 6 inches across.

REMARKS: I'll level with you. I included this species only because the docents at the Monterey Bay Aquarium demanded it. It is difficult to stand fast against an onslaught of pleading, nagging and appeals to a Higher Power.

Round Stingrays - Family Urolophidae

ROUND STINGRAY (UROLOPHUS HALLERI)

NAMES: *Urolophus* is
a Greek combina-
tion meaning "tail
crest"; *halleri* has a
more interesting
derivation. We quote
from Jordan and
Evermann, 1896, *The*

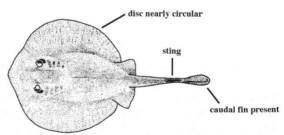

disc nearly circular

sting

caudal fin present

Fishes of North and Middle America: "Named for Mr. Haller, of Port Townsend, Washington, who, as a boy, was stung by this species at San Diego in 1862." And there you have it, ladies and gentlemen, the Rest of the Story.

IDENTIFYING CHARACTERS: These are sort of cute, small, round rays, brown or gray (rarely black), most often with yellow spots or other markings. Waders beware, they have a long slender sting at the base of their tails.

DISTRIBUTION AND BIOLOGY: Round stingrays are found from Eureka, northern California to Panama, but are rare north of central California. You will find them from intertidal waters to depths of 70 feet, usually on soft sand or mud. Off southern California, during much of the year, mature females occur slightly farther offshore (between about 40-60 feet deep) than males (less than 40 feet). In June, females move into very shallow inshore waters to breed with males, leave, then return to spawn in August and September.

Round rays reach 22 inches in length and they mature at 10-10.5 inches. Females spawn in protected, quiet backwaters, giving birth to as many as 8 young (the average is 3); young ones measure 4 inches at birth. They remain in waters shallower than 12 feet until 6-7 inches long, then move out into deeper, more exposed coastal environments. Adults are rare in very shallow water during winter. Small rays eat worms, shrimps, crabs and amphipods, while larger ones seem to really enjoy clams and lesser amounts of those other organisms. Northern elephant seals eat them.

FISHERY: Round rays are taken incidentally by shore and pier anglers and very occasionally by commercial fishermen. Currently, there is no market for this species.

REMARKS: In southern California, round stingrays are probably responsible for most wounds to waders. It's important to remember that rays do not attack humans; there has never been a ray that has swum up to someone, thrust out its butt and jabbed that person with a spine. People who get wounded have stepped on a ray, and if you shuffle your feet when walking in the surf it won't happen.

Eagle and Cow-nosed Rays - Family Myliobatidae

BAT RAY (MYLIOBATIS CALIFORNICA)

NAMES: *Myliobatis* means "grinder ray" in Greek, referring to the grinding teeth; *californica* refers to the catch location of the originally described fish.

IDENTIFYING CHARACTERS: Bat rays are very distinctive fish, with flat bodies, blunt, elevated heads and thick snouts. Bat rays are usually black, brown or blackish brown on top and white below. One albino

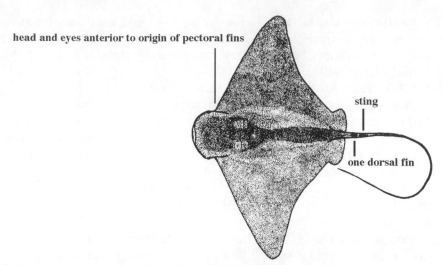

head and eyes anterior to origin of pectoral fins

sting

one dorsal fin

fish has been reported from Baja California. The stinging spine (sometimes there are 2 or 3) is located at the base of the long, thick tail.

DISTRIBUTION AND BIOLOGY: Bat rays are found from Oregon to the
Gulf of California, commonly from northern California southward.
You will encounter these rays in a wide variety of habitats, from intertidal mudflats in estuaries to open surf to kelp beds. The bays and
estuaries of central and northern California (such as San Francisco
Bay and Elkhorn Slough) are loaded with them, as are the Channel
Islands of southern California. Rays have been taken in water as deep
as 198 feet, but more commonly from intertidal regions to 100 feet.
Although you will routinely see these guys lying on sandy or muddy
bottoms, often more or less buried, you may run into them swimming in midwater or near the surface, very often at night. These are
big fish. A large one can blind-side you with the power of an NFL
linebacker. Bat rays can be found singly or in very large groups, sometimes numbering in the thousands. They travel inshore to spawn and
breed in summer, dispersing in fall and winter.

Bat rays are measured by width (fin tip to fin tip), not by length,
and rays as large as 6 feet across have been taken. These are fairly
long-lived fish; some live to at least 24 years. Females grow larger,
faster and live longer. Males may not live much longer than 6
years. A 2-foot-wide fish is 2-4 years, a 3-footer is about 7 years
and a 4-footer is about 12 years old. Male bats mature at 2 feet
across, females at about 3 feet. Females produce 2-12 young and
spawn during the summer. Unborn rays are carried by their mothers for 9-12 months and are 9-12 inches at birth (and cute as but-
tons too). Bats living on mudflats or sandy bottoms eat lots of
clams, crabs, shrimps and fishes (such as herrings, mudsuckers
and shiner perch). Those living over mud also consume unholy
quantities of the fat innkeeper, *Urechis caupo*, a worm-like animal

that lives in mud burrows. Bats flap their wing-like fins to remove sand and mud, exposing prey. Fish living in kelp beds are reported to eat snails, abalones and worms.

FISHERY: Bat rays are a common catch of shore, pier and vessel anglers, from northern California southward. A number of anglers, particularly night-time shore fishermen in southern California, target this species. There is a small, occasional, commercial market for bats in southern California; these are taken by gillnet and trawl fishermen who are targeting other species.

REMARKS: The skin surrounding a bat ray's sting is usually stripped off when the spine is used. However, the groove along the spine contains poisonous tissue that remains in place.

I have eaten bat rays and they are really tasty. They are also unbearably endearing creatures and I can't bring myself to do them in. In past years, unscrupulous fish merchants have cut round pieces of bat ray wings (and those of other rays and skates) and have sold them as "scallops."

The oyster farms of central and northern California are surrounded by fences to keep out oyster-loving bat rays.

Bat ray fossils have been found in Pliocene (over one million years old) deposits in southern California. They were a common part of the diets of Native Americans in California.

Shortnose Chimaeras - Family Chimaeridae

SPOTTED RATFISH (HYDROLAGUS COLLIEI)

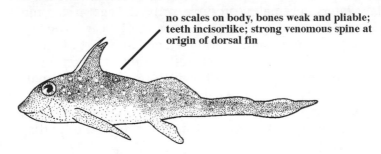

no scales on body, bones weak and pliable; teeth incisorlike; strong venomous spine at origin of dorsal fin

NAMES: *Hydrolagus* means "water hare" in Greek, referring to the rabbit-like appearance of these fish; *colliei* honors M. Collie, a naturalist.

IDENTIFYING CHARACTERS: This is an adorably bizarre fish; once you've seen it you will never forget it. It has a large head, resembling a rat's and a long tapering body, ending in a little pointy tail. Each fish has a long, venomous spine in front of its dorsal fin and its skin is scaleless. Spotted ratfish are usually brown, occasionally silvery, always with white spots. Their eyes are an exquisite green. Males have a *tenaculum*, a little club-like structure, in their foreheads. Really, this species looks like something that would trade puns with the March Hare in *Alice in Wonderland*.

DISTRIBUTION AND BIOLOGY: Spotted ratfish are taken over a wide geographic range (from southeast Alaska to Baja California, including the northern Gulf of California) and are abundant along much of this coast line. Although they are found from intertidal waters to 3,186 feet, they tend to be more common in shallow waters to the north and deeper waters to the south. They are often seen in 20-60 feet off British Columbia and in 200 feet off southern California, but are rare in less than 600 feet in the Gulf of California. Ratfish occur singly, in small groups or in aggregations, sometimes in very large ones. They occupy a wide variety of habitats, from sand and mud to rocky reefs. At least in Puget Sound, these fish make inshore migrations at night. In both Puget Sound and the Gulf of California, they move to shallow waters during spring and return to deep waters in summer and fall. One individual, appearing rather lost, was taken well up the Columbia River estuary. Off British Columbia, ratfish seem to like waters between 45-48° F.

Spotted ratfish reach 38 inches in length and no one has figured out a way of telling how old they are. Females mature when they are about 10 inches from the tip of their snouts to their vents and males mature at about 8 inches. This type of measurement is used, rather than total length, because ratfish tails are often broken. Females spawn year round, probably peaking in summer and fall, and at least some appear to spawn in intertidal and barely subtidal waters. Females produce only 2 eggs at a time and embryos may remain in the eggs cases for 1 year. The eggs are rather unique in appearance: long, ridged and sort of violin-case shaped, with stiff, hairlike structures jutting out from along the edges. Based on aquarium observations, it takes females an unpleasantly long time to extrude the eggs: 18-30 hours. The eggs are on long filaments, and these hang from the females for 4-6 days. Eggs may be planted vertically in the mud or perhaps are shed over rocks.

Ratfish eat a wide variety of organisms, including shrimps, clams, worms, fishes, brittlestars, gammarid amphipods and seastars. In turn, they are eaten by a number of predators, such as soupfin sharks, dogfish, Pacific halibut, pigeon guillemots, northern fur seals and northern elephant seals (the latter also eat the eggs.)

FISHERY: There is no sport or commercial fishery for this species. Ratfish are occasionally taken by sport anglers, particularly while fishing for rockfishes in deeper water, and are common in commercial trawl catches. Historically, ratfish have been used for mink food and in fish meal. Their liver contains an oil which makes an excellent lubricant.

REMARKS: Spotted ratfish spines are mildly poisonous and the toxin apparently only affects some people. They are also reputed to be edible, though bland and sort of mushy. Actually, they sound like the fish equivalent of tofu. On the other hand, the ovaries of spotted ratfish are toxic. So all of you lovers of Cajun fried ratfish ovary out there–cut it out.

The pits on the ratfish head are used to detect electric fields.

Lots of ratfish parts have been found in Native American middens in the Puget Sound region.

Sturgeons - Family Acipenseridae

GREEN STURGEON (ACIPENSER MEDIROSTRIS)

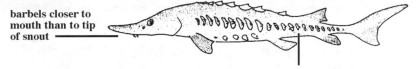

barbels closer to mouth than to tip of snout

midlateral plates 23-30

NAMES: In Greek, *Acipenser* means "bony cartilage"; *medirostris* is a combination of 2 Latin words "medium snout."

IDENTIFYING CHARACTERS: Sturgeon identification is fun; it's difficult to mistake this group with anything else. Sturgeons have 5 rows of scutes (thick bony plates). These are arranged as follows: 1 on the back, 1 on the middle of each side and 1 on each side of the belly. Sturgeons have underslung mouths, protrusible jaws, and barbels just in front of the mouth. Greens tend to be olive- colored, though some are grayish-white, and some have belly and side stripes. If unsure if you've got a white or green sturgeon, count the scutes on the midside row. Greenies have 23-30, whites have 38-48.

DISTRIBUTION AND BIOLOGY: Greenies are found from Japan and Korea to northern Baja California and are common at least from southern British Columbia southward to San Francisco Bay. These are bottom dwellers, found from inshore waters to 198 feet, mostly in the lower stretches of rivers, in estuaries and bays. Greenies are highly migratory fish. Both juveniles and adults appear to move extensively up and down the coast. Adults move from the ocean to estuaries and lower reaches of rivers between late winter and early summer. Fish tagged in the Sacramento-San Joaquin Delta were recaptured 1-3 years later in the Columbia River and in Grays Harbor, Washington.

Green sturgeons reach 7 feet in length. No one is too sure, but greenies may live as long as 60 years. Females are oviparous. The eggs are fertilized externally and probably stick to cobblestones. Spawning takes place in rivers, and the spawning season in California is spring and early summer. There is a report of gravid females in the Columbia River during the fall. Siberian females produce 60,000-140,000 eggs per season. Not much is known about the habits of larvae and juveniles, but the juveniles are found in freshwater, migrating to sea during summer and fall around their second birthday. Greenies are bottom feeders, inhaling shrimps, small fishes and other bottom species.

FISHERY: Greens are commonly taken in bays and estuaries by recreational fishermen, often by those fishing for white sturgeon. There is a small commercial fishery for greenies, particularly in Oregon and Washington.

WHITE STURGEON (ACIPENSER TRANSMONTANUS)

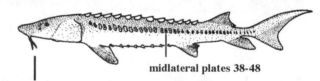

midlateral plates 38-48

barbels closer to tip
of snout than to mouth

NAMES:
Acipenser is Greek for "bony cartilage"; *transmontanus* is Latin for "beyond the mountain," probably a reference to its being thought to live only on the western side of the Rockies.

IDENTIFYING CHARACTERS: A white sturgeon is easily separated from anything else. It is grayish-white, with 5 rows of scutes (bony plates) on its body: one on back, one on each flank and one on each side of the belly. Very large fish have barely visible scutes. The mouth is underneath the head, with 4 barbels in the front. Green sturgeon are usually olive-green, occasionally gray, with 23-30 scutes along flanks (38-48 in whites) and 1 or 2 scutes after the dorsal fin (these are absent in white sturgeon).

DISTRIBUTION AND BIOLOGY: White sturgeon are found from the Gulf of Alaska to northern Baja California, primarily in freshwater and estuaries, infrequently meandering into the ocean. Most of the fish are found in river systems, with the Sacramento-San Joaquin and Columbia containing the largest populations. While most fish spend their lives in estuaries, going up rivers to spawn, some fish (for instance, those in Montana) spend their entire lives in freshwater. Basically, these are bottom fish, passing their days poking around sand and mud. However, on occasion they have been seen leaping out of the water, particularly in the spring. White sturgeon make several types of movements. Besides spawning migrations, Columbia River fish move into shallow, warm (63-64° F) water in summer and retreat to deeper pools in winter. While most fish seem to spend their lives in the same river system, one fish tagged in San Pablo Bay (San Francisco) moved 660 miles to the mouth of the Columbia River in Oregon. A go-hard tagged in the Columbia swam 200 miles northward to Willapa Bay, Washington.

These are by far the largest freshwater fish in the western part of North America. White sturgeon as large as 20 feet and 1,800 pounds have been reported; it is anyone's guess how accurate these old (pre-1900) reports are. They certainly reach 13 feet and 1,300 pounds and have been aged to 104 years. The study that reported the 104-year-old fish (1994, Transactions of the American Fisheries Society, p. 255-265) also noted that current aging techniques tend to underestimate true sturgeon ages. Males and females grow at about the same rate for a number of years, females eventually growing faster and larger. These fish also seem to grow much faster in the southern part of their range. In the Sacramento-San Joaquin system, sturgeon grow to about 25 inches in one year; they reach about 14 inches in the Columbia. Forty inch fish are 6-7 years old in the Delta, 8-10 years in the Columbia and 15 years old in the Fraser River of British Columbia.

In California, males mature after 10-15 years (3.6-6 feet); females, 12-20 years (4.6-6.6 feet). In British Columbia, males mature at anywhere from 11-22 years, females 11-34 years. Females produce between 100,000-4,700,000 eggs. Adults do not spawn every year; 4-11 years may pass between episodes. Spawning occurs from March-June in California and May-July further north. White sturgeon lay adhesive eggs on gravel or rock bottoms, and the eggs hatching in 1-2 weeks. Larvae stay near the bottom and are carried downstream to estuaries, where the juveniles remain until maturity. Juveniles eat mysid shrimps and amphipods, probing the mud and sand with their barbels. Larger fish eat lots of things, including shrimps, crabs, worms, clams, mussels, snails and a great variety of fishes (such as salmon, striped bass, gobies and herring). They are particularly fond of herring eggs and stuff themselves during herring spawning runs. Probably the most unusual food found in a white sturgeon was a house cat (honest). Exactly how a sturgeon got close enough to a house cat to eat it is unclear. I think it is likely the fish lured the cat into the water by making sounds resembling a can of Friskies Tuna and Liver Special.

FISHERY: White sturgeon are a major sport fish in estuaries and rivers from San Francisco Bay northward and are usually taken by boat and shore anglers fishing with shrimp. Commercial fishing is illegal in California, but considerable numbers are taken from Oregon to British Columbia.

REMARKS: White sturgeon are excellent eating, both fresh and smoked, and the eggs make a caviar which is just about as good as that pricey stuff from Russia and Iran. Commercial fishing for sturgeon, for meat, eggs and isinglass, was wide open during the latter half of the 19th Century, leading to widespread overfishing and severely reduced catches. (Isinglass is a gelatin-like material which comes from sturgeon swimbladders. It was used to make glues, jellies and to clarify beer. That makes sense, doesn't it? Here is a fish that has been around perhaps 200 million years, so what could be better than to clear beer with it?) By 1917, California banned all commercial fishing, opening the fishery to sportsmen in the 1950s. Thanks to improved management, the California sturgeon population has made something of a recovery over the years.

Sturgeon farming in California is on the brink becoming a profitable enterprise. A number of companies have been raising the fish for markets and restaurants, where there is strong demand. White sturgeon eggs make pretty good caviar; it retails for about $480 per pound. For an update on the sturgeon industry, send for NCRI News, June, 1995, from NCRI, 528 SW Mill, Suite, P.O. Box 751, Portland, Oregon 97207.

Native American middens around the Elkhorn Slough, San Francisco Bay, Sacramento-San Joaquin Delta and Puget Sound areas contain lots of sturgeon remains. One researcher believes sturgeon were second in importance only to salmon in the diets of Native Americans in the Puget Sound region.

Then there is this note on eating sturgeon heads by the coast Salish tribe of the Northwest: "J Ch said it was cooked for a long time; this took the plates off. Then it was sliced thin like bread and eaten. JM said the head was dried until hard, then boiled to soften before using". (J. Suttles. 1974. *The Economic Life of the Coast Salish of Haro and Rosario Straits.* Garland Publ., New York).

The U. S. Fish and Wildlife Service has listed the Kootenai River white sturgeon (found in the Kootenai River and Lake in Idaho, Montana and British Columbia) as endangered. This population has probably been isolated from their good buddies for about 10,000 years and their population is going to hell.

Here is a cheery note with which to leave you. Recent studies (summarized in Transactions of the American Fisheries Society, 1994, vol. 123, p. 565-573) have shown a large reduction in the levels of various radioactive materials in those white sturgeon living around the Hanford plutonium production facility on the Columbia River.

Morays - Family Muraenidae

CALIFORNIA MORAY (GYMNOTHORAX MORDAX)

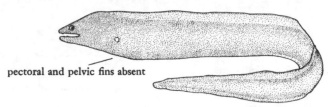

pectoral and pelvic fins absent

NAMES: *Gymnothorax* is formed from 2 Greek words meaning "bare thorax," *mordax* means "prone to bite" in Latin.

IDENTIFYING CHARACTERS: Morays are the only eels in our area without pectoral fins. They are colored light to dark brown or green, often with dark mottling. Other conspicuous characters include lots of sharp canine teeth and a small, round gill opening.

DISTRIBUTION AND BIOLOGY: Morays are found from Pt. Conception to southern Baja California, commonly from about Santa Barbara southward. The southern Channel Islands, Santa Catalina and San Clemente in particular, are loaded with them. Morays are rocky reef dwellers, living in crevices and caves from tidepools (rarely) to 130 feet in depth, most commonly from the shallow subtidal to about 60 feet.

California morays are reported to grow to 5 feet in length and probably live at least 30 years. A 12-incher is perhaps 2 years old. It is likely that the morays off southern California do not reproduce, probably because the waters are too cold. Rather, all the morays living there hatch off Baja California and drift north as larvae. Morays eat a variety of fishes, octopi, shrimp, crabs and the like.

FISHERY: These are occasionally taken by recreational anglers and divers. There are persistent rumors of a trap fishery for morays around Santa Catalina Island. The story is that these fish are being exported to Asia.

REMARKS: Divers are occasionally bitten by this eel, whose teeth can cause severe injury. Most of those bitten have either 1) stuck their hands in or near a moray's crevice or 2) speared one. While it may have happened, I know of no incidents where a moray has just swum out of a hole and bitten a swimmer or diver.

Herrings, Shads, Sardines - Family Clupeidae

AMERICAN SHAD (ALOSA SAPIDISSIMA)

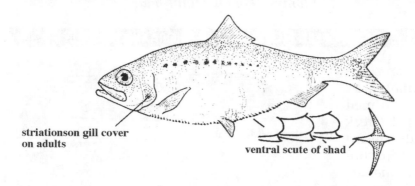

striationson gill cover
on adults

ventral scute of shad

NAMES: Common Shad, White Shad. *Alosa* comes from the Saxon word for the European Shad; *sapidissima* means "good to eat" in Latin.

IDENTIFYING CHARACTERS: These are deep-bodied, rather compressed fish, with blue backs and silvery sides. They have a very noticeable row of keeled scales on their bellies. A single row of dark spots on their backs distinguishes them from everything other than Pacific sardines, and these are rounder and do not have as sharp a series of belly scales.

DISTRIBUTION AND BIOLOGY: American shad are distributed from Kamchatka (Russia) and the Bering Sea southward to Todos Santos Bay, Baja California, most commonly from British Columbia to about Monterey Bay (central California). These fish are anadromous: they are born in freshwater, migrate to the ocean and live there for 3–5 years before returning to spawn. Spawning occurs in most of the major rivers and some of the smaller ones, from the Fraser in British Columbia to the Sacramento in California; the runs in the Fraser and Columbia Rivers and the Sacramento–San Joaquin River complex are quite large. This is a schooling fish, often found near the surface. It has also been taken in bottom drag nets down to about 1,200 feet. It is possible these nets caught the shad in midwater while being raised or lowered through the water. I have seen them caught in gillnets set on the bottom in about 120 feet. It is not clear where shad go, nor what they do while in the ocean; and though it is likely they move around a bit, no one knows how much. It is assumed they spawn within the same streams in which they were born (as do salmon), but this has not been proven.

American shad are the largest members of the herring family on the Pacific Coast, reaching 2.5 feet in length. Ninety percent of males mature at 3–4 years, 90% of females at 4–5 years; shad are 12 inches long or more when they mature. Many prespawning fish move into estuaries in the fall, overwinter there until water temperatures rise (they like 52°+ F), then move upstream. At least in the Sacramento–San Joaquin Delta, spawning occurs primarily from May to early July, when water temperatures range from 59–68° F. In the Sacramento–San Joaquin Delta, a few fish migrate upstream in March, with the run increasing in April and May. During spawning, a male shad nudges a female and they swim side by side, releasing sperm and eggs. Most spawning occurs at night and fish spawn repeatedly until all eggs are spent. Females produce 30,000–300,000 eggs. While almost all fish die after spawning, a few enjoy it so much that they survive to do it again the following year. The eggs drift downstream and the young hatch in 3–6 days. Juvenile shad remain in rivers or estuaries for up to a few months, when they are 3–8 inches. Almost all young–of–the–year move out of the Sacramento-San Joaquin Delta by December. Shad eat plankton.

FISHERY: A lot of people sport fish for American shad, primarily during the shads' freshwater spawning runs. Sport fishermen catch them in two ways, angling and "bumping." While I am reasonably sure you already are familiar with angling, bumping may be something of a mystery. In this technique, a dip net is held vertically in the water while the angler stands on a boat or on the shore. When a shad hits the net, the fisherman twists and scoops and the fish is trapped. At least in the past, most shad were either returned to the water (which is fine) or discarded dead (which is stupid). Hopefully, anglers will either return the fish to the water, alive, or take them home. They are good to eat, a bit bony to be sure, and make about the best smoked fish you can imagine.

Though commercial fishing for American shad is illegal in California, there is a fairly large fishery for them in the Pacific Northwest, primarily in rivers such as the Columbia. Most fish are taken by gillnet, although a limited amount is caught in the ocean by otter trawl. Shad have long been a great favorite on the East Coast, people in the West just haven't gotten their act together. Much of the commercial catch targets the species' roe, and the carcasses are sold for animal food or as bait for crabs.

REMARKS: American shad are not native to the West Coast. They were first planted on this side of the continent in 1871, in the Sacramento River. Further plants were made in the Columbia, Snake and Willamette Rivers in 1885 and 1886. All of these attempts were spectacularly successful and the fish quickly spread along the coast, establishing themselves in other rivers. Personally, I think that introducing non-native animals and plants is usually a dumb (often a very dumb) idea, and the well-meaning Bozos who do it often have no idea of the consequences. (However, ignorance is not going to save them. They will come back as accountants in their next life.) For instance, exactly how much do you really like all those snails munching away on your nasturtiums? Hey, give a big thank you to a misguided Frenchman; he brought them over from France and they took over. Was it a truly smart move to import mongooses into Hawaii in an attempt to kill rats? Well, the mongooses ignored the rats, but certainly did a number on the native birds. Various governmental agencies spend mucho taxpayer dollars getting rid of carp from lakes and rivers, and carp are an introduced species. ("Gee, everyone loves eating carp, don't they? Let's play Mother Nature and bring them over from the Old Country, so the entire nation can benefit!")

PACIFIC HERRING (CLUPEA PALLASI)

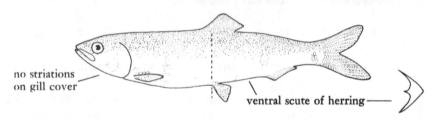

no striations on gill cover

ventral scute of herring

NAMES: Herring. *Clupea* is a Latin word for "herring"; *pallasi* honors the remarkable Russian naturalist and explorer of the North Pacific, Petrus Simon Pallas.

IDENTIFYING CHARACTERS: Pacific herring have compressed, somewhat elongate bodies and are bluish-green to olive on their backs and silvery on their bellies. Their pelvic fins are positioned underneath their dorsal fins. Herrings may be confused with the Pacific sardine, which usually have several dark spots on their sides and striations on their gill covers. The Pacific round herring (*Etrumeus acuminatus*) has its pelvic fin behind the dorsal fin.

DISTRIBUTION AND BIOLOGY: Pacific herring are found over a wide arc of the North Pacific, from Korea and Japan on the east, up to Arctic Alaska and down to northern Baja California. Herring in the northeastern Pacific (south and east of Kodiak Island) may be genetically isolated from those of the northwest Pacific and Bering Sea. Even within the northeast Pacific there may be a myriad of populations, including one or more off California, one off Oregon, 3+ in Puget Sound, 9+ off British Columbia, 5+ off southeast Alaska and 3 in the Bering Sea.

Along our coast, they are most abundant off British Columbia and Alaska. While these are schooling fishes, usually found at or fairly near the surface, there are reports of their having been taken at 990 feet or possibly to 1,568 feet. Herring may be found at different depths depending on season. During the summer, in the Gulf of Alaska, schools are found at depths of about 15-100 feet. By January and February, the fish have retreated to 150-250 feet. Herring schools may disperse at night. While most of a herring's life is spent along the open coast, sometimes at a considerable distance out to sea, the fish spawns in quiet bays and estuaries, returning to the same area to spawn every year. We don't know much about its movements at sea.

Pacific herring reach 18 inches in length and in Alaska live to at least 19 years. Off California they have been aged to 11 years. Generally, herring off British Columbia and Alaska live longer, grow faster and reach larger sizes. Off California, an 8 incher is 4–5 years old. The fish mature at 2–3 years (6.5–7 inches) off California and 3–4 years off British Columbia. Females produce between 9,000–134,000 eggs and those in the northern part of their range produce fewer eggs at a given size than do those to the south.

Spawning occurs from San Diego Bay northward, with major runs beginning in San Francisco Bay. Spawning takes place earliest off California and later to the north. Off California, minor amounts of spawning have been noted as early as late October and as late as April, but January and February are peak months. Off British Columbia, spawning occurs mostly from February to April, and in the Bering Sea during May and June. The earliest spawners are usually the largest fish. Some days or weeks before spawning, herring schools enter quiet bays and estuaries and sort of hang out. During these times they are often unresponsive to such stimuli as light, which normally attracts them. Most spawning occurs at night in very shallow, sometimes intertidal, waters down to 36 feet. The eggs are very sticky and are attached to a variety of marine plants, as well as rocks, pilings and virtually anything else that doesn't get out of the way. Eggs are usually layed in rows, 1 or 2 eggs deep. However, when spawning is intense, there is not enough room in the bay and egg masses as thick as 2 inches are produced. It's a bummer if you are one of the embryos at the bottom because your chances of hatching are poor when you are covered by a lot of other eggs. As females lay the eggs, males (who, like guys everywhere, are sort of clueless) emit sperm throughout the area and the water often turns milky colored. The eggs hatch in about 10-15 days, depending on water temperature.

In the fall, when herring reach 3–4 inches, they leave these shallow areas and head out to sea. Pacific herring eat zooplankton, including copepods, amphipods, krill and small fishes. In turn, they are eaten by a host of predators, including salmon, Pacific cod, dogfish, lingcod, lampreys, harbor seals, northern fur seals, Steller and California sea lions, sperm whales, Dall's porpoises and Pacific white-sided dolphins. Herring eggs are eaten by a number of birds (particularly gulls and such diving ducks as scoters), along with mollusks and amphipods. Lots of things eat the larvae, particularly jellyfish, they may really waste on the larval population. In one study off British Columbia, jellyfish reduced the number of herring larvae from an average maximum of 264 larvae per cubic meter to 3.5 in just 3 days.

FISHERY: There is a small sport fishery, by pier and shore anglers, as adults come in to spawn and by divers collecting egg-covered algae. The real action comes from the commercial fishery. Herring are an extremely, I might even say, hyper-valuable fish. Actually, the fish itself is not particularly sought after, though there are small fisheries (notably in Monterey, Puget Sound and off British Columbia) for herring to be used as bait and, occasionally, food. Rather, it is the herring eggs (roe) that are really valuable. Because the roe is considered a delicacy in Japan, it has a lively and very lucrative export market. In Japan, herring roe is consumed in two ways. *Kazunoko kombu* are lightly salted eggs still attached to edible algae. Along the Pacific coast, there is a fishery for kazunoko kombu, where divers collect egg–encrusted algae. The other, larger, fishery is the sac–roe fishery which targets the herring themselves. The egg sacs are removed from the herring, and, as *Kazunoko*, they are salted and shipped to Japan.

Along the Pacific Coast, from San Francisco Bay northward, the fishery is highly regulated. Sometimes fishermen are allowed to fish in a particular stretch of water for only a short period, occasionally only one day. The value of the fish is so great that a single purse seine or gillnet haul may be worth tens or even hundreds of thousands of dollars. As you might imagine, this fishery becomes sort of intense with a lot of boats in a very small area given only a little time to potentially make a lot of money. In such circumstances, fishermen have been known to say bad words as nets tangle with other nets, vessels collide and fishermen make sets on fish claimed by other fishermen. If you want to see this fishery in action, the San Francisco Bay herring fishery, which I understand is a little less cutthroat than in previous years, usually occurs December–March, right off Tiburon, Belvedere and nearby communities.

REMARKS: Want to pickle your own herring? Sure you do! It's as much fun for the whole family as regrouting your bathroom sink, and you can eat the results. (Of course, you can also eat grout, but there is more protein in herring.) Send for *Spiced and Pickled Seafood* (R. J. Price, UCSGEP 90–13, Food Sciences and Technology Extension, UC Davis, CA, 95616).

Here's an interesting tidbit from R. S. Croker's romantic report "Smoked, salted and dried sea foods of California" (*California Fish and Game*, 1936, vol. 22, p. 1-11). It seems that, in the past, brined and smoked herring were sold as "bloaters". Croker notes that before becoming this appetizingly-named product, "Alaska brine herrings are soaked in fresh water until there is no more than enough salt left to keep them from spoiling. Then they are given a short smoke, after which they are ready for sale." Personally, I'm saddened that the name "bloater" seems to have disappeared from the gastronomic lexicon of California. I can think of nothing more fun than going to a white linen restaurant for breakfast and having Morris, the ancient tuxedo-clad waiter, arrive with the meal, stating simply, "Your bloater, sir."

Native Americans have harvested herring at least back to 800 B.C. This species was also a very important food item in the San Francisco of Gold Rush days.

Pacific herring earbones have been recovered from 3 million plus year old deposits in southern California.

PACIFIC SARDINE (SARDINOPS SAGAX)

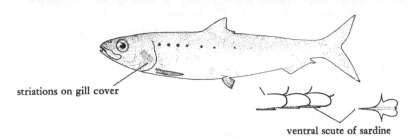

striations on gill cover

ventral scute of sardine

NAMES: California Pilchard, South American Sardine, Chilean Pilchard, Firecrackers (small ones), Pilchard. *Sardinops* comes from the Latin word *sardine* (meaning, to no one's intense surprise, "sardine") and the Greek word *ops*, which means "like;" *sagax* is Latin for "quick" or "alert."

IDENTIFYING CHARACTERS: Pacific sardines are elongated blue or green–backed fish, with silvery bellies. They almost always have dark spots on their upper sides, with striations on their gill covers. The Pacific herring has no spots or striations.

DISTRIBUTION AND BIOLOGY: Pacific sardines are found from Kamchatka (USSR) to southeast Alaska, southward to Guaymas, Mexico and possibly off Peru and Chile. Historically, sardines were abundant as far north as British Columbia, but the bulk of the population was (and is) centered from northern Baja California southward. These are schooling, pelagic fish, found from very near shore to hundreds of miles off the coast.

Pacific sardines reach 16.25 inches and they have been aged to 13 years. About 50% of all sardines mature at 7-8 inches and virtually all are mature by 9.5 inches. Studies made during the 1930s implied that sardines spawned primarily from late winter through summer, while recent ones showed some year-round spawning with a summer and fall peak. Females are oviparous and produce 30,000-65,000 eggs. The eggs hatch in about 2.5 days at 63° F and 2.5-4 days at 55-61° F. Considerable spawning occurs near shore, but some probably takes place out to at least 300 miles. Females spawn more than once per season. Greatest concentrations of sardine larvae are found from about Punta Baja, central Baja California to southern Baja California.

Sardines feed on various types of plankton and, in turn, are eaten by a host of fishes, birds and marine mammals. Harbor porpoises feed on sardines and one interesting episode was reported in Monterey Bay. Five to 7 porpoises formed a crescent and swept through a school, gobbling fish as they went. Immediately after they had run through the school, the porpoises dived beneath the sardines, forcing them to the surface. At the same time, other porpoises remained at the surface, splashing and jumping, keeping the fish bunched up. After each sweep, a new group of porpoises would line up and attack.

FISHERY: Pacific sardines are occasionally taken by sport anglers, primarily from piers, usually for bait. From the 1920s through 1940s, this species was the most important commercial fish in California waters, worth millions of dollars to the state's economy. Most of the fish were taken by purse seine or lampara net and canned or processed into fish meal and oil. For most of that period, Monterey was the center of the fishery, and Cannery Row was the place where it all happened. The fishery from central California to British Columbia collapsed in the 1940s and shifted briefly to southern California, only to collapse again in the early 1950s. Until about 1980, sardines were rarely seen in California waters. In the early 1980s, lots of sardine larvae were noted off southern California and soon both young ones and older fish (which swam up from Baja California) were common. By 1985, sardine populations were large enough to allow a small commercial take. Currently, sardines are taken by lampara net for the live bait industry and by purse seine. Some of the catch is sold whole, fresh and frozen, some is canned and some is turned into fish meal. Shelf life for fresh ones is about 5 days at 40° F and 9-12 months when frozen.

REMARKS: Why did the sardine population go to hell in a hand basket in the 1940s? Well, as easy as it might be to blame overfishing for the collapse, that would be too simple an explanation. Although overfishing probably hastened the process, it was not solely responsible. The sardine population off California goes through boom and bust cycles. Over the past 1,850 years, sardines have had 12 major periods of abundance; these last 20–150 years and are separated by 20–200 year periods of sardine scarcity. The pretty large population of the 1930s was really not particularly impressive, compared to what the numbers were like about 1,000 years ago. What happens is that conditions favoring sardine reproduction occur only sometimes off California; when they don't, few young ones survive and after a few years the population goes way down (remember, sardines don't live very long). The decline of the sardines that we saw in the 40s and 50s was the end of a process that began in 1890 (30 years before the fishery began). Interestingly, the collapse of the California sardine population was paralleled, year for year, with a similar one for the Japanese sardine.

Along with the unfortunate demise of the term "bloater" (see "Remarks" under Pacific herring), comes the tragic word that the "salacchini" industry has yet to recover (R. S. Croker, "Smoked, salted and dried sea foods of California", *California Fish and Game*, 1936, vol. 22, p. 1-11). In this marvelous publication, Croker (a really cool name for a Fish and Game biologist, yes?) writes: "The manufacture of salacchini, a salt and pressure-dried pack of sardines, was very important before the advent of prohibition. Many saloons served salacchini, as it is said to improve the flavor of light drinks at the same time tasting better itself when served with beverages. In 1918, the production was 2,000,000 pounds, but the industry declined markedly after the enactment of the Eighteenth Amendment. [Author's note: This was the infamous Anti-Salacchini Amendment, pushed through by OPWDLFNFII, the Organization of People Who Don't Like Food Names Ending In "I".] With the return of legalized drinking the sardine canneries that make salacchini as a side line are hopeful of the future, although the expected boom has not yet materialized."

Well, I think it is safe to say that the now-extinct sardine canneries are still sitting around on their metaphorical behinds, picking metaphorical lint from their metaphorical navels, eternally hopeful that the coming salacchini boom will propel them back into existence. I trust that this will serve as a wakeup call to all you brazen venture capitalists. The sardines have returned, the Eighteenth Amendment is gone: it's time to bring back salacchini.

In one of those supreme ironies that make life worth living, sardines have returned to a Monterey which is unable to can them. Most of the canneries have been converted to other uses: trendy fern bars (offering "Sea Otter Margaritas, $1, 4–6 PM"), little curio shops selling battery-powered sea otter dolls that smash plastic rocks against plastic abalones, and art galleries pushing "Mother Sea Otter and Baby" toilet paper holders carved from redwood burls.

Sardines were a major food of Native Americans.

Anchovies - Family Engraulidae

DEEPBODY ANCHOVY (ANCHOA COMPRESSA)

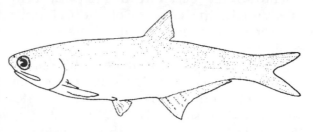

NAMES: *Compressa* is Latin for "compressed."

IDENTIFYING CHARACTERS: It's very easy to tell this one. It has a deep, very compressed body that is green or brown on back and silvery on belly. And (here is the big tip-off) they have a wide, silver stripe on each side of their flimsy little bodies.

DISTRIBUTION AND BIOLOGY: Deepbody anchovies have been taken from Morro Bay to northern Baja California, but they are more abundant south of Pt. Conception. Unlike northern anchovies, which positively relish being 30 miles from the coast in the middle of nowhere, this is a species of backwaters and bays. Adults migrate from the lower parts of bays into the upper regions during the spring-summer spawning season.

Deepbodies reach a mighty 7 inches long. They first mature at about 2.75 inches and a few live as long as 6 years. Females are oviparous and spawn from March to August (peaking April to June). Spawning occurs at night. Large females may produce over 28,000 eggs, and the eggs likely hatch in less than 4 days.

Deepbodies eat zooplankton of all sorts, including copepods, ostracods, amphipods and various larvae. There are no records of who eats these guys, but as usual, it's probably the same list of suspects - various fish-eating birds, fishes and maybe an occasional marine mammal.

FISHERY: No fishery to speak of, though once in a while you will find one in a party vessel bait tank.

NORTHERN ANCHOVY (ENGRAULIS MORDAX)

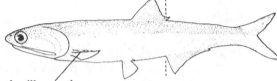

pectoral axillary scale

NAME: Pinheads (juveniles), Katakuchiiwasirui (Japanese). *Engraulis* is the ancient Greek name for a Mediterranean anchovy; *mordax* means "biting" in Latin.

IDENTIFYING CHARACTERS: This is a long, fairly thin fish, blue or green on back and silvery on belly. Its anal fin begins at the rear of its dorsal fin. Northerns have large, underslung mouths and sort of dopey, paranoid expressions (you would too if you realized everyone was trying to make a meal out of you). Slough anchovies (*Anchoa delicatissima*) are more compressed, the anal fin starts under the middle of the dorsal fin and, since they have been in therapy for some time, they look a bit more relaxed.

DISTRIBUTION AND BIOLOGY: Northern anchovies are found from Queen Charlotte Island (British Columbia) to the tip of Baja California and in the Gulf of California, most abundantly from Pt. Conception southward. Found from the surface to depths of over 1,000 feet and from the surf zone out to at least 300 miles, most live within about 100 miles of shore. They occasionally enter estuarine waters. The latest theory seems to be that there are 3 more-or-less genetically distinct populations along the Pacific Coast: one from north of San Francisco to British Columbia, one from north Baja California to San Francisco and one along the southern Baja California coast. Tagging studies show that fish move from San Francisco to Monterey, central California to southern California, southern California to central California and southern California to northern Baja California. Studies off southern California have shown that anchovies make extensive seasonal migrations. During fall, many of the fish are inshore in the northern part of the area, from about Santa Barbara to Newport Beach. In late winter, they tend to move offshore and down the coast, spreading out into small, numerous schools. Some time between March and June the fish begin to move north and inshore and start forming larger schools. These are just general patterns. There are lots of exceptions—please don't write me and explain them all. Anchovies are schooling fish and display a bewildering array of behaviors. Here are a few examples. During fall and winter, fish tend to form large schools, anywhere from near the surface down to about 180 feet. During other seasons, much of the population can be found in small, scattered schools, often 30–60 feet down. In general, fish disperse at sundown (probably to feed) and travel to the surface. They begin to reform later that night (often completing the process just before dawn) or in early morning. Very large schools may occur 360–720 feet below the surface along submarine canyons and over deep banks, particularly during fall. Submarine canyons, deep banks and basins all seem to be particularly good spots to find the fish.

Northern anchovies reach 9 inches in length, but anything over 7 inches is a rarity. They live to 7 years, but most die by 4–5 years. A one year old is 4.5–5.5 inches long, a 5 year old is 5–7 inches Central California anchovies may grow larger than ones off southern California and ones off southern Baja California seem to grow the slowest of any along the Pacific coast. The 1983 El Niño slowed growth rates of larvae, juveniles and adults, perhaps because food was in short supply during the warm water period. Off southern and central California some fish mature at the end of their first year and all are mature by age 4. Off Oregon and Washington, no fish mature until they are in their third year. Off southern California, spawning occurs all year, with peaks from December–May. Fish off Oregon and Washington spawn from mid-June to mid-August, much of it offshore of the Columbia River. There may be another spawning area off the Fraser River, British Columbia. Spawning occurs from near shore to over 200 miles from the coast, most often within about 150 miles offshore. Spawning usually occurs at night. Females are oviparous and spawn every 6-8 days during the peak season. Females emit between about 2,700-16,600 oval eggs per batch. They may produce as many as 130,000 eggs per year in southern California and perhaps 35,000 eggs a year in the more northern population. Most spawning occurs between Pt. Conception and Cabo San Lazaro, southern Baja California, with a peak between Punta Eugenia and Cabo San Lazaro. Spawning occurs mostly at temperatures between 54-59° F, usually within 30 feet of the surface. Eggs are found from the surface to about 175 feet, mostly in the upper 60 feet. Eggs take 2-4 days to hatch, with the young fish moving into very shallow water. Larvae transform into juveniles in about 70 days. Periods of calm water tend to benefit the survival of young, perhaps by keeping concentrations of food together.

Zooplankton (such as copepods, arrow worms and krill), phyto-plankton and small fishes make up much of their diet. As they prey on plankton, northern anchovies routinely eat northern anchovy eggs (leading, no doubt, to tremendous guilt feelings). In turn, anchovies are eaten by almost any fish, sea bird or marine mammal that can get their jaws around these guys. Brown pelicans are major eaters, along with California sea lions and northern elephant seals, as well as western gulls, tufted puffins, least terns, rhinoceros auklets, harbor porpoises, Dall's porpoises, Pacific white-sided dolphins and the list goes on and on.

FISHERY: Anchovies are occasionally taken from piers by anglers using shiny or yarn–covered hooks, but they are most important in the commercial and live bait fisheries. The use of anchovies as live bait goes back at least to 1910, when Japanese albacore fisher-men caught and held them in bait tanks. Sport fishing vessels quickly saw the effectiveness of live bait and began capturing them with nets carried on board. Soon, separate anchovy–netting vessels were developed. Today a number of lampara and purse-seine-equipped boats catch anchovies for the sport fishing industry in California, primarily in the central and southern part of the state. In an average year, 98–99% of the live bait catch is northern anchovy, with white croaker, queenfish, Pacific sardine, Pacific mackerel, jackmackerel, Pacific butterfish, squid and various perches making up the rest. Many sport anglers, such as those fishing for kelp bass and halibut, prefer the so-called "brown baits"—croaker, queenfish, and perch. All live bait catches are made with lampara nets and purse seines. As of the late 1980s, very small amounts of northern anchovy were also taken by commercial fishermen and reduced to fish meal and oil for poultry feed. Attempts have been made to can this species, but sales of this product were poor. The little salted anchovies used on pizzas are imported. Guess what—they are not salty if you eat them fresh.

REMARKS: A northern anchovy earbone was found in one million plus year old Pliocene deposits from Long Beach, southern California. Northern anchovies are very commonly found in Native American middens.

CUTTHROAT TROUT

Salmons, Trouts, Chars - Family Salmonidae

CUTTHROAT TROUT (ONCORHYNCHUS CLARKI)

NAMES: *Oncorhynchus* is Greek for "hooked nose"; *clarki* recognizes William Clark of the Lewis and Clark Expedition.

IDENTIFYING CHARACTERS: Probably the most obvious characteristic of this species is the orange or red streak on the lower jaw. Other than that, these fish resemble rainbow trout (see rainbow trout illustration). Sea-run individuals have greenish-blue or blue backs, silvery sides and bellies and lots of black spots on bodies and fins (though not the pelvics). Freshwater individuals are often greenish on their backs. Another good character is the teeth on the back of the tongue; these are not found in rainbows or in Pacific salmons.

DISTRIBUTION AND BIOLOGY: Cutthroats range from the Gulf of Alaska to the Eel River, northern California. Like the rainbow trout, some cutthroats are anadromous, spending time in the ocean, while others never leave their birth streams. Cutthroats tend to occupy the smaller coastal streams and tributaries. Perhaps this has evolved as a mechanism for avoiding some competition with steelheads and salmons. These trout tolerate temperatures between about 43-79° F, though they prefer 48-54° F.

The biggest cutthroat on record (not a sea-run specimen, by the way) was 2.5 feet long. The marine ones are smaller. Females are oviparous. As with steelhead, there is a very wide range of life-history parameters for sea-run cutthroats. Take maturity, for instance. While most probably mature at 3 or 4 years, the span for wild fish is 2-10 years, and some hatchery fish are in there spawning after one year. Spawning occurs in fall and winter, at temperatures of 43-63°, optimally around 50° F. Like other Pacific Coast trouts and salmons, these puppies spawn in gravel beds. Most cutthroat spawning occurs in small coastal streams in perhaps 4-6 inches of water. Females have been noted to produce anywhere from 226-4,420 eggs. Unlike the Pacific salmons, many cutthroats survive spawning and return in later years. Eggs take 28-40 days to hatch and the newly-hatched fish (alevins) stay under the gravel for 1-2 weeks, emerging as fry. There is a wide freshwater residence period for juvenile cutthroats, anywhere from 1-9 years. Somewhere around three years is the average residence time. Juveniles and post-spawning adults enter the ocean in spring and summer, depending on locality, and most return a few months later, in late summer and fall. Not all juveniles return as adults; some need more time to complete the process. The fish tend to stay in the lower parts of the streams for a bit, then press on during fall and winter. In rivers, juveniles eat the usual assortment of insects, small fishes and assorted crustaceans. While in the sea, fishes are the big items (e.g., northern anchovy, kelp greenling, rockfishes, salmons etc.), along with such zooplanktors as krill, mysid shrimps and crustacean larvae.

FISHERY: This is a very popular recreational species in the Pacific Northwest, from northern California northward. Cutthroats are not targeted by commercial fishermen, but they are occasionally taken in the salmon fisheries.

REMARKS: Cutthroats appear to be quite sensitive to environmental perturbations. There is evidence that a wide range of habitat alterations, including changes in temperature and turbidity, plant cover and siltation rates, all depress trout populations.

PINK SALMON (ONCORHYNCHUS GORBUSCHA)

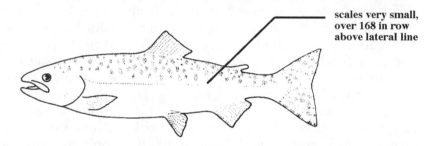

scales very small, over 168 in row above lateral line

NAMES: Humpback, tcas! (Native American - Tlingit). *Oncorhynchus* is Greek for "hooked nose"; *gorbuscha* was the Russian name for this species when the Russkies lived in Alaska.

IDENTIFYING CHARACTERS: A pink can be distinguished from other Pacific salmon by the very large black spots on all of the caudal fin and back. Coho salmon have no black spots on the lower part of their caudal fins and chinooks have small irregular black spots. The nickname "humpback" comes from the rather dramatic rounded back (along with a remarkable hooked upper jaw) that males develop prior to spawning.

DISTRIBUTION AND BIOLOGY: Pinks are the most abundant of the Pacific salmon. Pinkie Land extends from Honshu Island, Japan and North Korea, northward into the East Siberian Sea and Beaufort Sea and southward to La Jolla, southern California. The extremes of the spawning grounds are Hokkaido Island, Japan to the Sacramento River, northern California. Extensive runs occur in rivers stretching from the Amur of Russia to the Puyallup in Puget Sound, Washington. In North America, the area of greatest abundance is the central and southeastern parts of Alaska. Pinks usually stay near the surface; they have been reported to depths of about 120 feet.

Pinks are the smallest of the Pacific salmon, reaching 2.5 feet, but they do have the highest growth rate. Most pinks mature at 2 years, though there are populations that mature in 1 or 3 years. The oviparous females produce fewer eggs per female than other Pacific salmon. From June-September (mainly July-September) as the spawning season approaches, pinks migrate homeward and begin to bunch up in bays and estuaries near the spawning grounds. Several studies imply that during high population years, this migration occurs in the early part of this period. Spawning in streams and rivers takes place from June to October, (mainly August-October) depending on location. There are reports of just zillions of pinks crashing up river at the same time. How about this observation from Russian biologist I. F. Pravdin, quoted in *Pacific Salmon Life Histories* (University of British Columbia Press, 1991). "Although the weather was calm and sunny, an extraordinary noise could be heard coming from the middle of the river...similar to the noise of boiling water splashing in a gigantic cauldron...Standing there, the fishermen feasted their eyes upon a tremendous school of fish, which went up the river, making a very loud noise, as if a new river had burst into the Bolshaya; the fish jumped out of the water continuously. The noisy stretch of fish was at least one verst long [3,521 feet] and not less than 100 meters wide, so that the size of the school could be estimated at several million specimens." Neat, huh? But don't you just crave to make some pun, in a heavy Russian accent, about going from "bed to verst"?

Pinks migrate into freshwater during the day. Many populations spawn very near the coast, often only a mile or so upstream, and often in tidal areas. While they tend to spawn closer to the sea than other Pacific salmon, some move up quite a ways; the longest migration record I can find is a little over 400 miles, in the Snake River of Washington. Pinks are less able to negotiate waterfalls and other barriers than more athletic salmon, and that is often what limits their inland movement. During the initial migration, males tend to outnumber females, but by the end of the run, females often predominate. Spawning usually takes place in water temperatures of 45-65° F, in riffles a few inches to perhaps 2.3 feet deep. As a species, pinks produce fewer eggs per female than other Pacific salmon; anywhere from 800-2,800 eggs (depending on what study you read). As with other Pacific salmon, spawning takes place in gravel beds. A female excavates the nest (redd) with her caudal fin, the eggs are layed, fertilized and she covers them over. After the eggs leave the female, they are only fertilizable for about 30 seconds. At about the same time, the eggs become sticky (this lasts about 20 minutes), which helps keep them in the gravel until they are buried. After the eggs have been laid and covered over, the female guards the nest for as long as 13 days, primarily to prevent other females from inadvertently uncovering them. Females may mate with more than one male (as many as 6 at one time) and vice versa and females may dig more than one nest. Both males and females die soon after spawning.

Young ones hatch in about 2-6 months and emerge from the gravel after about another 3-4 months (in North America, that's mainly in late March to May). The newly-emerged fry pop out at night and usually begin to move downstream and head out to sea. In small coastal streams, where spawning may have occurred in intertidal waters, this migration may take just one night. In a few populations, young fish stay in freshwater for more extended periods. Once in the sea, the young ones stay near the coast until they are able to fend for themselves a bit. At some place around 2 inches, the juveniles tend to leave more protected climes and strike out for the open sea. There is a tendency for pinks produced between Puget Sound to southeast Alaska to initially migrate northwest for about a year. On the return leg home (around May to July), they head out to sea a bit, and turn back southeastward, eventually arriving back at their home streams. While they do not tend to migrate as far as some other salmon species, some do travel a ways, as much as 1,500 miles from their birth streams. About 10% of all returning fish "stray" and wind up in the wrong stream. At sea, pinks tend to aggregate in small groups or even in pairs. Juvenile pinks feed on various zooplankton. Older ones hit on krill, fishes, squids, copepods and other zooplankton. At sea, most feeding takes place at dawn and dusk. In streams, the little ones are eaten by various fishes (cutthroats, rainbows, coho, sculpins etc.), along with such birds as belted kingfishers, mergansers and probably small mammals. In the ocean, predators include lampreys, various salmon, and spiny dogfish, along with common murres, common mergansers, Caspian terns, harbor seals and northern fur seals.

FISHERY: If you look from Alaska to California, pinks usually make up about 10% of the total recreational salmon catch. Most are taken from south-central Alaska to British Columbia, and in Puget Sound. Pinks are a big time commercial fishery indeed and, as in the recreational fishery, most of the North American catch occurs from Alaska to Puget Sound, particularly off Alaska. Gillnets and purse seines catch the vast majority. Most fish are canned, a little is frozen. While it usually is worth the least per pound, the very large numbers caught make it a very valuable species.

REMARKS: People have spent considerable time and money trying to transplant pinks outside their natural range (Maine, Newfoundland, Hudson Bay, Chile) with almost zip to show for it. Ironically, the only really successful transfer, to the Great Lakes, was accidental. A number of pinks being hatched in an Ontario hatchery, prior to a release in Hudson Bay, were accidentally released into Lake Superior during loading into a float plane. Soon after, some bumblehead discarded a bunch of fingerlings down the hatchery drain, a drain that, again, eventually leads into Lake Superior. A few years later, adult pinks were noticed in Superior and they have since spread into all of the Great Lakes in considerable numbers.

Because pinks have a two-year life cycle, there are often two genetically distinct populations in the same stream, the "evens" and the "odds". Evens come back in even years, odds in odds and because of this they remain reproductively isolated from one another. In some cases, evens from different streams (and odds from different streams) are more closely related than are evens and odds from the same stream. Some streams also show dominance of one group, with even year runs being larger than those in odd years, or vice versa. When both strains are in the same river, odd fish generally spawn upstream and even ones spawn downstream. Odd fish are often larger than even fish in North American waters.

Hybrids between pinks and chums (they often spawn in generally the same vicinity) are not uncommon.

CHUM SALMON (ONCORHYNCHUS KETA)

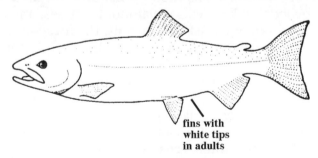

fins with
white tips
in adults

NAMES: Calico Salmon, Dog Salmon, Fall Salmon, Keta Salmon. *Oncorhynchus* is Greek for "hooked nose"; *keta* is the old name used for this species by the Nanai, inhabitants of what is now eastern Russia and northeastern China. Keta means "fish."

IDENTIFYING CHARACTERS: Unlike most other Pacific salmon, chums do not have large black spots, rather they may have tiny black speckling. Sea-run chums are metallic blue on their backs, with silvery bellies. Spawning individuals are blackish or dark olive on backs, reddish on sides, with dark bars or gray blotches (often described as a "calico" pattern).

DISTRIBUTION AND BIOLOGY: Chums are probably the second most abundant of the Pacific salmon (behind pinks) and have the widest distribution of this group. They are found from Japan and Korea northward to the Laptev Sea (northern Siberia) and Beaufort Sea (Northern Alaska) and southward to San Diego, southern California. DNA analyses indicate that there are three main population groupings: 1) Japanese, 2) Russian-Yukon River and 3) southeastern Alaska-British Columbia. These may reflect the areas of refuge for this species during the last glaciation. Spawning occurs from the Naktong River, Korea and on Kyushu Island, Japan across the Pacific to San Lorenzo River, central California. In North America, decent-sized runs occur from about Tillamook Bay, Oregon to Kotzebue Sound, Alaska. While most spawning occurs within about 50 miles of the coast, some fish migrate (as on the Yukon) 1,500 miles or more upstream.

Chums grow to about 40 inches long and mature at between 2-6 years old, most often 3-5. Fishes in the southern part of the range tend to spawn at 3-4 years of age, those in the north, 4-5. Females are oviparous and both sexes die after spawning. Chums spawn throughout the year, depending on where you are along the Pacific Coast, though in any particular stream or river the season may be only a few months long. There is a tendency for fishes in the southern part of the range to spawn later in the season. For instance, in the rivers entering Kotzebue Sound (Alaska), most spawning occurs in July and August. On the other hand, in Puget Sound spawning runs begin in early September and some continue into March.

In many streams, there are two fairly distinct runs. The early arrivers tend to spawn in the main parts of the natal rivers and streams; the later arrivals head to smaller tributaries. Late runners often seek out spring-fed tributaries, where water temperatures are relatively high (remember, it may be well into winter). North American females are reported to produce between about 2,000-4,000 eggs. Like other Pacific salmon, females dig nests in gravel, deposit eggs and the male fertilizes them. The following is one of those accounts that is sufficiently graphic that if it described any other animal, and the author lived in a state below the Mason Dixon Line, he or she could be prosecuted to the full extent of the law. From E. O. Salo (*Pacific Salmon Life Histories*, 1991, University of British Columbia Press), "When the female is ready to deposit her eggs, she will move into the nest and 'crouch'...with mouth agape. When she starts to crouch, the male immediately moves forward and lies next to her assuming a similar position. At this

101

point the reproductive products [another excellent name for a rock group - M. Love] are released with both partners vibrating their caudal peduncle and anal fin. Sometimes the female will perform several crouches in succession before releasing the eggs...The spawning act lasts, on average, 10 seconds." Immediately afterwards, the female covers over the eggs, moves a bit upcurrent, digs out another depression and the whole tedious process repeats itself. Once a female completes spawning, she defends the covered eggs until she dies. On the other hand, once spawning is complete, a male will search out other females with which to spawn. I will leave to others the pithy comparisons to human behavior. Males will mate with females for a total of 10-14 days, after which, with one assumes is a smile on their hooked beaks, they croak.

Fry emerge at night and quickly head downstream to the estuaries. The entire downstream migration may last 30 days or more, depending on how far they have to go. Generally, the farther south you are, the earlier it happens. Puget Sound fish do it in late winter and spring, while for those in the Yukon, late spring to autumn is the time. During their freshwater and estuarine sojourn they probably feed on insects and insect larvae. Some fry stay in estuaries for a month or more, then enter saltwater and quickly spread out along the coast, generally staying within about 20 miles of shore and feeding on copepods and amphipods. During this period, the fish move in a generally northerly direction along California, Oregon, Washington and British Columbia. Gulf of Alaska chums move westward or southwestward along the Aleutians and from Bristol Bay. After growing to about 18-24 inches, the fish head out to sea. Most North American fish move into the Gulf of Alaska in the fall, few migrate westward beyond the end of the Aleutians. Chums are champion migrators, travelling as much as 1,900 miles from their birth streams.

On the high seas, zooplankton (such as krill, amphipods, salps and other gelatinous animals) and fishes make up much of their diet. While it is likely that chums are eaten by a wide range of predators, there just isn't much data available. There are reports of sculpins, steelhead, coho salmon and other salmonids eating fry, and orcas, harbor seals, belted kingfishers, rhinoceros auklets and Pacific cods preying on them at sea. Bears and bald eagles eat the returning adults.
FISHERY: Not many chums are taken by recreational anglers–perhaps 1% of the total North American salmon catch. Most of these are taken in Cook Inlet and Prince William Sound, south-central Alaska. From Alaska to central Oregon, particularly off western and south-central Alaska, this is a big time commercial fish. Most are taken with purse seines and gillnets and the catch is sold fresh, frozen, canned and smoked.

REMARKS: Lots of chums are released from hatcheries around the North Pacific. The Japanese release incredible numbers; in some years, over 2 billion fry are released. In Japan, there are relatively few wild chum salmon left.

COHO OR SILVER SALMON (ONCORHYNCHUS KISUTCH)

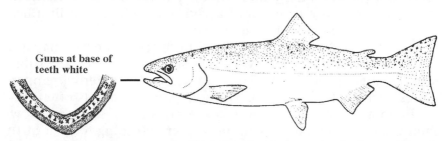

Gums at base of teeth white

NAMES: Young ones are called Bluebacks, particularly in British Columbia. Coho may be derived from Native American names, such as "kwahwult" or "kuchuks." *Oncorhynchus* is Greek for "hooked nose"; *kisutch* is what the 18th Century inhabitants of the Kamchatka Peninsula called this species.

IDENTIFYING CHARACTERS: Cohos have black spots on their backs and on the upper parts of their caudal fins. Their gums are white at the bases of their teeth. At sea, both sexes are blue on backs and silvery below. When they ascend rivers to spawn, males are green on backs and red on sides, sometimes blackish on bellies. Females are bronze to reddish on sides. Chinook salmon have black gums and spots throughout their caudal fins.

DISTRIBUTION AND BIOLOGY: Cohos are found from Korea and probably Japan to the Chukchi Sea and southeastward to Punta Camalu, northern Baja California. They are uncommon south of Monterey, with a center of abundance from Oregon to southeastern Alaska. Cohos, like all salmon, are anadromous. Hatching in freshwater, they migrate to the ocean and return to freshwater to spawn. Spawning occurs from Peter the Great Bay, Sea of Japan to the San Lorenzo River, central California. While the southernmost spawning stream is in northern Monterey Bay, few silvers run up the Sacramento River, despite numerous attempts to start runs there. Similarly, attempts to introduce cohos to the Atlantic Coast (between 1901-1948) have apparently been unsuccessful. On the other hand, plantings in the Great Lakes have been spectacularly successful. Annually, thousands of salmon-starved recreational fishermen flog these lakes to a froth.

A marvelous paper by Brown, Moyle and Yoshiyama (North American Journal of Fisheries Management, 1994, vol. 14, p. 237-

261), clearly shows that California coho salmon populations have gone, are going, and will probably keep going, right down the toilet. They estimate that the coho population of today is less than 6% of what it was in the 1940s. Of the 248 previously-known coho streams they were able to get data on, only 54% still contain coho. This is really pitiful. While there are all sorts of other reasons (overharvest, climate change, introduced diseases, etc.), the main problem is habitat destruction from logging and urbanization. It is always surprising to me that a civilization theoretically filled with adults can screw things up so completely.

Cohos reach 38.5 inches and 31 pounds and some fish may live as long as 5 years. They spawn in coastal streams or in the tributaries of larger rivers. They like cool water, rarely entering temperatures over 70° F. During spawning migrations, adults often stay in the mouths of streams until heavy rains increase stream flow, then the fish ascend to spawn, most often returning to their birth streams and birth areas. Most coho migrate during daylight hours. Cohos have been noted to leap over barriers higher than 6 feet. With a few exceptions in larger rivers, these fish rarely go upstream more than about 140 miles. The longest spawning run known is 1,320 miles, into the Yukon Territory. Spawning occurs over a very wide period, depending on location and year; for most populations it is October to March. More specifically, spawning takes place from early September-March in California, peaking in November-January, while in British Columbia, fish spawn in October and November. When a female finds a likely-looking gravel bed, usually at the head of a riffle, she digs out nests (called redds) and deposits her eggs (anywhere from 1,000-7,600). Cohos in Asia and Alaska tend to produce more eggs per body length than do fish in British Columbia and further southward.

After being laid, the eggs are fertilized by a male (sometimes by more than one) and the eggs are covered over. (If more than one male is involved, the additional males are likely to be so-called "jacks," small sex maniacs that have spent only 1 year at sea, instead of the usual 2 or 3.) After depositing some of her eggs, the female swims a bit upstream and digs another nest. This is done over and over until spawning is complete. Most females deposit all or nearly all of their eggs. However, retention rates of 20% or more of all eggs have been reported. After spawning, the adults, finally understanding that sex without commitment is unfulfilling, die. Most croak 3-24 days after spawning.

Under the gravel, the eggs hatch in 6–12 weeks, depending on water temperature, and the larvae stay buried for an additional 2–10 weeks. Young cohos remain in freshwater for 1–3+ years, with individual fish setting up little territories in pools or stream edges. At this age, they eat insects, insect larvae and small fishes. When found in the same water system, young cohos, steelheads and chinooks tend to keep out of each other's way. Cohos occupy stream pools, steelheads live in riffles and chinooks usually live in the warmer parts of the system. When cohos and chinooks do coexist, cohos are more aggressive and tend to dominate the clueless chinooks. Just prior to migrating to the sea, cohos, like all salmon, undergo smoltification, a physiological process which allows them to go from fresh to saltwater. In this process, the fish change shape, color and, most importantly, begin to excrete salts (handy if you live in a salty environment), rather than retaining them. Juveniles stay very near their home streams for their first year at sea. Cohos live in saltwater for 1–3 years, migrating as much as 1,000 miles from their birth streams. At sea, they feed on fishes (such as herrings, anchovies, sand lances and rockfishes) and on such invertebrates as krill and squids. A number of fishes and marine mammals, such as whitesided dolphins, eat cohos.

FISHERY: This is a very important recreational species. Overall, they contribute over half of the marine recreational salmon catch. The bulk of this fishery occurs from Vancouver Island to the Columbia River. Usually, chinooks make up the majority of the recreational salmon catch off California, but during some years cohos form almost half of the catch. Fishing for "blue backs," young coho salmon, is a popular springtime activity in some areas.

Cohos are also a major commercial fish, taken by trolling, purse seines and gillnets, primarily from Oregon northward. Through the North Pacific, they form about 10% of the total salmon catch. Off North America, catches are highest off British Columbia.

REMARKS: Here is an interesting quote from *Inland Fishes of Washington*, by R. S. Wydoski and R. R. Whitney (University of Washington Press, 1979): "This is the common salmon found in the backyards of residential areas. Along with the cutthroat trout, it manages to survive in the most unlikely neighborhoods—for example, alongside the supermarket in the section of stream channeled into a ditch where broken fluorescent lights have been dumped, or next door to the gas station where tires, oil cans, and broken auto parts have been discarded into the stream, and even in streams where fertilizers, herbicides, or pesticides used in landscaping on lawns might be poisoning the fish or the aquatic organisms they feed on."

Some cohos, termed "residuals," spend their entire lives in fresh water.

A bisexual coho was taken off Washington State.

Tony Gharrett, University of Alaska, Fairbanks, reports finding a white fleshed coho.

STEELHEAD OR RAINBOW TROUT (ONCORHYNCHUS MYKISS)

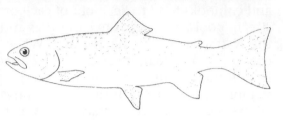

NAMES: Coastal Rainbow Trout, Half-Pounder, Salmon Trout, Truite Arc-en-Ciel (French). Half-Pounders are 10–14 inches, ones that have spent 1–3 years in fresh water and up to 1 year at sea. *Oncorhynchus* is based on 2 Greek words meaning "hooked nose."

IDENTIFYING CHARACTERS: At sea, steelheads have bluish backs and silvery bellies, with small black spots on their backs and on dorsal and caudal fins. Spawning males have a small red or pink stripe along their sides. Cutthroat trout usually have a red slash mark under the chin. Salmon have 14 or more anal fin rays (compared to 9–12 in steelheads).

DISTRIBUTION AND BIOLOGY: Steelheads have been taken from Japan to the Bering Sea and southward to northern Baja California. These are anadromous rainbow trout, hatching in freshwater, descending to the sea and returning to freshwater to spawn. In recent years, the furthest south they have spawned is in Malibu Creek, just north of Los Angeles. However, as late as the mid-1940s, these rainbows ran up San Mateo and San Onofre Creeks in San Diego County and in the Tijuana River. At sea, steelies are most abundant from Oregon to the Gulf of Alaska and the Aleutians, generally in water between 41° F and 59° F. These are highly migratory fish; many move north and west in late winter and spring, then southeast in late fall and early winter, occasionally motivating as much as 2,900 miles from their birth streams. Fish tagged in the Gulf of Alaska were later recovered off Grays Harbor and in Puget Sound, Washington. One go-hard tagged in Washington wound up at the tip of the Aleutian Islands, Alaska, a distance of 2,275 miles.

Steelhead as large as 45 inches and over 40 pounds have been taken; some steelies live at least 9 years. Young ones remain in fresh water anywhere from less than 1 year to 3 years. Fish tend to spend less time in freshwater in the southern part of their range and those that leave in less than 1 year are less likely to survive and return to spawn. Juveniles migrate to sea at anywhere from 6–10 inches, usually in spring, but throughout their range there are steelhead entering the ocean during every month. Similarly, these fish live for 1–4 years in the ocean before maturing and ascending streams for the first time. Fish in the north probably spend more time at sea than those in the south; the average steel-ie first returning to its home stream is 23 inches at Santa Cruz, California, 26 inches in Oregon and 29 inches in British Columbia. Most steelhead first spawn after 2–3 years in freshwater and 1–2 years in the ocean. Depending on the stream, steelies may be "summer" or "winter" migrators. "Summer" fish ascend from about May to August (spending the warm months in cool, deep pools), while "winter" ones go up from about November to April. As with salmon, steelhead tend to return to the same area in which they hatched. In some systems, males swim up to the spawning areas before females. Regardless of when the migration occurs, most spawning takes place from March to early May.

Length at maturity depends on the time they have spent at sea; one year fish are about 19 inches long, 2-year ones are around 28 inches and late-blooming 3-year olds are 32 inches. Some steel-head, primarily females, do not die after spawning, and may spawn as many as 4 times throughout their lives. Winter-run fish are more likely to be repeat spawners. Relatively few fish are repeat spawners in northern streams, and those that do spawn fewer times than the lucky ones that live to the south. Because females are more likely to live after spawning, there are more females present on most spawning grounds. (Reminds me of the line from "Surf City" by the Beach Boys, "Two girls for every boy.") Spawning occurs in gravel beds in both main rivers and streams and is similar to that of Pacific salmon (see the description under chinook salmon). Females usually produce anywhere from 200–12,000 eggs and these hatch in about 50 days (at 50° F). In contrast to most salmon, spawning steelhead do feed, chowing down on salmon eggs, insects and plants. Those at sea eat fishes, squids, krill and other planktonic critters. Northern fur seals eat them.

FISHERY: Steelheads are one of the most popular sport fish from central California northward, and winter steelhead fishing in the Pacific Northwest is particularly popular. As a kid, I grew up read-ing outdoor magazine articles extolling the mystique, the wonder and the glory of winter steelhead fishing. In the accompanying pictures, there were always some sodden, bedraggled characters, neck deep in a freezing, torrential steam, with 3 inches of sleet piled up on their heads. These pathetic figures, probably persons of at least moderate intelligence and maturity, were busily flaying the water with such dry flies as "Thompson's Redwing Midge #24" and "Ernest's Blackfooted Locust Larva Type B" or (if the fisherman was a craven lout) a salmon egg. Remember how your Uncle Phil regaled you with his tales of the "Battle of the Bulge" from World War II? Remember how he described that ghastly, bitterly cold December in 1944 Belgium, complete with frost bite, snow blind-

ness and Panzers? Fishing for steelhead in the winter is the equivalent of fighting the Battle of the Bulge over and over again. On a
happier note, in summer months, along much of their range,
10–14 inch "half-pounders" are a popular sport fish. All steelhead
caught by sport fishermen in British Columbia have to be returned
to the water. It is illegal to commercial fish for steelhead in
California waters. From Oregon northward, there is a fairly large
catch, mostly by gillnet and trollers.

REMARKS: Based on recent genetic studies, rainbow and cutthroat
trout split off from one another between 1 million and 2 million
years ago. Another recent study showed a slight genetic difference
between rainbow trout which do not go to sea and steelhead.

SOCKEYE SALMON (ONCORHYNCHUS NERKA)

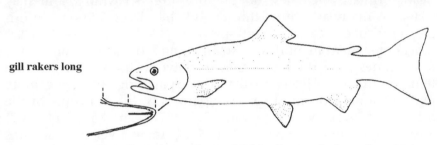

gill rakers long

NAMES: "Sockeye" comes from "Sukkai", used by the Native
Americans of southern British Columbia. Also, Red Salmon (Alaska),
Blueback Salmon (Columbia River), Nerka and Krasnaya Ryba
(Russia), Benizake and Benimasu (Japan), Kokanee (landlocked
form). *Oncorhynchus* is Greek for "hooked nose", referring to the
schnaz males develop as they migrate to their spawning grounds;
nerka is the Russian name for this species.

IDENTIFYING CHARACTERS: In the ocean, a sockeye is blue-black on
the top of its head, with a blue back and silvery sides. It does not
have distinctive black spots on its dorsal and caudal fins (unlike
pinks, cohos and chinooks - they do), though fine black speckling
may be present. Spawning colors are a very distinctive, *tres elegant*,
green head and bright red body (some females have green and yellow blotches on their bodies).

DISTRIBUTION AND BIOLOGY: Sockeyes live from northern Japan
and the Sea of Okhotsk northward to the Beaufort Sea (as far east
as Victoria Island) and southwards to Los Angeles, southern
California. They are not common south of about the Columbia
River. Most sockeyes are anadromous: they hatch in freshwater,
mature in the ocean and return to spawn in freshwater. There are
a number of landlocked populations (called kokanee or kickininee)

in North American, Japanese and Siberian lakes that never go to sea. Spawning runs have been noted as far south as the Sacramento River of California, but until you get to the Columbia River they don't amount to much. In fact, the most important spawning regions in North America are well to the north. These are the Bristol Bay, Alaska watershed and the Fraser River drainage, British Columbia. The Bristol Bay region alone may produce over 50% of all North American sockeyes. Other important areas are the Skeena, Nass and Somass Rivers of British Columbia and the Chignek, Karluk and Copper Rivers and tributaries of Cook Inlet in Alaska. Unique among Pacific salmon, most young sockeyes spend their early lives in lakes and these important river systems have many lakes associated with them.

The biggest sockeye on record was 33 inches long and weighed about 15 pounds. A few fish live to 6 years, commonly 4-5. Females are oviparous. Beginning in summer, ocean-run sockeyes move into streams and rivers. While some fish spawn close to the sea, most make fairly extensive migrations, some at least as far as 685 miles (Forfar Creek off the Fraser River of British Columbia). While most sockeyes spend at least 2 years at sea, some, termed "Jacks" and "Jills," return after one year. In most cases, Jacks make up most of the early returnees. However, in a few systems (such as the Okanagan River, off the Columbia), one-half of these early birds are Jills. In many cases, adult sockeye spend some time in their previous nursery lake before travelling up spawning streams. As with other Pacific salmon, females dig nests (redds)in gravel bottoms. J. L. Hart, in the redoubtable *Pacific Fishes of Canada*, reports that "A redd is likely to have three to 10 pockets (most commonly five) each containing an average of about 750 eggs but sometimes more than 1,600." He goes on to note that, while spawning most often takes place in streams near lakes, some sockeyes also spawn on lake shores, where springs well up. The fertilized eggs are heavier than water and sink into the holes, after which the fish loosely cover them with gravel. There is a great deal of variability as to how many eggs a female of a given size produces; this varies with year and area. North American sockeyes have been reported to produce anywhere from under 2,200 to over 4,300. Some Siberian fish produce over 5,000 eggs.

Under the gravel, the eggs hatch in anywhere from less than 50 to more than 150 days, depending on temperature (the warmer, the faster). The young stay under the gravel for at least 3 weeks, then emerge at night. Generally, the little ones pop out between April and July. However, in Lake Kuril (Kamchatka Peninsula, Russia) this may take place anywhere between March and September, peaking in July and August. In most cases, they immediately head down stream, and that takes them into their nursery lake or, occasionally, into the ocean. However, if the birth stream is at the outlet to a lake (downstream), the little ones swim up-current and enter the lake from that direction. How they know which way to travel is just one of those Mysteries of Nature you will have to adjust to. And just to confuse matters, some populations use stream areas for nurseries, never going into lakes. How long do young sockeyes spend in freshwater? Well, like just about everything else in this species' life, it's highly variable. Some spend just a few weeks, heading right out to sea, though this is rare. Others spend 1-3 years before heading out (most commonly, 1-2). During their freshwater sojourn they eat various aquatic insects, as well as zooplankton. The fish swim downstream head-first in quiet waters and tail-first where the current is swift.

During the 1-4 years they spend at sea, sockeyes will travel pretty far from their birth streams. Fishes from British Columbia and the lower U. S. tend to stay south of the Aleutian Islands, but are often found hundreds of miles out to sea. Bristol Bay sockeyes travel almost to the Asian mainland, while Asian fish migrate as far east as the central Aleutians. At sea, sockeyes probably move about continually; they may travel more than 2,000 miles per year. Many sockeye runs occur over a very discrete, rather short period. As an example, an estimated 80% of all Bristol Bay sockeyes pass through the fishery, located in Bristol Bay estuaries, over a 2-week period. And this period varies little between years. In B. B., it's generally within 6 days either way of July 4th. Sockeyes tend to remain in the upper part of the water column, most probably staying within 50 feet of the surface. While at sea, sockeyes feed primarily on zooplankton (such as krill and copepods), as well as small fishes and squids. They are eaten by rhinoceros auklets among other creatures.

FISHERY: In most areas, sockeyes are not a major recreational species. However, large numbers are taken by anglers in Lake Washington, Washington and in the Kenai River, Alaska. Coast-wide, sockeyes contribute about 12% to the recreational salmon catch.

The dark red color and firm texture of sockeye meat has made it a favorite commercial species for many years. In the early days, the salmon canning industry (begun in 1870 along the Fraser River, British Columbia, and spreading to Alaska by 1878) focused primarily on sockeyes. By the early 1900s, sockeye canning was a big industry on the Kamchatka Peninsula. Most of the sockeye fishery was aimed at the canneries until the 1960s when, to quote R. L. Burgner (*Pacific Salmon Life Histories*, 1991, University of British Columbia Press), "...salt cured salmon roe, 'sujiko', was developed as an export product to Japan, enhancing the value of the female salmon. In more recent years, improved refrigeration and freezing capabilities...have made it possible to develop a fresh and frozen market for sockeye salmon. By the early 1980s, about half the sockeye salmon catch in Alaska was marketed fresh or frozen."

In the commercial fishery, sockeyes are the third most important species, right behind pinks and chums. Between 1952 and 1976, sockeyes formed 17% by weight and 14% by number of all salmon taken. Sockeye are taken on the high seas by gillnetters. Closer to shore, gillnets, purse seines, traps and trolling are used. Much of the catch is made in river mouths and tidal areas. The Bristol Bay area, central Alaska and the region between British Columbia and Oregon account for most of the world catch. The largest Native American catch appears to be in the Fraser River. Here, from 1970-1982, annual subsistence catches averaged about 240,000 fish, equal to about 4.7% of the total Fraser River take. Some runs are extremely cyclical. As an example, catches on the Adams River, British Columbia, cycle over about 5 years, with peak catches as much as 250 times the smallest ones.

REMARKS: The Russian biologist, A. I. Smirnov, has suggested that the bright red color in spawning fish is due to the presence of carotenoid and lipoid pigments. Yeah, so what? Well, he goes on to speculate that since sockeyes tend to spawn in slower moving, lower oxygen waters, these pigments may help these fish more efficiently take up oxygen from the water.

Busy researchers have come up with a very clever method to help figure out the origin of sockeyes caught at sea. After a long and diligent search, and probably through dissecting more salmon than is emotionally healthy, biologists have figured out that there are two parasites that can be used as indicators of a sockeye's origin. Sockeye hatched in the Bristol Bay region have a larval tapeworm, *Triaenophorus crassus,* in their muscles, while Kamchatka fish have an intestinal nematode worm, *Truttaedacnitis truttae,* in them. So, the deal is, if you catch a salmon and it has one of these guys in it, you know where it came from. And if it doesn't? Hey, you're just out of luck.

CHINOOK OR KING SALMON (ONCORHYNCHUS TSHAWYTSCHA)

NAMES: Quinnat Salmon, Spring Salmon, Tyee Salmon, Winter Salmon, Masunosude (Japanese). Chinook is the name of a Native American tribe that lived along the Columbia River. Tyee usually refers to larger fish, while quinnat is an older name now somewhat in disuse. *Oncorhynchus* comes from the Greek, meaning "hooked

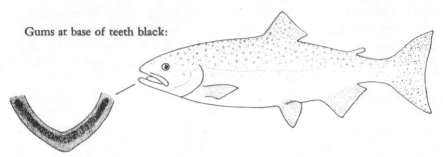

Gums at base of teeth black:

nose"; *tshawytscha* is an approximation of the name used by the native peoples of the Kamchatka Peninsula (filtered through the ears of Johann Julius Walbaum, a German scientist hired by Catherine the Great).

IDENTIFYING CHARACTERS: At sea, chinooks are bluish or greenish blue, gray or (as they mature) black on backs and silvery below. Spawning fish are olive-brown to dark red, and small males may be yellowish. Most important in its identification are the black gums at the base of the teeth in the lower jaw and the irregular black spots on the back and all over the caudal fin. A coho may be confused with a chinook, but coho have white lower jaw gums and no spotting on the lower part of their caudal fins.

DISTRIBUTION AND BIOLOGY: The natural range of chinooks is Japan to the Beaufort Sea and southward to San Diego, southern California. Beginning in 1872, many unsuccessful attempts have been made to transplant these salmon, but only plants in New Zealand and the Great Lakes have proven particularly successful. Along our coast, chinooks are common from about Pt. Conception northward. In some years, however, large numbers venture south of the Point and good fishing is had off Santa Barbara, Ventura and Pt. Mugu. Even further south, almost every year, there are chinooks in the cool waters of both Redondo and Newport submarine canyons. Although this species tends to stay fairly close to the coast, it has been found as much as 1,000 miles to sea and may swim as much as 2,300 miles from its birth river. Coastal movement is fairly extensive, with fish from the Sacramento–San Joaquin system migrating southward as far as southern California and northward to the waters off Washington. Many Columbia River fish move northward into Washington or even further north. Some fish have moved from Alaska to the Columbia River and from Vancouver Island to the Sacramento River. On the Asian side, chinooks spawn as far south as northern Hokkaido (Japan) and the Amur River in Siberia. In North America, chinooks may spawn way up on the Mackenzie and Coppermine Rivers of the Yukon Territory, but the northernmost authenticated site is Kotzebue Sound, Alaska. Today, the southernmost spawners head for the Sacramento-San Joaquin River system, though not too long ago chinook spawned as far south as the Ventura River, southern California. Chinooks tend to spawn in major rivers and streams; smaller coastal streams are the coho's province. While some fish spawn as close to the ocean as just above the tide line, others move upstream as far as 1,900 miles (up the Yukon).

Chinooks are the largest of the Pacific salmon, reaching 58 inches and at least 126 pounds. A few fish live to 8 years. There is great variability in age and size at maturity among chinooks, even in a single river. While the average fish spawns at 4–5 years of age and around 36 inches in length, some return to their birth streams earlier or later. At the extreme, a few males return after only one year, when they are around 6 inches long. These precocious kids are the only chinooks which do not die after spawning. Depending on the river system, chinooks ascend rivers to spawn during much of the year, and some rivers may have several distinct runs. Generally, the further south you go, the later will be the runs. For example, the Sacramento in the past had 3 runs, summer, fall and winter. In this river, the fall run is the largest, with the salmon moving upstream in the early fall and spawning between October and February. Winter run fish move up from December to February and spawn in May or June, while in the summer run (now lost because of dam construction), chinooks migrated upstream in May and June, summered over in deep, cool pools and spawned in late fall. This latter pattern is still prevalent further north. At least in Washington, there is evidence that summer and fall run salmon are genetically different from each other.

Upstream migration has been linked in at least one study to low barometric pressure. In some areas, upstream migration is limited to the first hour or so of daylight, while in others, travel takes place throughout the daylight hours. During this migration, chinooks are strongly repelled by extracts taken from mammalian skin, probably a good thing if you happen to be swimming through bear country. (The moral for salmon fishermen is that it is probably better to smell like an iguana if you can.) The salmon seek out gravel beds, primarily in larger streams, and carve out large depressions (called redds), some 10 feet long and 2.5 feet deep. Females produce between 273 and 20,000 bright red eggs, the number of eggs produced varies between years. The male fertilizes them and gravel is moved about to cover the eggs. Water temperatures over 57° F are detrimental to egg hatching. One study found that 50% of eggs hatched in 32 days at 61°F and as long as 159 days at 34°F.

In California, eggs laid in the fall hatch in the spring and those laid in the spring hatch in late August. The larvae, called *alevins*, remain buried in the gravel for 2–3 weeks. The fry, called *parrs*, stay in freshwater anywhere from a few days to (rarely) as much as 3 years. After their freshwater stay, the fry migrate (mainly at night and tails first), downstream, then spend some time in estuaries before entering the ocean. In California, most of the fry remain in freshwater for just a few weeks, and in estuaries for not much longer. They often enter the ocean at 2–4 months and 2–4 inches long. Chinooks further north, and those hatched far upstream, spend more time in freshwater and estuaries, often about a year. In freshwater, fry eat terrestrial and aquatic insects, while in estuaries, insects and crustaceans are fancied. In the ocean, chinooks eat primarily fishes (such as herrings, sand lances and rockfishes) and zooplankton (e.g. krill, amphipods and copepods). While most adults do not feed once they enter freshwater, a few fish have been found eating various organisms. Northern fur seals, least terns and likely lots of other things eat them.

FISHERY: By all odds, chinook salmon are just about the most popular recreational fish wherever they are found. They comprise about 40% of the recreational salmon harvest along the Pacific coast. Most of this catch is taken from party and private vessels, but some are also taken by shore anglers (particularly those fishing at river mouths) and pier fishermen.

While they are not taken in the same numbers as some other salmon species, chinooks are a prize catch for commercial fishermen. Trollers and gillnetters catch most of them. In California, chinooks are harvested only by trolling. They are sold fresh, frozen and smoked. Their shelf life is 5-7 days at 40° F and 9 months when frozen and kept at 0° F.

REMARKS: Chinooks, like salmon everywhere, have really taken a hit from habitat destruction. Water diversion, dams, spawning gravel siltation from logging–the list of damage just goes on and on. Due to poor water quality, pollution, low oxygen levels, high water temperatures and general screw ups on the part of the water managers in the State of California, chinook populations in the Sacramento-San Joaquin River system have hit all time lows. As an example, by 1990, the entire winter run salmon population on the Sacramento River, once numbering many thousands of animals, had been reduced to less than 500 fish. In this case, because of poor water management, cold water that was needed for egg and larval survival was not released from dams at the proper times and the fish just did not survive.

From my exotic sex file: a bisexual chinook, containing functional male and female reproductive systems, was captured off Fort Bragg a number of years ago.

Also, chinooks occasionally mate with cohos (probably causing consternation and some heartache in both families).

Chinooks come in red and white-fleshed forms. White flesh chinooks are more common in Alaska and British Columbia and rare in Washington, Oregon and probably California. In the lower Fraser River, British Columbia, about 54% of all chinooks had white meat. The color of the meat seems to be due primarily to genetic factors rather than differences in diet.

Mitochondrial DNA studies suggest chinooks have been around for 3-4 million years. Chinooks are most closely related to cohos.

Chinooks have been successfully transplanted to New Zealand, Tasmania and possibly Chile. A freshwater population now exists in the Great Lakes.

Having painted a bleak picture of the chinook population, I should mention that 1995 saw one of the greatest salmon runs in southern California history. Even anglers who had no conceivable right to catch a salmon, on either moral, ethical or spiritual grounds, just creamed them.

For a truly awe-inspiring bunch of Pacific salmon facts, go get a copy of *Pacific Salmon Life Histories*, edited by C. Groot and L. Margolis, UBC Press, 1991, ISBN 0-7748-0359-2.

Smelts - Family Osmeridae

SURF SMELT (HYPOMESUS PRETIOSUS)

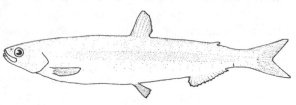

NAME: Silver Smelt, Pacific Surf Smelt, Day Smelt (because they spawn during the day–get it?) *Hypomesus* means "below the middle" in Greek, referring to the middle of the body position of the pelvic fins; *pretiosus* means "precious."

IDENTIFYING CHARACTERS: These are small, slender fish, blue-green on backs and silvery on sides and bellies, with a silvery band along their sides. Some time before spawning, adult males develop a golden tinge, little lumps on their snouts and think themselves really hot stuff. Surf smelt mouths are small, with their upper jaws ending before the middle of their eyes. Surf smelts may be confused with delta smelts (*Hypomesus transpacificus*), which, however, have 10–12 pectoral fin rays, rather than the 14–17 found on surf smelt.

DISTRIBUTION AND BIOLOGY: Surf smelts are found from Prince

William Sound (Gulf of Alaska) to Long Beach (southern California), often near shore, sometimes in brackish water. This is a schooling, pelagic form, common from central California northward (the southernmost spawning ground seems to be near Scott Creek, Santa Cruz County). This species is noteworthy for the large numbers of distinct, local spawning populations, with perhaps 10 different spawning stocks in Puget Sound alone. Surf smelt schools are often composed of only one sex.

Surf smelt grow to about 10 inches. Females live to at least 5 years but males don't seem to be able to hobble past 3 years. Females grow faster than males. These fish mature at between 1 and 2 years of age, with females producing 1,300–37,000 eggs (depending on size, population and sincerity). Along much of its range, spawning occurs throughout most of the year (in Puget Sound they don't do it in April; it's a philosophical thing). However, a particular population probably spawns for only 4–5 months per year. Most spawning takes place on fine gravel or coarse sand beaches, in the upper intertidal zone, often in locations where nearby trees or boulders provide shade. Typically, these beaches also have freshwater seepage. In some localized areas, with very heavy spawning, most of the "beach" actually consists of smelt eggs. These daytime spawners (hence the common name, day smelt), prefer high tides, espically in the late afternoon. Prior to spawning, a smelt school will swim to within about 3 feet of shore. When spawning, a female, joined by 2-5 males, swims in with the waves, and both sexes spawn in a few inches of water. Spawning beaches may contain 2–4 (up to 8) batches of eggs spawned on different days. Females are oviparous and will spawn on several consecutive days. There is evidence that some females may come back to spawn later in the season. The eggs stick to the bottom on neat little stalks, looking sort of like the lollipop trees you drew in the first grade. After some days (it varies, so I'm hedging here) the eggs detach and are washed seaward down to the gravel of the lower intertidal. While surf smelt eggs usually hatch in 8–28 days (depending on temperature), very cold water will delay the process to as much as 90 days. Wave action seems to stimulate hatching. Young-of-the-year stay near shore. Surf smelt eat a wide variety of plankton, including copepods, amphipods and krill as well as larval fishes. In turn, they are eaten by various fishes, such as salmon, birds (such as terns) and marine mammals (including harbor seals, northern fur seals, and Dall's porpoise).

FISHERY: From northern California northward, there is a large and enthusiastic recreational fishery for this species during the spawning run. In many years, greater numbers of surf smelt are taken by fishermen than any other species in northern California, as thousands of pounds are hauled in by waders armed with nets and rakes.

These are also important commercial fish, taken by gillnet and purse seine from central California northward. There aren't a lot of precise figures, but about 51 tons are taken yearly in the Washington fishery. The combined recreational and commercial catch in California is estimated at 400,000-600,000 pounds per year. Surf smelt are marketed fresh and frozen, usually as whole fish. Fresh smelt have a shelf life of 5 days at 40° F; frozen, it's 9-12 months at 0° F. Asian markets are perhaps the largest buyers of smelt for food. Much of the commercial catch is sold as animal food to zoos and aquariums. For a very nice review of the California commercial fishery, see Mick Kronman's article in the March 1995 edition of National Fishermen.

REMARKS: Males and females have asymmetrical gonads; the left one is more developed.

EULACHON (THALEICHTHYS PACIFICUS)

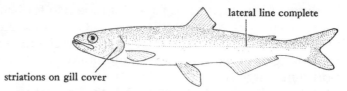

NAMES: Variants of Eulachon (Oolakan, Oolachon etc.), Candlefish, Hooligan. Smallfish, Sak, Ssag (Native American Tlingit), Yuurachon (Japanese). *Thaleichthys* is a combination of 2 Greek words and means "rich fish," referring to the large amounts of oil in the body; *pacificus* describes the species' geographic range.

IDENTIFYING CHARACTERS: These are small, slim fish, which are bluish or blue-silver on backs and silvery below, with tiny black dots on backs and sometimes on caudal fins. At spawning time, they turn gray-brown and males develop tubercles on their heads and on the scales along the lateral line. There are circular grooves on the gill cover (unique to this smelt).

DISTRIBUTION AND BIOLOGY: Found from the eastern Bering Sea, and along the Aleutians, southeast to Monterey Bay (central California), eulachons are abundant from the Klamath River, northern California, northward. This is a pelagic species, living in dense schools on the outer continental shelf. Taken from the intertidal zone to possibly as deep as 2,063 feet, it is encountered most frequently in depths between 150 and 750 feet. These are anadromous fish, born in fresh water, spending most of their days in the ocean and entering rivers and streams to spawn. Spawning occurs from the Klamath River (northern California) northward; the smelt ascend only a few miles before depositing their eggs. There are at least 2 populations in British Columbia and possibly others along the rest of the coast.

Eulachon reach 10 inches in length and live at least 4 years. The fish mature after 2-3 years and most, but not all, die after spawning. Spawning usually takes place at night, in the lower parts of streams and rivers. In British Columbia, spawning occurs from March-May. Females are oviparous and produce between 7,000-40,000 eggs. These stick to sand grains on cute little stalks and hatch in 19-40 days, depending on water temperature. Eulachon spawn at water temperatures ranging from 39-50° F. After hatching, the larvae are carried downstream and flushed into the sea. Eulachon eat plankton, primarily krill and copepods. During spawning migrations, when great masses of these smelts head for coastal rivers, they are eaten with abandon by all sorts of predators, including spiny dogfish, sturgeon, Pacific halibut and arrowtooth flounder, salmon, harbor seals, orcas, finback whales, northern fur seals, Pacific white-sided dolphins and various sea birds.

FISHERY: Eulachon are popular recreational fish, taken in the surf by dipnets. They have been a major food fish for Native Americans for thousands of years (see Remarks). Currently, there is a moderate-sized gillnet, trawl and dip net commercial fishery along much of its range. In particular, the Columbia and Klamath Rivers support quite large runs.

REMARKS: Use of eulachons by Northwest Native Americans goes back into antiquity. These smelts, and particularly their oil, were a very important part of the diets of these indigenous people. The oil, which is very high in vitamin D, was (and is) used as a condiment with many foods. The oil and meat were carried inland along well-beaten paths (called "kleena" or grease trails), and traded with inland tribes. Some reduction of eulachon to oil still goes on, particularly in British Columbia. After I read a description of the process, I thought you would like to hear it.

In spring, Native American families encamp on river spawning sites and, using beach seines, net thousands of pounds of smelt. These are placed in pits and left to decompose for 8–14 days. Water is heated to about 170° F in large wooden tanks, and the fish are soaked for about 30 minutes. After this, they are broken up with large wooden forks, which releases the oil. The oil is pushed to one side of the tank, scooped up and allowed to settle in large containers. Later, it is filtered through canvas and stored in dark bottles (in the early days, oil was stored in kelp floats). The oil is still important in the diets and traditions of the local people and it is a favored gift on various ceremonial occasions.

Speaking of Native American (or in this case First Nation) practices, here is a truly unique quote I saw on the wall of the Museum of Anthropology, at the University of British Columbia. It was written in 1918, by William Holliday, a Canadian Indian Agent. He was discussing the need for abolishing the potlatch, a traditional ceremony of the Haida, Tlingit and other indigenous peoples. "During these gatherings they lose months of time, waste their substance, contract all kinds of diseases and generally unfit themselves for being British subjects in the proper sense of the word."

I don't know, it sounds pretty good to me.

You know, the more I think about it, the more I am convinced that rendering eulachon oil just might be the activity for you. It would be a great way to get your family reconnected, instead of vegetating in that air-conditioned, three-bedroom, two-and-one-half bath split-level (with the sunken conversation pit). Just imagine everyone, from Gramps to Little Susie, hefting massive wooden forks and breaking up 500 pounds of boiled eulachon there in the hot tub.

There is so much oil in these smelts that a dried one, with a wick inserted, can be lit and used as a taper (hence its name, candlefish). Curiously, one major oil in eulachon is squalene, a very light oil usually found in sharks and rays.

Lizardfishes – Family Synodontidae

CALIFORNIA LIZARDFISH (SYNODUS LUCIOCEPS)

NAME: Chile (Mexico), *Synodus* is Greek for "teeth meeting"; *lucioceps* is Latin for "pike head."

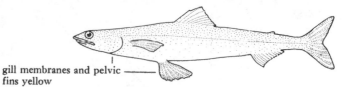

gill membranes and pelvic fins yellow

IDENTIFYING CHARACTERS: These are cylindrical, elongate fish with small, lizard-like heads and mouths filled with good-sized canine teeth. They are brown on backs and silvery on bellies, with yellow fins.

DISTRIBUTION AND BIOLOGY: Found from Cape Beal, British Columbia to Guaymus, Mexico, lizardfish are occasional from Monterey Bay, central California southward and are common south of Pt. Conception. They have been taken from 5–750 feet, most commonly from 30–180 feet. These are sand or mud bottom dwellers, often found resting on the bottom with their pelvic fins.

Occasionally, they bury themselves in the sand.

California lizardfish reach 25 inches and they appear to mature at around 12 inches. Females are oviparous and produce pelagic eggs. On the Pacific Coast, spawning occurs from central California to Cabo San Lucas, southern Baja California, peaking between Punta Baja, northern Baja California and Cabo San Lazaro, southern Baja California. Spawning season is probably August to March, with a September-December peak. The larvae are generally found within 100 miles of the coast. From February to May, young-of-the-year first recruit to nearshore waters, forming very large schools. Larger fish are more common in deeper water. Lizards undergo real boom and bust cycles, with only a few little ones surviving during some years and huge numbers making it in others. Lizards eat fishes (including topsmelt, anchovies and white croakers), squids, mysid shrimps and krill. California sea lions eat them.

FISHERY: Mostly in Southern California, lizards are frequently taken by sport anglers from party and private vessels, particularly when fishing for halibut and barred sand bass. Young ones are often caught from piers, particularly during spring and summer months. There is no commercial fishery for this species, although they are common in trawl and gillnet hauls. I have been told that lizards are quite tasty, but pretty bony.

Cods and Haddocks - Family Gadidae

PACIFIC COD (GADUS MACROCEPHALUS)

NAMES: Alaska Cod, Gray Cod, Madara (Japanese), Tara (Japanese). *Gadus* is the Latin name for "cod"; *macrocephalus* is formed from 2 Greek words meaning "long head."

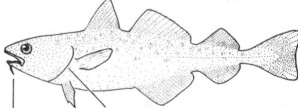

barbel longer than diameter of eye (rarely slightly shorter)

gill rakers 41–42

IDENTIFYING CHARACTERS: These are brown or gray fish, covered on backs and sides with brown spots. They have 3 dorsal and 2 anal fins and a large, distinctive chin barbel (about as long as their eye diameter). Pacific tomcod have a smaller barbel (about one-half the eye diameter) and walleye pollock have no (or a minute) barbel.

120

DISTRIBUTION AND BIOLOGY: Pacific cod are found from Manchuria, Korea and the Sea of Japan to the Bering and Chukchi Sea and southward to Santa Monica (southern California), and are rare south of about Cape Mendocino (northern California). They have been taken from shallow subtidal waters to 2,889 feet, but most live in 150–900 feet. This is a schooling species, found over soft or gravel substrate, usually near the bottom. Pacific cod move into deep water in autumn and winter, preparatory to spawning. Then, having done this to keep us in fish and chips, they cruise into shallower waters in late spring and early summer to feed. Spawning depths become shallower to the south: they are about 500-600 feet in the most northern areas, 300-500 feet off Canada, 200-250 feet south of Vancouver Island and even shallower in Puget Sound. The species also makes considerable alongshore movements. Cod tend to stay in water less than about 50° F and, in fact, their eggs and larvae may be damaged above this temperature.

Pacific cod reach 45 inches and some may live as long as 13 years. A 10-incher is about 1 year old and they grow to 18-20 inches in 2 years. Size and maturity vary between areas. Most Pacific cod mature at 2-4 years. Fifty percent of the males reproduce by 19-22 inches, females by about 22-23 inches. Females are oviparous and produce as many as 5,000,000 eggs. Spawning occurs between January and July, depending on area. In the Gulf of Alaska, fish in spawning condition have been noted over bottom depths of 240-875 feet, mostly between 500-825 feet. Cod eggs stay near the bottom, but probably do not stick to the substrate as people once believed. The eggs hatch in 8-28 days depending on water temperature. Larvae tend to stay near the surface (0-100 feet), but some may descend to about 150 feet at night. Juveniles are found in shallower waters than adults (usually at 200-500 feet), occasionally coming inshore. Pacific cod eat a variety of small animals, including fishes (such as walleye pollock, herring and sandlances), krill, shrimps and crabs. In turn, they are eaten by such predators as northern fur seals, harbor seals, sperm whales and Pacific halibut.

FISHERY: Pacific cod are taken by recreational fishermen from boats, piers and jetties in the northern part of their range; Puget Sound is a good spot. They are a major commercial species, captured primarily by trawl gear from northern Oregon to the Sea of Japan, with the Bering Sea yielding up the biggest hauls.

REMARKS: There is some evidence that Pacific cod, which love to munch on snow crabs, are the major source of death for at least one crab species in its first year of life. Within this species, one study estimates that as many as 95% of all crabs 1 year old or less are eaten by Pacific cod.

Pacific cod ear bones are found in the middens of Puget Sound Native Americans.

PACIFIC TOMCOD (MICROGADUS PROXIMUS)

barbel about ½
diameter of eye
or shorter

gill rakers 22–28

NAME: Whiting, California Tomcod, Piciata, Wachna (in Alaska). In southern California, white croakers are called "tomcod." Just as a friendly warning, people who continue to do this will be severely punished, once I take over. *Microgadus* means "small cod" in Greek; *proximus* is "near or next to" in Latin, a reference to this species' close resemblance to *Microgadus tomcod* in the Atlantic.

IDENTIFYING CHARACTERS: These are small fish, with 3 dorsal fins, 2 anal fins and a small chin barbel. They tend to be greenish or brown on backs with white bellies. Pacific cod usually have a larger barbel and are spotted; Pacific hake are silvery with no barbel and walleye pollock usually have no barbel and a slightly projecting lower jaw.

DISTRIBUTION AND BIOLOGY: Tomcod are found from the Bering Sea southward to Pt. Sal (central California), commonly from about San Francisco Bay northward, over sand and mud. These are schooling, bottom dwellers, abundant in estuaries, bays and on the outer coast. While they have been caught from the shallow subtidal to 908 feet, they are most common down to about 500 feet. Larger individuals move out of estuaries in the winter and return in the spring. Juveniles are most abundant in estuaries and near-shore waters.

Relatively little is known about this species. It reaches 1 foot in length and at least some fish mature at 2 years and about 9 inches. They spawn from January-June off San Francisco, in winter and spring off Oregon, in spring off Washington and in Puget Sound, and probably in late spring off Alaska. Females are oviparous and spawning likely lasts at least a few months in each locale. Females produce around 1,000 eggs. The eggs stay near or on the bottom, are reported to be adhesive to the substrate and hatch at temperatures between 37-43° F. Young ones swarm into shallow water in summer and fall; larger ones are usually found in deeper water. Tomcod eat shrimps and other bottom-living invertebrates, as well as small fishes. They are eaten by larger fishes (including salmons, lingcods, white sturgeons and rockfishes), marine mammals (for instance, harbor seals, northern fur seals, harbor porpoises, Dall's porpoises) and sea birds (e.g. Brandt's and double-crested cormorants).

FISHERY: Most tomcod are taken by shore, pier and small boat anglers, particularly when juveniles come into shallow water in summer and fall. At this time, anglers from about San Francisco north just clean up on these little suckers, even though most anglers don't want to catch them. Tomcod tend to be on the small side and most fishermen over the age of 10 want to catch something a bit larger. Tomcod are actually quite tasty and either should be taken home to be eaten or thrown back, alive. It is mega-bad karma to catch a fish and let it dry out on the deck, even worse than removing the "Do Not Remove" tags from pillows. Tomcod are also commonly taken by commercial fishermen, mostly in trawls. These are usually discarded or occasionally sold for animal food. Before 1925, there was a pretty good sized commercial fishery for tomcod in California. Of course, the Great Depression hit soon after, but it was probably unrelated to tomcod consumption.

REMARKS: Fossil tomcod ear bones have been found in Pliocene deposits, in Long Beach, southern California. What is fun about this discovery is that today tomcod are virtually never found off Long Beach, indicating that ocean temperatures were considerably colder at the time the bones were laid down. (Okay, it's not as much fun as bumper bowling, but *I* liked it.)

Native Americans in the Pacific northwest ate a lot of them.

WALLEYE POLLOCK (THERAGRA CHALCOGRAMMA)

NAMES: Pollock, Alaska Pollock, Big-eye Pollock, Pacific Pollock. Suketodara (Japanese),

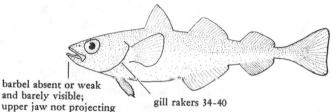

barbel absent or weak and barely visible; upper jaw not projecting

gill rakers 34-40

Sukeso (Japanese), *Theragra* is a combination of 2 Greek words meaning "food beast," because pollock are a major prey of marine mammals; *chalcogramma* is Latin for "brass line."

IDENTIFYING CHARACTERS: Walleye pollock are olive-green or

123

brown on backs and silvery on sides; young ones have 2-3 yellow stripes on sides. They have 3 dorsal fins and 2 anal fins and either no chin barbel or a very small one. Pacific cod and Pacific tomcod have large barbels.

DISTRIBUTION AND BIOLOGY: While found from the Chukchi Sea (north of the Bering Sea) to the southern Sea of Japan and to Carmel (central California), walleye pollock are particularly abundant from Japan northeast to the Gulf of Alaska and Bering Sea (typically along the edge of the continental shelf). These are schooling, midwater to bottom-dwelling fish, living anywhere from the shallow subtidal to 3,220 feet, most commonly from about 300-900 feet. They are occasionally taken near the surface and may rise in the water column at night. The species seems to make considerable seasonal movements, particularly from inshore feeding to offshore spawning grounds. Generally, fish move onshore during summer and offshore during winter. As an example, in the Gulf of Alaska, pollock are found mainly at 300-600 feet during the winter and 150-450 feet in the summer. Tomcod like it cool and while they tolerate water of 0-50° F, most are found in 36-41°. There appear to be at least 2 genetically distinct populations, one in the Bering Sea and the other within the Gulf of Alaska. One study suggests that there are 3 reproductively isolated populations in the Bering Sea, each one spawning at a different season.

Lucky walleyes reach a length of 3 feet and some live at least 17 years. While their growth rates vary widely throughout their range, a 12-incher is about 3 years old and a 2-footer has been kicking around 8-12 years. A few fish mature at 2 years and all reproduce at 4 years. Males and females seem to grow and mature at the same rate and size. And, depending on where they live, their spawning season is variable. In the Bering Sea alone, pollock may form 3 spawning groups; one from January-March, another March-June and a third from June-August. Typically, any one season is quite short. For instance, in the Shelikof Strait of Alaska, spawning occurs over a 10-20 day period. Spawning depths seem to be between 150-1,200 feet, usually 300-750. Females are oviparous, produce between 20,000-1,750,000 eggs and spawn once per year. There is some evidence that the eggs stay in deep water. In lab studies, they hatch in 9 and 21 days. Larvae settle out on the bottom and metamorphose into juveniles when they are between 1.5 and 2 inches. Young-of-the-year, at about 2 inches long, swarm into shallow water in summer and fall. Juveniles feed at night on the surface and descend to midwater or the bottom during the day. Older fish eat a variety of planktonic animals, including krill, shrimps and copepods, as well as fishes (they like younger pollock). A very wide range of larger animals snack on them. Harbor seals and Steller sea lions are major predators, as are northern fur seals, various whales, sea birds and such fishes as Pacific cod and arrowtooth flounder.

FISHERY: Young walleye pollock school in inshore waters, where they are taken in some numbers by sport anglers from boats, piers and jetties. As of the late 1980s, the commercial fishery for pollock was the largest single species fishery in the world. Stretching from the coast of British Columbia to the Asian mainland (but centered in the Bering Sea), a vast armada of trawlers, gillnetters and longliners from many nations search out pollock schools. The Russians catch the most pollock, with Japan, Korea, China and the U. S. scooping up most of the rest. In the past, most of the catch was reduced to fish meal or used to feed minks.

At present, three other uses have caused a great expansion in the fishery. Pollock roe is very popular in Japan and a considerable fishery targets this species only for its roe. This has led to the unfortunate habit of "roe stripping," where the roe is removed from the fish and the remainder is chucked overboard, unused. Get it together, fellas—it's just not acceptable. A second use is as a substitute for cod and haddock as frozen fillets or fish sticks. Lastly, a lot of pollock goes into surimi production. Surimi is processed fish flesh that is shaped and flavored into pretend seafood (seafood analogues), including crab, lobster and scallops. In the surimi process, fishes are mechanically filleted, the meat minced and then intensively washed in chilled water. The washing removes all sorts of gunk (blood, fat, enzymes) and increases the amount of certain rather elastic proteins. The product is then dewatered in a press and the resulting flesh is white, odorless and, when extruded into various shapes, it has a texture similar to crab, lobster, etc. Adding various flavors, colors and additives completes the transformation. When you see them in the market, they are usually called something like King Karl's Kustom Kooked Krab or King Karl's Inkredible Krispy Krustacean Kutlets. I hate that. Apparently misspelling the stuff makes it taste more like the real thing. How about a refreshing blow for honesty here? How about calling it Pretty Good Pretend Crab and be done with it?

Ah, there's good news tonight! And here, courtesy of Japan's National Surimi Association, is the estimated annual world surimi production. In the 5-year period, 1985-90, Japan fell from being the Godfather of surimi makers to sharing joint honors with...Tah Dah!, the good ol' U S of A! It's true, we may not be able to build cars, cameras, boom boxes or mechanical pencils as well as the Japanese, but by golly, they are actually importing tons of our fish paste! De Tocqueville wrote that: "America is a land of wonders...No natural boundary seems to be set to the efforts of man; and in his eyes what is not yet done is only what he has not yet attempted to do." Obviously, U. S. surimi manufacturers have taken de Tocqueville's observation to heart.

Merluccid Hakes - Family Merlucciidae

PACIFIC HAKE (MERLUCCIUS PRODUCTUS)

NAMES: Hake, Pacific Whiting, Heiku (Japanese), Merurusa (Japanese). *Merluccius* is an ancient word meaning "sea pike;" *productus* is Latin

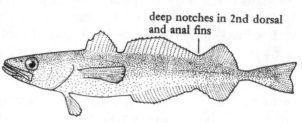

deep notches in 2nd dorsal and anal fins

for "drawn out," a reference to this species' elongated body.

IDENTIFYING CHARACTERS: Hakes are cod-shaped fish, silvery in color with black speckles on backs and black mouth linings. The fish have no fin spines and the second dorsal and anal fins are deeply notched. Cods have 3 dorsal and 2 anal fins, while sablefish are colored dusky or black, have 2 dorsal fins and spines in the first dorsal.

DISTRIBUTION AND BIOLOGY: Found from the Bering Sea to Bahia Magdalena, Baja California, Pacific hake are abundant throughout much of their range. They live in 35–4,380 foot depths, most commonly, based on trawling studies, from 150–600 feet, in dense midwater schools. Some of these schools are, as we say in biology, really, really big. Schools can vary in length from several hundred feet to 12 miles, be up to 7.5 miles wide and have a depth of 20-70 feet. There are 3 or perhaps 4 distinct Pacific hake populations. The "coastal" one occurs from northern Baja California to the Bering Sea. A second group lives in the Strait of Georgia, between British Columbia and Vancouver Island, while a third resides in Puget Sound. Fish living off central and southern Baja California may form a fourth group, composed of dwarf hake which grow to a relatively small size. The coastal group makes extensive annual migrations. Adults spawn from central California to northern Baja California in winter and early spring and the young are found in the inshore waters of southern and central California. During the 1983 El Niño, large numbers of little ones moved northward into northern California, away from their normal haunts. When hake mature they begin a seasonal migration from the southern spawning grounds. Adults appear off San Francisco in early March, off Oregon and Washington in April and off Vancouver Island in May. By early September, the fish begin to head south and most are gone by fall, returning to their winter spawning grounds.

Pacific hake reach 3 feet in length and at least 23 years in age. Females grow slightly faster than males and probably reach a larger size. In the coastal stock, a 12-incher is about 2 years old, but one twice as long is around 12 years. Coastal hake mature at around 16 inches and 3–4 years. In the Strait of Georgia, fish grow more slowly, reach a smaller size and mature at around 14 inches and 4 years. Mature females as small as 6 inches have been found off southern Baja, in the supposed dwarf population. Females are oviparous. In the coastal population, spawning occurs well offshore, at depths of 350–1,550 feet from central California to northern Baja California and spawning schools have been spotted at least 200 miles offshore. The coastal population spawns from at least December–April (perhaps stretching from October - June), probably peaking in January and February, while Strait of Georgia hake spawn from March to May. Hake eggs hatch in about 3 days. Hake eggs and larvae seem to congregate at 130–330 feet below the surface. Larvae have been taken at least 400 miles offshore.

Pacific hake appear to feed mainly at night and eat just about whatever comes by. Juveniles feed extensively on krill, while adults eat a lot of krill, fishes and shrimp. Hake often feed at night, heading upwards in the water column as dark descends. Near dawn, the fish move back towards the bottom. Juveniles and adults are eaten by many fishes (dogfish, rays, sablefish, lingcod, rockfish, tuna), marine mammals (including northern elephant seals, northern fur seals, California sea lions, harbor porpoises, Pacific whitesided dolphins, killer and sperm whales) and sea birds (western gulls, common murres, Brandt's cormorants).

FISHERY: Hake are occasionally taken by salmon trollers and rockfish anglers fishing in deep water. However, because the meat softens quickly, hake are usually discarded by sport anglers.

Until recently, there was no large commercial fishery for the coastal hake population. The fish had very little value and most of what was taken (by otter trawl) was processed into fish meal or used as mink food. In the mid-1960s, the U. S. Bureau of Commercial Fisheries showed that truly horrific quantities of hake could be taken by midwater trawls (how about 60,000 pounds in a half hour trawl?) Soon after, a large foreign fleet, composed of vessels from the USSR, Poland, East and West Germany, Japan and Bulgaria, was busily trawling large quantiiies from off our shores. These large factory ships were able to catch and quickly process the hake, helping to prevent the meat from softening. Since the late 1970s, some U. S. vessels have taken large numbers, then transferred these at sea to foreign processing ships. Today, Pacific hake are fished at optimum levels. They comprise the largest single resource in the groundfish fishery off California, Oregon and Washington.

REMARKS: The reason coastal hake are difficult to market for human food is that they contain a parasitic protozoan in their muscle which softens the fish after death. The organism, *Kudoa paniformis* produces an enzyme that can liquify muscle tissue. When the hake is alive, the animal removes this enzyme from its muscle quickly enough to prevent damage. However, when the fish die the parasites live on for a while, continuing to produce the substance, with devastating effect on the muscle tissue. Interestingly, fish from the Strait of Georgia population are not infected by *K. paniformis*, and do not suffer from muscle softening. The parasite is not harmful to humans, even if swallowed alive. Of course, if the fish is cooked the parasite is dead. So stop whimpering and eat your hake.

In 1989, many young-of-the-year (yoy) hake were found stranded on the beaches of northern California. These had probably come into unusually shallow water to feed on yoy shortbelly rockfish. The rockfish had been driven into shallow water by unusual southerly winds. Open-water hake are not adapted to living around structures and probably injured themselves at night, slamming into kelp and rocks while feeding on the rockfish.

Remains of Pacific hake have been found in Pliocene deposits over one million years old in southern California. Hake ear bones are occasionally found in Native American middens.

Cusk-eels - Family Ophidiidae

SPOTTED CUSK-EEL (CHILARA TAYLORI)

NAMES: *Chilara* is a modern Greek word for several cusk-eel species; *taylori* honors A. S. Taylor, this species' discoverer.

IDENTIFYING CHARACTERS: Bill Eschmeyer, in the rightly-celebrated *A Field Guide to Pacific Coast Fishes of North America* describes cuskeels as "tapered, like a letter opener." Indeed they are, with long dorsal and anal fins, joined at the tail. Spotteds are brown to ecru (so look it up) with lots of dark spots.

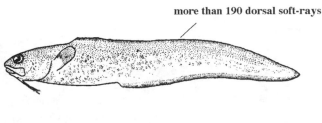

more than 190 dorsal soft-rays

DISTRIBUTION AND BIOLOGY: Reports of these little charmers have come in from Willapa Bay, Washington to central Baja California. These are bottom fishes of soft sediment, found anywhere from 4 to 3,702 feet, living in burrows they enter tail-first.

The biggest spotted cusk-eel on record was 14 inches long. They may live to at least 4 years. Females are oviparous. Spawning occurs primarily from July to November, though a little spawning may also occur through March. Peak spawning occurs from about Punta Baja (central Baja California) to Cabo San Lazaro (southern Baja California) and most larvae occur within 150 miles of the coast (a few out to 300 miles). Spotted cusk-eels feed on shrimps, crabs, amphipods and occasionally fishes. Jim Allen, of the Southern California Coastal Water Research Project, has seen them swimming just over the bottom, dragging their pelvic fins through the muck; apparently these guys feel for their prey, rather than look for it. Gammarid amphipods, shrimps and crabs are mostly what they eat. Elephant seals, harbor seals, harbor porpoises, Dall's porpoises, Pacific striped dolphins, Bonaparte's gulls and northern fulmers eat them.

FISHERY: As Monty Python would say, in the "Cheese Shop" routine, "Not as such."

REMARKS: Cusk-eels are normally nocturnal, though in deep water they have been seen out and about during the day. They also come out of their burrows on overcast days.

Ear bones from these fish have been taken from Pliocene deposit in Long Beach, southern California.

Toadfishes - Family Batrachoididae

PLAINFIN MIDSHIPMAN (PORICHTHYS NOTATUS)

NAMES: *Porichthys* is Greek for "pore fish," based on the numerous photophores on the body; *notatus* is Latin for "spotted." Curiously, scientists did not realize that photophores were light-producing organs until about 50 years after this species was described.

IDENTIFYING CHARACTERS: These fish are very distinctive and fairly

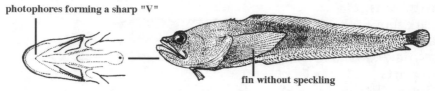

photophores forming a sharp "V"

fin without speckling

unattractive, with large, flattened heads, a sharp spine on each gill cover and rows of dots on their sides and bellies. These dots are photophores, which produce a blue-green light. Throat photophores in this species form a V-shape. Plainfins are brown, gray or sort of purple on backs, silvery on sides and sometimes yellowish on bellies. The specklefin midshipman (*P. myriaster*) closely resembles this species; however, it has spots on its dorsal and pelvic fins and a U-shaped pattern to its throat photophores. You can tell the sex of your midshipman by looking at its external genital papilla. Male ones are elongated and conical.

DISTRIBUTION AND BIOLOGY: Plainfins are found from Sitka, Alaska to Bahia Magdalena, southern Baja California, commonly from Vancouver Island southward. For obscure reasons, very few have been taken between northern California and Cape Flattery, Washington, although there seems to be plenty of suitable habitat. They are very abundant in Puget Sound, however. Sand and mud bottoms are preferred by these guys, and while they have been found from the intertidal zone to 1,200 feet, they are most abundant between about 150–450 feet. Plainfins bury themselves in the substrate during the day, leaving only their beady little eyes and toothy mouths exposed, looking like the Cheshire Cat with a hangover. When adults emerge from the bottom, they inflate their swimbladders, only to deflate them as dawn approaches. Active primarily at night, aggregations rise into the water column, usually near but occasionally as much as 450 feet above the bottom. Plainfins make extensive spawning migrations. Beginning in late winter, males start to move inshore, reaching the intertidal zone or shallow subtidal in May; females follow soon after. Both sexes return to deep water in fall. There is some evidence that not all mature males move into shallow water to spawn every year.

Plainfins reach 15 inches, and some live to at least 7 years. Males grow larger than females. Both sexes are about 4 inches long at 1 year; males are 8 inches and females 7 inches at about 4 years. Most fish mature at around 5.5 inches and 2 years; some males mature when as small as 3.5 inches. Females produce between 80 and 200 eggs per season. Off central California, spawning occurs from May–August (peaking in May and June) and from May–September off Santa Barbara. Beginning in May, males dig out nests under rocks in the intertidal zone from central California northward and in shallow subtidal water below Pt. Conception. Females join them, lay their eggs on the overhanging ledges (often more than one female will lay eggs in a single nest) and depart. Ed Demartini estimates that 5-6 females per nest is the average, but the numbers may occasionally go as high as 20.   A male guards the eggs until they hatch in about 15 days, then guards the larvae that are stuck on to the rocks for about one month. Occasionally, one of the eggs will split just after fertilization, leading to twins; these larvae remain attached by their yolks until they leave the nest. Even during very low tides males stay with the eggs and larvae, when the young are exposed to the air. Plainfins are able to breathe air for at least short periods.

Besides living off their yolks (just like Jack Benny), the attached larvae also feed on passing plankton. Once detached, juvenile plainfins hang around inshore waters until winter, then gradually migrate into deeper water. Plainfins will lunge from hiding and snap at prey during the day, but most feeding activity is at night. Krill, mysid shrimps, amphipods and squids make up most of their diet. Plainfins are eaten by a simply astounding number of animals. Here is a short list: kelp bass, northern elephant seals, California sea lions, northern fur seals, Pacific white-sided dolphins, Steller sea lions, pygmy sperm whales, harbor porpoises, Pacific striped dolphins, cormorants (Brandt's, double-crested, pelagic), western gulls, common murres, artic loons and pink-footed shearwaters. On Vancouver Island, plainfins may be the dominant food of mink during the summer. The mammals make subtidal excursions for the little spiny treats. During very low tides, herons, gulls and crows eat the males guarding nests.

FISHERY: Plainfins are taken incidentally by sport fishermen from boats, piers and jetties. There is no commercial fishery for this species, although they are taken in some numbers by otter trawlers (particularly in the shrimp fisheries off California). They are edible, but opinions of their flavor range from the good, to the bad, to the ugly. John Richards, until recently the Santa Barbara area marine advisor in the University of California Cooperative Extension Program, tried one and says he was not impressed.

REMARKS: Midshipmen make a wide array of sounds, including a sort of grunt and a very noticeable hum. At night, during spawning season, males produce a very loud, rather monotonal hum to attract apparently tone-deaf females. An individual male may continue his serenade for over an hour, and when a whole bunch of the fellows get together and perform "Louie Louie," the sound can be pretty intense. The males are the terrors of Sausalito during late spring and early summer, humming so loudly that house boaters on the Bay can barely enjoy their Late Harvest Riesling.

The spine on a midshipman gill cover is venomous. You won't die after being pricked, but it is distinctly unpleasant.

Though midshipmen remains are occasionally found in Native American middens, it does not appear as if they were a hot culinary item.

As mentioned earlier, plainfin midshipman produce a blue-green light, and light production is a rarity among shallow water fishes. The light, may be used for communication between individuals or species or as countershading (producing light which matches that coming downward, allowing the fish to blend in with the surrounding environment). Based on these possible uses, you would think that light production would be very important to this species. However, none of the fish in Puget Sound and only some off northern California produce light. The fish have all the necessary apparatus, but they appear to lack a chemical needed for light production. This chemical is found in a specific ostracod (a type of zooplankton crustacean) which does not live in Puget Sound and which is not abundant in the northernmost part of California. When the Puget Sound fish are given the ostracod (or chemicals from it), they can produce light.

Your science tax dollars at work.

Clingfishes - Family Gobiesocidae

NORTHERN CLINGFISH (GOBIESOX MAEANDRICUS)

NAMES: Two Latin words, meaning "goby pike" make up *Gobiesox*; *maeandricus* is Latin for "streaks", referring to the chain-like pattern on the sides.

IDENTIFYING CHARACTERS: Clingfishes are elongated little fishes, with depressed heads and a sucking disc on their breast regions, formed from their pelvic fins. This species is relatively easy to distinguish. Usually it has a distinctive chain-like pattern and dark lines radiating from the eyes. It is also the only clingfish to grow larger than 3.5 inches.

DISTRIBUTION AND BIOLOGY: A relatively wide-ranging form, northern clingfish manage to cling from southeastern Alaska to Baja California (abundant as far south as central California) and from intertidal waters to depths of 26 feet. They can be commonly found on the underside of rocks in the boulder fields of very shallow pools.

These are small fishes (though giants for the family), growing to 6.25 inches. Females are oviparous. They lay a single layer of eggs on rocks (usually intertidal) during the winter and spring. For their part, the males guard the eggs until the little ones hatch. Females produce between 194 and 382 eggs per season; these take 30 days to hatch at 48-52° F. At least in Washington, larval northern clingfish settle out and transform into juveniles on blades of bull kelp (*Nereocystis*) in shallow subtidal waters. These small fish then move into the intertidal zone. Northerns feed on isopods, worms, gammarid and caprellid amphipods, isopods, crabs and occasionally fishes. On San Juan Island, Puget Sound, gopher snakes go into intertidal waters and eat these fish.

Sauries - Family Scomberesocidae

PACIFIC SAURY (COLOLABIS SAIRA)

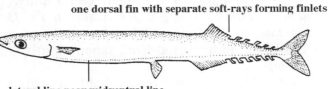

one dorsal fin with separate soft-rays forming finlets

lateral line near midventral line

NAMES: I like this one. *Cololabis* is formed from two Greek words, meaning "defective forceps" probably referring to the fact that the upper and lower jaws are uneven lengths; *saira* is Japanese for "spear fish".

IDENTIFYING CHARACTERS: These are skinny little suckers, with 5-6 finlets behind the dorsal and anal fins. They are usually green or blue above and silvery on sides and belly. Bar Betting Tip #1: If you are wagering on the identification of sauries, look for the finlets and bet big bucks. Bar Betting Tip #2: If you are wagering with a guy named Keghead, who dresses in army fatigues and believes the Small Business Administration is busily draining his brain, try to lose.

DISTRIBUTION AND BIOLOGY: Sauries are found throughout the

North Pacific, from Japan and the Gulf of Alaska as far south as the Revillagigedo Islands of Mexico. Within this range, there may be 3 somewhat separate populations that, nevertheless, extensively mix. The Pacific Coast stock extends from the Gulf of Alaska to Baja California, and one study showed that the bulk of the population occurred north of San Francisco, in a band 40-120 miles offshore. There is some evidence that many sauries (particularly older adults) migrate northward from California waters during the summer. Sauries seem to prefer a relatively narrow range of fairly cool temperatures (57-63° F), often associating themselves with upwelling areas. While sauries often stay at or near the surface, they have been taken down as deep as 660 feet.

These silvery little beauties grow to 14 inches. A few live to at least 6 years. Off the Pacific Coast, sauries apparently mature after a little over 1 year and at about 8 inches. Females are oviparous. Females spawn during different seasons all along their geographic range. Off California and Baja California, saury larvae are found from about San Francisco southward to Cabo San Lazaro, southern Baja California. Highest larval concentrations occur well offshore of central California. At least a few saury larvae are found nearly every month off our coast, but most spawning seems to occur from about April to June. This is an oceanic species; few larvae are taken closer than 40 miles from shore, and most are found at least 100 miles from the coast.

FISHERY: There is no U. S. fishery for sauries. Sus Kato, who knows all about these things, states that, in California, Pacific sauries are only popular among the Korean community. (S. Kato, 1994, *Study of Ethnic Markets for California's Underutilized and Undermarketed Fish Species*, California Seafood Council). All sauries in the U. S. are imported from Japan, South Korea, Taiwan and Thailand.

REMARKS: Most of you have probably already read this, but for those few who have not, the May-June 1991 issue of the Pakistan Seafood Digest notes that the consumption of sauries in Japan is about 1.3 pounds per person. This compares to a consumption rate of sauries in California (I got this from the National Marine Fisheries Service) of .05 pounds per person. Now, while I certainly do not wish to enflame passions any more than necessary, it appears to me that we have here all the makings of a classic "saury gap."

Killifishes - Family Cyprinodontidae

CALIFORNIA KILLIFISH (FUNDULUS PARVIPINNIS)

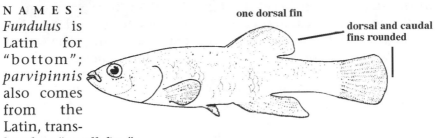

one dorsal fin

dorsal and caudal
fins rounded

NAMES: *Fundulus* is Latin for "bottom"; *parvipinnis* also comes from the Latin, translated as "small fin."

IDENTIFYING CHARACTERS: These are very pretty, quite distinctive fish. They have brown-green backs and brown or yellow-brown sides, a rounded caudal fin and dark, vertical bars.

DISTRIBUTION AND BIOLOGY: California killifish have been taken from Morro Bay, central California to at least Bahia Magdalena, southern Baja California. These are estuarine fishes; though you will occasionally find them in bays, only rarely do they live on the open coast. Young fishes tend to form schools, but adult ones are less inclined to that behavior. California killifish tolerate a wide range of salinities, from fresh to twice+ sea water. When disturbed, these killies often bury themselves head-first in the mud.

This species reaches 4.25 inches. A study in Anaheim Bay, southern California, showed that most fish live about 18 months, though about 3% of adults survived for about 30 months. Both sexes mature at a minimum length of 1.8 inches. Females are oviparous, spawn from April to September (probably with an April-June peak) and spawn more than once in the season. Females produce between about 60-440 eggs. Most adults probably do not survive past the spawning season, and males may die within 1 month of spawning. These are tough little fish: fertilized eggs successfully develop into larvae at temperatures between 62-83° F and salinities between nearly freshwater and almost twice sea-water. Development time is between about 18-55 days, depending on temperature. Insects, amphipods, copepods and ostracods make up most of the diet. Algae, worms, fish eggs and snails have also been found in their stomachs.

REMARKS: Here is a very good story uncovered by Kevin Lafferty and Aaron Morris, both of the University of California, Santa Barbara. The story involves the digenetic trematode, *Euhaplorchis californiensis*; a tiny worm-like parasite whose adult stage lives in the gut of several fish-eating birds. The birds contract the parasite by eating California killifish that are infected with juvenile

Euhaplorchis. In fact, *Euhaplorchis* must live in a killifish (they infect the brain) and must be eaten by a bird in order to complete its life cycle. The problem facing the worm is that not all California killifish are eaten by birds; an uneaten fish means a worm that does not get to reproduce. So the worms have (metaphorically speaking) figured out a way to even the odds a bit. Remember, the worm larvae infect killifish brains. The worms actually alter the normal behavior of these fish, causing them to come to the surface, meanwhile vibrating, jerking and contorting; all ways of saying to your local cormorant "I'm in Show Biz, Eat Me".

Silversides - Family Atherinidae

TOPSMELT (ATHERINOPS AFFINIS)

NAMES: Old names, now more or less out of service, include Bay Smelt, Little Smelt, Rainbow Smelt, Least Smelt, Capron, Jack Pescadillo and

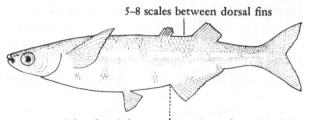

5–8 scales between dorsal fins

origin of anal fin under insertion of 1st dorsal fin

Panzarotti (I love that one; it sounds like it should be the tenor in Rossini's *Barber of Seville*.) *Atherinops* is derived from a Greek word meaning "appearance"; *affinis* is Latin for "related."

IDENTIFYING CHARACTERS: Topsmelts are green on backs, with silvery stripes along their sides. The anal fin begins below the first dorsal, there are 5–8 scales between the dorsal fins, and the jaw teeth are forked. This contrasts with the closely-related jacksmelt, in which the anal fin begins behind the dorsal, there are 10–12 scales between dorsal fins, and the jaw teeth are unforked.

DISTRIBUTION AND BIOLOGY: Topsmelt are found from Vancouver Island, British Columbia, to the Gulf of California, commonly from about Tillamook Bay, Oregon, southward. These are schooling, surface-dwelling animals, very common in estuaries (often they are the most abundant fish), kelp beds, along sandy beaches and, occasionally, offshore. They usually hang out near the surface, though they have been seen to depths of 30 feet. On calm days, you can often see them dimpling the water. These fish are very tolerant of drastic swings in water salinity, and they can tolerate anything from freshwater to water with a salt content almost three times that of sea water. (They routinely live in the salt evaporating ponds of San Francisco Bay.) Topsmelt are active during the day and become quiescent at night. Generally, many of these fish move into estuaries during spring and summer and into shallow, open coasts in fall and winter.

Topsmelt reach a length of 14.5 inches and some live to about 8 years. A 4-incher is 1 year old, a 6-incher is 2. The fish mature in the second and third year. Females are oviparous, spawn in batches and produce 200-1,000 eggs per season. Topsmelt spawn in estuaries and along the open coast. In Newport Bay, southern California, spawning occurs from February-June, peaking in May and June. In San Francisco Bay, things are a bit different, with a range between April-October, again with a May and June peak. Spawning temperatures generally range from 50-77° F and females lay their sticky egg strands onto many kinds of aquatic plants; eelgrass seems to be a favorite. Topsmelt are primarily nighttime spawners. Their eggs hatch in 35 days at 55° F and less than 9 days at 81°. Plankton, algae and insect larvae are all on the Blueplate Special for this species. A large number of fish eaters target topsmelt. These include California sea lions, harbor seals, least terns, and Brandt's and double-crested cormorants.

FISHERY: See Jacksmelt, below.

REMARKS: This was a big food item for Native Americans. Topsmelt remains are very common in Native American middens.

Although there are supposed to be a number of subspecies in California, no one has proven this to my satisfaction.

In the lagoons of Baja California, topsmelt clean whale lice from the skins of gray whales.

I have often seen topsmelt thrown on shore (only to wiggle back into the water) when entering and leaving the Goleta Slough through a narrow, fast-flowing channel.

On one occasion off La Jolla, California, a number of researchers noted topsmelt leaping out of the water, then scraping themselves on a floating stick (the fish, not the researchers). Well, I agree it's not the most interesting thing you could do on a Thursday afternoon, but remember, this was years before Nintendo.

JACKSMELT (ATHERINOPSIS CALIFORNIENSIS)

NAMES: California Smelt, Silverside, Horse Smelt, Bluesmelt, Pescado Del Rey, Peixe Rey, Pesce Rey. As in *Atherinops*, *Atherinopsis* comes from a Greek word meaning "appearance"; *californiensis* refers to the capture locality of the first individual known to science.

IDENTIFYING CHARACTERS: These fish are greenish-blue on backs,

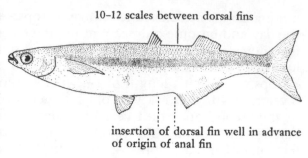

10–12 scales between dorsal fins

insertion of dorsal fin well in advance of origin of anal fin

with silver stripes on their sides. The anal fin begins behind the first dorsal fin, there are 10–12 rows of scales between the dorsal fins and the jaw teeth are unforked. Topsmelts are similar, but the anal fin starts below the first dorsal fin, there are 5–8 scales between the dorsal fins, and the jaw teeth are forked.

DISTRIBUTION AND BIOLOGY: Jacksmelt are found from Yaquina Bay, Oregon, to at least Bahia Magdalena, southern Baja California, most commonly from about Coos Bay, Oregon, southward. These are schooling, pelagic fish, usually found near shore, but occasionally venturing away from the coast a few miles. They occur in estuaries, in bays, around kelp beds and in open water. Jacksmelt often school with topsmelt. While they have been seen from the surface down to depths of 95 feet, they are most common between 5 and 50 feet.

Jacksmelt are the largest of the silversides on the Pacific Coast, reaching 19 inches (this last from Mike Shane at Hubbs-Sea World Research Institute) and sometimes living as long as 11 years. They grow to 5 inches in one year and 6-8 inches in 2 years, and most mature at 2 years. Females are oviparous, laying long strands of pretty pink and orange eggs (the size of bb's) on estuarine and marine plants and other floating objects. Spawning season is variable, depending on location, and here are some examples: Southern California, October to March; San Francisco Bay, October to August; San Pablo Bay, September to April; Tomales Bay, January to March. Their eggs are pretty tough, they will hatch in water that is almost fresh. Eggs hatch in 7-19 days, depending on temperature. Larvae and juveniles survive best and grow fastest in brackish water. Jacksmelt eat plankton and small fishes and are themselves preyed upon (and thoroughly enjoyed) by the usual assortment of marine fishes (including yellowtail), marine mammals (harbor seals, northern fur seals) and sea birds (brown pelicans, western gulls, least terns, Brandt's and double-crested cormorants).

FISHERY: Jacksmelt and topsmelt are popular catches with pier fishermen throughout California (topsmelt are also important further north). Both species, especially jacksmelt, also are taken by shore and boat anglers. Along with shiner perch and white croaker, these species are a major catch of anglers under the age of 10.

A number of pier anglers specialize in catching jacksmelt, which eagerly go for various small lures and yarn–wrapped hooks. Historically, there was a medium–sized commercial fishery for all silversides, particularly jacksmelt. Most were taken by purse seine and lampara net; some were also captured in gill nets. By the late 1930s, the fishery had sort of petered out and today they are taken only incidentally in gill and lampara nets and purse seines, and small quantities are sold fresh.

REMARKS: A fossilized jacksmelt earbone was found in a deposit over one million years old in southern California. This species was commonly harvested by coastal Native Americans.

GRUNION (LEURESTHES TENUIS)

NAMES: *Leuresthes* is formed from 2 Greek words, "smooth" and "to eat," referring to their toothless jaws; *tenuis* is Latin for "slender."

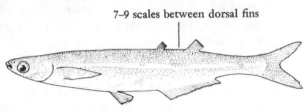

7–9 scales between dorsal fins

IDENTIFYING CHARACTERS: Grunion are small, slender fish, greenish on backs with a silver-blue stripe on sides. They have few or no teeth, and their anal fins begin below the first dorsal fins.

DISTRIBUTION AND BIOLOGY: Found from off San Francisco to southern Baja California, grunion are most abundant from Pt. Conception southward. These are pelagic, schooling fish, usually seen from just behind the surf line to depths of about 60 feet. They don't seem to migrate much, generally staying off the same piece of real estate for extended periods.

Grunion reach 7.5 inches in length, and some may live as long as 4 years. They mature when 1 year old, at about 5 inches; growth stops during the spawning season. Undoubtedly what is most unusual about this species, and the reason most people have heard of it, is its habit of spawning on sandy beaches, out of the water. Spawning occurs only on 3 or 4 nights following each full or new moon, and then only for 1 3 hours immediately after the high tide, from late February to early September (peaking late March to early June). The female swims onto the beach, usually with one or up to 8 males accompanying her. If no males are present, a female will return to the water, usually muttering fairly unflattering things about us guys. If males are present (it does happen occasionally, honest), the female swims as far up the beach as possible. By thrusting herself vertically (head up) and wiggling her tail back and forth, she digs herself into the wet sand, burying herself up to her pectoral fins or above. The male or males curve around her with vents touching her body, and when the female lays eggs beneath the sand, the males emit sperm which flows down her body and fertilizes the eggs. As you might expect, this behavior is illegal in six states (and Guam) and, although grunion have been arrested numerous times, the ACLU has always managed to spring them. Females spawn 4–8 times per season, at about 15 day intervals, producing 1,000–3,000 eggs. While spawning has been noted as far north as Monterey Bay, it occurs more frequently from Morro Bay southward. Eggs hatch at temperatures between 57–83° F, ideally in 61–81° F. The eggs remain in the sand until they are liberated by the next tide high enough to reach them (10+ days). In fact, the embryos require agitation such as wave action before they will break loose from their shells. These are plankton feeders. Least terns and double-crested cormorants (among others) eat them.

FISHERY: The sport fishery for grunion is unusual in that, by law, it must be conducted entirely with hands; no other gear is permitted. Of course, if you were a real man or woman, you would use your mouth. These fish are occasionally taken in the live bait fishery.

REMARKS: Every spring and summer, thousands of people on countless southern California beaches spend altogether too much time waiting for these little fish to come ashore. Occasionally someone will even catch one. Now, I can understand getting cold, tired and wet while smelling of stale beer or cheap wine if there were something truly outstanding about to happen (like watching the Earth collide with an asteroid or waiting for a piece of really good cheesecake). But how excited can I get about losing my beauty sleep over slimy 5 inch long fish?

It's difficult to know how to relate this last tidbit, but here goes. It seems, based on a fairly extensive experiment, that under the right conditions male grunion will mate with ... well ... mate with ... a stick. Now, we aren't just talking about any stick, mind you. No, indeed. First, remember that female grunion thrust themselves vertically and wiggle around in the sand. Researchers theorized that male grunion key in on females by looking for the only vertical things on the entire beach, a wiggly female. During the spawning runs, the researchers placed wooden dowels (1 inches in diameter and 2 feet long) in the sand near individual males. While stationary sticks were not too effective, wiggled sticks, which create a soft, puddled sand, did the trick. Apparently, the sight of a thin, 2 feet high "female grunion" was more than the males could resist.

As you might suspect, grunion were important foods for Native Americans.

Opahs - Family Lamprididae

OPAH (LAMPRIS GUTTATUS)

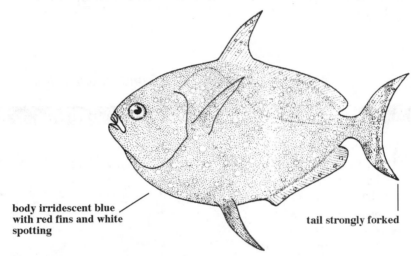

body irridescent blue with red fins and white spotting

tail strongly forked

NAMES: Poisson Lune (French). *Lampris* is Greek for "radiant"; *guttatus* is Latin for "spotted."

IDENTIFYING CHARACTERS: What would have happened if Picasso had eaten too many chocolate-covered almonds at Gertrude Stein's Paris flat? Yep, he would have created this polka-dotted beauty. They are oval, with bright red fins and mouth, a blue body and big, white spots.

DISTRIBUTION AND BIOLOGY: Opahs are found throughout the world in both temperate and tropical seas. In the north Pacific, they live from Japan and the Gulf of Alaska southwards to the Gulf of California. This is a pelagic species, usually found away from the coast, from surface waters down to 1,690 feet.

Opahs get big; the largest one on record was 4.5 feet long. People really don't know doodly about this species. Females are oviparous and produce pelagic eggs that turn into pelagic larvae. Spawning probably takes place in the spring and the eggs take about 3 weeks to hatch.

FISHERY: Opahs are occasionally taken by recreational anglers pursuing albacore. Caught commercially worldwide, opahs are moderately-important along the Pacific Coast. While most are taken

141

in the swordfish drift gillnet fishery, others are caught by salmon trollers. Quoting from Robert Price's admirable work, *"A Guide to California Seafood,"* (1994, California Seafood Council) we note that "Opah meat is multicolored. Meat from behind the head and along the backbone is amber red; meat toward the belly is pale pink; meat from the cheeks is red; and meat from inside the breast plate is bright ruby-red...The texture is oily, firm and delicate." It certainly is tasty. Most opah are caught in fall and winter, and most are marketed fresh, as fillets. Fresh opah has a pretty long shelf life, 7-10 days, at 40° F; frozen, it will hold up for 9 months at 0° F.

Scorpionfishes and Stonefishes - Family Scorpaenidae

CALIFORNIA SCORPIONFISH (SCORPAENA GUTTATA)

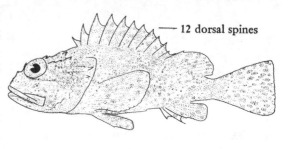

12 dorsal spines

NAME: Sculpin, Lupón (Mexico). The ancient Greeks called their scorpionfishes by a variant of *Scorpaena*, which means "scorpion," referring to the poison spines; *guttata* is Latin for "speckled."

IDENTIFYING CHARACTERS: California scorpionfish are spiny, thick-bodied fish, with large, flexible fins. Their color is variable, ranging from bright red through light brown, occasionally with lavender streaks, particularly on the head. Black or dark brown spots cover the entire body and fins.

DISTRIBUTION AND BIOLOGY: These puppies live from tide pool depths to about 600 feet (usually about 20–450 feet) from Santa Cruz (central California) south along Baja California and into the Gulf of California. Preferring warmer water, scorps are common as far north as Santa Barbara, and while they are most abundant on hard bottom (such as rocky reefs, sewer pipes and wrecks), they also perch on sand and mud. California scorpionfish make extensive spawning migrations in late spring and early summer, when most adults move into 120–360 feet, forming large spawning aggregations on or near the bottom. Spawning occurs in the same areas year after year (from June to August) and it is likely that the same fish return each time. When spawning ends in August, the aggregations disperse and many (though not all) of the fish move into shallower waters. As an example of how far they travel, spawning fish that I tagged off Huntington Beach, California were recaptured over 25 miles away. In other studies, the fish moved as much as 220 miles. While they rarely leave the bottom during the day, scorps rise to the surface at night to spawn.

California scorpionfish grow to 17 inches and some live at least 21 years. A 10-incher is about 6 years old. They are about 2 years old and 8 inches long when they mature. Females produce eggs imbedded in the gelatinous walls of hollow pear-shaped structures which are transparent or greenish and float near the surface. Within these structures, the eggs hatch in about 5 days. Young-of-the-year appear in shallow waters in summer and fall and usually hide out on the bottom in heavy cover. Small crabs are probably the most important food of larger juvenile and adult scorpionfish, although other items, such as small fishes, octopi, shrimps and even pebbles (lots of roughage there) are sometimes eaten. These animals are primarily nocturnal and catch food at night.

FISHERY: California scorpionfish are a fairly important part of the commercial and sport fishery in southern California and off Ensenada, Baja California. They are taken primarily aboard party and private vessels, occasionally from piers and jetties, mostly from Santa Monica Bay southward. Many fish are taken during the spring and summer, when the vessels target spawning aggregations. However, during some years, peak catches occur in other months. This may occur if party vessels find other species lacking and target scorpionfish. The commercial catch is made by hook and line, gillnet and otter trawl. Commercial fishing for this species has declined over the last 50 years, with only a few fishermen (notably the Newport, California dory fishermen) actively fishing for this species. However, the recent start of a live fish fishery (where fish are delivered alive to restaurants and fish markets) has increased interest in this species, as it is very hardy and quite popular with consumers. Scorpionfish are seen most commonly in Asian markets.

REMARKS: The sharp spines on the dorsal, anal and pelvic fins are quite poisonous. The toxin is produced in glands which lie at the base of each spine and run up to the tip through a groove. Although a stab from one of these fish is almost never fatal, it can be quite unpleasant and you should probably avoid it unless you are fond of pain. The most effective way to decrease or end the pain is to bathe the wound in hot (not scalding) water. The heat alters the toxin's structure, making it harmless. Care should always be taken when handling these fish, as the poison remains effective even after the fish is dead and even if the fish is frozen. The flesh of California scorpionfish is not hazardous and, in fact, is quite tasty.

Oh, my. Here is quite a story from my bud, Paul Nakatsuka. "The scorpionfish's hardiness makes it good for live display in tanks at sushi bars. I occasionally go to a restaurant in West Los Angeles that prepares *ikizukuri*, sashimi from a live animal. For $25-$45, depending on size, a scorpionfish is scooped out of a tank and hit over the head to subdue it. The flesh on each side is carefully filleted, then thinly sliced and spread out on a plate. In the center of this display, the remainder of the fish is placed on its belly on a bed of sea algae. The fish continues to open and close its mouth while the diner consumes the sashimi."

PACIFIC OCEAN PERCH (SEBASTES ALUTUS)

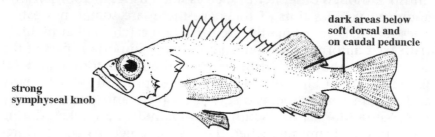

NAMES: Long-Jawed Rockfish, Arasuka Menuke (Japanese). *Sebastes* is Greek for "magnificent"; *alutus* is Latin for "unwashed," probably a reference to this species' light saddling.

IDENTIFYING CHARACTERS: Not one of your more distinctive rockfish, these have light-red backs and sort of silvery bellies. After capture, you might see dark saddles on the back and sometimes an olive-green patch below the soft dorsal fin. These also have a fairly prominent knob on their chins.

DISTRIBUTION AND BIOLOGY: Found from Japan and the Bering Sea southwards to central Baja California, POPs are relatively rare south of Cape Mendocino, northern California. Basically, this is a deep-water species (they have been caught down to 2,723 feet), mainly an inhabitant of the upper continental slope and lower continental shelf. Though they have been taken near the surface, adults are usually found below about 600 feet. They like rocky, high relief bottom. Off British Columbia, maximum adult abundance occurs in waters between 42° and 43° F; throughout their range they have been taken in waters between about 36-44°F. During the day, POPs tend to school between about 3 and 100 feet off the bottom, migrating upwards 120-250 feet and dispersing at dusk. They probably move vertically to follow the krill and deep-water fishes they prey on. They don't like light; on sunny days they stay closer to the bottom than on cloudy ones. During the summer, males and females hang out in their relatively shallow (600-1,200 feet) feeding grounds. After mating, the females, and a few politically correct males, move into deeper water (1,500-2,100 feet) at the mouths of submarine canyons. In the spring, the females release their young and return to shallow waters, much to the relief of the abandoned males, who were wondering if the femmes would ever come back.

POPs reach a length of 20 inches and live to 90 years. Females grow larger and somewhat faster than males. However, the really hot news, moderately fresh from the word processor of Bruce Leaman (Fisheries and Ocean Canada), is that the females that grow the slowest live the longest.

POPs in the northern part of their range seem to mature at smaller lengths than those in the southern end. Fifty percent of Bering Sea fish are mature at 8.5-10.5 inches, while the 50% mark is reached by those off British Columbia and Washington at 13.5-14.0 inches. There is some debate over how old they are when they mature. Estimates of half maturity range from 4-8 years in the Bering Sea to 11-12 years off British Columbia to 13-15 years in the Gulf of Alaska. The new, improved estimates for British Columbia, made by the aforementioned Bruce Leaman, are that half of males are mature at 6-8 years, females 7-9 years. Fertilization is internal and females may be primitively viviparous. The larvae inside the females may receive some nutrients from her. Females produce between 90,000-510,000 eggs per season and spawn in the spring. Spawning reportedly occurs at dusk. Smaller POP eat mainly krill and copepods; larger ones eat krill, shrimps and fishes. Among their finny foods are walleye pollock, flatfishes, lanternfishes and smelts. They are eaten by Pacific halibut, sablefish, arrowtooth flounder, sperm whales and various other marine mammals.

FISHERY: There is no recreational fishery for POPs. On the other hand, during the 1960s, there was a very intensive trawl fishery that slammed the population good. Today, POPs are still an important commercial species, taken primarily from the Aleutians, in Queen Charlotte Sound (British Columbia) and off Vancouver Island. Most of the catch is filleted and frozen.

KELP ROCKFISH (SEBASTES ATROVIRENS)

NAME: Dumb Bass, Rocot (Mexico). *Sebastes* is Greek for "magnificent"; *atrovirens* means "black and green" in Latin.

IDENTIFYING CHARACTERS: Like many rockfish, kelps are spiny,

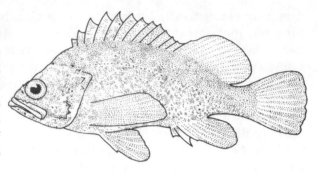

deep-bodied fishes, usually colored tan or pinkish-brown with dark mottling. You will occasionally see a reddish one if you were particularly good in a previous life.

DISTRIBUTION AND BIOLOGY: Kelp rockfish live from shallow subtidal waters (maybe 10 feet) to at least 150 feet. Russian scientists report taking them from depths of over 900 feet. Although the Russians are usually quite good observers, I have my doubts about these reports. Most fish live in waters between 15 and 50 feet. Kelp rockfish range from central Baja California to Sonoma County, northern California, but are abundant from northern Baja California to central California. While I have seen them living in rocky areas without algae, these fish really prefer kelp and other algae. During the day, they are usually right in the algal blades, sometimes sitting on them, often upside down. At night, when they are most active, they will sometimes chase food slightly away from this plant habitat. Rarely moving from place to place, these fish may migrate into slightly deeper water or retire to rock caves during winter storms. Although they do not school, occasional aggregations of hundreds are seen.

Kelp rockfish reach 16.75 inches. Spawning takes place from late winter to spring, and juveniles settle out of the plankton into kelp beds in summer, from April through August (earliest in southern California and Baja California). Young-of-the-year first settle in the fronds of kelp beds and as they grow, they spread out, away from the canopy. Kelps eat a variety of prey, most of which are found swimming about in the water. Important foods include small fishes (such as juvenile rockfishes), shrimps, amphipods and isopods.

FISHERY: Kelps are often taken in the sport fishery, commonly in kelp beds and occasionally from piers and rocky shores. Because you can just about swim up to a kelp rockfish and give it a big hug, they are quite important in the sport diver catch (particularly from Santa Barbara, southern California, to northern California). Commercial fishermen infrequently take them in traps and gillnets.

BROWN ROCKFISH (SEBASTES AURICULATUS)

NAMES: Commercial fishermen along much of the coast call them

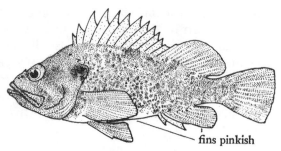

fins pinkish

Bolinas and Rocot in Mexico. *Sebastes* is Greek for "magnificent"; *auriculatus* means "eared" in Latin, probably referring to the brown patch on the gill cover. IDENTIFYING CHARACTERS: Browns are deep-bodied, squat rockfish, with well-developed head spines (Plate 7). They are brown or orange-brown with darker mottling, and most have a dark patch on their gill covers which tends to fade in older fish. Kelp and grass rockfish resemble browns, but neither has the dark gill cover blotch.

DISTRIBUTION AND BIOLOGY: Found from southeast Alaska to central Baja California, browns are most abundant from Puget Sound to southern California. These fish are found from shallow subtidal waters to 444 feet, most commonly from 20 feet down. These are bottom dwellers, living on hard bottom or sand, near structure of some kind. While they are not usually found on high reefs, browns seem to enjoy aggregating near rocks, oil platforms, sewer pipes, and even old tires. There is no evidence that browns make extensive movements; however, juveniles gradually move into deeper water as they mature. In a study by the National Marine Fisheries Service, juvenile browns were tagged around a dock in San Francisco Bay and most showed little movement over a number of months. However, at about 7.5 inches the fish left the dock and at least one was later taken from the open coast outside the Bay. These fish also showed a strong homing tendency; a number of them were transported away from the dock, and some returned to the same site soon afterward.

Browns reach 22 inches, and a 21 incher I aged was 18 years old. Males and females probably grow at the same rate and mature at similar ages and lengths. Fifty percent are mature at 12 inches (5 years), and all are mature at 15 inches (10 years). Off Oregon, females spawn in May and June; the spawning season is longer off central California, from at least December to July. Females produce anywhere from 42,000-266,000 eggs. Off southern California, females spawn more than once per season. Browns eat fishes and crustaceans such as crabs.

FISHERY: Browns are a small part of the sport catch, comprising 1-5% of the total marine recreational catch in some areas. They are most commonly taken from party and private vessels, but are also caught from piers and shore, primarily from Mendocino County,

147

northern California, southward. Divers also take a few. Most of the fish taken in shallow water are juveniles. Commercial fishermen harvest minor numbers, usually as an incidental catch in crab and lobster traps, but also in trawls. They are a valuable hook and line species in various locales, where they are kept alive and sold at high prices to the local Asian markets.

REMARKS: Browns may hybridize with copper rockfish in Puget Sound.

AURORA ROCKFISH (SEBASTES AURORA)

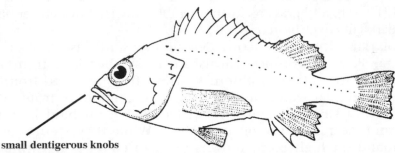

small dentigerous knobs

NAMES: *Sebastes* is Greek for "magnificent"; *aurora* is Latin for "dawn," perhaps referring to this species' red coloration.

IDENTIFYING CHARACTERS: This is another sort of undistinguished species. They are fairly spiny, bright pinkish-red or orangish-red, without much in the way of markings. They have a small protrusion at the tip of each upper jaw.

DISTRIBUTION AND BIOLOGY: Aurora rockfish are found from west of Langara Island, British Columbia to Isla Cedros, Baja California. This is a deep-water form, living in 413-2,520 feet. Trawl studies indicate they are most common in depths from about 1,000-1,500 feet.

A medium-sized species, auroras grow to 15.5 inches. Like other rockfishes, it is possible that females are primitively viviparous. Based on limited studies, auroras mature at around 11 inches and 5 years. Females spawn from March-May off central and northern California and sometime later than June off British Columbia. Aurora larvae have been taken from about San Francisco, northern California to Punta Baja, northern Baja California, with heaviest numbers off central California. Larvae have been taken in all months except September and October, with a peak period in the spring.

FISHERY: Once in a while, when they least expect it, deepwater rockfish anglers catch this one. They are taken by deepwater trawlers targeting thornyheads and splitnose rockfish.

REDBANDED ROCKFISH (SEBASTES BABCOCKI)

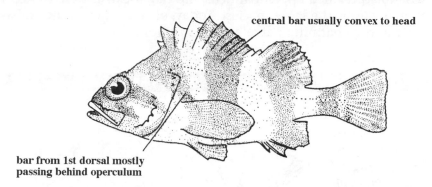

central bar usually convex to head

bar from 1st dorsal mostly
passing behind operculum

NAMES: Hatazoi (Japanese). *Sebastes* is Greek for "magnificent"; *babcocki* comes from John P. Babcock, described by J. L. Hart (*Pacific Fishes of Canada*) as an "enlightened fishery administrator in California and British Columbia." What exactly does "enlightened fishery administrator" mean? Did he give all fishes Friday afternoon off?

IDENTIFYING CHARACTERS: You will never mistake redbandeds for any other rockfish species except one. Redbandeds are deep-bodied fish, with 4 quite distinctive wide red bars. The only species that causes confusion is the flag rockfish and here's how you tell the difference. First, flags tend to be a bit sleeker; in particular the front of their heads come to more of a point. Second, in redbandeds the red bar under the front part of the spiny dorsal extends backwards. In flags, this bar goes pretty much straight down.

DISTRIBUTION AND BIOLOGY: Redbandeds live from the Bering Sea to off San Diego, southern California, often in fairly deep water (162-2,062 feet). They are most abundant in depths of about 450-1,200 feet. Found occasionally off central California, they become more abundant to the north. In our observations from submersible vehicles, we have seen them in rocky, high relief areas, particularly ones with caves and other shelter.

Redbandeds reach 25 inches. In general, the big zip is known about them. Females are possibly primitively viviparous. Males mature at 10.5-12.5 inches (3-5 years); females, 13-16.5 inches (3-6 years). Females spawn in April and May.

FISHERY: Recreational anglers do catch these deepwater fish once in a while, as do commercial fishermen. Their contribution to the catch is nowhere large, though the further north you go, the more common in the catch they become. I have frequently seen them in the Chinese markets of San Francisco.

REMARKS: Until Ace Ichthyologists Lo-Chai Chen and Dick Rosenblatt teamed up, redbandeds and flag rockfish were thought by many to be the same species. Today, of course, we smile knowingly at the charming naivete of this notion.

SILVERGRAY ROCKFISH (SEBASTES BREVISPINIS)

NAMES: Gin Menuke (Japan). *Sebastes* is Greek for "magnificent"; *brevispinis* is formed from the Greek words for "short spine."

IDENTIFYING CHARACTERS: This is a fairly sleek species, with a large mouth and small head spines. Its back is gray and sides are silvergray. Only the bocaccio closely resembles it and bocaccio are reddish.

DISTRIBUTION AND BIOLOGY: Silvergrays have been caught from the eastern Bering Sea to Bahia Sebastian Vizcaino, central Baja California; they are rare south of about Oregon. These are aggregating fish, usually found over high relief, mostly above the bottom. They live anywhere from the surface to 1,440 feet, most commonly between about 300 and 900 feet.

Twenty-eight inches is the maximum size for this species. They live to 80 years; males and females grow at similar rates. There is just not a lot known about them. Studies off British Columbia imply that the length at which 50% of these individuals are mature ranges from 1.3-1.7 feet. Spawning occurs from May to July.

FISHERY: They are an occasional catch in the recreational fishery but a common trawl-caught species, particularly off British Columbia.

I have seen good numbers of these for sale in the Asian markets of Vancouver, British Columbia.

GOPHER ROCKFISH (SEBASTES CARNATUS) AND BLACK-AND-YELLOW ROCKFISH (S. CHRYSOMELAS)

NAME: China Cod, Gopher Cod, Rocot (Mexico). *Sebastes* means "magnificent" in Greek; *carnatus* means "flesh-colored" and *chrysomelas* means "black and yellow" in Latin.

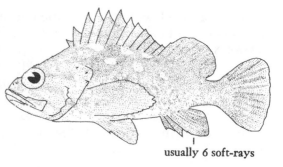

usually 6 soft-rays

IDENTIFYING CHARACTERS: Both species are heavy bodied, thick rockfish with large head spines. Gophers tend to be brown or dark brown, interspersed with large pink or whitish blotches. Two brown lines extend backwards from the eyes. Black-and-yellows are black or dark brown, with yellow areas on back. They resemble each other so closely that I have lumped them together under one heading.

DISTRIBUTION AND BIOLOGY: Both gophers and black-and-yellows are found from Eureka (northern California) to central Baja California. Gophers are common from about Mendocino County (northern California) southward to perhaps Santa Monica Bay, and black-and-yellows on down to about San Diego. Though gophers have been taken from nearly intertidal waters to 264 feet, the adults are most abundant from 30 to about 120 feet. Black-and-yellows are also found down to 120 foot depths, but are most common in less than 60 feet. When found together, the two species segregate somewhat by depth, with the more aggressive black-and-yellows holding forth in shallower water. These are solitary, territorial reef fishes, found right on the bottom.

Gophers reach 15.5 inches and some live to 13 years, while black-and-yellows grow to 15.25 inches and have been aged to about 15 years. Spawning takes place in spring and young-of-the-year first appear in kelp beds in May and June. Young-of-the-year at first live right among the fronds, later descending down the plant and eventually leaving its protection. Small gophers and black-and-yellows eat such zooplankton as copepods and crab larvae. Larger fishes eat crabs, shrimps and occasionally fishes and octopi.

FISHERY: In general, both species are minor parts of the party and private vessel recreational rockfish catch in both California and northern Baja California. They are usually taken by vessels fishing for kelp bass and shallow water rockfishes. However, studies by the California Department of Fish and Game show that gophers are an important species from about Monterey to Avila Beach, central California. In some years, gophers comprise 7-11% of the total marine recreational fish catch. Once in a while, black-and-yellows are caught by rocky shore fishermen. While in the past they were rarely taken in the commercial catch, both species are now targeted by hook and line commercial fishermen for the market and restaurant live fish trade.

REMARKS: These two species are *very* closely related, so closely that color is the only way we know to tell them apart. This is a poor way of separating species (after all humans come in different colors and we are all one species). It is possible that these two forms are so closely related that only the use of very sensitive genetic techniques (which resemble black magic to me) will separate them.

COPPER ROCKFISH (SEBASTES CAURINUS)

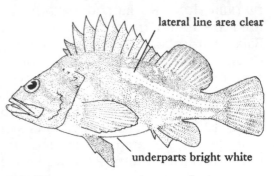

lateral line area clear

underparts bright white

NAMES: Chucklehead, Whitebelly Rockfish, Never Die (because they survive in air for quite a while), Rocot (Mexico). *Sebastes* means "magnificent" in Greek; *caurinus* comes from the Latin for "northwestern," referring to its being first described in Puget Sound, Washington.

IDENTIFYING CHARACTERS: Coppers are short, fairly squat rockfish with extensive head spines. They come in an assortment of colors, which has lead to some confusion. Adults can vary from whitish to pink or orange-red to brownish or even almost black. All have patches of other colors, often copper or yellow (Plate 12). Juveniles are often most intensely colored; occasionally they are brick-red. There are usually two yellow, copper or orange stripes running backward from the eyes, and in a majority of fish the lateral line sits within a white line.

DISTRIBUTION AND BIOLOGY: While coppers have been found from the Gulf of Alaska southward to central Baja California, they are most abundant from British Columbia to southern California. These are solitary, bottom-dwelling reef fishes which commonly live on such high relief as pinnacles and wrecks. Although coppers have been taken from about 20–600 feet, adults are most common in water shallower than 400 feet. Because they avoid warm water, adults live in deeper depths off southern California (usually below 150 feet) than farther north. Conversely, off British Columbia, they are found in quite shallow water, mostly less than 60 feet. Juveniles tend to live in shallower water, up to about 20 feet. Once adults find a good reef, many don't seem to move about much. In northern waters, these fish probably withdraw deep within crevices in winter to avoid storms. I have seen them as much as 10 feet above the rocks on a number of occasions.

Coppers have been reported to reach 22.5 inches and 14 years, though it is very likely they live considerably longer. Fifty percent are mature at 13–14 inches (4–6 years); all are mature by 16 inches (8 years). Spawning occurs in late winter to early spring, from about February–April south of British Columbia and from March–July in southeast Alaska. Young-of-the-year first appear in kelp and other algae in April off Monterey and August off British Columbia. These small fish are found near the bottom over sand, along rock-sand interfaces, often associating with drift algae. Juveniles eat plankton; adults feed on such bottom organisms as octopi, shrimps, crabs and small fishes.

FISHERY: Coppers are a moderately important part of the recreational fishing catch from southern California (particularly the Santa Barbara Channel) northward to at least southeast Alaska. They are commonly taken by party and private vessels and the young are occasionally taken from piers, jetties and rocky shores. Off California and Oregon, they may comprise as much as 15% (commonly 1-3%) of the total marine recreational catch. Similarly, they form a part of the "red" rockfish commercial catch off California, taken primarily by hook and line and gillnet and sold whole. They are quite important off British Columbia and California, where they are sold at high prices to the Asian live fish markets.

REMARKS: This species comes in such a wide array of colors that, until recently, it was classified as two forms, the copper and whitebelly rockfishes.

Coppers have been sighted sharing caves with giant Pacific octopi (not that they have much choice).

Coppers may hybridize with brown rockfish in Puget Sound.

GREENSPOTTED ROCKFISH (SEBASTES CHLOROSTICTUS)

NAMES: Bosco, Chucklehead, Scrub. *Sebastes* is Greek for "magnificent"; *chlorostictus* is Greek for "green spotted."

IDENTIFYING CHARACTERS: This is a spiny, dumpy rockfish, with a yellowish-pink or pink body, lots of round, green spots (particularly on back) and 3–5 whitish or pinkish-white blotches on back. The underside of the lower jaw has a few fine scales or no scales at all. This species closely resembles the greenblotched rockfish which has irregular green vermiculations that often connect with each other and rough scales on the underside of the lower jaw.

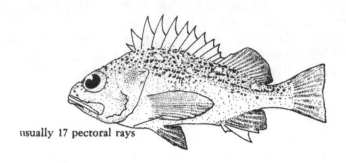

usually 17 pectoral rays

DISTRIBUTION AND BIOLOGY: Greenspotteds are found from Copalis Head, Washington southward to central Baja California and are abundant as far north as about Monterey, central California. They occur between depths of 100 and 900 feet (most often from about 300-650 feet). Juveniles are found mostly between 100 and 300 feet. This is a solitary, rather sedentary species; it spends most of its time on or near the bottom. When it comes to habitat preferences, greenspots are really open to suggestion. Off Monterey, we have seen them over rocks, hard bottom, sand, mud, vertical faces, horizontal plains, you name it.

Greenspotteds are reported to grow to 19.75 inches We don't know how long they live, nor how fast they grow. A 10 incher is around 13 years old. Off southern California, about half are mature at 9 inches; all are mature at about 13 inches. Off central and northern California, all are mature at 15 inches. Spawning takes place from February–July (peaking in April) off southern California and April–August (peaking in May) off central and northern California. I have found as many as 760,000 eggs in a female. Greenspotteds eat mainly invertebrates, such as crabs and shrimps, but I have also found them eating fishes, squids and octopi.

FISHERY: Greenspotteds are an important part of the recreational fish catch, taken from party and private vessels in southern, central and northern California, at least as far north as Mendocino County. In the Santa Barbara Channel, the "Elephant Burial Ground" of greenspotteds, this species may comprise 10% of the total marine recreational catch. They, along with rosies and starries, are often the only rockfishes taken over reefs from which more mobile species, such as bocaccio or chilipepper, have moved or been removed. These are a moderately important part of the commercial rockfish catch, commanding a high price in the Asian market and restaurant "red snapper" trade.

REMARKS: Don't be put off by the black-lined gut cavity. It in no way affects the flesh.

STARRY ROCKFISH (SEBASTES CONSTELLATUS)

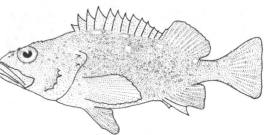

NAMES: Spotted Rockfish, Rocot (Mexico). *Sebastes* is Greek for "magnificent"; *constellatus* is Latin for "starred," a reference to the myriad cute little spots on their chubby little bodies.

IDENTIFYING CHARACTERS: These are really pretty, spiny fish, red-orange on back and sides, profusely covered with whitish or yellowish spots with 3–5 whitish blotches on their backs.

DISTRIBUTION AND BIOLOGY: Starries are found from Cordell Bank, northern California to Thetis Bank, southern Baja California (commonly from about Monterey southward), exclusively over hard bottoms, usually around large rocks or wrecks. With an overall depth range of 80–900 feet, adults are most abundant from 180–450 feet, with juveniles common from 90–250 feet. These fish live right on the bottom, often in crevices, and rarely go more than a foot or two above the rocks. While usually solitary, you may occasionally find them in small aggregations. Starries are sedentary couch potatoes; it's unlikely they move from reef to reef.

Starries reach 18 inches in length and live at least 28 years. Males and females grow at about the same rate. Starries spawn from February–July in southern California (peaking in May) and April to May off central California. Males mature at a slightly smaller size than females. About half of males are mature at about 8 inches (6–7 years), females at about 10 inches (8–9 years). Females may have as many as 230,000 eggs. Small fishes, along with crabs, shrimps and other small invertebrates make up their diet.

FISHERY: Starries are a minor, though aesthetic, part of the party and private vessel sport fishery from southern to northern California, commonly taken by vessels targeting medium-depth rockfish. Most recreational catches occur from Monterey Bay, central California, southward. In some regions, starries may contribute as much as 3% to the total marine recreational catch. Since their bright orange color makes them particularly appealing to various ethnic groups, they form a small (but lucrative) part of the commercial catch. Almost always sold whole, they are taken primarily by hook and line and gillnet.

REMARKS: Starry remains have been found in Native American middens in Ventura, California. Some anglers call them "starry eyes." This annoys other anglers and must be stopped.

DARKBLOTCHED ROCKFISH (SEBASTES CRAMERI)

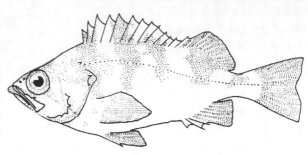

NAMES: Yotsujim-amenuke (Japanese). *Sebastes* is Greek for "magnificent"; *crameri* honors the 19th Century Stanford University rockfish biologist, Frank Cramer.

IDENTIFYING CHARACTERS: Darkblotches are somewhat oval rockfish, with 4-5 dark saddles on their backs. Underwater, they have pale backgrounds and brilliant red bars.

DISTRIBUTION AND BIOLOGY: Darkblotches have been taken from the Bering Sea to near Santa Catalina Island, southern California. We start to see fair numbers of them as far south as Monterey Bay. These are deep-water fishes and even though they have been taken from 17-2,982 feet, don't expect them in water shallower than perhaps 300 feet. Almost all darkblotches live between 150-1,300 feet. Darkblotches like to hang around rocks, right near the bottom. However, they are not strictly rock-dwellers. You will also see them along mud-rock interfaces.

Darkblotches reach 22.5 inches and live at least 66 years. Various studies off British Columbia, Oregon and California have given somewhat different results regarding size and age at first maturity. Several studies imply that males tend to mature earlier and smaller than females; one study does not. Taken together, it appears that half of males are mature at anywhere from 10.5 to 14 inches (4-5+ years old), while half of females mature at 10.5-15.25 inches (4-8 years old). Females may be primitively viviparous. They spawn from November to March and smaller ones tend to spawn later in the season. Females spawn once per season. Thus far, anywhere from about 20,000-610,000 eggs have been found per female.

FISHERY: Generally too deep for recreational anglers, commercial trawl fishermen catch substantial numbers.

CALICO ROCKFISH (SEBASTES DALLI)

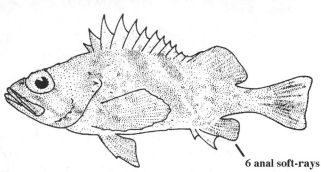

6 anal soft-rays

NAMES: *Sebastes* is Greek for "magnificent"; *dalli* refers to the Smithsonian zoologist, William H. Dall. **IDENTIFYING CHARACTERS:** For a rockfish, this is a pretty easy one. They are small, relatively spiny and have a bunch of diagonal, brownish bars on their backs and sides.

DISTRIBUTION AND BIOLOGY: These little puppies are known from San Francisco to central Baja California. While they have been taken from 24-840 feet, they seem most abundant from about 150-300 feet of water. Calicos are bottom-dwellers, often found on the sand-rock interface.

One of the dwarf rockfishes, calicos get no bigger than 8 inches and probably live to about 11 years. Males and females mature after about 4 years at around the same length, generally 3-4 inches. Females are possibly viviparous. Based on a seemingly endless study I conducted on southern California rockfishes, calicos spawn from January to May, peaking in February. Females produce anywhere from 3,900-18,000 eggs per season. Calicos feed on a variety of prey; copepods, gammarid amphipods, bivalves and crabs are all important.

FISHERY: Despite its diminutive size, calicos are commonly taken by shallow water rockfish anglers, particularly from Santa Barbara, southern California, southward. They are not of commercial importance.

SPLITNOSE ROCKFISH (SEBASTES DIPLOPROA)

NAMES: *Sebastes* is Greek for "magnificent"; *diploproa* is formed from two Greek words meaning "double prow," referring to this species' deep notch in its upper jaw.

IDENTIFYING CHARACTERS: Splitnoses are pink fish with, as the name implies, two knobs on their upper jaw, one on each side of the snout. That, and big eyes, are the giveaways here.

DISTRIBUTION AND BIOLOGY: A species with a very wide geographic distribution, splitnoses live from southeastern Alaska to central Baja California. Pelagic juveniles congregate around drifting kelp

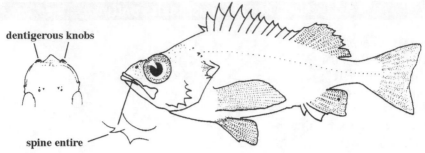

dentigerous knobs

spine entire

mats. While juveniles are found in shallow water, adults are usually deeper. Splitnoses have been taken down to 2,982 feet. Trawl studies show that most occur between 300 and 1,500 feet. From submersibles, we have seen them singly (often sitting in little depressions in the mud or sand) or in near-bottom aggregations.

Splitnoses don't get very big, 18 inches is the maximum size and around 84 years is the maximum age. Just to put that in perspective, one 12 inches long could be anywhere from about 20 to over 80 years old. Splitnoses lucky enough to live in the northern part of their range tend to grow faster than those in more southerly climes. In Tina Wyllie-Echeverria's admirable, one might say exhaustive, study of rockfish spawning, male splitnoses matured at 8-11.5 inches (7-10 years) and females at 7-9 inches (6-9 years). Females are possibly primitively viviparous. It is likely that, throughout their range, some splitnose is spawning during every month of the year. However, most females spawn from January-September, peaking in July. George Boehlert, currently the Mister Big of the Monterey Laboratory of the Pacific Fisheries Environmental Group (National Marine Fisheries Service), found that splitnose pelagic juveniles live around drifting kelp mats and hang under them until they are about one year old; then, they migrate to the bottom in depths of 600 feet and greater. It is likely that during this migration juveniles spend some time in midwater. Spitnoses eat krill, copepods and squids.

FISHERY: Splitnoses are taken only occasionally in the recreational fishery, probably because these are primarily plankton eaters, live in deep water and just don't want to gnaw on a bait almost as big as they are. From central California northward to at least Washington, they are a major commercial species, taken almost entirely by trawls.

GREENSTRIPED ROCKFISH (SEBASTES ELONGATUS)

NAMES: *Sebastes* is Greek for "magnificent"; *elongatus* is Latin for "elongated," a comment on the greenstripes' sleek physique.

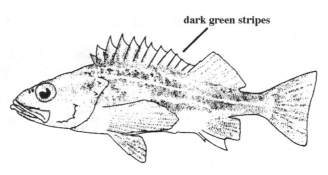

dark green stripes

IDENTIFYING CHARACTERS: A fairly slim species, pinkish with green stripes. DISTRIBUTION AND BIOLOGY: Greenstripes are found from Cherikof Island in the Aleutian chain to central Baja California. These are rather solitary rockfish, often found on mud, cobble or mud-rock inter-face, from 83-1,632 feet of water, most commonly from 150 to 800 feet.

Greenstripes are relatively small fish, reaching 15 inches. They live to 25 years and females grow faster than males. A 10-inch female is about 10 years old, a similar-sized male is 15. Males and females mature at about the same length, 6-10 inches (4-10 years). Females may be primitively viviparous. Spawning season is January-July in southern California (peaking in April) and May-July in central and northern California (peaking in May). Females in southern California may spawn more than once per season and produce 10,600-295,000 eggs. Calanoid copepods, shrimps, squids, gammarid amphipods and krill are common prey.
FISHERY: Greenstripes are very common in the deeper-water recreational rockfish fisheries of California and Oregon, particularly from Cape Mendocino southward. They are taken incidentally in commercial fisheries.

PUGET SOUND ROCKFISH (SEBASTES EMPHAEUS)

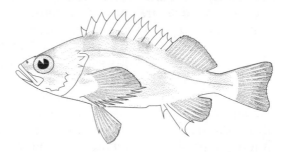

NAMES: *Sebastes* is Greek for "magnificent"; *emphaeus* is Latin for "display."
IDENTIFYING CHARACTERS: This is one of the dwarf rockfishes, and unless you are diving in their habi-tat, they just are not seen too often. They are reddish, with sort of greenish blotches on backs and sides.
DISTRIBUTION AND BIOLOGY: Pugets are at home in the area from the Kenai Peninsula, Alaska to northern California. They are found around rocks in 33-1,200 feet of water. Adults are usually

found in small groups, often in crevices and caves, just over rock surfaces.

They don't get big, 7.2 inches tops. And they don't seem to live too long; 4 years may be about the maximum. Pugets mature beginning at about 5 inches in length and 2 years of age. Females may be viviparous and, in Puget Sound, they spawn in August and September, producing from about 20,000-57,000 eggs. In the one published study, zooplankton, mostly cope-pods, was the preferred food.

WIDOW ROCKFISH (SEBASTES ENTOMELAS)

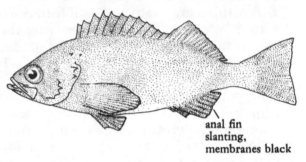

anal fin slanting, membranes black

NAMES: Brown Bombers, Brownies, Widowfish. *Sebastes* means "magnificent" in Greek; *entomelas* is a combination of 2 Greek words translated as "black within," alluding to the species' jet black body cavity lining.

IDENTIFYING CHARACTERS: These are bass-shaped rockfish, with few head spines, brassy-brown or brown on sides, white or pinkish-red on bellies. The spiny dorsal fins are tan and other fins are blackish. Fish less than about 10 inches often have orangy-brown streaks.

DISTRIBUTION AND BIOLOGY: Widows are wide-ranging, found from near Kodiak Island, Alaska to southern Baja California, usually over rocky reefs and other hard bottoms (e.g., oil platforms and wrecks). Widows are most abundant from central California to southern Washington. Juveniles enter shallow water (often in kelp beds); adults are found from 80–1,237 feet, though almost all adults live in 150–1,000 feet. Adult widows tend to be in shallower water in the northern part of their range. These are schooling fish (sometimes found with boccacio, black, canary, yellowtail and silvergray rockfish) living in aggregations of thousands or tens of thousands. They seem to move extensively, but we don't know much about these movements. Widows form tight, midwater schools at night that usually break up during the day. Schools appear on depth sounders as tall, slender columns.

Widows reach 24 inches and live at least 59 years. Females grow larger and may live slightly longer than males. An 18 inch fish is around 15 years old. Most fish are mature at 8–9 years and

17 inches. Females spawn from December–May, with a February peak, some producing over a million eggs. We see juveniles settling out of the plankton beginning in April. Reproduction seems most successful (the most larvae survive) during years when there are violent winter storms and above average water temperatures. Widows are daytime feeders, eating plankton (particularly krill, crab larvae and gelatinous creatures such as salps) and such fish as deep sea lanternfish. Northern fur seals eat them.

FISHERY: Widows are usually a minor part of the party vessel sport fish catch from the Santa Barbara Channel northward to at least Oregon. In many areas, they form around 1% (occasionally as much as 7%) of the total marine recreational catch. However, off San Francisco and Bodega Bays, they are an important part of the winter rockfish fishery and occasionally recreational vessels will target them. During some years, juvenile and subadult widows are extremely abundant around the offshore oil platforms in the Santa Barbara Channel. During this period, recreational fishermen, particularly on party vessels, haul them in by the bushel.

Widows form a major commercial fishery, particularly between northern California and Washington, where they are taken almost entirely by midwater trawl towed during the night. They are also captured by gillnet and hook and line. Few widows are sold whole. Most are filleted and sold fresh and frozen as "rockcod," "rockfish" or "Pacific snapper." Widows have a refrigerated fillet life that is reported to be shorter than many other rockfishes.

REMARKS: The commercial fishery for widows is a true "boom and bust" story. In 1979, a trawl fisherman off Oregon discovered large, previously undetected schools of widows–undetected because these fish school only at night and no one had looked for them then. Fishing with a midwater trawl, the fisherman started making average catches of 31 tons/hour, a lot of widows however you look at it. Coastwide, widow catches went from about 1,000 tons in 1978 to 28,000 tons in 1981. To no one's intense surprise, the fishery soon collapsed and strict catch quotas now exist.

Why do you suppose the body cavities of these fish are black? Oh, time's up Mr. Ditweiler, you did not answer the question in time. Tanya, would you show this hapless bozo what he could have won? Yes, Mr. Ditweiler, if you had known why the body cavity of a widow rockfish is lined with black pigment, these wonderful prizes could have been yours. First, an all-expenses paid vacation for 2 to Eastern Zolonia, the land that Time has not only forgotten, but does not wish to be reminded! You would have flown to Eastern Zolonia via Air Zolonia, the "14th Safest Airline in Central Europe," and enjoyed the glorious accommodations of the Heroic Turkey-Lip Sausage Makers Commune Number 14 Bed and Breakfast Hostel! Second, an oak veneer pseudo. Victorian knick-knack cabinet filled with pseudo-Victorian knick-knacks from Spavined and Sons of Patterson, New Jersey, makers of fine pseudo-Victorian furniture for over 200 years! And last, but assuredly not least, this beautiful mink coat from Mr. Ernest's Fine Furs of Muncie, Indiana, composed entirely of live minks! And to go with your coat, a 1-year supply of minced haddock, from the Fish Boutique of Encino, California, to feed those minks!

And now the answer to the question, "Why do widow rockfish have black-lined body cavities?" Actually, no one knows for sure, but one possibility has to do with what these fish eat. Widows occasionally feed on fishes or invertebrates which produce light. If these organisms are swallowed quickly, they will still be glowing when down in the fish's stomach. This might cause the fish's stomach region to glow, allowing predators to spot them.

YELLOWTAIL ROCKFISH (SEBASTES FLAVIDUS)

NAMES: Bass, Yellow Bass, Yellowtail Bass. Kiobui Menuke (Japanese). *Sebastes* means "magnificent" in Greek; *flavidus* comes from the Latin for "yellow."

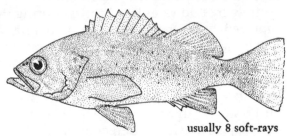

usually 8 soft-rays

IDENTIFYING CHARACTERS: Yellowtail rockfish are bass-shaped and elongated, with few spines on their heads. They can be colored greenish-olive, brown or gray on backs and sides and almost silvery below. There are usually whitish blotches on their backs, particularly near the dorsal fins. Reddish-brown flecks are found on the scales of small and medium-sized fish; these tend to fade in large animals. The fins are yellowish (particularly the tail fin): yellow-orange in small individuals and dirty yellow in larger ones. Olive rockfish, which occur more commonly off southern and central California, are frequently mistaken for yellowtails. Olives do not have yellow tails or reddish-brown flecks on scales and tend to be more olive in color.

DISTRIBUTION AND BIOLOGY: Yellowtail rockfish are found from Unalaska Island (Aleutian Islands) southward to San Diego, California, commonly from the southeastern Alaska–British Columbia region to about Pt. Conception, California (including San Miguel Island). This is a midwater, schooling fish, usually found over rocky and hard bottoms, but also occasionally over sand and mud. It has been taken in depths between the surface and 1,812 feet. These fish can be found throughout much of the water column, from near the bottom to more than 100 feet above it. In a study conducted between central California and Alaska, yellowtail rockfish were most frequently taken over bottom depths between 300–450 feet. However, during some years, large parts of the population may return to deeper water. These fish often associate with canary, widow, black and silvergray rockfishes. Young-of-the-year come into shallow water, often into kelp beds, and usually migrate into deeper water as they mature. In cold-water areas, such as southeastern Alaska, adults are apt to be in shallower water than off such warmer areas as central California. Tagging studies off Alaska, British Columbia and in Puget Sound imply that both immature and mature fish can make long distance movements, sometimes more than 200 miles.

These are medium-sized rockfish, reaching about 26 inches and living to at least 64 years. An 18-incher is about 10 years old. With nothing in nature being particularly straightforward, it is not surprising that the size and age at which these fish mature is highly variable. Off Alaska, half are mature at about 16–18 inches (11–15 years), while off California half are mature at around 14 inches (6 years). Females are perhaps primitively viviparous and produce anywhere from 56,000-1,993,000 eggs per season. Off California, females less than 15 years old show interannual differences in egg production. Curiously, this does not occur in older California fish, nor for any age yellowtail off Washington. Looking up and down the coast, it appears that these fish are primarily winter spawners, with a peak period around February. The longest season reported is January-July off central and northern California. Young-of-the-year appear in kelp beds beginning in April, and little yellowtail rockfish live in and around kelp in midwater during the day, descending to the bottom at night. Large juveniles and adults eat fishes, along with krill and other planktonic animals. Pigeon guillemots and pelagic cormorants eat them.

FISHERY: This is a very important species in both the recreational and commercial catch, from central California to southeastern Alaska. As an example, in the Mendocino County region, northern California, yellowtails have comprised between 5-12% of the total marine recreational catch. In some recent years, it has been the leading rockfish in the U. S. and Canadian commercial rockfish fishery. Most of the catch is made by trawl, with lesser amounts taken by gillnet and hook and line. Most fish are sold as fillets.

REMARKS: Yellowtail rockfish are known for their remarkable homing ability. In southeastern Alaska, researchers captured and released them at various distances from their original reef. Some individuals travelled as far as 12.5 miles back to the capture point.

Here's an interesting bit of fluff. During a severe storm off Monterey, yellowtail rockfish were left stranded on shore by giant waves. Hey, I know it's not earth shaking, but I thought you would want to know.

CHILIPEPPER (SEBASTES GOODEI)

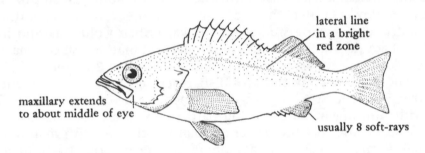

lateral line in a bright red zone

maxillary extends to about middle of eye

usually 8 soft-rays

NAMES: Chili, Red Snapper. *Sebastes* means "magnificent" in Greek; *goodei* honors Dr. George Brown Goode, an ichthyologist and fisheries biologist of the 19th Century.

IDENTIFYING CHARACTERS: Chilis are bass-shaped rockfish, with few spines on their heads. Large ones are pinkish-red on backs and sides with white bellies. Small ones may be pink, tan or olive on back, and the lateral lines sit in a red or pink stripe. Chilis closely resemble bocaccio, which are much darker in color, often a brownish or reddish-brown, and have larger mouths.

DISTRIBUTION AND BIOLOGY: Chilis range from Queen Charlotte Sound, British Columbia to southern Baja California, commonly from northern California southward. They are found from near the surface to 1,452 feet. Almost all adults live between 150–1,000 feet and most juveniles occupy waters between 100–250 feet (occasionally down to 300 feet). A few young-of-the-year occur in kelp beds off central and northern California. These are aggregating, midwater or near-bottom fish, usually found over reefs and along drop-offs. While we know they move about a great deal, we do not know how far they travel or their migration paths. Aggregations are particularly apparent during spawning seasons.

Chilis live to at least 16 years and reach 22 inches. A foot-long fish is 4–5 years old and most fish mature at 12–13 inches. Females mature slightly later than males and then grow faster and larger and live longer. Females produce as many as 530,000 eggs. In southern California, chilis spawn from September through April, peaking in December and January. In central and northern California, they spawn from November through June, also peaking in January. Young-of-the-year appear in shallow waters in spring and early summer. Chilis eat krill, squids and small fishes.

FISHERY: Chilis are pretty important to the recreational party vessel fleet, at least from about Mendocino County, northern California, southward. In many regions, they form 2-6% (as much as 17%) of the total marine recreational catch. In southern California, the largest catches are made from late fall to spring, corresponding to the period when party vessels tend to fish for deeper-water rockfishes. A California Department of Fish and Game survey showed that hot spots for chilis were in the Santa Barbara Channel and along the outside of the Santa Rosa Flats, south of Santa Rosa Island.

Key species in the commercial rockfish catch off central and northern California, chilis are also important off southern California. Most chilis are taken by trawl and gillnets, but hook and liners catch them too. They are considered part of the "brown rockfish" catch and are less valuable than redder species. Most are filleted prior to sale. Compared to some other rockfishes, chilis are known for their relatively long shelf life, a fact that they can scarcely resist mentioning to their neighbors.

REMARKS: Native Americans must have caught chilis occasionally since their bones have been found in middens.

ROSETHORN ROCKFISH (SEBASTES HELVOMACULATUS)

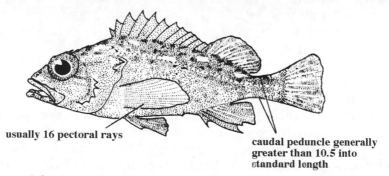

usually 16 pectoral rays

caudal peduncle generally greater than 10.5 into standard length

NAMES: *Sebastes* is Greek for "magnificent"; *helvomaculatus* comes from 2 Latin words "light yellow, spotted."

IDENTIFYING CHARACTERS: This is one of a number of species with 4-5 light blotches on the back. Rosethorns are light pink and greenish yellow; the blotches are white or pink. Two closely related species, rosies and swordspines, might be confused with this

165

one. Rosies are purple and chunkier (and usually found in shallower water). Swordspines are easy to differentiate, with their long 2nd anal spine, just about reaching to, or surpassing, the edge of the soft anal rays.

DISTRIBUTION AND BIOLOGY: Kodiak Island, Alaska to central Baja California is the range from this relatively deep-water (83-1,800 feet) species. In the northern part of their range, they are common in relatively shallow water, while off southern California, we don't often see them in less than 600 feet. Overall, they are most abundant from about 300-1,000 feet. This is a relatively solitary, rocky-bottom species. Off Monterey deeper than 600 feet, if there is a little rock outcrop surrounded by mud there will often be a rosethorn tucked underneath it.

Rosethorns don't grow too large, and 16 inches is the world record. In central and northern California, males and females mature between 9-11 inches (7-10 years). Spawning season is reported to be February-September along the southeast coast of Alaska and May-June off central and northern California. Females may be primitively viviparous.

FISHERY: They are taken fairly commonly in the deep-water recreational rockfish fishery, particularly from central California northwards. Rosethorns are taken incidentally in commercial fisheries.

SQUARESPOT ROCKFISH (SEBASTES HOPKINSI)

NAMES: *Sebastes* is Greek for "magnificent"; *hopkinsi* refers to Timothy Hopkins, founder of the Hopkins Laboratory, now the marine facility of Stanford University.

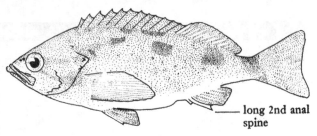

long 2nd anal spine

IDENTIFYING CHARACTERS: Squarespots are small, perch-shaped rockfish, yellowish-brown or tan on backs and sides, with more or less square brown or reddish-brown blotches on their backs.

DISTRIBUTION AND BIOLOGY: Squarespots are found from southern Oregon to central Baja California and Guadalupe Island in 60–600 feet of water. These guys are always over high rocky reefs and boulder fields, usually in 120–350 feet, particularly from Monterey southward. On some southern California reefs they may be the most abundant fish. These are schooling, midwater or benthic rockfish, often found in groups of hundreds or even thousands, usually swimming from near the bottom to perhaps 60 feet above it. You will often see them with halfbanded and pygmy rockfishes. Very small young fish are in the shallowest part of the species' depth range, often in 90–150 feet.

Squarespots are a dwarf species, reaching only 11.5 inches. Any fish over 10 inches is a real trophy. The oldest one I have aged was 19 years. Like many other rockfish species, females grow more quickly than males, grow to a much larger size (a 7 inch male is a giant) and live longer. These fish mature at about 6 inches (2 years for females and 4 for males). Off central California, they spawn in February and March; off southern California, spawning occurs from January to April, peaking in January and February. I have found as many as 39,000 eggs in a female. These fish feed entirely on plankton, primarily copepods, krill and crab larvae.

FISHERY: Squarespots are quite important to the party and private vessel sport fishery in southern California. Anglers fishing for shallow water rockfish often load up on squarespots using very small yarn-covered hooks. They are rare in the commercial catch.

SHORTBELLY ROCKFISH (SEBASTES JORDANI)

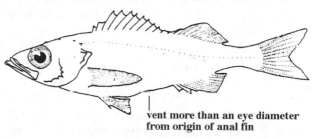

NAMES: *Sebastes* is Greek for "magnificent"; *jordani* honors David Starr Jordan, one of ichthyology's old time greats.

vent more than an eye diameter from origin of anal fin

Rather thoughtfully, I would say, Dr. Jordan titled his autobiography *The Days of a Man*. Now, while some might feel this was egotism run amuck, I prefer to believe this was mere thoughtfulness on his part. How else would we be able to distinguish his book from David Starr Jordan *The Days of a Skink*, David Starr Jordan *The Days of a Toaster Cozy* or David Starr Jordan *The Days of One of Those Little Things at the End of Your Shoelaces*?

IDENTIFYING CHARACTERS: Shortbellies are slender and pink, with small mouths and deeply forked caudal fins. The big tipoff is that a shortbelly's anus is midway between its pelvic and anal fin (instead of right up against the anal fin, as with other, more decorous rockfishes).

DISTRIBUTION AND BIOLOGY: Shortbelly rockfish hold sway from the Gulf of Alaska to southern Baja California. These are schooling, semi-pelagic fishes, found in very large aggregations, often well off the bottom. Young-of-the-year are found inshore, sometimes even in kelp beds. Adults are found from about 300-1,524 feet. They are grotesquely abundant off central California, far more common than any other rockfish species. While conducting a submersible study of rockfishes off San Miguel Island, I saw simply amazing numbers of these puppies.

They reach about 15 inches and live to at least 22 years. Males grow more slowly and grow to a smaller maximum size. One study noted that the oldest females were smaller than some younger females, perhaps implying that genetically-smaller individuals live longer. Males and females mature at the same size, 5-8 inches, and at the same age, 1-5 years. Females may be primitively viviparous. A study off central and northern California found that shortbellies spawn from February-April, peaking in February. Shortbelly larvae have been found as far south as about Punta Eugenia, central Baja California; highest densities have been noted off central California. Larvae are taken from November to May, with peaks from January to April. While a few larvae drift as much as 250 miles offshore, most larvae are found relatively near the coast, between 10 and about 30 miles off the beach. During periods of intense upwelling, pelagic juveniles tend to stay in deeper water. This probably helps prevent them from being carried out to sea by the offshore current. Shortbellies are plankton eaters; krill and copepods are the hot items. They are probably eaten by lots of predators. Shortbelly parts have been found in king salmon, bocaccio and chilipepper, as well as pigeon guillemots and Brandt's cormorants.

FISHERY: Their little bitty mouths preclude anglers from hauling in too many shortbellies, and they are only an occasional catch. Though there is currently no commercial fishery, their huge numbers make them a recurrent fantasy for many entrepreneurs. The problem is that shortbellies are pretty diminutive, have lots of small bones and they are too small for economical filleting. So what can you do with them? Turning them into surimi (fish paste, see the thrilling discussion under walleye pollock) seems like one potential answer. The wonderful world of bone softening might be another. In *"Bone Softening", a Practical Way to Utilize Small Fish* (M. Okada et al., Marine Fisheries Review, 1988, vol. 50, number 3, p. 1-7), the good news is put forth that pressure cooking shortbellies softens their bones to the point that head and gutted fish can be eaten right from the cooker.

REMARKS: June, 1988, saw a massive stranding of young-of-the-year shortbellies along the northern California coast. Zillions of dead fish washed up and zillions more lay dead on the bottom, just off shore. What caused this unusual occurrence? During an average spring, these juvenile rockfishes are well off the coast, kept there by strong winds blowing from the north; these "northerlies" help push water offshore. However, during this particular June, winds came from the south and the offshore water flow was replaced by one moving inshore, carrying shortbellies with it. These pelagic fish were not adapted to life in the more rugged near-shore water and so croaked in large numbers.

COW ROCKFISH (SEBASTES LEVIS)

N A M E S : Cowcod, Cow. *Sebastes* is Greek for "magnificent"; *levis* is Latin for "capricious" or "fantastic." (It's also English for

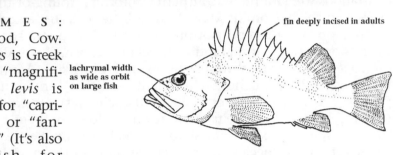

"How to make big bucks selling overpriced pants to gullible consumers.")

IDENTIFYING CHARACTERS: These are very spiny rockfishes; the large ones may be orangish, pink or almost red, sometimes with indistinct black bars on their sides. Small ones tend to be white, pale pink or yellow with black bars (Plate 6). In large fish, the membranes between the dorsal spines are deeply grooved.

DISTRIBUTION AND BIOLOGY: Cows are found from Newport, Oregon to central Baja California and Guadalupe Island, commonly from central California southward. While they have been taken from 100–1,200 feet, adults are rare in less than 300 feet in depth. (One sport fishing skipper told me he caught a large adult in 60 feet off Pt. Conception.) Juveniles are found from about 100-600 feet and although juveniles occasionally live over sand or mud, adults only inhabit hard or rocky bottoms. In fact, based on our observations, cows really like areas with caves, crevices and other places to hide. Even 20-pounders routinely wedge themselves so far into holes that only their dorsal fins are visible. Here's how addicted cows are to crevices. I saw one monstrous one with only its head in a little cave; the poor beast felt that, as long as its eyes were in a hole, its body could take care of itself. These fish tend to stay on or near the bottom, a few venturing up as much as 40-50 feet above the substrate. Cows can be seen either singly or in aggregations.

These are *big* rockfish, one of the largest in the world. They have been reported to reach 37 inches, but fish over about 35 are rare. On the other hand, I saw one from a research submarine that was easily longer than 37 inches. It looked like the Goodyear Blimp. I am not sure how long cows live, but they reach at least 25 years and probably a lot more. About half are mature at 18 inches; all reproduce when 22 inches long. Males mature at the same size as females. I have found as many as 1,925,000 eggs in the female. Spawning occurs off southern California from November through May, with a January peak. In larval fish surveys conducted from northern California to southern Baja California, the greatest concentrations were found off southern California. Young-of-the-year appear on the bottom in May. I saw a little one, just as cute as a button, on a sand-mud bottom in Carmel Canyon sharing a depression with a shrimp and a stripetail rockfish. Juveniles feed on copepods, mysid shrimps, fishes and the like. Adult cows inhale everything in the environment, and that turns out to be primarily fishes (such as rockfishes and anchovies) and squids.

FISHERY: Though they are taken in relatively low numbers, the fact that cows are the size (and shape) of Volkswagon Beetles make them a popular species in the central and southern California recreational fishery. Some anglers target cows on party and private vessel rockfish trips using whole, large fishes as bait. For some reason that escapes me, these fish seem particularly susceptible to black lures. Catches aboard party vessels peak between late fall and early spring, when these boats target deepwater rockfishes.

Cows form a minor part of the commercial catch and are taken by gillnet, hook and line and trawls. Trawls outfitted with roller gear, allowing them to be towed over rocks, take substantial numbers. The reddish color of cow rockfish puts them into the "red rockfish" category and increases their value. More than one fish processor has marketed them as "seabass," taking advantage of their very firm flesh to pull off a naughty little deception.

REMARKS: These are my favorite fish and to commemorate my love and devotion I have a tattoo of one on my arm (glossies available for $10 per copy).

QUILLBACK ROCKFISH (SEBASTES MALIGER)

NAMES: *Sebastes* is Greek for "magnificent"; *maliger* is formed from two Latin words meaning "I bear a mast," referring to the high dorsal fin.

IDENTIFYING CHARACTERS: Quillbacks are short dumpy rockfish with heavy head spines. Their basic body color is brown or blackish, with orange splotches on back and sides. Generally, the first part of the body is orangish, the rear darker. Orange or orange-brown spots cover the animal's front half. DISTRIBUTION AND B I O L O G Y : Quillbacks have been found from the Gulf of Alaska southward to San Miguel Island, southern California and are com-

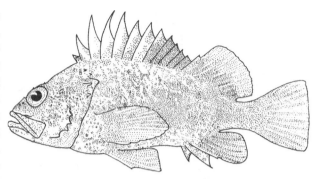

mon from southeastern Alaska to northern California. These are solitary bottom dwellers, living among rocks or sometimes on coarse sand or pebbles next to reefs, particularly in areas with lots of flat-bladed kelp. Although they are usually found on or near the bottom, they occasionally will rise as much as 30 or 40 feet into the water column. Taken from barely subtidal waters to about 900 feet, most live at depths between 40–250 feet. Quillbacks do not make extensive migrations and may stay on the same reef for long periods. Smaller ones begin to poop out at around 120 feet. Similarly, larger ones are more common at greater depths.

Quillbacks have been reported to grow as large as 2 feet, but anything over 20 inches is rare. So far, the oldest one aged was 32 years, but they almost certainly live longer. This species seems to grow at different rates along its range. Off southeastern Alaska, a 12-year-old is about 12 inches long, off California, it's 7 inches. Similarly, off southeastern Alaska, half of the fish are mature at 12 inches, compared to only 9 inches off California. Depending on where you are along the Pacific Coast, spawning occurs from March to July. Quillbacks feed primarily on crustaceans—shrimps and various kind of crabs.

FISHERY: Quillbacks are an important part of the inshore sport fishery from northern California to southeastern Alaska and are taken by party and private vessels and by divers. While they are taken in low numbers compared to many other rockfishes, these rockfish are a valuable commercial species. Most are taken by hook and line and sold at premium prices to ethnic markets in both the U.S. and Canada. Off British Columbia, fishermen keep this species alive, destined for the Asian markets of Vancouver.

BLACK ROCKFISH (SEBASTES MELANOPS)

NAMES: Bass, Black Bass, Black Snapper, Gray Rockfish, Pacific Snapper, Snapper. *Sebastes* means "magnificent" in Greek;

melanops is formed from 2 Greek words meaning "black face."

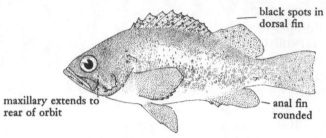

black spots in dorsal fin

maxillary extends to rear of orbit

anal fin rounded

IDENTIFYING CHARACTERS: Black rockfish are fairly slim, bass-shaped fish with few head spines (Plate 10). They are black or blue-black, mottled with gray or blue-gray, with black spots on their backs and dorsal fins. Blue rockfish resemble blacks, but are somewhat more oval, have smaller eyes, an upper jaw which extends to the middle of the eye (not the rear) and, not surprisingly, tend to be blue.

DISTRIBUTION AND BIOLOGY: Black rockfish are found from Amchitka Island (Aleutian Islands) southeast to San Miguel Island and Santa Barbara in southern California, commonly from central California to southeastern Alaska. These are usually midwater and surface-dwelling schooling fish, but have been captured down to 1,200 feet. From Oregon to southeastern Alaska they can be found in schools numbering in the thousands, usually associated with reefs and schooling with yellowtail, dusky (*S. ciliatus*), silvergray or blue rockfish. Young-of-the-year are found in very shallow water (occasionally in tide pools), most often in kelp beds. As they grow older, black rockfish tend to leave the shallowest reefs for somewhat deeper haunts, and adults are most abundant in waters with bottom depths of perhaps 40–300 feet. These are relatively mobile rockfish. Tagging studies show that some may move hundreds of miles (345 miles is the record, from Tillamook Hook, Oregon to Cape Mendocino, California).

The largest black rockfish on record was 25 inches; the oldest one aged was 36 years. Off southeastern Alaska, half are mature at about 18 inches (9–13 years); off California, at about 14–16 inches (6–7 years). Males mature at a smaller size than females. Females are viviparous. These are winter-spring spawners. Mating occurs from September-November and females usually store the sperm for a few months before fertilizing their eggs. They release young from January–May, peaking in February off California. Young-of-the-year first appear in kelp beds and tide pools in April. In these beds, very small fish live in midwater around kelp plants during the day, settling to the bottom at night. Juveniles eat fish larvae and plankton such as mysid shrimps; older ones eat mainly fishes (such as juvenile rockfishes, sablefish, sandlances) and zooplankton. Among other predators, lingcods, rockfishes, sea lions and pigeon guillemots eat them.

FISHERY: Black rockfish are an increasingly important part of the party and private vessel recreational catch, particularly from San Francisco, northern California, to southeastern Alaska. In some localions off northern California and Oregon they may comprise 37% of the total marine recreational catch. Divers take substantial numbers, as do pier and rocky shore anglers. Black rockfish are also an important segment of the commercial rockfish catch from Oregon to southeast Alaska. However, their fillets have a shorter lifespan under refrigeration than do many other rockfishes.

BLACKGILL ROCKFISH (SEBASTES MELANOSTOMUS)

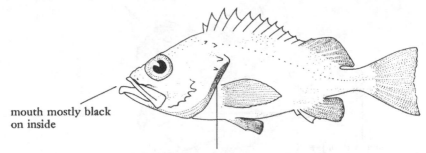

mouth mostly black
on inside

gill membranes jet-black

NAMES: Deepwater Red, Blackmouth Rockfish, Red Rock, Deepsea Rockfish. *Sebastes* means "magnificent" in Greek; *melanostomus* comes from 2 Greek words meaning "black mouth."

IDENTIFYING CHARACTERS: Blackgills are short, heavy bodied, spiny rockfish, red in color with (most important) a black slash along the rear edge of the gill cover. Bank rockfish might be confused with blackgills; however, banks have black fin membranes while blackgills have red ones.

DISTRIBUTION AND BIOLOGY: Knowledge about blackgills is still pretty spotty. They are distributed from about Washington (maybe further north, there is some dispute about this) to central Baja California. These are *deep*-living fish, ranging from 413–2,520 feet. In the northern part of their range, adults are found from 750–1,800 feet, while off southern California mature fish are rarely taken in less than 900 feet. Juveniles prefer shallower water, starting in about 600 feet. Blackgills usually choose rocky or hard bottom habitats along steep drop-offs such as the edges of submarine canyons and over seamounts. An aggregating species, blackgills are rarely taken at more than 30 feet above the bottom.

The largest blackgill on record was 24 inches in length. About 50% of all fish are mature at about 14 inches (7–8 years). Spawning occurs from January–June (peaking in February) off southern California and in February off central and northern California. I have found as many as 770,000 eggs in female black-gills. This species eats mostly fishes and krill.

FISHERY: Until recently, this species was rarely taken by any fishermen. While it is still relatively unusual in sport catches, it is now a mainstay of the commercial rockfish catch in southern and central California, taken by trawl, gillnet and hook and line.

REMARKS: I often see these in Vietnamese and Filipino markets.

VERMILION ROCKFISH (SEBASTES MINIATUS)

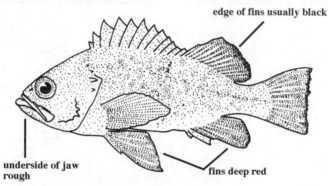

edge of fins usually black

underside of jaw rough

fins deep red

NAMES: Red Snapper, Rasher, Scarlletino, Rasciera, Shu Menuke (Japanese). *Sebastes* is Greek for "magnificent"; *miniatus* is Latin for "vermilion."

IDENTIFYING CHARACTERS: Vermilions are typical rocky reef rockfishes, with thick bodies and heavy head spines (Plate 13). They vary somewhat in color, ranging from bright red to orange-red, with gray or black mottling on backs and sides; a few fish are so dark red they appear almost black. Smaller fish have more distinct dark mottling and their fins are red and black-edged. Underwater photos show that this species is occasionally covered with white blotches. This species looks a lot like the canary rockfish, and when I was a kid I thought canaries were washed-out looking vermilions. Canaries are basically gray with a lot of orange markings.

DISTRIBUTION AND BIOLOGY: Vermilions are found from Zaikof Bay, Prince William Sound, Alaska to central Baja California and are most abundant from northern California southward. They range in depth from shallow subtidal waters to 1,440 feet. Juveniles are usually found in the shallowest depths; very young ones appear in kelp beds from central California northward, while most adults inhabit waters of 180 to perhaps 750 feet. In general, these fish live in shallower waters where temperatures are colder—for instance, north of Pt. Conception and off San Miguel and Santa

Rosa Islands in southern California. They usually are found over rocks, along drop-offs and over hard bottom, often in aggregations. In the inshore waters north of Pt. Conception, large solitary fish also may be found lounging about large rocks. Most of their time is spent on or near the bottom; occasionally, they rise 20 feet or so above a reef. It is likely that this species makes some movements from reef to reef, particularly in deep water, but how far they move is anyone's guess.

Vermilions are reported to grow as long as 2.5 feet, and they have been aged to 22 years. An 18-incher is about 10 years old. Half are mature when about 14 inches long (5–6 years old). Spawning occurs in southern California from September to December (peaking in November) and from at least September through November off central and northern California. I have found as many as 2,680,000 eggs in a female. Young-of-the-year appear in inshore waters beginning in February. These fish prey on other fishes (such as anchovies, lanternfishes, small rockfishes), octopi, squids and krill.

FISHERY: Oh, my. Vermilions are a very popular fish in both the recreational and commercial fisheries. They are highly prized by party and private vessel anglers from Bahia San Quintin, northern Baja California, northward into Oregon. The majority of the catch occurs from Monterey Bay southward. In areas of highest abundance, they often form 2-4% of the total marine recreational catch. Divers on the central California coast occasionally take large, solitary individuals. Juveniles are caught from piers from about Santa Barbara northward.

Vermilions, taken by hook and line and gillnet, make up a substantial part of the "red" rockfish commercial catch and bring high prices. In fact, this is a perfect example of how cultural factors influence what fishes we buy. Why brightly-colored rockfishes should be more valuable than drab ones is beyond me. The reality is that, despite small differences in texture and flavor, once a rockfish hits the plate, it's all about the same. I know your great-aunt Netty claims she can tell apart all 60-odd species, even after they are covered in a bechamel sauce, but can you really trust a person who still believes Nixon was framed?

BLUE ROCKFISH (SEBASTES MYSTINUS)

NAME: Blue Bass, Blue Fish, Aomenuke (Japanese). An old name, seemingly out of commission, is Priestfish. *Sebastes* is a Greek word for "magnificent"; *mystinus* is Greek for "priest," an allusion to the dark color of this fish and the dark color of a priest's garb.

175

BLUE ROCKFISH

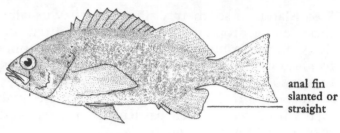

IDENTIFYING CHARACTERS: These are perch-shaped, sort of oval fish with only a few head spines. They

anal fin slanted or straight

are blue or bluish-black, with blackish fins. Very small fish are gray, with reddish streaks and black spots and speckles. They closely resemble black rockfish, to which they are related. Blacks tend to be darker colored, somewhat slimmer, have larger eyes and an upper jaw that goes to the rear of, or beyond, the eye.

DISTRIBUTION AND BIOLOGY: Blues are found from northern Baja California northward to at least Vancouver Island. There are records of blues further north to the Aleutians, but these may have been mis-identifications. Blues are extremely abundant along much of Oregon and California, though they begin to drop out by Dana Pt. (southern California). Found from tide pools to depths of 1,800 feet, they are most abundant in 15–200 feet. These are midwater or even surface-dwelling fish, swimming in schools of hundreds or thousands over reefs and around kelp. Blues north of Pt. Conception school with olives and black rockfish; south of the Point they mix it up with kelp bass, olives, blacksmith and half-moons. Adults tend to be resident on a reef for extended periods, though blues on deeper reefs seem to wander about more than do their shallower brethren. Young ones also stay within a very small chunk of the reef.

Blues reach 21 inches in length and live to 24 years. Females grow slightly faster than males. A 12-incher is 8-9 years old. Half of males are mature at about 10 inches (5-6 years old), and females when about 11 inches and 6 years old. All fish are mature by 12 inches. Females may be primitively viviparous; they produce as many as 300,000 eggs per year, spawning them all at once. Rockfishes have internal fertilization and blue rockfish males transfer sperm to females in October. Spawning occurs from November-March, with a January or February peak. Beginning in April, young-of-the-year appear in kelp beds and over rocky reefs. Off central California, according to hotshot biologist Mark Carr, these little ones prefer hanging out over rocks devoid of kelp, usually staying near the bottom. Blues eat zooplankton (such as jellyfish, krill and copepods), fishes, hydroids and kelp. Larger ones eat relatively more fishes. Young blues are often one of the most abundant fish over the shallow reefs of central and northern California and are a very important food for many other fishes, as well as sea birds and mammals.

FISHERY: Blues are one of the most important fish in the California party and private vessel recreational sport catch, from the Santa Barbara Channel northward. Once you turn the corner into central California, they are the most important species, well into Oregon. During some years, in some areas, as much as 31% of all fishes taken in the marine recreational fisheries are blues. Blues are frequently taken by divers and occasionally hooked by pier and jetty fishermen, particularly in central and northern California. Because blues do not move much and because they have been fished so intensively, this species has been over-harvested in many areas. There is only a limited commercial fishery, much of it by hook and line. Blues are sold both whole and filleted. One reason for the small commercial fishery is the short time these fish can be refrigerated before tasting a bit suspect.

CHINA ROCKFISH (SEBASTES NEBULOSUS)

NAME: China cod, Yellowstripe Rockfish. *Sebastes* means "magnificent" in Greek; *nebulosus* is Latin for "clouded."

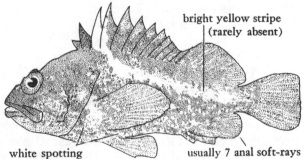

bright yellow stripe (rarely absent)

white spotting

usually 7 anal soft-rays

IDENTIFYING CHARACTERS: These are gorgeous fish (Plate 8). They are sort of squat and spiny, but what they lack in grace they make up for in color. They are basically black and are mottled or flecked with yellow or yellow-white. A large yellow stripe runs from near the beginning of the dorsal fin down to midbody, then swings backward to the tail.

DISTRIBUTION AND BIOLOGY: Chinas are found from southeastern Alaska southward to Redondo Beach (southern California) on the mainland and San Miguel Island (southern California) offshore. These rockfish are abundant from southeastern Alaska to about Sonoma County, northern California, always on rocky reefs. They are sedentary, probably territorial, fish and have been taken in 10–420 feet, though they are most common from 30 to about 300 feet. Chinas spend virtually all their time sitting on the bottom, often sheltering in crevices. They rarely move from home sites, and it is likely that fish remain around these spots for years.

Chinas reach 17 inches in length. About half are mature at 11 inches; all are mature at 1 foot. Males and females mature at the same size. Throughout most of its range, spawning occurs from January–July, with a January peak; off southeastern Alaska, spawning is April–July, peaking in May. Chinas eat a wide range of bottom-dwelling animals such as brittle stars, shrimps and fishes.

FISHERY: These moderately important sport fish are taken by party and private vessels from central California to southeastern Alaska. They are also occasionally speared by divers and taken by rocky-shoreline anglers. Chinas are valuable in the commercial rockfish fishery, bringing high prices in ethnic markets. Most of the commercial catch is by hook and line.

REMARKS: One very large, bright yellow individual has been reported.

TIGER ROCKFISH (SEBASTES NIGROCINCTUS)

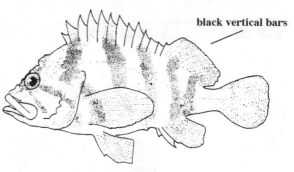

black vertical bars

NAMES: Black-Banded Rockfish. *Sebastes* is Greek for "magnificent"; *nigrocinctus* means "black" and "girdle" in Latin.

IDENTIFYING CHARACTERS: This is a very striking species, with 5 dark black or red bars against a red or pink background (Plate 9).

DISTRIBUTION AND BIOLOGY: Southeast Alaska to the Tanner-Cortes Banks, southern California, in 180-900 feet, is home to this rather reclusive species. They like high relief with crevices to hide in. Most of the time you will see them by themselves, but Tory O'Connell, rockfish guru of Alaska Fish and Game, tells me she has often seen individual tigers holed up with single yelloweye rockfish.

Tigers reach 2 feet in length. Females may be primitively viviparous. Along southeast Alaska, females spawn from February-June, peaking in April. Tigers eat stuff off the bottom. Shrimps, crabs, gammarid amphipods and fishes are the most important prey.

FISHERY: Despite their solitary nature, tigers are commonly taken by recreational anglers. They are a fairly significant part of the shallow water longline and handline catch, particularly in British Columbia.

SPECKLED ROCKFISH (SEBASTES OVALIS)

NAMES: Bank Perch, Widowfish, Viura, Cinnamon Bass. *Sebastes* is Greek for "magnificent"; *ovalis* is Latin for "oval," describing this species' body shape. **IDENTIFYING CHARACTERS:** These are perch–shaped rockfish with small head spines. They are tan or pink and covered with small black

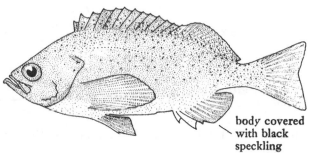

body covered with black speckling

spots. Small bank rockfish, which have the same shape, may be mistaken for speckleds, but banks are red or red-gray and have their lateral lines sitting within a pink channel.

DISTRIBUTION AND BIOLOGY: Speckleds range from northern Washington to northern Baja California, commonly from central California southward. These midwater rockfish are found over rocks, normally from near the bottom to about 30 feet above the reefs. Although speckleds have been taken between 100 and 1,200 feet, adults usually live between 250–500 feet, with juveniles most common in 100–250 feet. Speckleds probably move from reef to reef, though we don't know how far they travel.

Speckleds grow as long as 22 inches and live for at least 37 years. Females grow larger and live longer than males. A 12-inch male is around 20 years old; a similar-sized female is about 12 years. Off southern California, these fish spawn from October–May, peaking in January and February. Spawning was noted in May off central and northern California. I have found as many as 160,000 eggs in a female. Speckleds feed primarily on plankton, although they will occasionally eat small fishes.

FISHERY: Speckleds form a nominal part of the party and private vessel recreational fishery, particularly from the Santa Barbara Channel southward. They are occasionally taken by commercial fishermen, primarily in gillnets. Depending on the port, speckleds are sold either whole or as fillets.

BOCACCIO (SEBASTES PAUCISPINIS)

NAMES: Grouper, Salmon Grouper, Slimy, Merou, Jack, Tom Cod (juveniles), Bara Menuke (Japanese), Bokachio (Japanese). *Sebastes* means "magnificent" in Greek; *paucispinis* is Latin for "few spines."

IDENTIFYING CHARACTERS: Bocaccio are bass-shaped, elongated fish with large mouths. They have few or no spines on their heads and tend to be brown or reddish-brown on back, pink or brown on sides and silvery on bellies. Small ones are brown-red with dark spots on sides. They resemble chilipeppers, but chilis are pinkish,

179

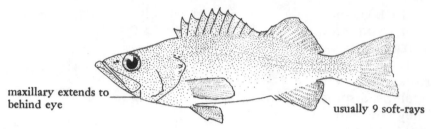

maxillary extends to
behind eye

usually 9 soft-rays

have smaller mouths and their lateral lines sit in red or pinkish streaks.

DISTRIBUTION AND BIOLOGY: Bocaccio are extremely widespread, found from Stepovak Bay, Alaskan Peninsula to central Baja California, most abundantly from British Columbia and southern Alaska southward. Bocaccio have been taken from the surface (juveniles) to 1,568 feet, but most live between 150–1,000 feet. In southern California, most adults are taken in water deeper than 250 feet, though where water is cold, such as off San Miguel Island or at the head of Redondo Canyon, they will come into water as shallow as 60 feet. Young-of-the-year come into 30–90 feet in southern California and into even shallower waters off central and northern California. Many small ones live for months under drifting kelp mats which have broken free from beds. As bocaccio grow, they gradually swim into deeper waters. This is an aggregating, bottom species, found primarily over hard and rocky bottom, but also occasionally over sand and mud. I have seen absolutely humongosoid ones in caves on the edge of Monterey Submarine Canyon. While they commonly hover a few feet above the bottom, I have taken them over 100 feet above reefs. This species moves about considerably. Juveniles tagged at an oil platform off Santa Barbara were later recovered at such locations as Santa Cruz Island (12 miles), Santa Monica Bay (60 miles) and off the Santa Maria River (80 miles).

A relatively large rockfish, bocaccio grow to 3 feet in length and live to about 35 years. Females grow faster than males, mature at a slightly larger size and probably live longer. A 2-footer is about 8 years old. Off southern California, about half are mature at 14 inches and all reproduce by 18 inches. Further to the north, fish mature at a larger size, with all males mature at 22 inches and all females at 2 feet. Females may be primitively viviparous; they produce as many as 2,300,000 eggs per season. Off southern California, the resulting larvae are spawned in 2 or more batches; this is rarely the case further north. In southern California, there is some spawning by bocaccio nearly all year, at least from October to July, although the peak month is January. Off central and northern California, spawning takes place from January to May, with a February peak. Further north, spawning is more restricted, primarily January-March. While larvae have been taken as far out as 300 miles, most are within 150 miles of the coast. Based on larval surveys along California and Baja California, there is substantial spawning from about the U. S.-Mexican border northward, peaking off northern California. Young-of-the-year first appear in inshore waters in February. Larger juveniles eat small fishes, particularly juvenile rockfishes. Adults feed on fishes (i.e., rockfishes, sablefish, anchovies) and squids. Marine mammals (such as harbor seals and northern elephant seals) are major bocaccio eaters. Sea birds, such as least terns, get the juveniles.

FISHERY: Bocaccio are important recreational and commercial fish. They are taken by party and private recreational vessels throughout California and less commonly off Oregon. Most party vessel catches are made from Mendocino County, northern California, southwards. Bocaccio may comprise as much as 14% of the total marine recreational catch. Year in and year out, they are the most important rockfish in the southern California recreational catch.

Taken by trawl, gillnet and hook and line, these guys are also a major part of the commercial rockfish catch, particularly in California. This is a "brown" rockfish (also called a "junk" fish) and, on average, is worth only half as much as those fortunate rockfish categorized as "red." Most bocaccio are sold as fillets. Along with chilipeppers and bank rockfish, bocaccio have longer shelf lives as fresh fish than many other rockfishes.

REMARKS: Two color variants are known for bocaccio. One is a golden form, with color resembling that of garibaldi. This variant has been seen off San Miguel Island, California and off British Columbia, and I expect it exists throughout the species' range. For some unknown reason, bocaccio also develop black (melanistic) blotches as they grow older. These affect the skin only and have no effect on the fish's edibility.

During some years, large schools of juvenile boccacio swarm around the piers of central California. In the 1950s, before strict bag limits were enforced, I saw families catch literally thousands of 6–inch long "red snapper" off the pier at Cayucos, near Morro Bay. Similarly, huge aggregations can sometimes be found around the oil platforms in the Santa Barbara Channel.

All rockfish have dorsal, anal and pelvic spines that are mildly poisonous. In general, the toxin causes only minor pain, which usually subsides quickly. A number of fishermen have said that bocaccio spines cause the most severe and long-lasting pain of all the rockfishes.

I think bocaccio have a very distinctive, sort of sickly-sweet odor quite different from other rockfishes. If you have hung around party vessels or commercial ships long enough, you can just tell when they have loads of bocaccio. In fact, even their swimbladder gas tastes different from other rockfishes. I spent a good part of my college career tagging rockfishes. When one is caught from waters deeper than perhaps 90 feet their swimbladders expand, and they must be deflated to allow them to return to depth carrying their tag. A quick way to deflate them is to stick a hypodermic needle into their bladders and quickly suck the gas out. I could always tell when I was deflating bocaccio, even with my eyes closed.

CANARY ROCKFISH (SEBASTES PINNIGER)

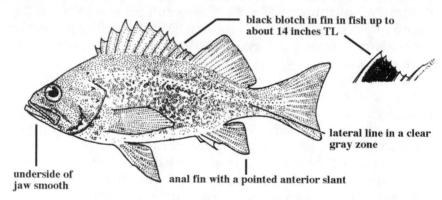

black blotch in fin in fish up to about 14 inches TL

lateral line in a clear gray zone

underside of jaw smooth

anal fin with a pointed anterior slant

NAME: Fantail, Red Snapper, Swallowtail, Orange Rockfish, Red Rock, Pacific Red Snapper, Orenji Menuke (Japanese). *Sebastes* is Greek for "magnificent"; *pinniger* is Latin for "large-finned."

IDENTIFYING CHARACTERS: Canaries are fairly spiny, thick-bodied rockfish, basically orange with a lot of gray mixed in. Their fins are usually light orange and their lateral lines sit in a gray stripe. While vermilion rockfish may be confused with canaries, vermilions are usually much redder, their lateral lines are not in a gray band and they have scales on the underside of their lower jaws.

DISTRIBUTION AND BIOLOGY: Canaries are found from the western Gulf of Alaska to northern Baja California, but they are abundant from southeastern Alaska to central California. They have been taken from tide pools (young-of-the-year) to depths of 2,748 feet. Juveniles descend into deeper water as they mature, and almost all adults are found between 150–750 feet, most frequently between 300–450 feet. These are densely aggregating fish, usually associated with pinnacles and sharp drop-offs. They are found near, but usually not on the bottom, often associating with yellowtail, widow and silvergray rockfishes. An Oregon tagging study showed that immature ones move about a fair amount.

Canaries reach lengths of 30 inches and live to at least 75 years. A 20-inch fish is about 10 years old. Off central and northern California, half are mature at 7–9 years and 16–17 inches and all are mature by 13 years and 23 inches. While females seem to grow faster than males and mature at a larger size, it appears that males live longer than females. Off central and northern California, canaries spawn from December–March, peaking in December. Females may be primitively viviparous and they produce between 69,000-1,113,000 eggs. They probably spawn slightly later to the north; off southeastern Alaska, spawners were found in February and March. Beginning in April, young-of-the-year appear in tide pools and kelp beds. Canaries eat mostly planktonic creatures such as krill, and occasionally nibble on fishes.

FISHERY: Canaries are moderately important in the party and private vessel recreational fishery from the Santa Barbara Channel, southern California, northwards. They really kick into the fishery north of San Francisco. In some areas, canaries form as much as 13% of the total marine recreational catch. They are a major constituent of the North Pacific commercial fishery, again from central California northward to at least southeastern Alaska, but particularly off Oregon, Washington and British Columbia. Most fish are caught by trawl, with lesser amounts by gillnet and hook and line. Trawl-caught fish are usually filleted. The rest are often sold whole.

REMARKS: There may be 2 populations of canaries, one north and the other south of central Oregon.

GRASS ROCKFISH (SEBASTES RASTRELLIGER)

NAMES: Grass Bass. *Sebastes* is Greek for magnificent; *rastrelliger* is a combination of 2 Latin words meaning "I bear a small rake," which refers to the fish's small gill rakers.

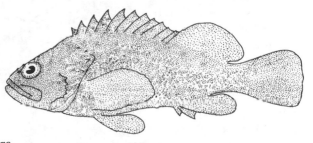

IDENTIFYING CHARACTERS: These are short, squat, dumpy little rockfish, with heavy head spines. Grasses are green with black or gray mottling. Kelp rockfish resemble them, but are brown or gray-brown, while brown rockfish are brown with a dark blotch on their gill covers.

DISTRIBUTION AND BIOLOGY: Grasses have been found from Yaquina Bay, Oregon to central Baja California (commonly from northern California southward), wherever there are jumbles of rocks or other structures and abundant plant life. These are shallow water rockfish, and though they have been taken down to 150 feet, they are most common from tide pool depths to about 20 feet. Although tide pools usually contain only juveniles, I have seen some very large ones come out of pools the size of bath tubs.

Grasses reach 22 inches and some live at least 13 years. Not a heck of a lot is known about these little buggers. Spawning occurs in winter and young-of-the-year appear in shallow water during spring and summer. These fish love to eat crabs, shrimps, fishes and octopi. Midshipmen, migrating into shallow water in spring to spawn, are a common part of their diets.

FISHERY: Throughout coastal California and occasionally off Oregon, where rocks meet the sea, recreational anglers catch grass rockfish. They are a common part of the shore, pier and small vessel catch and, because they are too slow get out of their own way, they are speared right and left by divers. Party vessels fishing near shore for bass and shallow water rockfish also catch substantial numbers.

Grasses form the basis of a hot new fishery, one that targets shallow water fishes and keeps them alive. Most of these are taken on long lines, and the prices to the fisherman are relatively astronomical.

REMARKS: Grasses were an important part of the Native American catch.

ROSY ROCKFISH (SEBASTES ROSACEUS)

NAMES: *Sebastes* means "magnificent" in Greek; *rosaceus* is Latin for "rosy."

usually 16 pectoral rays

caudal peduncle generally greater than 10.5 into standard length

IDENTIFYING CHARACTERS: Rosies are small, spiny rockfish that are colored red-purple with purple mottling on their backs and orange or red sides. There is a purple saddle across the head behind the eyes and 4 or 5 light blotches (bordered with purple) on their backs. This guy can be confused with the rosethorn rockfish, which has white blotches surrounded by red and, particularly, with the swordspine rockfish, which has a scaly underside to its lower jaw.

DISTRIBUTION AND BIOLOGY: Rosies have been reported from Puget Sound to central Baja California. They are definitely known from at least the Cobb Seamount, southern Washington. These are solitary, bottom-dwelling rockfish that are always found over hard, high relief. Though they have been taken in depths between 50 and 420 feet, adults are most common between about 180 and 350 feet with young ones usually living shallower (100–200 feet).

While rosies have been reported to reach 14 inches, anything over about 10 inches is rare. They have been aged to 13 years and it is likely they live even longer. A 6-incher is about 7 years old. Off southern California, half are mature by 6 inches and all are mature at 8 inches. Off central and northern California, half are mature at 8 inches; all by 10 inches. Spawning occurs in southern California from January–September, peaking in May and farther north takes place from April–July, peaking in June. I have found as many as 95,000 eggs in a female. Rosies feed primarily on small, bottom-dwelling animals such as shrimps and crabs.

FISHERY: These small rockfish are a common catch aboard recreational party fishing and private vessels in southern, central and northern California to almost Mendocino County. They are occasionally taken in the commercial hook and line rockfish fishery, where they bring in high prices as "red" rockfish. In the party vessel catch, they often comprise 1-3% of the total recreational marine catch.

GREENBLOTCHED ROCKFISH (SEBASTES ROSENBLATTI)

NAMES: *Sebastes* is Greek for "magnificent"; *rosenblatti* honors Richard Rosenblatt, big-time ichthyologist at Scripps Institution of Oceanography.

IDENTIFYING CHARACTERS: This is a rather dumpy, heavy-bodied species. It is pink, with 5 light blotches and lots of green wavy lines on the back, and scales on the underside of the lower jaw. The closely-related greenspotted rockfish has distinct spotting and no scales on the jaw. The even more closely related pink rockfish (*S. eos*) usually has 18 pectoral rays (rather than usually 17) and 30 or more gill rakers on the first gill arch (rather than 30 or less for greenblotched).

DISTRIBUTION AND BIOLOGY: Greenblotches are found from Pt. Delgada, northern California to Ranger Bank, central Baja California. Greenblotches are relatively deep-dwelling rockfishes.

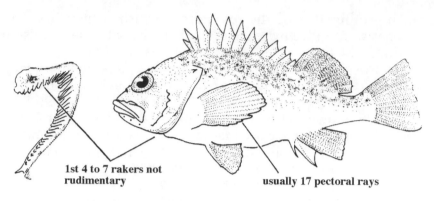

1st 4 to 7 rakers not rudimentary

usually 17 pectoral rays

Though they are taken from 200-1,300 feet, they are abundant from about 500-900 feet. These are bottom dwellers, occupying high relief bottom; they seem to prefer areas with lots of caves and crevices.   From a submersible, I have noted that greenblotches have really craggy heads, particularly compared to the closely-related greenspotted rockfish.

Greenblotches grow to 19 inches and live about 30 years. Males and females grow at the same rate, mature at the same size and have similar life spans.   A one-footer is about 12 years old, a 15-incher has been around about 22 years. Half are mature at one foot (12 years), all are at 14 inches (16 years). Spawning occurs from December-July, peaking in April, and females may spawn more than once per season. Females are possibly viviparous. Little females produce as few as 31,000 eggs, great big ones as many as 655,000.   Small greenblotches eat plankton, such as copepods. Larger fish feed on or near the bottom and eat all sorts of things, including shrimps, fishes and squids.

FISHERY: Greenblotches are common in the deep-water recreational catch, particularly in southern California. They are taken with some regularity by commercial fishermen, particularly trawlers with roller gear (allowing for trawling over rocky bottoms), as well as those fishing with gillnet and hook and line.

YELLOWEYE ROCKFISH (SEBASTES RUBERRIMUS)

NAMES: Red Snapper, Turkey-red Rockfish, Rasphead, Swallowtail. *Sebastes* is Greek for "magnificent"; *ruberrimus* is Latin and means "very red."

IDENTIFYING CHARACTERS: This is a big rockfish, one of the largest. It has the typical short, squat shape of a bottom-dwelling species, with many spines on head and cheeks. Individuals longer than about 1 foot have file-like raised areas on the head. The most

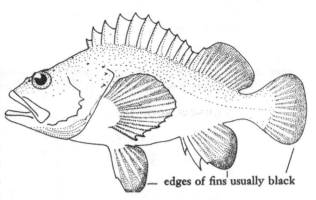

edges of fins usually black

obvious characters are the bright yellow eyes. Yelloweyes go through a rather dramatic color change from juveniles to adults. Juveniles are basically red with 2 white stripes, one on the back, one on the side. Most fins, except for the spiny dorsal, are tinged with black. As the fishes grow, they lose the stripes and their body color turns to a golden yellow or orange. Underwater, you will often see some large, white blotches on their backs. So different are the juveniles and adults that they were thought to be 2 species for many years.

DISTRIBUTION AND BIOLOGY: Yelloweyes have been reported from the Aleutian Islands, Alaska to northern Baja California; commonly from central California (and San Miguel Island in southern California) northward to the Gulf of Alaska. While found from about 60–1,800 feet, a California to Alaska survey found that they were most frequently taken in 450–600 foot depths and almost all occurred between 150–1,200 feet. These are generally solitary, rocky reef fish, found either on or just over reefs. They really like areas with big boulders and/or large crevices.

Yelloweyes reach 36 inches and a mind boggling 114 years old. Off Alaska, a 2-footer may be 40–80 years old. Males and females probably grow at about the same rates. Off central and northern California, half of all fish are mature at 16 inches and all reproduce by 18 inches, while off southeast Alaska, half are mature at 20 inches or more. Yelloweyes have a pretty long spawning season, releasing young from February–September. These fish eat just about anything they can handle, including fishes, crabs, shrimps and snails. In Alaskan waters, important prey include rockfishes, cods, sand lances and herrings.

FISHERY: This is a popular sport fish, taken with increasing frequency by sportsmen as one travels from southern California to Alaska. While they are only a minor part of the commercial rockfish catch throughout most of their range, yelloweyes are the most important rockfish off southeastern Alaska. Here they are targeted by longline fishermen for eventual air shipment to Seattle and beyond. Their bright orange color and large size make them a particularly sought-after species.

I have seen them in almost every Asian fish market worth the name on the Pacific Coast.

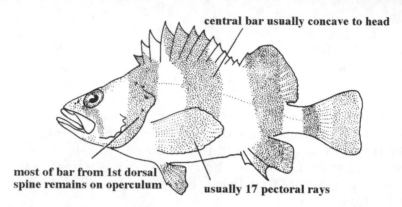

FLAG ROCKFISH (SEBASTES RUBRIVINCTUS)

central bar usually concave to head

most of bar from 1st dorsal spine remains on operculum

usually 17 pectoral rays

NAME: Barber Pole. *Sebastes* is Greek and means "magnificent"; *rubrivinctus* is formed from 2 Latin words and means "red banded."

IDENTIFYING CHARACTERS: This is a brilliantly colored, somewhat oval and spiny rockfish. It's colored pinkish-white or white with wide red or orange-red bars on both body and tail fin. The bars can be almost black in fish less than 2–3 inches.

DISTRIBUTION AND BIOLOGY: From 1928 to 1972, flags were thought to be identical with the redbanded rockfish. Reports of very large flags, flags taken from Oregon to Alaska and flags caught in deep water probably refer to mis-identified redbandeds. Flags have been authenticated from San Francisco to northern Baja California and are common from central California southward. They are known from about 100–1,380 feet in depth, with young ones in the shallower part of the range. As adults, these are strictly solitary, bottom-dwelling reef fish, often found among sea anemones. Almost any hard bottom seems acceptable; they commonly live on the sewer lines off southern California. Young-of-the-year juveniles, on the other hand, are often found sheltering under drifting kelp mats. I have seen hundreds of 1–2 inches flags hovering inside these mats, often many miles from the coast. It is not clear how (or if) these fish find their way to the shallow coastal waters they inhabit as older juveniles and adults.

These rockfish reach lengths of 20 inches, but 16-inchers are about as big as you are likely to see. Relatively little is known about them. I aged a few individuals, and the largest one I examined, a 16-incher, was 18 years old. A 12.5 inch one was 12 years old. Half of these fish are mature at 12–13 inches and all are mature by 15 inches. Flags are probably summer spawners, which is unusual for the rockfishes. As mentioned, young-of-the-year are very common under drifting mats, first appearing in August, leaving the mats in January and February. Based on my examinations, flags eat mostly bottom dwellers, such as crabs (including hermit crabs), shrimps and an occasional fish and octopus.

FISHERY: Flags are a moderately important sport fish in both the party and private vessel catch along both central and southern California. Their bright colors make them a particularly popular species. They are occasionally taken by gillnetters and hook and line commercial fishermen and bring in the high prices of the "red" rockfishes.

REMARKS: On a number of occasions I have seen flags sitting among large white anemones. Both the tropical anemonefish and the painted greenling also sit on or among anemones, and both have orange or red bars alternating with lighter ones. It has been suggested that this pattern helps the fish blend into the anemones, like zebras in tall grass.

BANK ROCKFISH (SEBASTES RUFUS)

NAMES: Commonly referred to as "Red Widows" by commercial fishermen and fish processors. *Sebastes* is Greek for "magnificent"; *rufus* means "red" in Latin.

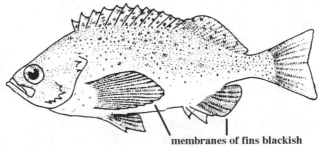

membranes of fins blackish

IDENTIFYING CHARACTERS: A fairly oval species with reduced head spines. Banks come in a range of colors and patterns. They can be anywhere from reddish to gray and may or may not have black spots on backs and fins.

DISTRIBUTION AND BIOLOGY: Found from central Washington to central Baja California and Isla Guadalupe. Don't let the depth range (102-1,470 feet) fool you; these are deeper-dwelling fishes, and most are taken in 600 feet or more. Usually, these are schooling or at least aggregating fishes, often found on the sides of sheer, rocky walls. I have seen isolated small ones under ledges along Monterey Submarine Canyon.

Banks don't get very large; a 20-incher is the record. There is some question as to whether males and females mature at the same length; one study says yes, the other says males mature at a smaller size. One way or the other, about half of fish are mature at around 13 inches, and all are mature at about 16 inches. Females are possibly primitively viviparous. Along the California coast, banks spawn from December-May, with a January peak in southern California and a February one further north. Off southern California, many females produce more than one batch of larvae per season. Females produce anywhere from 65,000-608,000 eggs per season.

FISHERY: Banks are reasonably important in the party vessel recreational catch, particularly off southern California. In the southern California fishery, most banks are caught during winter and spring, corresponding to the peak of the deep-water rockfish fishery. Banks are often taken in the commercial catch, mostly by deepwater trawlers and gillnetters who catch a complex of species, including darkblotches, splitnoses and blackgills.

STRIPETAIL ROCKFISH (SEBASTES SAXICOLA)

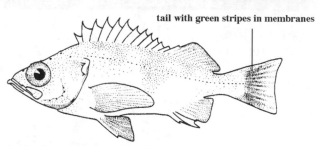

tail with green stripes in membranes

NAMES: Olive-Back Rockfish. *Sebastes* is Greek for "magnificent"; *saxicola* means "I inhabit rock" in Latin. Pretty cute, but not particularly accurate–see below.

IDENTIFYING CHARACTERS: These are elongated fish, usually pink or yellow-pink, with very faint darker saddles on the back. The best character is the greenish stripes on the caudal fin.

DISTRIBUTION AND BIOLOGY: Stripetails live from southeast Alaska to central Baja California. They live over soft mud-pebble or mud-cobble bottom. As Mary Yoklavich (an *eminence grise* of submarine rockfish observers) notes, stripetails often sit on the bottom in little depressions, evenly spaced and all facing the same way. Found from 33-1,320 feet, the young are usually found in the shallower part of the species' depth range. Most fish are found in waters between about 300 and 1,000 feet.

A fairly small species, stripetails reach 15.25 inches. While males seem to live for only about 6 years, females just keep going, and going and going...to at least 22 years. Both sexes mature at 4-7 inches (3-4 years). Like other rockfishes, females may be primitively viviparous, but the research has not been done on most species. Off southern California, females spawn from September to February, peaking in December. As with many rockfishes, the season is later in central and northern California, January-March, peaking in January. Females produce anywhere from about 1,200-131,000 eggs per season. Females produce one brood per season. Stripetails feed mostly on planktonic creatures; krill and copepods are the big items here.

FISHERY: For several reasons, recreational anglers only occasionally take stripetails. First, they have fairly small mouths and probably don't find big gobs o' bait that attractive. Second, they are most common over soft bottoms, which rockfish anglers stay away from like the plague. Trawlers catch fair quantities of stripetails, though some are discarded because of their small size.

HALFBANDED ROCKFISH (SEBASTES SEMICINCTUS)

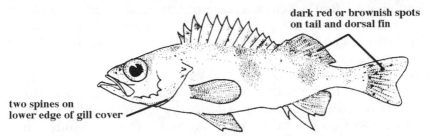

dark red or brownish spots on tail and dorsal fin

two spines on lower edge of gill cover

NAMES: *Sebastes* is Greek for "magnificent"; *semicinctus* means "half-banded" in Latin.

IDENTIFYING CHARACTERS: This one can be confused with stripetails; their coloring and overall shape is similar. However, halfbandeds have two very distinctive black, brown or red-brown blotches on their sides; these are not present on stripetails.

DISTRIBUTION AND BIOLOGY: Halfbandeds are found from northern Washington to central Baja California in 48-1,320 feet of water. These are schooling fish, usually found within a few feet of the bottom. They like cobble-mud or cobble-sand bottoms. These are one of the most abundant of rockfish species. You can see just jillions of them, often with squarespots and pygmies.

This is another dwarf rockfish species. They reach 10 inches and live perhaps 15 years. Females grow faster and larger than males. Halfbandeds mature at 4.5-6 inches (3-4 years of age). Like other rockfishes, females may be primitively viviparous; they produce one brood per year. Females spawn from December to March, peaking in February, and produce 3,400-31,000 eggs.

FISHERY: Halfbandeds are very occasionally taken by recreational anglers. They are not a commercial species.

OLIVE ROCKFISH (SEBASTES SERRANOIDES)

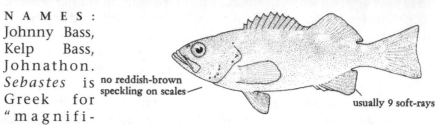

no reddish-brown speckling on scales

usually 9 soft-rays

NAMES: Johnny Bass, Kelp Bass, Johnathon. *Sebastes* is Greek for "magnificent"; *serranoides* is a combination of Latin and Greek and means "resembling a bass."

IDENTIFYING CHARACTERS: These are bass-shaped fish, often mistaken for kelp bass or yellowtail rockfish. They are olive-brown or brown with olive, brown or yellowish fins and a series of pale blotches on the backs (which may be difficult to see in fish larger than about 1 foot). Kelp bass do not have spines on the rear part of their cheeks; yellowtail rockfish have very yellow or orange fins, and their bodies are flecked with tiny golden brown or reddish stipples.

DISTRIBUTION AND BIOLOGY: Olives range from Redding Rock, northern California southward to central Baja California and are abundant from southern California northward to about Mendocino County, northern California. They are found from very shallow water (10 feet or less) to 570 feet, most commonly from about 15–180 feet. These are midwater fish, almost always living over hard, high relief (such as reefs, wrecks, oil platforms or pipes). They may form large aggregations of hundreds of fish but are often found singly in blue rockfish schools. Although olives will occasionally sit on the bottom, they spend most of their time anywhere from a foot or two to 40 feet or so above the substrate, and I have often seen them break the surface chasing small fishes. On some reefs, particularly in southern California, olives are the most abundant species. These are fairly sedentary fish; in a study I conducted off Santa Barbara, California, few olives moved between reefs, even after several years.

Olives live at least 25 years and reach 2 feet in length. Most are mature at about 6 years and 14 inches. Spawning occurs from January–March, peaking in February. Beginning in April, newly-settled olives appear over rocky reefs. Young-of-the-year tend to aggregate over low rocks, in areas with reduced water movement, particularly over drift algae. While these young olives tend to live

Plate 1. *Basking sharks,* Cetorhinus maximus, *busily scarfing up plankton off Santa Barbara, California.*

Plate 2. *Marc Chamberlain found this blue shark,* Prionace glauca, *near San Diego.*

Plate 3. *A pensive moment for a Pacific angel shark,* Squatina californica.

Marc Chamberlain

Plate 4. *A schnoz-eye view of a shovelnose guitarfish,* Rhinobatos productus.

Marc Chamberlain

Plate 5. *Off British Columbia, a male greenling,* Hexagrammos decagrammus, *hangs out.*

Plate 6. *A cow rockfish,* Sebastes levis, *sits in 600 feet of water in Monterey Bay.*

Plate 7. *The brown rockfish,* Sebastes auriculatus, *in its preferred habitat.*

Plate 8. *A rather dramatic China rockfish,* Sebastes nebulosus, *on a shallow British Columbia reef.*

Plate 9. *A striking tiger rockfish,* Sebastes nigrocinctus, *erects its fins in response to a diver's intrusion.*

Plate 10. *Black rockfish,* Sebastes melanops, *are common on nearshore reefs in the northeast Pacific.*

Plate 11. *From southern California southwards, honeycomb rockfish,* Sebastes umbrosus, *are abundant on mid-depth reefs.*

Plate 12. *Pt. Lobos, California, is home to this copper rockfish,* Sebastes caurinus.

Plate 13. *An attractive vermilion rockfish,* Sebastes miniatus, *from San Miguel Island, California.*

Plate 14. *Just an elegant little fish, this is a juvenile California sheephead,* Semicossyphus pulcher.

Plate 15. *Female California sheepheads are pink all over with white chins.*

Plate 16. *A male California sheephead, complete with characteristic blunt forehead.*

Plate 17. *Off southeast Alaska, a lingcod,* Ophiodon elongatus, *hunkers onto a pinnacle.*

Plate 18. *Kelp bass,* Paralabrax clathratus, *are big time recreational fish in southern California and northern Baja California.*

Plate 19. *Almost lost among anemones and tubeworms, a painted greenling,* Oxylebius pictus, *sits on a reef near the Coronado Islands, Baja California.*

Plate 20. *About as blotchy as its background, a red Irish lord,* Hemilepidotus hemilepidotus, *surveys a British Columbia rock.*

Plate 21. *A school of juvenile jackmackerel,* Trachurus symmetricus, *graces the waters of San Clemente Island.*

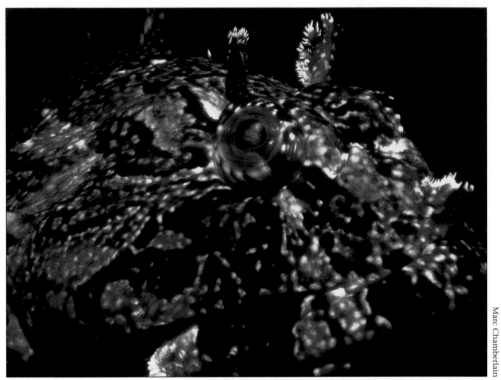

Plate 22. *The head of a male cabezon,* Scorpaenichthys marmoratus, *from Santa Cruz Island, California.*

Marc Chamberlain

Plate 23. *A sleek yellowtail,* Seriola lalandi.

James Watt

Plate 24. *A simply gorgeous dolphinfish,* Coryphaena hippurus.

Plate 25. *Blacksmith,* Chromis punctipinnis, *looking to be cleaned by a few senorita,* Oxyjulis californica.

Plate 26. *A whole bunch of black perch,* Embiotoca jacksoni.

Plate 27. *A nearly-psychotic male garibaldi,* Hypsypops rubicunda, *guards a red algae nest.*

Plate 28. *Male garibaldi remove anything from the nest that is not red algae, including a stone put there by a mischievous diver.*

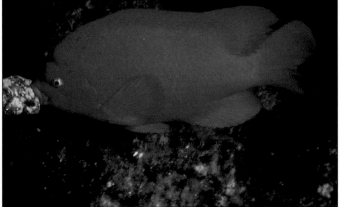

Plate 29. *Mission accomplished, the stone has been removed. But look at the expression on that garibaldi's face. He looks like Felix in the Odd Couple. "Oscar, Oscar, you put a rock in the nest again!"*

Plate 30. *Oh, my. Is this just the cutest thing you have ever seen, or what? It's the business end of a wolf-eel,* Anarrhichthys ocellatus.

Plate 31. *They are bad and they should be California's state marine fish. Sarcastic fringehead,* Neoclinus blanchardi, *usually live in beer bottles, but this one is slumming inside a shell.*

Plate 32. *The curled lip of a Pacific halibut,* Hippoglossus stenolepis, *photographed as it lounged inside an extinct submarine volcano off southeast Alaska.*

Plate 33. *Normally fairly reclusive, this zebra goby,* Lythrypnus zebra, *gives us its best profile.*

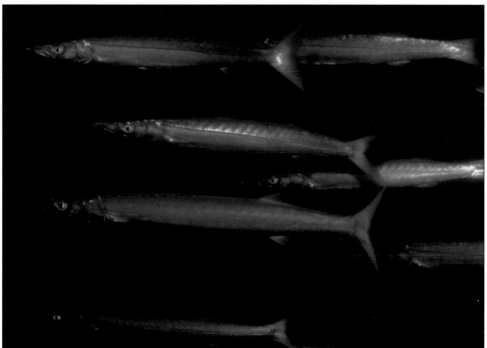

Plate 34. *A very aesthetic school of Pacific barracuda,* Sphyraena argentea.

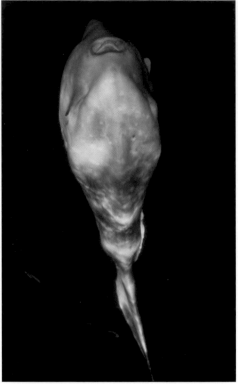

Plate 35. *Quick now, and don't look at the end of this caption. What is this fish? Wrong, it's the underside of an ocean sunfish,* Mola mola, *and I asked you not to look.*

Plate 36. *A more formal view of an ocean sunfish.*

Plate 37. *Very spiff indeed - a yellowfin,* Thunnus albacares, *motivating off Clipperton Island.*

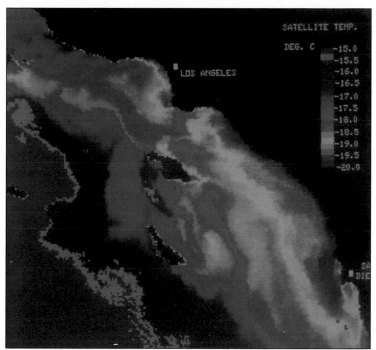

Plate 38. *Sea surface temperatures off southern California on 19 July 1982, a non-El Niño year. The redder it is, the hotter. It's warm off San Diego and cools off to the north.*

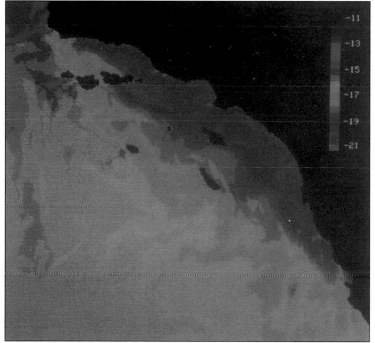

Plate 39. *That naughty El Niño. Pretty much the same view as above, but on 9 July 1983, the year of the Big One. Note that all of southern California is covered by warm water.*

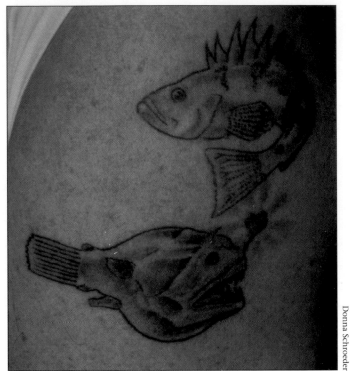

Donna Schroeder

Plate 40. *The wonderful world of fish tattoos. The upper one is a cow rockfish, the lower a deep-water anglerfish. The anglerfish is a female, with a small, parasitic male attached underneath.*

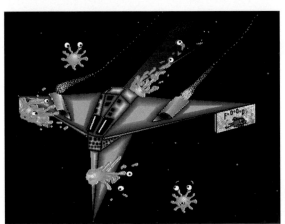

Elan Love

Plate 41. *The Kwarkarkian space ship under attack by Xandarians, the official bookies of the Lesser Magellenic Cloud. See "About the Author" on page 381 for the gruesome details.*

between the bottom and mid-water column, they occasionally venture near the surface. Young ones descend to the bottom at night. Larger juveniles and adults are nocturnal, pursuing prey primarily after sunset. Major prey include fishes (particularly juvenile rockfishes), octopi, squids and such planktonic organisms as copepods and crab larvae.

FISHERY: Olives form a respectable part of the party and private vessel recreational catch. While they are taken from northern California southwards, our drab little friends really contribute to the fishery in a big way from about Santa Cruz, central California, to the Santa Barbara Channel, southern California. Here they may form as much as 6% of the total recreational catch. Divers spear substantial numbers and juveniles are taken from piers.

On the other hand, they are only occasionally found in the commercial catch, taken primarily by hook and line and gillnet. In previous years, when shallow gillnet sets were legal, they were netted in substantial numbers. While some are marketed whole, much of the catch is filleted.

REMARKS: Olives are particularly abundant around oil platforms in the Santa Barbara Channel. These fish are 1–4 year old juveniles and occasionally are found by the thousands.

TREEFISH (SEBASTES SERRICEPS)

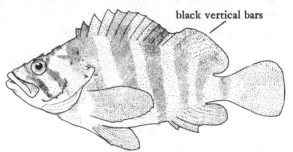

black vertical bars

NAMES: *Sebastes* means "magnificent" in Greek; *serriceps* is formed from 2 Latin words meaning "saw head," referring to the very large head spines.

IDENTIFYING CHARAC-
TERS: Treefish are very distinctively patterned rockfish, with compact little bodies and large head spines. They have a series of black or dark green bars alternating with yellow or olive ones. This, combined with pink lips, make them look like something your teenage daughter is dating.

DISTRIBUTION AND BIOLOGY: These are solitary, reef-dwelling fish, found from San Francisco to central Baja California. They are common from about Santa Barbara southward, almost always in caves and crevices. They are most common between 20 and 140 feet, with a maximum depth of 150 feet..

Trees reach 16 inches. They are probably either dawn and dusk or nighttime predators, feeding on bottom invertebrates (such as shrimp and crabs) and small fishes. They probably spawn in late winter. Young ones often are found in drifting kelp mats, which have broken free from beds and are traveling with the currents. Least terns eat the juveniles.

FISHERY: Treefish are occasionally taken by party and private vessel anglers and by divers, mostly from Santa Barbara southward. Once in a while, they are taken in lobster traps.

REMARKS: Trees are highly territorial. When two meet, they flare their mouths and gill covers. The reddish color of the lips is probably used to warn off other fish.

HONEYCOMB ROCKFISH (SEBASTES UMBROSUS)

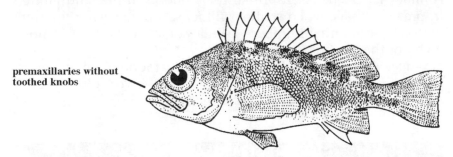

premaxillaries without toothed knobs

NAMES: *Sebastes* is Greek for "magnificent"; *umbrosus* is Latin for "shady."

IDENTIFYING CHARACTERS: A small, sort of chunky species with large head spines. They are orangy-brown or pinkish-yellow with a honeycomb pattern on their sides (Plate 11).

DISTRIBUTION AND BIOLOGY: Though they are found from Pt. Pinos, central California to south-central Baja California, honeycombs are uncommon north of about Pt. Conception. You find them all over medium-shallow reefs from Santa Monica Bay southward. They inhabit waters ranging from 98-390 feet. These are rocky substrata dwellers; they live right on the bottom.

Honeycombs are small fishes, reaching 10.5 inches. Males and females grow at the same rate and they live to at least 15 years. Females spawn from March to July and young-of-the-year seem to settle to the bottom in the fall.

FISHERY: They may be small, but they are important in the southern California recreational party vessel catch. A mid-1980s survey showed that honeycombs comprised about 4% of the rockfish catch in southern California, most taken during trips that target shallow-water rockfishes.

PYGMY ROCKFISH (SEBASTES WILSONI)

NAMES: *Sebastes* is Greek for "magnificent"; *wilsoni* honors Charles B. Wilson, who discovered and described a truly numbing number of parasitic copepods.

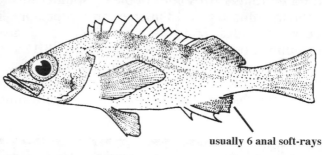

usually 6 anal soft-rays

IDENTIFYING CHARACTERS: Pygmies are a fairly elongated species. They are red-brown with a reddish stripe along their sides and a number of darker saddles on their backs.

DISTRIBUTION AND BIOLOGY: Pygmies have been taken from southeastern Alaska to Cortes Bank, southern California, most commonly from central California northward, between 100 and 1,056 feet. Off central and southern California, we have seen clouds of pygmies mixed with squarespot and halfbanded rockfishes over cobble or boulder bottoms.

Pygmies are well-named; the world record is 8.25 inches long. And not much else is known about them.

FISHERY: Are you kidding?

SHARPCHIN ROCKFISH (SEBASTES ZACENTRUS)

NAMES: *Sebastes* is Greek for "magnificent"; *zacentrus* is formed from 2 Greek words forming "very spiny."

IDENTIFYING CHARACTERS:

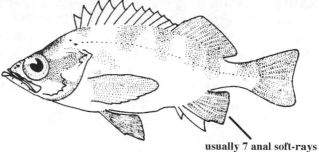

usually 7 anal soft-rays

Another one of those pinkish species, with the usual dusky blotches on the back. One good character is the 2 bars that radiate back from the eye to the back edge of the gill cover.

DISTRIBUTION AND BIOLOGY: Found from the Gulf of Alaska to San Diego, southern California, sharpchins are common from central California northward. These are deeper-water fishes. Though they have been taken from 83-1,632 feet, they are more abundant in waters deeper than perhaps 600 feet. They like mud bottoms, but mud bottoms with some cobble or boulder mixed in.

Sharpchins reach 13 inches and problably live to about 45 years. Females may be primitively viviparous. Off British Columbia, both sexes mature at around 8-10 inches and females spawn in June and perhaps later.

FISHERY: Only rarely taken by recreational anglers, they are an incidental take in trawl fisheries throughout much of their range.

SHORTSPINE THORNYHEAD (SEBASTOLOBUS ALASCANUS) AND LONGSPINE THORNYHEAD (S. ALTIVELIS)

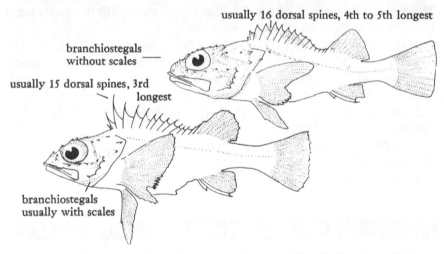

usually 16 dorsal spines, 4th to 5th longest

branchiostegals without scales

usually 15 dorsal spines, 3rd longest

branchiostegals usually with scales

NAMES: Channel Rockfish, Hardhead, Idiotfish, Spinycheek Rockfish, Shortspine - Arasukakichiji, Longspine - Hirenagakichiji (Japanese). *Sebastolobus* is formed from 2 Greek words meaning "*Sebastes* lobed," referring to the lobed pectoral fins; *alascanus* means "Alaskan"; *altivelis* is Latin and translates to "high sail."

IDENTIFYING CHARACTERS: Both shortspines and longspines are red or pink; longspines may have some black on bodies and have mostly black gill chambers. Both species have a row of spines along their gill covers and look quite similar. Longspines usually have 15 (not 16) dorsal fin spines and the 3rd spine is longest (not shorter than the 4th spine).

DISTRIBUTION AND BIOLOGY: Shortspines are found from the Sea of Okhotsk (Asia) to the Bering Sea and southward to Isla Cedros, Baja California. They are common from at least southern California northward. This is a soft substrate, bottom-dwelling species, found from 55 to 5,000 feet, most commonly from about 450–1,900 feet. Juveniles tend to live in shallower water than do adults. Probably in response to cooler inshore water temperatures, shortspines live in shallower water in the northern part of their range. We see them mainly on mud bottoms, often sitting in little depressions they seem to have carved. However, it seems they still like to be near structure of some sort; there is usually a rock, sponge or other something in the vicinity.

Longspines range from the Aleutian Islands, Alaska to southern Baja California; they are abundant from at least southern California northwards. Like shortspines, these fish live on soft sand or mud bottoms, but they are most common in waters deeper than that preferred by their close relatives. Longspines have been taken in 858-5,280 feet, most commonly from about 2,000-4,000 feet. Off central California, the vast majority of reproductive longspine females live between about 1,700-3,300 feet.

Shortspines grow to 29.5 inches, while longspines reach 15 inches. Most research on shortspines has occurred off Alaska and some fish there live at least 62 years. In Alaskan waters, a few shortspines mature at around 5 years (6 inches), half are mature at 12 years and 9 inches, and all have spawned by 16 years and 10 inches. On the other hand, longspines mature at 4-7 inches. Along much of their range, both species spawn from about January to May. However, off California and Baja California, larvae have been taken in every month except December, with a very sharp March peak. Females are oviparous and produce between 20,000 and 450,000 eggs per season. Female longspines produce 2-4 batches of eggs per season. Female thornyheads extrude hollow, gelatinous egg masses that float near the surface until the eggs hatch. Off California and Baja California, larvae are most often found 30-250 miles off the coast. Larvae are much more common north of Pt. Conception, implying that most spawning takes place to the north. Before they set up housekeeping on the bottom, juvenile shortspines spend 14-15 months and longspines around 18-20 months in midwater. Shortspines settle out at about 1.5-2.25 inches, longspines at .75-1.0 inch. Off central California, longspines settle out at about 1,900-3,800 feet. Shortspines eat a variety of invertebrates, such as shrimps, crabs and amphipods, as well as fishes and worms.

FISHERY: In central and northern California, recreational fishermen catch small numbers of shortspines. Longspines are rarely taken. On the other hand, there is a pretty hefty commercial trawl fishery, particularly from central California northward. In 1993, about 9,000 metric tons (worth about $10 million) were taken along the Pacific Coast. A very high percentage of these fish are exported to Japan, where thornyheads bring big bucks. Both shortspines and longspines are taken with Dover sole and sablefish.

REMARKS: Even though thornyheads are very abundant in southern California waters, they may not spawn there. Thornyhead larvae are very rare in that area, and based on some limited research I conducted, females do not seem to have ripe eggs. If this is the case, almost all the fish found south of about Pt. Conception drift or swim down from northern waters.

Sablefishes and Skilfishes - Family Anoplopomatidae

SABLEFISH (ANOPLOPOMA FIMBRIA)

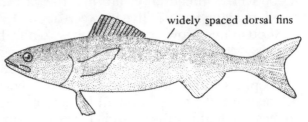

widely spaced dorsal fins

NAMES: Just about every commercial fishermen and fish processor on the coast calls them Blackcod. As usual in these matters, sablefish are not cods, are not closely related to cods, and, in fact, do not wish to be seen with cods on social occasions. Among other names, they are also called Coal Fish, Coal Cod, Butterfish, Candlefish, Blue Cod, Bluefish, Deep Sea Trout, Black Candlefish, Beshow, Gindara (Japanese), Hokuyumutsu (Japanese). *Anoplopoma* means "unarmed operculum" in Greek, referring to the smooth gill cover; *fimbria* means "fringed," but I have no idea why this name was given.

IDENTIFYING CHARACTERS: Sablefish are sleek fish. Adults are dark gray, greenish-gray or blackish, sometimes with a latticework pattern on their backs. Very small juveniles are blue-black on backs with white bellies; larger juveniles are greenish or grayish with faint stripes on backs. Yellow ones and albinos have been reported. True cods have 3 dorsal fins (not 2) and 2 anal fins (not 1). Pacific hake are silvery and have a notch in the second dorsal and anal fins.

DISTRIBUTION AND BIOLOGY: Sablefish have been reported from east-central Honshu Island, Japan north into the Bering Sea and southeast to Isla Cedros, Baja California. They are abundant at least from southern California northward, although their largest concentrations start kicking in north of Cape Mendocino, northern California. Large adults appear to be uncommon south of Pt. Conception. Sables live from surface, inshore waters to about 9,042 feet. These are schooling fish, living on or near the bottom, usually over sand or mud. Juveniles rarely occur in water deeper than about 600 feet and adults don't like to come in much shallower than this depth. While various reports give a range of figures, most adults are found from 600–3,000 feet. As a rule, the deeper you go, the larger will be the sablefish.

In general, sablefish do not make extensive movements, remaining in an area of a few tens of miles. Having said that, it appears that a small percentage really do hoof it; one fish tagged off of Washington wound up at the tip of the Aleutians, a distance of over 1,700 miles. In at least some areas (such as Monterey Bay), larger fish move into somewhat shallower water in summer. Tagging experiments off California and Alaska show that smaller fish move around more than larger ones, while data from Oregon and Washington did not indicate this. On the Asian coast of the Bering Sea, sablefish seasonal migrations may be more prominent than those on the North American side. Some sablefish may make inshore-offshore movements. As an example, in 1983 at least some of the population shifted downslope into cooler waters, apparently to escape that year's El Niño. Generally, sables seem to prefer waters between 37-46° F.

The largest sablefish on record was 40 inches long; some live to at least 55 years. Females grow faster, larger and live longer. Both sexes just about stop growing by about 10 years. In the first year they reach about 11 inches. A 10-year-old female is about 30 inches long; a 5-year-old male is 25 inches. About half of all females mature at 5–6 years (24 inches) and half of males at 4–6 years (around 20 inches). Some populations of sablefish grow faster than others, and fast–growing fish mature at a younger age than slow growers. Females are oviparous and spawn in batches, 3-4 times per season. Spawning occurs in deep waters (900-2,000 feet in the Gulf of Alaska, over 1,000 feet off British Columbia, 1,700 feet off Monterey, California). Spawning season seems to be highly variable, depending on where you are and perhaps who you are. In the Gulf of Alaska, it appears to be January-June, peaking in June and July. Another study along the Washington-California coast noted spawning from August-November. Yet more research, this time off central California, came up with October-February. Eggs have been found as much as 150 nautical miles offshore. The eggs and larvae stay deep; most are below 600 feet. On the other hand, most young-of-the-year swim into inshore waters and are pelagic, living at or near the surface. Two-inchers appear off our coast in summer. After about one year, the fish move down to the bottom and slowly migrate into deeper water as they mature. Small sables eat small fishes and squids; when they descend to the bottom, fishes are still important prey, but such invertebrates as amphipods and krill are added to their diets. Large ones eat mainly fishes (such as rockfishes and herring), krill, salps and octopi. In turn, they are eaten by such sea birds as least terns and rhinoceros auklets (these just love the young-of-the-year), fishes (for instance Pacific cod, Pacific halibut, lingcod, arrowtooth flounder, spiny dogfish) and marine mammals (northern elephant seals, California sea lions, harbor seals and northern fur seals). Orcas really seem to like them; they have been reported to preferentially take sablefish off of long lines, ignoring other species.

FISHERY: Sablefish are a minor sport fish throughout most of their range, often taken by deep water rockfish fishermen after the boats drift off reefs. However, juveniles—which often swarm into shallow water— are a common catch from piers and boats from northern California northward. Very occasionally, large schools of juveniles move inshore in central California, as occurred in 1947. For 2 weeks the pier at Monterey was surrounded by thousands of these small fish. Apparently the local populace went semi-berserk, lining the rails and hauling in fish after fish on any bait or lure available. Ah yes, many were the tales told by weather-beaten office managers of 6-inch-long fish hauled in by the ton.

Sablefish are a big, big commercial species along much of our coast, but particularly within the Gulf of Alaska where fish are taken by otter trawl, fish trap or longline. The fishery is closely regulated, and various groups of fishermen (trappers, trawlers, hook and liners) are allotted percentages of the total annual quota. Inevitably, no one is happy with their allotment, and there is a fair amount of grumbling in one's beer. The sablefish fishery did not really hit its stride until the late 1960s when Japan began to take substantial quantities off Alaska and British Columbia. Other nations (the USSR, Republic of Korea, U. S. and Canada) joined in; as of 1988, the U.S. share of the fishery was worth almost $100 million. A large part of the catch goes to Japan, where this oily species is very popular with sashimi buffs. I have been told that sablefish are graded for sashimi by their oil content (the higher the oil, the better) and that deeper-dwelling fish have more oil. Sablefish are also sold fresh and frozen (usually as "black cod") and they make one of the best smoked products you can imagine. Fresh sables have a relatively short (3-5 days) lifespan when refrigerated at 40° F. Frozen at 0° F, they last 6-9 months.

REMARKS: My associates have seen considerable numbers of juvenile sablefish sheltering under drifting kelp mats in southern California.

Greenlings - Family Hexagrammidae

KELP GREENLING (HEXAGRAMMOS DECAGRAMMUS)

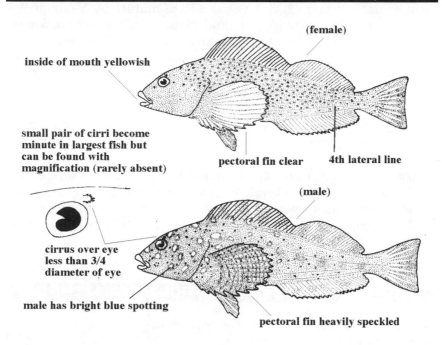

(female)

inside of mouth yellowish

small pair of cirri become
minute in largest fish but
can be found with
magnification (rarely absent)

pectoral fin clear

4th lateral line

cirrus over eye
less than 3/4
diameter of eye

(male)

male has bright blue spotting

pectoral fin heavily speckled

NAME: Seatrout, Arasukaainame (Japanese). *Hexagrammos* is formed from 2 Greek words meaning "6 lined"; *decagrammus* is also Greek and means "10 lines," referring to the total number of lateral lines on this species.

IDENTIFYING CHARACTERS: This is one of the few fish around with 5 lateral lines on each side, so identification should be a snap. Females are gray in color and are profusely covered with reddish-brown or orange spots. Males are gray or brown with a few blue spots on the front parts of their bodies (Plate 5). Each blue spot is surrounded by a ring of reddish-brown spots.

DISTRIBUTION AND BIOLOGY: Kelp greenlings have been taken from the Aleutian Islands to La Jolla, southern California, from tide pools to 150 feet. While rare south of Santa Barbara, California, they are common from central California northward. These are rocky reef fish, found right on the bottom, often in dense algae. Between Alaska and central California, most of them live from lower intertidal waters to about 50 feet, with females tending to live in shallower waters than males. In Puget Sound, females are most common in about 10–25 feet, while males prefer 20–35 feet. These critters tend to be solitary, territorial fish, given to chasing away other greenlings.

The largest kelp greenling on record was 21 inches long. They have been aged to 12 years, but a few probably live a bit longer. A typical 10-incher is 6–9 years old. Females grow faster than males. Some females mature at 3–4 years; all are mature by 5 (about 9.5 inches). Females are oviparous and these fish are fall spawners, with nesting noted in October–November off Washington and British Columbia. Females migrate down to the males, lay pale blue eggs in nests, and the males guard these until they hatch. These fish are true gourmands, eating just about anything that isn't nailed to the bottom. High on their preferred menu are shrimps and crabs, worms, octopi, brittle stars, snails and small fishes. Feeding occurs during the day and they are inactive at night.

FISHERY: Kelp greenling are a major sport species from central California northward, taken by rocky shore, pier, private and party vessel fishermen. They are also targeted by divers. Although they are yummy to eat, there never has been much of a commercial market.

LINGCOD (OPHIODON ELONGATUS)

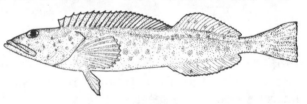

NAMES: Cultus Cod, Cultus, Blue Cod, Ling, Greenlinger, Slinky Linky (really, I am not making this up), Kin Mutsu (Japanese), Lincod or Bacalao (Mexico). *Ophiodon* is formed from 2 Greek words meaning "snake tooth"; *elongatus* means "elongated" in Latin.

IDENTIFYING CHARACTERS: These are elongate fish, with large mouths filled with canine teeth. Lingcod come in an assortment of colors, from nearly black or brown to blue and green (Plate 17). They often have orange or yellow spots.

DISTRIBUTION AND BIOLOGY: Lingcod are found from the Shumagin Islands (western Gulf of Alaska) southward to at least Ensenada, northern Baja California and, at the northern end of their range, possibly into the Bering Sea. A cold water species, they are most abundant from southeast Alaska to central California and the northern Channel Islands in southern California. Although lings have been recorded from the intertidal zone to depths of 1,620 feet, they are rarely taken in more than 1,000 feet. Lingcod live in shallower water (occasionally even in tide pools) from central California northward, while in southern California adults are rarely taken in less than 100 feet. Until they reach about 3 inches, juveniles are more or less pelagic and can be attracted to the surface at night with lights. Larger juveniles live on the bottom in a wide range of habitats, including sand, gravel and eelgrass beds, from bays and estuaries out to at least 200 feet. Adults also can be found on soft bottoms, particularly in deeper water, although many move onto rocks as they grow. Males tend to live in shallower water than females.

Lingcod are bottom dwelling, more or less solitary animals, and while they tend to stay near the bottom, I have seen them rise 20–30 feet to the surface, attacking hooked rockfish. While immature fish seem to move about somewhat, it is unclear whether most adults make extensive migrations. Some research, such as that off Cape Flattery, Washington (Transactions of the American Fisheries Society, 1995, vol. 124, p. 170-183), shows that there is a great deal of movement into, and out of, a particular area. On the other hand, Jeff Marliave of the Vancouver Aquarium feels that lings inhabiting the isolated shallow reefs of British Columbia fjords may not leave these structures at all. Various studies imply that lings prefer water temperatures between about 44-50° F.

Lingcod reach 5 feet, and the oldest one I know of lived for 20 years. Females grow faster and attain a larger size than males. In their first year, lings grow to one foot, and reach 3 feet in 7-10 years. Off British Columbia, males first mature at 20 inches, females at 30 inches. In a study off central California, the smallest mature male was 15 inches, the smallest mature female 20 inches. Most males matured by 20 inches and most females by 24 inches. In general, it appears that lingcod off central California mature at a smaller size than off British Columbia. Off central California, over 60% of 2-year-old males and virtually all 4-year-olds were mature, while the youngest mature female was 3 and all had matured at 7. Females are oviparous and produce between 6,000 and at least 500,000 eggs per season. Spawning varies with location; British Columbia, February-April; Puget Sound, December to April (perhaps to June); California, November to April, peaking in late December to early February. Males guard the eggs for 8-10 weeks until they hatch. The eggs masses, which start off pink and later turn white, can weigh 15 pounds and be 2.5 feet across. Eggs are laid in crevices, caves and under rock ledges from the intertidal zone to at least 60 feet (and probably deeper). Given half a chance, the eggs are preyed upon by a variety of animals, including snails, hermit crabs and sculpins. In particular, snails seem to be eaten by guarding males. Lingcod are voracious predators and eat almost any fish in the vicinity, as well as squids and octopi. Northern fur seals, Steller sea lions and California sea lions eat them.

FISHERY: Lingcod are very popular recreational fish from at least Ensenada, northern Baja California, northward. They are taken primarily by anglers aboard party and private vessels and by divers, but a substantial number are also captured from piers and by rocky shore fishermen. Starting north of Pt. Conception, lings begin to form more than 1% of the recreational catch. In northern California and Oregon, they may comprise 3-7% of the total take.

Along much of the Pacific Coast, commercial fishermen also take substantial numbers, although many more are taken from Oregon northward. A substantial part of the northern lingcod catch is make by hook and line, particularly by lures. In the southern part of the fishery, gillnets and trawls catch most of the fish. Lingcod are marketed either fresh or frozen, as fillets or steaks. Shelf life is 5-7 days at 40° F. You can keep them frozen at 0° F for 6-9 months and still flash that appealing grin when you eat them.

REMARKS: Lingcod are neither lings (an Atlantic fish) nor cods, are not closely related to lings or cods and do not particularly resemble (are you ready?) lings or cods.

Probably to your great relief, the green color occasionally found in lingcod flesh disappears with cooking and is harmless.

Lingcod were commonly eaten by Native Americans.

PAINTED GREENLING (OXYLEBIUS PICTUS)

NAME: Convict Fish. *Oxylebius* more or less means "sharp greenling" in Greek; *pictus* means "painted."

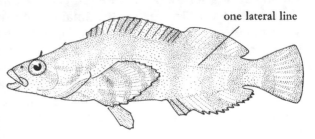
one lateral line

IDENTIFYING CHARACTERS: Painted greenling (Plate 19) are one of the few fish on the Pacific Coast with alternating bars on their sides. These red or red-brown bars alternate with a gray or white background color. Some individuals are heavily sprinkled with tiny white spots. Adult males are more brightly colored than females, particularly during spawning season. All fish have little cirri (fleshy tufts) on their heads, one above each eye and one between each eye and the dorsal fin.

DISTRIBUTION AND BIOLOGY: These fish have a wide geographic range, from Kodiak Island, Alaska, southward to north-central Baja California and range in depth from the intertidal to 307 feet. In northern waters, they start to poop out north of the Strait of Georgia; southward, they become rare south of about La Jolla,

California. In southern California, they are most abundant from depths of 50–100 feet, while from central California north they primarily inhabit 15–70 feet. Painteds are solitary bottom dwellers found on or near hard bottom. While they are usually associated with rocks, they also are found on oil platforms and sewage pipes. Adults are territorial and seem to stay in the same area for years. Yet another example of grouchy fish, adults have been seen nipping at fish many times their sizes. Males prefer high relief rocky bottoms, while females and juveniles are often found on sand-rock boundaries. These fish are inactive (sheltering in holes) during the coldest and stormiest months (February–March in California, December–March in Puget Sound).

Painted greenling grow to 10 inches and live to at least 8 years. Females live longer and grow larger, as do fish in the northern part of their range. A 4-incher is about 1 year old; a 6.5-incher off Monterey and an 8-incher in Puget Sound are about 6 years old. Females mature at 3 years and most males at 2. Spawning occurs during the summer in Puget Sound, from September to March off Monterey and perhaps year round in southern California. Females are oviparous and lay egg masses in nests on exposed rock surfaces which are then guarded by males. Females produce between 12,000-28,000 eggs per season. Egg masses contain as many as 2,200 eggs and a male may guard numerous egg masses in the same nest. Painteds are inactive at night, spawning probably occurs at dawn. These fish mainly eat bottom-dwelling invertebrates such as crabs, shrimps and amphipods and curried tofu. (Are you awake out there?) Brandt's cormorants eat them.

FISHERY: These peanuts are occasionally taken by party and private vessel fishermen, fishing over rocky reefs.

REMARKS: I've seen these fish in aquaria sitting on top of the large, white anemone, *Metridium*, apparently without ill effects. Flag rockfish, which have similar alternating reddish and white bars, also occasionally nestle in these anemones. Both have color patterns similar to those of tropical anemonefish, which also reside in anemone tentacles.

ATKA MACKEREL (PLEUROGRAMMUS MONOPTERYGIUS)

NAMES: Kitanohokke (Japanese). *Pleurogrammus* is formed from 2 Greek words "side line"; *monopterygius* is also from the Greek, "one fin."

IDENTIFYING CHARACTERS: A somewhat elongated species, with 5 lateral lines and no cirri (those little flap doodles found in the related greenlings) on the head. Males and females are differently colored, or sexually dimorphic. This is particularly obvious during the sum-

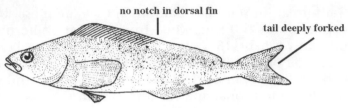

no notch in dorsal fin

tail deeply forked

mer. Males are golden-yellow or orange with black or brown transverse stripes; females are dull grayish-green. Males also have larger pelvic and pectoral fins and greater body depth.

DISTRIBUTION AND BIOLOGY: While atka mackerels are known from the Sea of Japan and Bering Sea to Redondo Beach, southern California, they are uncommon south of Washington. These are rocky reef dwellers and they have been taken from the lower intertidal to 1,898 feet. Trawl surveys show they are most abundant in waters between about 150-1,000 feet. Both juveniles and adults may make vertical migrations, coming to the surface at night.

Nineteen and one-half inches is the record size for this one. Atkas live to at least 11 years and mature at 3-4 years. Females are oviparous and, in inshore waters, lay masses of demersal adhesive eggs in rock crevices and among stones. Russian researchers working off the Kamchatka Peninsula report that spawning occurred in very specific locations, in about 50-100 feet of water. Spawning occurs from June-September in the Bering Sea, perhaps to October elsewhere. Nests, composed of eggs from more than one female, are guarded by males. The previously-mentioned Russian scientists also observed that, during spawning season, large, brightly-marked males are the ones that guard nests and hold territories. Smaller, paler, but still mature males school with mature females. They may fertilize eggs but do not guard them. There are various figures for fecundity, ranging from 3,700-43,000 eggs per season. Females may spawn twice per season. Larvae and juveniles are pelagic and have been found as much as 500 miles offshore. Fishes, particularly walleye pollock and sandlances, and krill are the big foods for this species.

FISHERY: Atkas are occasionally taken by recreational fishermen. They are a moderately important commercial species, taken primarily by trawls off North America and by purse seines, gillnets and hook and line off Asia. Most of the North American commercial catch is made around the Aleutian Islands, Alaska. A sharp decline in population was noted in the late 1970s, perhaps due to a large Soviet fishery.

LONGSPINE COMBFISH (ZANIOLEPIS LATIPINNIS) AND SHORTSPINE COMBFISH (ZANIOLEPIS FRENATA)

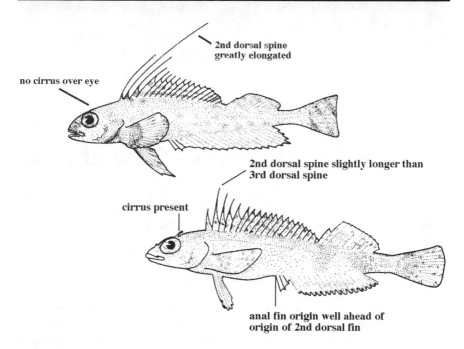

no cirrus over eye

2nd dorsal spine greatly elongated

2nd dorsal spine slightly longer than 3rd dorsal spine

cirrus present

anal fin origin well ahead of origin of 2nd dorsal fin

NAMES: *Zaniolepis* is formed from the Greek words forming "comb scales"; *latipinnis* is Greek for "broad fin"; *frenata* is Latin for "bridled."

IDENTIFYING CHARACTERS: Both species are very slender and elongated, with tiny scales that give them a slightly rough feeling. As the name implies, longspines have a long dorsal spine (number 2, to be precise), shortspines don't.

DISTRIBUTION AND BIOLOGY: Longspines are known from Vancouver Island, British Columbia to Bahia Tortugas, central Baja California; shortspines from southern Oregon to Bahia San Cristobal, central Baja California. Both species are found over sand or other soft substrates and both species spend most of their time lying on the bottom. Longspines have been taken from 24-1,380 feet of water, while shortspines are known from 24-3,168 feet.

Longspines grow to 1 foot, shortspines reach 10 inches. Females of both species are oviparous and the eggs are demersal. Longspine females spawn in the fall and winter. Overall, most combfish larvae (both species combined) are found from October to April. Based on sort of limited numbers of larvae, southern California harbors the heaviest concentrations of combfishes along the Pacific coast. Most larvae are found within 50 miles of the coast. Gammarid amphiphods, copepods, fishes and worms are the big food items for longspines; gammarid amphipods, isopods, worms, mysid shrimps and other small prey are favored by shortspines.

FISHERY: No.

REMARKS: Both species curl up when captured.

Sculpins – Family Cottidae

SCALYHEAD SCULPIN (ARTEDIUS HARRINGTONI)

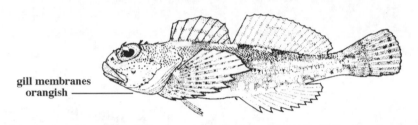

gill membranes orangish

NAMES: *Artedius* is for Petrus Artedi (see *A. lateralis* below); and here is the derivation of *harringtoni*, as stated by its describer, Edwin C. Starks, in 1896, "I take pleasure in naming this species for President Mark Walrod Harrington of the University of Washington." Whoa, E. C., a little kissing up to the Prez, eh?

IDENTIFYING CHARACTERS: Look, I'll level with you. I can't tell most sculpins apart and it would be the height of hubris for me to pretend that I can. (Not that I wouldn't indulge in that if I could get away with it.) If I have to key one out I go to Bill Eschmeyer's *A Field Guide to Pacific Coast Fishes of North America* (Houghton Mifflin, 1983) and you should too. But here's an interesting tidbit not mentioned by Bill, from Ragland and Fischer (Copeia, 1984, p. 1059-1063): "During the breeding season, males have a bright orange branchiostegal membrane, red-brown spots inside the mouth and a brown anal fin with small yellowish-white spots that resemble [scalyhead] eggs in color, shape and size."

DISTRIBUTION AND BIOLOGY: Scalyheads have been taken from Kodiak Island, Alaska to southern California. While they live down to at least 231 feet, they are common in both the intertidal and subtidal. In some areas, such as in the kelp beds of Barkley Sound, British Columbia, scalyheads are one of the most common benthic species. In the San Juan Archipelago, Puget Sound, they (with longfin sculpin) may be one of the few sculpins common in the subtidal kelp-rock habitat. In Puget Sound, subtidal scalyheads prefer living around clumps of giant acorn barnacles or over cobble. Scalyheads prefer living within the barnacle clusters and in the recesses of the cobble.

Scalyheads reach 4 inches and probably live at least 2 years. Females are mature at about 2 inches, and probably when one year old. Females are oviparous and fertilization is internal. Spawning occurs from December to late April in Puget Sound. Females probably produce more than one egg clutch per season. Males guard nests, often containing several egg masses. Eggs hatch in 11-18 days. Scalyheads search for food over a fairly small area, perhaps 3 feet by 3 feet. They tend to hide between rocks or barnacles and jump out at prey; gammarid and caprellid amphipods, crabs and shrimp are popular items. Copper rockfishes and pigeon guillemots have been seen eating them, but it is likely they also have other predators.

REMARKS: Collections made in a study of the fishes of the kelp beds of Barkley Sound, British Columbia showed a very strange pattern. Of the 485 scalyheads collected, 484 were female.

SMOOTHHEAD SCULPIN (ARTEDIUS LATERALIS)

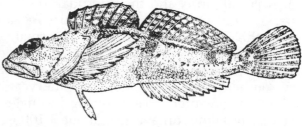

NAMES: *Artedius* is Petrus Artedi (a bud of Linnaeus), sometimes called the "Father of Ichthyology"; *lateralis* is Latin for "of the side," noting the scales on the sides.

IDENTIFYING CHARACTERS: See the *mea culpa* above, under scalyhead sculpin.

DISTRIBUTION AND BIOLOGY: Smoothheads are found from Kodiak Island, Alaska to northern Baja California, commonly from at least British Columbia to central California. They are common in the intertidal zone and shallow subtidal, down to 43 feet. In the intertidal, they are most abundant in the middle or lower zone. Limited studies show that they may have a strong homing instinct.

Smoothheads reach 5.5 inches and live to at least 3 years. They may mature in their first year, perhaps at about 1.5 inches. Females are oviparous and lay adhesive eggs on the underside of rocks. Spawning season is winter and spring in British Columbia and has been noted in June in Puget Sound. Eggs held at 61° F hatched in 11-12 days. Off Washington State, young ones recruit to the intertidal from June to October. Gammarid amphipods, isopods, fishes (such as pricklebacks, gunnels, sculpins and juvenile rockfishes), shrimps and crabs are commonly eaten.

ROUGHBACK SCULPIN (CHITONOTUS PUGETENSIS)

NAMES: *Chitonotus* is from the Greek for "tunic" and "back," referring to the dorsal saddle pattern; *pugetensis* come from Puget Sound, Washington, the site of its first capture.

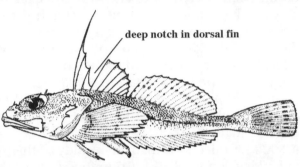

deep notch in dorsal fin

IDENTIFYING CHARACTERS: The backs and heads of roughbacks are almost completely covered by large scales. They have large, antlerlike spines on their cheeks, an elongated first dorsal spine and a deep notch between the third and fourth dorsal spines.

DISTRIBUTION AND BIOLOGY: Northern British Columbia to southern Baja California and the intertidal to 474 feet is home to this one. They live on, and reportedly bury in, sand.

Roughbacks grow to 9 inches. The smallest mature female in one study was 2.75 inches long. Females are oviparous and fertilization is internal. The eggs are adhesive and layed on the bottom. Off southern California, there is some year round spawning; it peaks in late winter to early spring. Females produce 3 clutches per year totalling, on average, about 3,100 eggs per year. In one study, the eggs hatched in 14 days at 54° F. This little bottom grubber eats crabs, shrimps and gammarid amphipods. In turn, it is probably eaten by a number of fishes, birds and sea mammals, but only pigeon guillemots have been identified.

SHARPNOSE SCULPIN (CLINOCOTTUS ACUTICEPS)

NAMES: *Clinocottus* is a combination of clinus, the kelp fishes, and cottus, an ancient word for a sculpin that lives in Europe; *acuticeps* is formed from 2 Latin words for "sharp head."

IDENTIFYING CHARACTERS: I don't know, this species just does not seem to have a particularly sharpnose compared to some other sculpins. Admittedly, it's head is not as round as some, but that's about as far as it goes. Probably better characters are the lack of scales on the body, the single spine on the preoperculum (cheek),

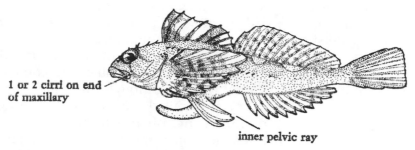

1 or 2 cirri on end
of maxillary

inner pelvic ray

the cirrus over each eye and the dark patch at the front end of the dorsal fin.

DISTRIBUTION AND BIOLOGY: Sharpnoses are found from the Bering Sea to off the Big Sur River, central California, commonly as far south as northern California. This one is mostly intertidal, often in the high intertidal, but it has been reported to 66 feet.

Tiny is our friend the sharpnose–2.5 inches is its length. Off British Columbia, spawning occurs from January-April. Females are oviparous, fertilization is internal and they lay circular, single layer egg masses in the high intertidal. Once laid, neither sex guards the eggs. In one study, nests contained from 18-98 amber or olive-green eggs. Sharpnose females select smooth rocks that are near marine plants, particularly *Fucus* and *Endocladia*. At low tide, the eggs are exposed to the air, but the fronds from the near-by plants flop over on them, protecting them from desiccation. Young sharpnose recruit to the intertidal from July-September along Washington shores. Gammarid amphipods, isopods and harpacticoid copepods are the most commonly eaten items.

WOOLLY SCULPIN (CLINOCOTTUS ANALIS)

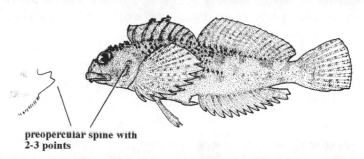

preopercular spine with
2-3 points

NAMES: *Clinocottus* is a combination of clinus, the kelp fishes, and cottus, an ancient word for a sculpin that lives in Europe; *analis* refers, in Latin, to the large papilla that is located near the anus.

IDENTIFYING CHARACTERS: Woollies are densely covered with cirri and prickles on backs, cirri on heads and 1–2 cirri at the rear of the upper jaw. The upper preopercular spine has 2–3 points. These little fish come in a variety of colors, ranging from gray-green to brown to reddish, with white, yellow or pink markings.

DISTRIBUTION AND BIOLOGY: Found from Cape Mendocino (northern California) to central Baja California, woollies are common from central California southward. Although they have been taken down to 60 feet, they are limited almost entirely to tide pools. They are the most abundant fish in southern California pools. At low tide, the youngest ones are found in the highest pools; as they grow, they seek deeper enclosures. Woollies live in a variety of rock pool habitats, including ones with bed rock, gravel and sandy bottoms. Youngsters are typically found in small, shallow pools with lots of coralline algae, while the big honkers are more casual about their living arrangements and frequently can be found in large open pools. With high tide, woollies move toward shore, usually occupying the most turbulent zone. They retreat to home pools as the tide ebbs, and exhibiting a good ability to home, return to the same pools day after day. Larger ones tend to stick to specific pools longer than smaller ones, and many fish seem to stay in the same general locality for weeks at a time. Woollies are capable of breathing air for a bit.

Woollies grow to 7 inches. A nearly 7-incher was at least 8 years old. Males appear to grow faster and larger and live longer than females. These sculpins mature at the end of their first year, at about 2.5 inches. Spawning occurs during all months and peaks from September–November. Females are oviparous, fertilization is internal, and they can store sperm in their bodies for up to 2 months. The eggs are layed in nests, but neither parent guards them. The eggs hatch in 13-18 days, depending on temperature. Young ones first appear in pools from November–May. This species eats a wide variety of food, with crustaceans (i.e., amphipods, copepods, isopods), algae, worms, chitons, snails and crabs high on the hit list.

REMARKS: The blood plasma of woolly sculpins is a deep green due to the presence of biliverdin, a chemical produced when hemoglobin degrades. Most animals quickly remove biliverdin from the blood, but for unknown reasons, this species does not.

MOSSHEAD SCULPIN (CLINOCOTTUS GLOBICEPS)

NAMES: *Clinocottus* is a combination of clinus, the kelp fishes, and cottus, an ancient word for a sculpin that lives in Europe; *globiceps* is Latin for "globe head."

IDENTIFYING CHARACTERS: I like mossheads because, for a smarmy

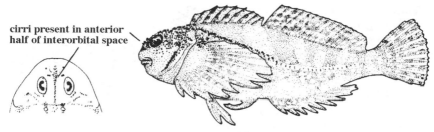

cirri present in anterior half of interorbital space

little sculpin, they are pretty easy to identify. They have a rounded, blunt head and a single, rounded preopercular (cheek) spine. Best of all, they have lots of cirri on their heads, between the eyes. Mossheads come in a wide range of colors, from solid black to reddish brown to olive-green. They often have irregular white patches or vertical bands.

DISTRIBUTION AND BIOLOGY: Mossheads live from Kodiak Island, Alaska to Gaviota, southern California. You can find lots of them from at least British Columbia to northern California. This is an intertidal species, found occasionally as much as 8 feet above zero tide level, but much more commonly in middle to lower zones. One study in Washington found they had a distinct preference for living in mussel beds and seemed to stay away from algal cover. Larger fish tend to be lower in the intertidal than smaller ones. Mossheads are most commonly found in high surf areas. They can breathe air for extensive periods. It appears that mossheads can return to specific tidepools, even if moved to other tidepools 30 feet or more away.

They grow to 7.5 inches and may live as long as 6 years. Females produce demersal eggs and it is likely they (the females, not the eggs) are oviparous. Young ones recruit to the intertidal from April to October. In a Washington State study, they ate a lot of algae (primarily greens, but also reds and browns), along with gammarid amphipods, ostracods, worms and other small animals.

BUFFALO SCULPIN (ENOPHRYS BISON)

NAMES: *Enophrys* is formed from 2 Greek words meaning "on" and "eyebrow," for the ridges over the eye; *bison* is, of course, the North American bison, referring to the horn-like spines on the head.

IDENTIFYING CHARACTERS: Buffalo sculpin are pretty easily identified by their very long upper preopercular (cheek) spine, the lowest cheek spine (near the jaw) points downward. These fish are scaleless except for a bunch of large, thick ones along the lateral line. Colors of these rather remarkable sculpins are black to green, often with 3 dark saddles across the back.

DISTRIBUTION AND BIOLOGY: Buffalos are found from Kodiak Island, Alaska to Monterey Bay, central California, from the intertidal to 743

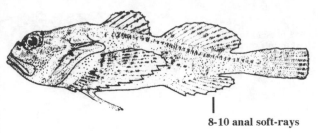

8-10 anal soft-rays

feet, often on rocks but also over sand.

This is a fairly large species reaching 14.5 inches. Females are oviparous, produce two egg batches per season and spawn from January to May. Females spawn about 19,000-32,000 eggs and lay multilayered egg masses in a roughly circular pattern on rocks or other hard surfaces, from the lower intertidal down to depths of at least 45 feet. Typically, females lay eggs in areas exposed to tidal currents. Ed Demartini, who did a lot of this reproductive stuff, noted that females laying their eggs on dock pilings placed them in the direction of the ferry boat propeller wash. Males probably spawn with more than one female per season, perhaps as many as 9 at a time. Males guard the nests until they hatch, as long as 39 days. Ed observed that eggs laid in really shallow waters were occasionally abandoned. Males sometimes fan the eggs with their pectoral fins and guard them against predation by such species as striped seaperch. Eggs exposed to the air at low tide may not be eaten very often. The eggs are brightly colored (purple, pink, yellow, orange, red and tan), perhaps implying that they are toxic (as are cabezon eggs). Buffalo sculpin seem to eat just about anything too slow to get out of the way. Shrimps, crabs, gammarid and caprellid amphipods, isopods, hydroids and algae are among the food items. They are eaten by harbor seals.

FISHERY: A common catch by nearshore recreational anglers, from northern California northward.

RED IRISH LORD (HEMILEPIDOTUS HEMILEPIDOTUS)

NAMES: *Hemilepidotus* is formed from 2 Greek words meaning "half scaled."

IDENTIFYING CHARACTERS: Two distinct scale bands help differentiate RILs from other sculpins. There are 2 major bands, one above the lateral line (4-5 rows wide) and one below the lateral line (up to 10 rows wide). They come in a variety of colors, often red, with black, white and brown spots and blotches mixed in (Plate 20). Males have black and white pelvic fins, females have white ones.

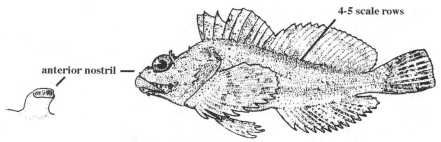

4-5 scale rows

anterior nostril —

DISTRIBUTION AND BIOLOGY: Found from Kamchatka, Russia to Monterey Bay, central California, from the intertidal to 908 feet. This is a fish of rocks, wharfs and other hard substrate.

RILs grow to 20 inches and live at least 6 years. They probably mature at around 4 years. Males are mature at a minimum of 8.5 inches and females at 11.5 inches. Adult RILs aggregate just before spawning season, males getting together first. Females tend to come into nesting areas shortly before spawning. It is likely that some males and females come back to the same area to spawn year after year. The Puget Sound spawning season is from October to January. Females lay pink eggs from the mid-intertidal to shallow subtidal on rocks and man-made structures. Females produce between about 59,000 and 126,000 eggs per year and probably spawn once per season. Males probably spawn more than once per season. Eggs masses are roughly circular. As with buffalo sculpin, females lay their eggs in higher current areas, mostly on reef crests or channel entrances receiving maximum wave and tidal action. While both females and males guard the eggs, females do it most of the time; laying on top or near them, but not fanning or cleaning them. While a single female is usually the only guard, occasionally a male (sometimes as many as 4) will help out, lounging a few inches to a few feet away. These appear to be "backup" guards; if the female is removed, one of the males fills the breach. Guards may occasionally leave the nests, perhaps to feed. Striped seaperch and small sculpins have been seen nabbing unguarded eggs. Eggs take 22-26 days to hatch. Though they are not particularly active at night while guarding eggs, during much of the year RILs may be nocturnal feeders. Benthic crustaceans, including hermit crabs and tanner crabs, are important food items; shrimps, worms and fishes are other occasional prey.

FISHERY: RILs are commonly taken by recreational anglers from Oregon northwards, and occasionally off northern California.

YELLOWCHIN SCULPIN (ICELINUS QUADRISERIATUS)

NAMES: *Icelinus* is the slightly distorted name of the Greek god of sleep, a reference to the slow moving nature of these fishes; *quadriseriatus* means "4-rowed" in Latin, probably from the 4 rows of scales (2 on each side).

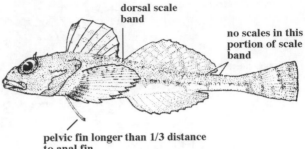

dorsal scale band

no scales in this portion of scale band

pelvic fin longer than 1/3 distance to anal fin

IDENTIFYING CHARACTERS: These are perky little fishes, with a double row of scales on their sides running from near the beginning of their dorsal fins to their tails. When you catch one, they flare out their cheek spines, making it difficult to pry them free of the net. Males have bright yellow chins.

DISTRIBUTION AND BIOLOGY: Found from Sonoma County, northern California to southern Baja California, they occasionally live in the intertidal, more commonly in somewhat deeper water, to 660 feet. We commonly take them in otter trawls off southern California.

They are pretty small; 3.5 inches is the record. Not much is known about them. The smallest mature female on record was 2.5 inches long. Females are oviparous and produce about 850 eggs per average female per year. They probably spawn throughout the year, peaking from late winter to early spring. Females produce perhaps 3 clutches per year. Gammarid amphipods, worms, shrimps and fishes make up much of their diet.

REMARKS: Yellowchins make a buzzing sound and distinctive vibration when picked up. Could this be an anti-predator response?

LONGFIN SCULPIN (JORDANIA ZONOPE)

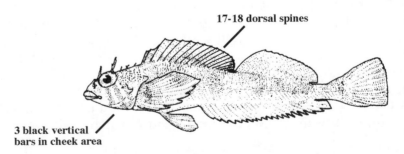

17-18 dorsal spines

3 black vertical bars in cheek area

NAMES: *Jordania* honors, yet again, David S. Jordan, the Big Kahuna of ichthyology in the late 19th and early 20th Century; *zonope* is formed from 2 Greek words meaning "zone window," referring, albeit rather obscurely, to the banded eyes.

IDENTIFYING CHARACTERS: This one is long and slender, with long dorsal and anal fins, scales covering the body above the lateral line and plate-like scales below the line. Also, look for the 3 dark bars under the eye.

DISTRIBUTION AND BIOLOGY: Longfins live from Baranof Island, southeast Alaska to Diablo Canyon, central California. While they have been taken from the intertidal to 126 feet, they are common in shallow subtidal waters, often on steeply sloping or vertical rock faces. Along with the scalyhead sculpin, this is the most common species among subtidal kelp and rocks in the San Juan Islands, Puget Sound. Also like scalyheads, longfins are most abundant around giant acorn barnacles and over cobble. Longfins tend to live on the fringes of the barnacle masses and on the exposed cobble surfaces. These fish are highly territorial against both their own species and such others as scalyhead sculpins.

Longfins grow to 6 inches and live to 5 years. Females guard egg nests. Considering their size, longfins tend to search out prey over a relatively large area, as much as 30 feet by 30 feet. Longfins are visual feeders: they sight a prey, slowly "walk" toward it on pectoral and pelvic fins, then grab it in a short burst. Gammarid and caprellid amphipods, shrimps, crabs, worms, isopods and nudibranchs are all eaten. One study noted that these small fish will even go after shrimps their own size. When one attacks a shrimp, other longfins, and sometimes scalyhead sculpins, join in. Not much is known about their predators; they are eaten by smoothhead sculpins.

PACIFIC STAGHORN SCULPIN (LEPTOCOTTUS ARMATUS)

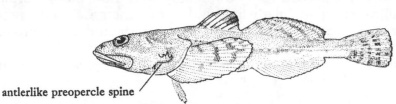

antlerlike preopercle spine

NAME: Bullhead, Kajika-Rui (Japanese). *Leptocottus* is formed from 2 Greek words which mean "slender cottus" (cottus is an ancient word for a European sculpin); *armatus,* Latin for "armed," refers to the spines on the gill covers.

IDENTIFYING CHARACTERS: Staghorns are relatively large, green-brown or gray fish, with flattened heads and long, branching cheek spines.

DISTRIBUTION AND BIOLOGY: Staghorns are found from the southern Bering Sea to north-central Baja California, usually in shallow water, but occasionally as deep as 906 feet. Sitting on the bottom and waiting for a meal to come by, they are most common in the sand or mud of bays and estuaries. Very young ones are found in the lower parts of streams and larger ones in protected ocean environments. These are aggregating animals; where you find one, you usually find a bunch. Recently hatched fish often recruit into fresh water for a short time, moving into more saline conditions by about 3 months of age. In estuaries and marshes, staghorns follow the tides, coming onto mudflats at high tide to feed. Not having accurate time pieces, the little bozos sometimes find themselves stranded on the flats. When this unfortunate event occurs, the sculpins bury themselves in the mud and await the next tide. Fortunately, staghorn can breath air. Unfortunately, blue herons, which eat large quantities of staghorns, can search out buried ones, apparently with ease. There must be a moral here somewhere.

Staghorns grow to 1.5 feet (a 10-incher is about 3 years old), mature at about 1 year old (5 inches) and live to the ripe old age of 10. Spawning occurs in bays and perhaps in the open ocean–in California from October-March, peaking in January and February. Females are oviparous and produce between 2,000-11,000 eggs. Though a complete study has not been done, males may protect the eggs after they are laid. Eggs hatch in 9-14 days and young ones recruit to fresh waters at lengths of .75-1.0 inch. Staghorns are feeding generalists. They eat shrimps, worms, crabs, gammarid amphipods, clam siphons and whatever else is available. Besides being eaten by the aforementioned blue herons, loons, cormorants (pelagic, Brandt's, double-crested), least terns and harbor seals also get in on the act.

FISHERY: Staghorns are very commonly taken from piers, shore and small vessels, particularly in bays, from southern California northward. They are used extensively for bait, primarily by striped bass fishermen.

REMARKS: Lots of staghorn remains have been found in Native American middens from Puget Sound.

TIDEPOOL SCULPIN (OLIGOCOTTUS MACULOSUS)

NAMES: *Oligocottus* is formed from the Greek words for "small" and "cottus," an ancient word for a European sculpin; *maculosus* is Latin for "spotted."

IDENTIFYING CHARACTERS: First of all, tidepools have no scales, an excellent beginning. They have a single preopercular (cheek)

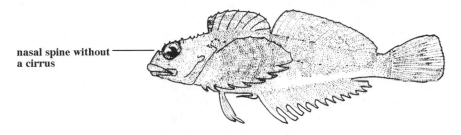

nasal spine without
a cirrus

spine and it is usually forked, but occasionally is cleaved in thirds. In males, the first 3-4 rays of the anal fin are extra large. This species comes in a wide range of colors, including gray, green, brown, and 2-5 saddles or vertical bands are usually present. Then there may be a wide range of white, tan, pink, green, brown or black speckles.

DISTRIBUTION AND BIOLOGY: Found from the Sea of Okhotsk, Russia and the Bering Sea southward to Los Angeles County, southern California, this one is abundant from British Columbia to central California. It is widely distributed throughout the intertidal, most commonly in the middle and upper zones. Wave action seems to be an important factor. Where waves are heavy, this fish seems to favor the high intertidal, away from the brunt of the combers. Younger ones tend to be found in higher pools, older ones in both higher and lower pools. While it does inhabit pools with lots of algae, it is also found in relatively open ones, and even on open sandy areas of some pools. Jeff Marliave of the Vancouver Aquarium notes that tidepool sculpins are also quite abundant on fjord beaches, where they are routinely stranded under logs or rocks at low tide.

Tidepools are able to withstand large changes in temperature, and they can live in waters at least as cold as 33° F, the winter temperatures in upper pools. Many larger individuals remain in the same pools for extensive periods, perhaps a year or more. Experiments show that tidepools, particularly middle-sized, middle-aged ones (2 years) have a strong ability to home. If they are removed from home pools and placed even as much as 100 yards away, they are quite successful at returning to their favorite haunts. How do they find their way back? One clever study, by II. W. Khoo, found that these little ones may use their sense of smell to sniff their way home. They have some ability to breathe air.

Yet another small sculpin, this one grows to 3.5 inches. Though there is some question about this, they may live as long as 5 years, certainly as long as 3 years. Tidepools mature at 1 year. Females are oviparous, lay adhesive eggs in the intertidal zone and may lay as many as 3 egg batches per season. Spawning season in Puget

Sound is from April to July. Fertilization is internal and adults do not guard eggs after they are laid. They really like gammarid amphipods, isopods, shrimps, copepods and worms.

REMARKS: In another clever study, M. A. Chotkowski showed that tidepool sculpins can detect kelp greenlings (a potential predator) by smell. Aquarium-held sculpins exposed to water that had previously contained a kelp greenling reduced their activity levels and were more likely to seek shelter. There was some evidence that sculpins in tidepools tended to leave the pools when kelp-greenling water was introduced.

Will the clever tidepool sculpin studies never end? D. M. Hugie, et al. (*Ethology*, 1991, p. 322-334) report that chemicals from injured tidepool sculpins cause nearby members of the same species to decrease movement and feeding rates and to search for cover.

Here is yet another snazzy observation, by the man I like to call Mr. Marliave, for that is his name. Jeff states that tidepool sculpin eggs laid on wave-exposed areas tend to be "burgundy," while those in more protected areas are green. Don't even think about writing: I don't know and neither does Jeff.

FLUFFY SCULPIN (OLIGOCOTTUS SNYDERI)

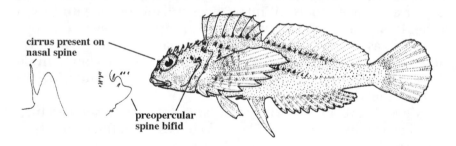

cirrus present on nasal spine

preopercular spine bifid

NAMES: *Oligocottus* comes from the Greek words "small" and "cottus," an ancient word for a European sculpin; *snyderi* honors J. O. Snyder, curator of fishes at Stanford U. (long, long ago, when it was Leland Stanford Junior University).

IDENTIFYING CHARACTERS: Like several other members of this genus, fluffies have smooth bodies, without scales or prickles. Look for the forked preopercular (cheek) spine and the cirri along the base of the dorsal fin and along the lateral line. Fluffies seem to be able to change color in response to their environment. There are two main color morphs, bright green and red, but they may also come in lavender, pink, orange or other colors.

DISTRIBUTION AND BIOLOGY: Fluffies are found from Sitka, Alaska to northern Baja California (they are very abundant from central

California to British Columbia), always around rocks and algae. They are common in the middle and lower intertidal zone, and very occasionally in the shallow subtidal, primarily in areas of heavy algal cover, such as eelgrass (*Phyllospadix*) beds. Water temperature is a very big factor in how high in the intertidal you will find fluffies. They don't like it hot, and this prevents them from occupying the highest tide pools. Fluffies probably occupy a "home range" comprised of several adjacent pools. And, based on pretty neat research, fluffies are very fond of their home turf. If transported away from their familiar pools, they will often swim back; larger ones are better at it than smaller ones. In one experiment, fluffies were deposited in pools 150-200 feet away from their pools and had to swim across a large expanse of sandy bottom to reach home. A number of individuals succeeded. Fluffies can breathe air.

Fluffies reach 3.5 inches and probably live about 1.5 years. They may mature before their first birthday. What I am about to say may not be proper for impressionable youths, and I don't want some Congressperson from Happy Skunk, South Carolina, going ballistic on me and taking me to task on the Floor of the House. So, if you are under 18 years, please close your eyes. Are your eyes closed? Are you sure? Okay, for the adults in the audience, I should let you know that male fluffies have a well-developed penis and fertilization is internal. Okay, you can open your eyes now. Females are oviparous and lay eggs on the substrate. Off northern California, they have a long spawning season, at least October-May and possibly June. Females probably spawn more than once per season, and it is possible that neither males or females guard the eggs after they are laid. Young-of-the-year first appear in shallow waters in spring, probably peaking in the summer. Fluffies eat a variety of small organisms, including gammarid amphipods, polychaete worms, shrimps, isopods and copepods.

REMARKS: Here's more on fluffy sex, so all you young'uns close your eyes again. The first anal fin ray of males is very long and actually prehensile. During copulation, the male reaches around the female and holds her close with this fin ray. Pretty amazing, yes?

Okay, open your eyes.

GRUNT SCULPIN (RHAMPHOCOTTUS RICHARDSONI)

NAMES: *Rhamphocottus* is Greek for "snout" and "cottus", an ancient word for a European sculpin; *richardsoni* honors John Richardson, a naturalist and explorer.

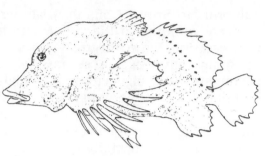

IDENTIFYING CHARAC-
TERS: They are sooooo
cute. Gosh, are they
cute. A short, deep body,
pointed snout and lots
of body prickles are good
things to look for. These
guys are colored like a
tropical species. The base
body color is cream or tan, but they have streaks of brown. The
big tip-off is the bright red streak on the caudal peduncle.

DISTRIBUTION AND BIOLOGY: These are primarily shallow subtidal
sculpins, but they have been taken from the intertidal down to
540 feet. Look for their little, pointed schnozes sticking out of
crevices.

Grunt sculpins reach 3.25 inches. In an aquarium, grunties
matured at 2 years. Females are oviparous and seem to prefer to
lay eggs in dead barnacle shells. Spawning takes place from fall to
spring. Males are the primary nest guarders, though the female
takes over if the male is indisposed. The definitely coolest story
about them was told to me by Jeff Marliave, the maven of little
fish ecology at the Vancouver Aquarium. When a larval grunt
sculpin is about to break out of the egg, the guarding parent lifts
it up in its mouth, swims into the water column and spits it out.
This breaks the egg shell, sending the larva on its way. This helps
prevent the larva from hatching near the substrate, where it is
more likely to be snarfed by a predator. Grunties eat such crustaceans as crabs and shrimps. Among their predators are pigeon
guillemots.

REMARKS: This one is for devoted reader Susan Crane. She took me
to task for not including this cutie in the first edition.

Another over-emotional statement from Jordan and Evermann,
1898, *The Fishes of North and Middle America*: "A most singular
fish."

CABEZON (SCORPAENICHTHYS MARMORATUS)

NAMES: Marbled Sculpin. *Scorpaenichthys* is formed from 2 Greek
words meaning "scorpaena fish," probably referring to this
species' resemblance to scorpionfish, genus *Scorpaena*; *marmoratus*
is Latin for "marbled."

IDENTIFYING CHARACTERS: Cabezon are large, scaleless, brown, red
or green sculpins covered with darker mottling (Plate 22). They
have a flap of skin on their snouts and long, branched flaps over

each eye. Ninety-two percent of adult males are reddish and 97% of adult females are green. Juveniles are occasionally bright red.

DISTRIBUTION AND BIOLOGY: Found from Sitka, Alaska southward to central Baja California, cabezon are abundant from Washington into southern California. They are hard-bottom dwellers, found over natural and artificial reefs, oil platforms (they like the crossbeams) and wrecks. Although you generally see these fish sitting on the bottom, often in crevices, they occasionally venture up into the kelp canopy. Living from the intertidal to 362-foot depths, they are most common down to about 90 feet. Cabezon seem to be sedentary fish, living on the same reef for extensive periods.

These fish reach 30 inches and live to more than 13 years. A 12-incher is about 2 years old, while a 2-footer is about 9. Females live longer and grow larger and faster than males. Males mature at 2-3 years of age and females at 3-5 years. Females are oviparous and produce 49,000-98,000 eggs per season; they may spawn twice in that time. Off California, spawning may occur at low levels throughout the year, but it probably peaks from October-April. In Puget Sound, it's from November-September, peaking in March-April. Nests are made on exposed surfaces of rocks and may measure as much as 18 inches across. These fish occasionally nest in the intertidal, and the eggs (which have been described as red, maroon, green, or amber) may be exposed at low tide. Nests have been seen from the intertidal down to depths of 55 feet, and the same nesting sites are used each year. Males guard the eggs until they hatch. Off California and Baja California, larvae have been noted as far south as southern Baja, but the largest concentrations occurred off central California. Few larvae are seen more than 50 miles from the coast. Young, pelagic cabezon are silvery and are surprisingly common underneath drifting kelp mats. Beginning in March, young-of-the-year about 2 inches in length recruit from the plankton into tide pools; most leave before they mature. However, large fish will enter pools at high tide to feed. Small fish in tide pools eat such small crustaceans as amphipods, shrimp, crabs and isopods. Adults feed heavily on crabs, followed by fishes, abalone, chitons, octopi and the like. What is really neat about these guys is their ability to knock abalone off rocks (we don't know how), eat them whole, then spit out the shell at their leisure. Cabezon are eaten by sea otters, pigeon guillemots, least terns and Brandt's cormorants.

FISHERY: The cabezon is an important sport fish throughout much of its range. Because it primarily inhabits shallow water, it is most commonly taken by rocky shore and pier fishermen, although larger fish are most often bagged by party and private vessel sport fishermen and divers. Despite their blue flesh, which scares away the more timid fish buyer, there is a small but consistent commercial market for these guys. Most of the catch is made incidental to fishing for other species and occurs by trap, gillnet and hook and line.

REMARKS: The eggs of cabezon are poisonous, not only to humans but also to many other mammals and birds. Carl and Laura Hubbs (famed ichthyologist, and famed wife of famed ichthyologist, respectively) became quite ill after dining on cabezon roe in the 1920s. "An unhappy gastronomic experience" is the way Dr. Hubbs put it. And, as it led to the two Hubbs being "violently ill throughout the rest of the night, with rapidly alternating chills and fever and with frequent vomiting and diarrhea," it seems like a reasonable description to me. That's how I felt after the 1980 U.S. presidential election. This may explain why cabezon can lay their eggs in very shallow water, where they are exposed to the air at low tide, without minks, raccoons, crows, etc. eating the roe.

Kids, don't try this at home. When injected into small rodents, the toxic substance in cabezon eggs is lethal in 18-48 hours.

The blue color of cabezon flesh is harmless and disappears when the meat is cooked. The color may come from copper–based compounds in the shellfish they consume.

Cabezon remains are common in Native American middens.

MANACLED SCULPIN (SYNCHIRUS GILLI)

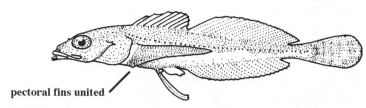

pectoral fins united

NAMES: *Synchirus* is from the Greek for "together hand," referring to fused pectoral fins; *gilli* is after Theodore Gill, an old-time stud in rockfish research.

IDENTIFYING CHARACTERS: These sculpins are easy to identify. They are the only ones on this coast that have their pectoral fins fused across the belly. Both sexes are olive-green to brown and males have a prominent silvery stripe along their sides. Both sexes have pale blotches on the back.

DISTRIBUTION AND BIOLOGY: Prince William Sound, Alaska to San Miguel Island, southern California, in intertidal and shallow subtidal waters is home to these animals. They live on both giant and bull kelp, as well as other lower-lying algae.

Manacleds reach 2.75 inches and may mature at about 1.5 inches. Females are oviparous and lay egg masses (15-20 eggs per mass) on *Laminaria* and other algae. Spawning season is January-April off British Columbia. Manacled sculpins have internal fertilization and it is possible that neither parent protects the eggs after they are layed. Males have a relatively large penis. During mating, a male holds on to a female crossways in mid-body, with his lower jaw around the female's dorsal fin and his fused pelvics glomming on to her belly region. The male has a curved lower jaw, complete with a wrinkled pad. Both aid in holding on to the wet female. So tight is a male's grip that mating couples can be picked up out of the water for a few seconds before they disengage. R. Krejsa, the voyeur who first noted all of this, also commented that the male of one forcibly separated pair tried to mate with his right index finger. I can certainly relate to that. Gammarid amphipods and isopods seem to be eaten with some regularity.

Striped Basses and Relatives - Family Moronidae

STRIPED BASS (MORONE SAXATILIS)

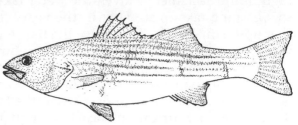

NAMES: Bar d'Amérique (French). When Mitchill first created the genus *Morone*, in 1814, he neglected to explain what the name meant; *sax-atilis* means "living among rocks" in Latin.

IDENTIFYING CHARACTERS: Stripers are usually greenish on backs and silvery on sides, with 6-9 black stripes on flanks. On our coast, small stripers might possibly be confused with salemas, which have orange-brown stripes.

DISTRIBUTION AND BIOLOGY: Along the Pacific Coast, stripers are found from Barkley Sound, British Columbia to Ensenada, northern Baja California. They also abound along the east coast of North America. These bass are anadromous; they hatch in rivers and spend most of their lives in estuaries, bays and coastal waters, and return to spawn at maturity. On our coast, the vast majority of striped bass live either in San Pablo and San Francisco Bays or just outside these enclosures along the shallow, open coast. Almost all the rest live between Monterey Bay (central California) and southern Oregon, although every year a few fish are taken as far south as Morro Bay. Spawning occurs in rivers between the Sacramento–San Joaquin complex and the Siuslaw in Oregon. These are schooling fish, found in shallow water throughout the water column. While some individuals wander along the coast, most appear to stay in or near their home river and estuary system.

Stripers reach 4 feet in length along our coast and 6 feet in the Atlantic; they probably live longer than 30 years. Females live longer and grow faster and larger than males. A 1-year-old is 5–6 inches, a 2-year-old is maybe 13 or 14 inches and a 4-year-old is a hefty 22 inches. A few males mature at one year, most at 2–3 years. Females are slower on the uptake and most mature when 4–6 years old. In a study of stripers off Oregon, a fair number were found to be hermaphrodites, fish having both male and female sexual organs. While this had been noted in San Francisco Bay fish, the percentage of hermaphrodites in Oregon was considerably higher. *What are you people putting in your water?* Spawning occurs in rivers during the spring, from April to June, peaking in May and early June. Water temperatures are a critical factor in striper spawning. The fish aren't in the mood until it gets up to 58° F and they really prefer 60–68° water. For more on reproduction we turn to Peter Moyle's really admirable book *Inland Fishes of California* (University of California Press): "When flows are high in the Sacramento River, the water takes longer to warm up so spawning takes place later in the year. It also takes place further upstream than is usual, since the bass migrate upstream while waiting for temperatures to rise. When flows are high in the San Joaquin portion of the Delta, spawning may actually occur further downstream than usual, since the salt water is pushed further downstream. Years of high flow when the large volume of runoff dilutes the salty, irrigation waste water that normally makes up much of the river's flow, are virtually the only time when successful spawning occurs in the San Joaquin River upstream from the Delta."

There are two main spawning areas in the Delta: the Sacramento River from about Sacramento City upstream to Colusa and the San Joaquin River from Venice Island down to Antioch. Stripers spawn in large groups near the surface, usually as light begins to fade in the late afternoon and early evening. Females are oviparous and produce 11,000–2,000,000 eggs per year. The eggs hatch in around 2 days, and both eggs and larvae concentrate near the bottom. In the Sacramento–San Joaquin complex, eggs and larvae are carried downstream into the estuarine waters of Suisin Bay and the lower Delta. Juvenile stripers eat plankton and small fish. As the fish grow, they feed more and more on fish, with invertebrates decreasing in importance.

FISHERY: In California, striped bass are reserved for sport fishermen, who avidly search them out. Most of the fishery takes place in San Pablo and San Francisco Bays and surrounding environs, from boats and from shore. A fairly large number of these fish are also taken by pier anglers in the Bay. In 1935, the commercial fishery for stripers was closed in California; Oregon followed suit in 1976. The Oregon fishery was located primarily in the tidal regions of the Coos and Umpqua Rivers, where gill netters took both stripers and shad. The current law allows shad to be taken in these waters; the gill netters use netting strong enough to hold shad but which will break if a striper gets into it.

REMARKS: Striped bass are an introduced species, planted in the Sacramento–San Joaquin Delta in 1879 and 1882, and they have done very well for themselves in the Golden State. Within 25 years of introduction, the species was a major commercial target and had spread into southern Oregon. For truly insightful comments on introducing species, please see my remarks under American Shad.

Since the 1960s, the striped bass population in the San Francisco Bay region has really declined, and a number of truly creative and probably not very important reasons have been offered. One explanation that seems to have merit comes from California Fish and Game studies from the 1960s and 70s. This research found that a major factor in striped bass survival was summer river water flow levels in the Delta. The more water passing through the Delta, the more larval fish live to become juveniles. What may be more crucial is the percent of the water that is directed out of the river, versus how much is allowed to flow to the Bay. A reasonable explanation, one which is politically unappetizing, is that each year millions of gallons of water, along with zillions of larval striped bass, are unceremoniously sucked up and transported into the Delta, San Joaquin Valley and points south. In years with relatively low water flow, proportionately more water is sucked up and larval bass have less chance to make it to their nursery grounds. Possible solutions, such as not pumping when little striped bass are around or just not directing as much water away from the Delta, are considered treasonous, blasphemous and fattening by some elements of the political establishment in Sacramento.

Striped bass were planted in Newport Bay from 1974 to 1977. A study in the late 1970s showed that, although some of the fish had survived and were living in the Bay, they were not reproducing and appeared to be in relatively poor condition.

The red "strawberry" marks or lesions often seen on the right sides of striped bass are caused by a parasite. Adults of the tapeworm *Lacistorhynchus tenuis* live in sharks, such as the leopard shark. The eggs of the worm are eaten by small crustaceans, in which the worm becomes a larvae. The crustaceans, with the worm larvae inside, are then eaten by striped bass. The worm larvae penetrate the intestinal walls of the fish and lodge in the muscle and other areas, where they die. If large numbers of these dead worms are near each other, the bass's immune system encircles them with a tissue "raft." If this raft touches the wall of the body cavity, it causes an inflammation and the red area noted on the outside of the fish.

Wreckfishes - Family Polyprionidae

GIANT SEA BASS (STEREOLEPIS GIGAS)

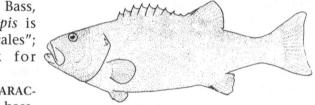

NAMES: Black Sea Bass, Jewfish. *Stereolepis* is Greek for "firm scales"; *gigas* is Greek for "giant."

IDENTIFYING CHARACTERS: These are bass-shaped fish, which when given the time, reach truly gargantuan sizes. Young ones, in the few inch range, are perch-shaped, red with black spots, have huge pectoral fins and are just the cutest little devils. By the time the fish are maybe 9 inches or a foot long, they have elongated and are brown with black spots, turning gray or dark brown as adults.

DISTRIBUTION AND BIOLOGY: Giant sea bass have been reported from Humboldt Bay, northern California to the Gulf of California, from depths of 18 to at least 150 feet. Before this species was overfished, it was common from Pt. Conception southward, particularly along the Baja California coast and throughout the Gulf of California. In southern California, fair numbers can still be found around the offshore islands as far west as Santa Rosa, and occasionally along the coast (particularly smaller individuals). These fish are usually bottom dwellers, though they will come into the midwater or even to the surface when searching for food. At Santa

Cruz Island, I had one just about come out of the water chasing after a sheephead I had hooked. Where abundant, giant sea bass are usually found in small groups of up to 10 individuals. While researching sandy bottom fish off southern California, I have taken a number of very small ones (2–6 inches) in 18–30 feet, usually in areas where drifting kelp littered the bottom. Juveniles to about 50 pounds are often found over hard bottom, often in pretty shallow water (perhaps as deep as 100 feet). A typical area is off the foot of Sunset Boulevard in Santa Monica Bay. Here a mixture of boulders and sand flats, with some low–growing algae attached, seem to attract larger juveniles. Adults are usually found over high relief (over rocky reefs, and on the outer margins of kelp beds) from 100 feet down.

The largest giant sea bass on record was 7.4 feet long. The oldest fish was about 75 years old, but it is likely they get older. A 7-footer which was found beached at San Clemente weighted 539 pounds. The fish are reported to mature at 11–13 years, at 50–60 pounds. Spawning occurs primarily from July to September. A 320 pound female contained 60 million eggs. These guys eat fishes of all sorts, along with spiny lobsters, rock crabs and squids. A stingray sting was found in the swim bladder of one fish, having worked its way out of the stomach of the animal. Giant sea bass are very fast over a short course and routinely run down bonito.

FISHERY: Until recently, giant sea bass were a very desirable sport fish, taken aboard party and private vessels, primarily around the offshore islands of southern California and southward. Due to severe overfishing, it is now illegal for sport fishermen to keep any giant sea bass; all must be returned. The fish tend to float if cranked out of more than about 60 feet, since the gas in their swim bladders expands and acts as a floatation device. When this occurs, it may be necessary to deflate the swim bladder with a syringe or sharp knife by inserting the instrument along the fish's flanks, ideally just behind the point where the pectoral fin meets the body. Commercial fishermen take sea bass in gillnets; it would be preferable if they also released any living fish.

REMARKS: Giant sea bass populations have been severely knocked down throughout much of the species' range, even into the Gulf of California. It would be nice (although hardly likely) if all fish were released. They do seem to be making a comeback, thanks to some good survival of little ones and stricter game laws.

Oh, where is C. F. Holder now that we really need him? Holder, a tireless promoter of southern California at turn of the century, wrote a number of books about fishing around the Channel Islands. I just can't get enough of that remarkably purple prose. Here he describes fishing for black sea bass off Catalina (*The*

Channel Islands of California, 1910, Hodder and Stoughton). "Like the charge of the Furies it strikes you...From absolute quiet the angler is hurled into a maelstrom of excitement. That unknown, unseen fish has headed out to sea for a deeper haunt where the long, snake-like kelp vines coil and writhe in the blue Kuro Shiwo as it sweeps down the island shores." Nice, huh?

Sea Basses and Groupers - Family Serranidae

KELP BASS (PARALABRAX CLATHRATUS)

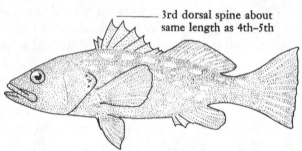

3rd dorsal spine about same length as 4th–5th

NAMES: Bull Bass (big ones), Calico Bass, Cabrilla (Mexico). *Paralabrax* comes from 2 Greek words meaning "near Labrax," (Labrax is a name of a bass in Europe); *clathratus* is Greek, referring to the lattice-like markings on the sides.

IDENTIFYING CHARACTERS: These are handsome fish (Plate 18), brown, gray-brown or olive on backs and sides, alternating with pale blotches (hence the name "calico"); the colors are much more vibrant in small fish. Some breeding males, usually the smaller ones, have bright yellow snouts and chins. Barred sand bass are gray or greenish-brown, usually with freckles on their snouts; their third dorsal spine is much longer than the fourth (unlike in kelp bass). Olive rockfish have spines on their cheeks; kelp bass have a row of fine serrations.

DISTRIBUTION AND BIOLOGY: Kelp bass occur from the mouth of the Columbia River (Washington) to southern Baja California. Although they are most abundant from Pt. Conception southward, they are taken in some numbers as far north as Monterey Bay during warm water periods. Kelp bass love to live around structure and almost any kind of stuff will do. Kelp, rocks, sewer pipes and oil platforms, it hardly matters. The most interesting question is whether kelp bass require kelp at all. The answer seems to be a resounding "probably not." True, little kelp bass are very abundant in the kelp beds off much of southern California. However, they may also be extremely common where kelp does not grow, say along the breakwater of King Harbor, Redondo Beach, California. What seems to be happening is that larval kelp bass, drifting along in the plankton, seem to prefer to settle out where there is a lot of structure. Kelp plants, one end anchored on the bottom and the other floating on the surface, provide a lot of structure for a larval kelp bass to find. The plants probably act as giant sieves, "straining" larvae out of the water. But larval kelp bass will also settle out in bottom algae, which can be abundant in areas without any kelp at all. Actually, my friend Mark has shown that these larvae will even settle out on plastic plants, if the plants are placed near the surface, where larvae are likely to be.

You can find kelp bass as solitary individuals, morosely hanging around reefs; in small, loose aggregations, morosely hanging around reefs; or, during breeding season, in large, fairly compact schools, morosely hanging around reefs. Living from very shallow subtidal waters to depths of at least 200 feet, they are most abundant in 10–70 feet and will come out of the water when chasing food. Do kelp bass migrate? Well, it sort of depends on whom you ask. A California Department of Fish and Game tagging study, carried out in southern California in the 1950s, showed relatively little movement and concluded that the fish hang around the same area for very extended periods. However, my observations and those of my colleagues imply that fish in some locales may be more mobile than was suspected previously. There are several lines of evidence which support this statement. First, at any given time, there are about 400 kelp bass on Naples Reef, a very prominent structure just north of Santa Barbara. However, over a year's time, a single sport fishing party vessel will take 5,000 bass off that reef. Unless kelp bass bud off of kelp fronds, they have to be moving in from some place. Second, skippers of sport fishing vessels in the area report that kelp bass aggregations swarm onto offshore reefs during certain periods, particularly (but not limited to) spawning season, and then disappear. I have seen pelagic schools of kelp bass miles offshore, determinedly heading some place, at a relatively rapid rate. Lastly, a recent tagging study undertaken in the Santa Barbara area showed that fish tagged during the summer, at oil platforms and local reefs, started moving away from these sites during the fall, with some moving many miles. Overall, it is likely that kelp bass behave differently in different circumstances. For instance, fish living in a food-rich environment may live there for years. Ones which find themselves in an area where food comes and goes may move around more.

Kelp bass reach 28.5 inches and some live at least 33 years. They are 4 inches long at 1 year, 12 inches at 6 years and 17 inches at 9 years. Some mature at 7 inches (2–3 years), the rest when they are a little older and longer. All are mature by 10.5 inches. Spawning occurs from April to November and peaks during summer. During spawning periods, the fish form large aggregations and may move into slightly deeper water. As with many fish species, the largest females spawn the earliest in the season. Kelp bass eggs are pelagic and after fertilization drift about for 1–2 days before hatching. Larval bass take about one month to metamorphose into juveniles; these fish recruit inshore to kelp and other algae (and probably to rocky bottom if nothing else is available) in late summer and fall. Small kelp bass are active during the day and shelter at night; they eat plankton and very small algal-associated invertebrates. Subadults feed mainly during the day, but are also somewhat active at night; they eat larger invertebrates (such as amphipods, brittlestars and shrimps) and small fish. Adult kelp bass are most active at dawn and dusk; they feed on a wide variety of mid-water and bottom dwelling organisms, including fish, octopi, squids, crabs, shrimps and algae. Some research indicates that adult fish have two major feeding periods: in late spring, just before spawning season and in fall, just after. However, fish in breeding aggregations can be very aggressive, snapping at anything that comes near.

FISHERY: Arguably, kelp bass are the most important recreational species in the southern California party vessel fishery. From Santa Barbara to Bahia San Quintin, northern Baja California, anglers spend a lot of time and energy catching these guys. While most are caught from party and private vessels, a fair number are taken from piers, jetties and in the surf (where rocky reefs run near the shore). It's illegal to sell kelp bass, barred sand bass and spotted sand bass taken in California, but twas not always so. Until 1947, there was a medium-sized fishery for these species, particularly for kelp bass and barred sand bass. Much of this "commercial" catch was made by recreational fishermen selling their catch.

REMARKS: The question of whether kelp bass require kelp is of more than academic interest. Every time there is an El Niño, much of the kelp in southern California dies back, causing some folks to run around in terror, believing that the kelp bass population (and other fish as well) will suffer (and parenthetically that the sky is falling). It turns out that relatively few fish species depend on kelp. Kelp beds which sit on flat, featureless bottom actually have relatively few fish. It is the beds anchored on nice rock reefs which contain the most fish. In fact, rock reefs without kelp (maybe the kelp was lost in a big storm or due to an intense El Niño) often have large fish populations, including kelp bass. Just to beat this discussion to death, oil platforms, which have no kelp and are not even natural formations, often harbor hundreds of kelp bass and other "kelp bed" fish.

My, how times have changed. Today, kelp bass are a very popular recreational fish, but listen to what C. F. Holder had to say about them a while ago (*The Channel Islands of California*, 1910, Hodder and Stoughton): "The rock bass [kelp bass] is a poor fighter at best...no one cares for the rock bass; as game he is considered a delusion and a snare. Some days at San Clemente when the professional [commercial] fishermen were in hard luck, and they had given us bait, we caught rock bass for them, and it was merely a question of baiting and hauling them in. We never could reduce the numbers of these pests". I don't know, C. F., sounds like pretty strong words to me.

The longest movement of any tagged kelp bass was 282 miles, from southern California well down the Baja California coast.

Examination of Native American kitchen middens in southern California indicate that kelp bass were a part of these people's diets.

SPOTTED SAND BASS (PARALABRAX MACULATOFASCIATUS)

NAME: Johny Verde, Cabrilla (Mexico). *Paralabrax* is formed from 2 Greek words meaning "near Labrax" (labrax is a European sea bass); *maculatofasciatus* is a fusion of 2 Latin words for "spotted" and "banded."

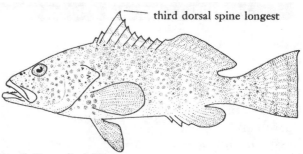

third dorsal spine longest

IDENTIFYING CHARACTERS: This is a very nice-looking fish, with a brown, olive or gray body, liberally covered with black spots. Young ones are pretty, with several dark strips running along their sides and a row of dots near their bellies.

DISTRIBUTION AND BIOLOGY: Spotteds have been taken from Monterey, central California, into the Gulf of California, to Mazatlan. They are a warmer water species and are not common north of about Newport Bay, southern California. There are simply bozillions of them in the bays and backwaters of central Baja California (such as around Guerrero Negro) and in the northern and central Gulf of California. There are old reports from the late 19th Century of spotteds taken in San Francisco Bay. Ocean waters may have been considerably warmer back then, as a number of subtropical species, no longer found there, were reported at that time. Although they have been taken in waters as deep as 200 feet, these are shallow water fish, usually living in 2-20 feet. Preferred habitats are back bays, lagoons and quiet sections of open coast, where there is extensive cover such as eelgrass or rocks.

Spotted sand bass reach 22 inches in length and live to at least 14 years. Larry Allen, the guru of spotted sand bass, provides the following information. Females may mature before their first birthday and all are mature at age 1. Half are mature by about 6 inches long. Males mature a bit later, all of them can reproduce by age 3; half of them are mature by 7 inches long. Females are oviparous. Some individuals change sex, from female to male; this seems to be the norm in the Gulf of California. However, off southern California, it appears that only some individuals change sex. In southern California, spawning occurs from June-August. Spotteds mostly eat crabs and clams, but they will also go for small fishes.

FISHERY: Spotted sand bass are a major quarry of bay and lagoon fishermen from Newport Bay southward.

REMARKS: Occasionally, spotted sand bass remains are found in the middens of southern California Native Americans.

BARRED SAND BASS (PARALABRAX NEBULIFER)

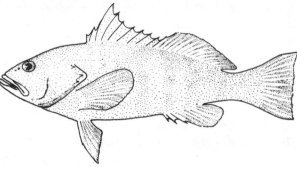

NAME: Sand Bass, Cabrilla (Mexico). *Paralabrax* means "near Labrax" in Greek (labrax is a European sea bass); *nebulifer* is Latin for "I bear clouds," a rather poetic reference to the blotches of color on this species' sides.

IDENTIFYING CHARACTERS: Barreds are greenish to gray with dusky bars on sides. Small ones are more brilliantly colored; large ones are faded out. Most have freckles on their snouts. Kelp bass closely resemble barreds, but are usually brown with white blotches and have a shorter third dorsal spine.

DISTRIBUTION AND BIOLOGY: Found from Santa Cruz (central California) to southern Baja California, barreds are occasional as far north as Morro Bay and common from Santa Barbara southward. This bass loves the sand-rock interface; you'll rarely see it over high relief, and they are a major species on artificial reefs. While inhabiting waters from shallow subtidal to 600 feet, barreds are common from about 10 to 120 feet. Younger ones are most abundant in quite shallow water, perhaps 5–30 feet. While an occasional solitary one can be found, barreds seem to prefer the company of at least a few others. They mass up during spawning season, often leaving their normal haunts for flat, sandy bottoms. After spawning, gaunt and listless fish return to their reefs. Barreds probably do not move around too much, though a few tag returns show movements of up to 40 miles.

Barred sand bass reach 25.5 inches and 24 years. A few mature at 7 inches (2 years), all are mature by 10.5 inches (5 years). Spawning takes place from April into the fall, probably peaking around July. Bass eggs and larvae are pelagic, drifting about in open water; juveniles appear in shallow water from late summer to early winter. Small ones eat small invertebrates such as amphipods and mysids; big ones concentrate on fishes (such as midshipmen), crabs and octopi.

FISHERY: Barreds form a major part of the sport fishery in southern California and northern Baja California. During some years, in some locations, they comprise as much as 17% of all fish taken in the southern California marine recreational catch. Barreds are occasionally caught as far north as Morro Bay. Most of the catch is made from boats, but a substantial number of fish also are taken from jetties, piers and even in calmer surf areas. Party and private vessels concentrate their efforts on the summer spawning aggregations found along the coast. Commercial fishing for this species is illegal.

REMARKS: One albino barred sand bass has been reported.

Tilefishes - Family Malacanthidae

OCEAN WHITEFISH (CAULOLATILUS PRINCEPS)

NAMES: Blanquillo, Pez Blanco (Mexico). *Caulolatilus* is a Greek combination meaning "stem *Latilus* " (this is one of your more obscure names, probably meaning

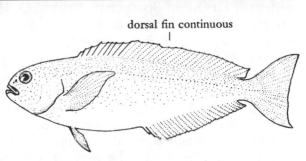

dorsal fin continuous

"closely related to the fish *Latilus*"); *princeps* is Latin for "leader."

IDENTIFYING CHARACTERS: This is a very attractive, elongated fish, with long dorsal and anal fins and a small mouth. Ocean whitefish are brown or tan on backs and sides and white below, with fins that are striped with light yellow and blue.

DISTRIBUTION AND BIOLOGY: While ocean whitefish have been taken from Vancouver Island, British Columbia to Peru (including the Galapagos Islands), they are most abundant from Pt. Conception southward. Commercial fishermen say they occasionally catch them as far north as Piedras Blancas, central California. In particular, shallow reefs off such Channel Islands as Santa Catalina, Santa Barbara and San Clemente are just loaded with these guys, and some of the biggest ones I have seen were from Santa Rosa Island. Found in aggregations, ocean whitefish live from near the bottom to about 15 feet above it, almost always over rocks, kelp or other high relief. While this fish lives from the shallow subtidal to at least 450 feet, I have noted the largest concentrations in about 90–200 feet, with smaller fish abundant in shallow water and bigger ones seeming to prefer deeper depths.

Ocean whitefish are reported to grow to 40 inches, and some have been aged to at least 13 years. Males and females grow at the same rate. A 12-incher is 2 years old; one 24 inches has been around for 6 years. Females mature at 3–4 years (16–19 inches); males at 4–5 years (19–22 inches). It looks like there is some question about whitefish spawning. One study showed that, off southern California, spawning occurred from early spring through summer, and perhaps into fall. However, another paper found no whitefish larvae off southern California, but quite a few off Baja California, implying that the whitefish off California swim up from the south. Moreover, whitefish larvae were found off Baja California in all months except December, indicating that at least some fish spawn year round. So, the complete answer is still unknown. One possibility is that whitefish spawn off southern California, but their larvae quickly die. Another explanation is that space aliens, having sucked up Elvis, are sucking up ocean whitefish larvae off southern California. These fish eat a wide variety of bottom invertebrates, such as worms, shrimp, crabs, octopi and squids, as well as small fishes.

FISHERY: Ocean whitefish are an important part of the party and private vessel recreational catch in southern California and Baja California; anglers catch an occasional individual as far north as central California. Catches peak in summer and fall, coinciding with an emphasis by party vessels on catching shallow water species. Historically, some of the largest whitefish in the California recreational fishery have been taken off the northern Channel Islands, particularly Santa Rosa. Occasionally, whitefish make up as much as 7% of the total marine recreational catch in some southern California areas. There used to be a pretty large commercial fishery for this species, particularly in the 1920s and 30s, with fishermen targeting shallow or medium depth rockfish and taking quite a few whitefish on the side. With the decline in that fishery, whitefish catches diminished, and today relatively few fish are taken.

REMARKS: Here's a florid, but fun, quote from C. F. Holder's *The Game fishes of the World* (1913, Hodder and Stoughton) about fishing for whitefish at San Clemente Island: "Possibly the finest game fish of this region among the small fishes is the Blanquillo or whitefish...When fishing with Dr. Gifford Pinchot in 1910 we found a rock one day rising to within ten feet of the surface then dropping to a great depth...The zone of thirty or forty feet was evidently devoted to the blanquillo...some weighed ten or twelve pounds. I took so many whitefish that day on the side of that beautiful mountain of the sea, up whose sapphire sides Queen Gulnore might have appeared at any moment, that I have never felt quite the same regarding a blanquillo." So, what's the deal with this Queen Gulnore and why does she like whitefish so much?

Jacks, Amberjacks, Pompanos - Family Carangidae

YELLOWTAIL (SERIOLA LALANDI)

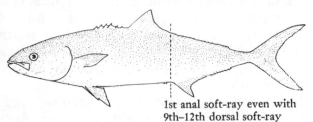

NAMES: Jurel (Mexico). *Seriola* is the Italian name for a wide ranging amberjack; *lalandi* refers to M. Delalande, a natu-

1st anal soft-ray even with 9th–12th dorsal soft-ray

ralist who collected fishes for Cuvier (who described this species) in Brazil.

IDENTIFYING CHARACTERS: Yellowtail are really handsome torpedo-shaped silvery fish, with a yellow to dusky stripe along their sides (Plate 23). A dark bar extends through each eye.

DISTRIBUTION AND ABUNDANCE: Found from British Columbia to Chile, and worldwide in temperate and subtropical seas, yellowtail are common off our coast from about Santa Barbara southward. Along the northern Channel Islands, they are occasionally taken as far west as Santa Rosa. These jacks usually school, though you will often see single individuals or small groups, particularly under drifting kelp mats. Although they are usually thought of as open water animals, yellows are most often found in association with some kind of structure, such as kelp, rocky reefs or oil platforms. In open water, they are attracted to kelp mats and various other

237

flotsam. Yellows usually hang out within 10 or 20 feet of the surface, although I have seen them caught from at least 120 foot depths. These are highly migratory fish and their migrations seem to be linked to water temperatures. Most yellows in southern California migrate there from central Baja California, usually during the spring, but in some years they begin their migration as early as late winter. Tagging studies from the 1950s and 60s show that many of the fish entering southern California come from around Isla Cedros. Some fish, particularly larger ones, remain in southern California year round. Such areas as Anacapa Island and Cortes Bank were, in previous years, famous for their very large, apparently resident, fish.

Yellows as long as 5 feet have been taken. The oldest one known was 12 years old but was only about 4 feet long. These are fast-growing fish; they reach 18 inches in one year and a 3-footer is 7 years old. Some yellows mature at 2 years of age (about 22 inches), while all spawn by their third year, at 28 inches. Yellowtail produce between 458,000–3,900,000 eggs per season. In the northeast Pacific, spawning takes place from May–October, peaking in July and August, mostly off of central Baja (particularly between Punta Eugenia and Cabo San Lazaro), but also off southern California during warm-water years (such as 1983–84). Larvae are usually found within 200 miles of shore. Young-of-the-year yellows first appear around September. A variety of small fishes (such as Pacific mackerel, sardines, northern anchovies, jack mackerel) and squids fill out their diet. They also scarf pelagic red crabs (*Pleuroncodes*), if these are about. Least terns have been noted eating little ones.

FISHERY: This is one of the premier sport fish in southern California. From Naples Reef, near Santa Barbara, and south, this is one of the "exotic" species that anglers get excited about. Most sport catches occur from southern Santa Monica Bay to Baja California, usually beginning in late spring and ending in fall. Peak months vary annually, but usually are between April and August. Most of the yellowtail taken in the southern California fishery are between 1 and 7 years old, and many of these are 2-3 years old. Because there is relatively little yellowtail spawning in southern California, this fishery depends on an annual migration of fish from northern and central Baja California. The average sea surface temperature for catching this species in southern California is 63° F. In some years, substantial catches are made in winter. During warm water years, yellowtail are abundant as far north as Pt. Conception, and they are occasionally taken well into central California. Almost all the fish are caught from party and private vessels, although divers spear some, particularly at Santa Catalina and San Clemente Islands. Anglers are well aware of the charming habit many schools have of "breezing," moving quickly near the surface, usually ignoring all bait. There is only a minor commercial catch, due mainly to poor demand. Yellowtail are taken by commercial fishermen with gillnets and occasionally by hook and line; it is illegal to catch them with purse seines and lampara nets.

REMARKS: Yellowtail have been seen chaffing themselves against blue sharks. In a sighting off Baja California, 8–15 yellows rubbed themselves against the rear part of a blue shark, perhaps to dislodge parasites, while the blue disdainfully ignored the whole operation. This same behavior has been reported off southern California, where it was interpreted as the yellows trying to kill the shark.

Here's a neat story. Yellowtail may act cooperatively to capture food. As an example, divers observed 7 yellowtail off Catalina herding a large school of jackmackerel. After splitting off a small group and chasing them up against a cliff in shallow water, the yellows spread themselves out, 3–6 feet apart and faced the small fish. Suddenly, a single yellow chased into the prey, causing them to scatter outward, toward the other waiting predators.

Another neat story. Richard Herrmann, whose photos are on the cover, was once diving on a kelp mat drifting off San Diego. While slowly gliding down the plant, he came across the rear end of a 20 pound yellowtail sticking out of the foliage. Now, yellows are open–water fish and they do not normally stick their derrieres out of kelp mats, so this was a novel sight indeed. Thinking the fish was dead, Richard pulled it out, only to have it promptly hurtle back in, this time at an angle that caused its tail to stick out of the water. While there was always the possibility that the fish had seen Richard, suddenly realized it was unclothed and in a burst of modesty tried to hide, this seemed unlikely. A more reasonable explanation soon came by in the form of a pod of pilot whales circling the mat. Richard surveyed the area a bit more and found drifting bits of large fish, including gill covers and gills, implying that the yellowtail had a right to be a tad edgy.

You don't really get the picture about how fishing has changed until you read about what it was like in the Good Ol' Days. "I shall never forget my first view of Avalon Bay (Santa Catalina Island) when I landed, in 1886. Men and boys were standing on the beach catching yellowtail with cod hand-lines. As fast as they could cast they had strikes. The fish ranged from twenty to thirty-five pounds in weight, and every few moments there would be a wailing and gnashing of teeth as a yellowtail would break the rope they were fishing with." (C. F. Holder, *The Channel Islands of California*, 1910, Hodder and Stoughton).

Many vertebrae of large yellowtail have been found in the middens of southern California Native Americans. That yellowtail and bonito were important food fishes for the Native Americans of southern California can be seen in a quote from the journal of A. Menzies. Menzies was a naturalist with the Vancouver expedition of the Northwest in the late 18th Century. On November 9, 1772, the expedition stopped off at Santa Barbara, southern California. In his diary, Menzies wrote. "There was a Village of Indians close to the place where we daily landed from the Vessels to whose industrious inhabitants we were greatly indebted for a regular supply of fish; they were always seen out by the dawn of the day either examining their fish pots in the Bay or fishing in the middle of the Channel where they never failed to catch a plentiful supply of fish of different kinds particularly Boneto and a kind of Herring with a yellow tail and in the forenoon they always came along side of the Vessels and for a few beads supplied each with whatever quantity was wanted for all hands." (California Historical Society Quarterly, 1924, vol. 2, p. 265-340). The "herring with a yellow tail" is almost certainly the Pacific yellowtail and the "Boneto" is probably the Pacific bonito (*Sarda chiliensis*).

JACKMACKEREL (TRACHURUS SYMMETRICUS)

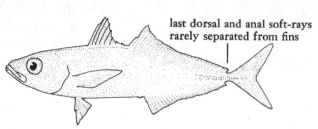

last dorsal and anal soft-rays rarely separated from fins

NAMES: Horse Mackerel, Spanish Mackerel, Mackerel Jack, Jackfish, Pacific Jack Mackerel, California Jack Mackerel. *Trachurus* is the ancient name of a jack which lives in Europe and is formed of 2 Greek words meaning "rough tail"; *symmetricus* comes from the Greek for "symmetrical."

IDENTIFYING CHARACTERS: Jackmackerel are streamlined fish, blue or green on backs and silvery below (Plate 21). They have a dark spot on the upper gill cover and projecting scales (scutes) along the lateral line.

DISTRIBUTION AND BIOLOGY: Jackmackerel are found from the Gulf of Alaska southward to at least the tip of Baja California and out to about 1,200 miles. Young fish (0–5 years old) inhabit inshore waters, primarily from southern California to central Baja

California and out 90 miles.

These young ones form dense schools and are often found over shallow reefs, near kelp beds or piers. On the other hand, older fish, 15-30 years old (20-24 inches), move offshore and are solitary or form loose aggregations. These are found from Baja California to the Aleutian Islands. Occasionally, these large folks move back inshore, where they are an important part of the recreational and commercial fishery. Jackmackerel are usually found near the surface, but occasionally they descend as deep as 1,330 feet. Older and larger fish are found in deeper waters than young ones. Older fish appear to move northward in response to warming water temperatures.

Jackmackerel reach 32 inches and live about 35 years. They grow quickly during their first year (reaching 8 inches), then slow down. A 14-incher is 4 years old. Most fish mature at around their first birthday. Spawning occurs from January-November, with a February-July peak, and takes place both inshore and offshore (more than 400 miles off the beach), at least as far north as British Columbia. Very large fish, found in southern California and Baja California, spawn first, from March-June; fish farther north spawn later in the season. The small inshore ones do their thing later in the summer. Females are oviparous and release their eggs into the water column. Most spawning occurs at water temperatures of 57-61° F. The eggs hatch in 2-5 days, depending, as usual, on water temperature. Interestingly (at least to me, but I'm easily impressed), most young-of-the-year are found between southern California and central Baja California. This implies that even those fish that hatch hundreds of miles offshore and to the north find their way to southern coastal waters. (How do they know where to go?) Jackmackerel feed on a variety of planktonic organisms, such as krill and copepods as well as juvenile squid and fishes. They are eaten by various marine mammals (such as Pacific white-sided dolphins, Dall's porpoise, California sea lions and Steller sea lions), giant seabass, angel and blue sharks, albacore, as well as Pelagic and Brandt's cormorants.

FISHERY: Jackmackerel are a moderately important part of the recreational catch, taken incidentally aboard party and private vessels and from piers. Most of the catch is of small (to 1 foot) fish. Only occasionally will larger, older adults come inshore, where they are a popular catch. The young ones (less than 6 years old) are an important commercial species, taken by purse seine and lampara net in both southern California and Baja California, with lesser numbers as far north as Monterey, central California. Jackmackerel became an important commercial species in 1947, with the collapse of the Pacific sardine fishery and the decline in the Pacific mackerel population. One problem was that the popular name for jackmackerel was "horse mackerel," a moniker that most agreed was somewhat lacking in aesthetic appeal. In 1948, the name was changed to "jack mackerel," and the rest is fishing history.

Despite their apparent abundance, there is no directed commercial fishery for the larger, offshore fish, although these are taken by salmon trollers and by trawlers fishing for Pacific hake. Jackmackerel are often canned, but you do see them occasionally in fish markets. Fresh ones stay yummy for about 5 days at 40° F; frozen ones are good for 4-6 months at 0° F. Canned, they are primo for about 1 year.

People do occasionally come down with scombroid poisoning after eating jackmackerel; see the discussion under albacore.

Dolphinfishes - Family Coryphaenidae

DOLPHINFISH (CORYPHAENA HIPPURUS)

NAMES: Mahi mahi is what they call them in Hawaii, and a while back this is what fish markets and restaurants started using to avoid having the public think they were dining on

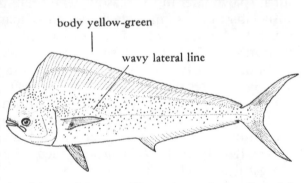

body yellow-green

wavy lateral line

Flipper. This name (mahi mahi, not Flipper), and the Spanish "Dorado," are commonly used by California anglers. Because they are found throughout the world, dolphinfish have acquired a nice variety of names, including the ever popular Bakhti Bakhti of Syria; the romantic Coriphene of France; the mysterious Fei Niau Fu of Taiwan; the colorful Ca Nucheo of North Vietnam and the downright tongue twisting Dakaunomoutas of Cyprus. *Coryphaena* is the name given by Aristotle to this fish and comes from 2 Greek words meaning "showing a helmet"; *hippurus* is Greek for "horse tail."

IDENTIFYING CHARACTERS: These are truly gorgeous fish, long and sleek with very long single dorsal and anal fins. They tend to be gold or yellow-green, with flashes of metallic blue and green on backs and sides, and white and yellow on bellies (Plate 24). Many fish have blue, green and/or black spots. Dark vertical bars cover the sides of small individuals. At around 18 inches, males develop a pronounced crest on their foreheads, giving them a very steep, blunt profile (think of Winston Churchill in about 1942).

DISTRIBUTION AND BIOLOGY: Dolphinfish are found worldwide, primarily in tropical and subtropical waters. They don't seem to like water less than 68° F. In the eastern Pacific, they have been found from Grays Harbor, Washington to Chile. Some place around Palos Verdes (southern California) is about as far north as you are likely to see them on a regular basis. These are pelagic, oceanic fish which usually live near the surface in small schools, occasionally descending as deep as 660 feet. They migrate north from Baja California during warm water years in the late summer and fall.

Dolphinfish are reported to reach 6.75 feet in length. These fish grow like bats out of hell and grow rapidly throughout their lives. Current wisdom is that they live for a maximum of 4 years. Males may grow slightly faster than females. Off Hawaii, a 6-month old fish is about 28 inches long, while a one-year-old is over 4 feet. Both sexes mature well before their first birthdays, most are mature when about 24 inches long. Spawning seasons vary with location. In tropical waters they may spawn throughout most of the year, but restrict such activities to warm water months in subtropical or temperate regions. The eggs are pelagic and at 75–77° F they hatch in about 60 hours. They eat fishes and squids.

FISHERY: Worldwide, these are very popular recreational fish, taken almost entirely from boats. In southern California, almost all are caught around drifting kelp mats and other floating matter. Southern California catches are highest during warm-water years and the warmest-water months. Catches tend to peak in August. Wherever they are common, dolphinfish are also a major commercial fish. In many locations around the world, dolphinfish are attracted to bundles of bamboo or cork planks, then encircled with nets. (Examples are the Shiira–zuke fishery of Japan, the Kannizzali fishery of Malta and the Matas fishery of the Balearic Island.)

REMARKS: Dolphinfish have a definite thing about floating objects; they just love to hang out near them. Off southern California and northern Baja California, they are most commonly seen under or near the drifting kelp mats which break free from nearshore beds. However, the fish are also attracted to boats, logs, boxes– in fact almost anything that stays at the surface. It is not clear why this species (along with yellowtail, various tunas, etc.) are so fond of these structures: there is often no food around them and small bits of flotsam provide little protection from predators.

Grunts - Family Haemulidae

SARGO (ANISOTREMUS DAVIDSONI)

NAMES: *Anisotremus* is formed from 2 Greek words which mean "unequal aperture," referring to the pores on the chin; *davidsoni* honors George Davidson, a San Francisco astron-omer of the 19th Century.

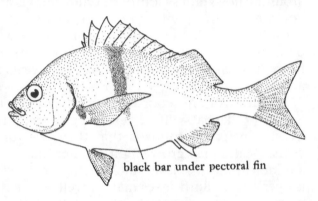

black bar under pectoral fin

IDENTIFYING CHARACTERS: Sargos are deep bodied, perch-shaped fish. Adults almost always have a vertical dark bar on their sides, near midbody. They are usually silvery, although an occasional one is golden, brassy or even albino. I know, they look like a pile or rubberlip seaperch, but here is how to tell the difference. Pile perch have a really high, peaked soft dorsal fin, while rubberlips have thicker lips. Juvenile sargos have 2 dark stripes along their flanks.

DISTRIBUTION AND BIOLOGY: Sargos have been found from Santa Cruz (central California) to southern Baja California, and there is an isolated population in the northern Gulf of California. They were planted in the Salton Sea in 1951 and have done well there. Rare north of Santa Barbara, they are quite abundant from Santa Monica Bay southward. These are schooling fish, found near the bottom from shallow subtidal waters to 198 feet, most often in 40 feet or less. While they like to be around structures, such as rocks, kelp, oil platforms and pier pilings, they often school along the sand or cobble margins of these features.

The largest authenticated sargo was 19.7 inches long. A 23-incher has been reported, but if true, that fish must have been a mutant. There is no complete study on their biology, but a few odds and ends are known. Based on some aging work I did, a 10-incher is about 4 years old, a 13-incher is 12 and I have read of one around 17 inches that was 15 years old. They may mature at about 7 inches and 2 years. Spawning occurs from late spring through summer. The eggs are pelagic, drifting near the surface. One-inch-long young-of-the-year move inshore into shallow waters in late summer and fall; they often school with young-of-the-year salema and black croaker, both of which have similar black striping. The stripes on sargos disappear and the bars emerge when the fish are around 6 months old. Sargos spend quite a bit of time desultorily poking around substrate and eating various invertebrates such as isopods, amphipods, shrimps and kelp scallops. Least terns eat them.

FISHERY: In marine waters, sargos are a common catch of shore and pier fishermen in southern California, particularly from about Newport Beach southward. They have been a mainstay in the Salton Sea, almost since their introduction in 1951. Sargos are an occasional commercial catch, taken incidentally in gill and lampara nets and are marketed with perch.

REMARKS: A sargo otolith was recovered from a Pleistocene deposit over 20,000 years old in southern California.

Sargos can tolerate, and in fact thrive, in water somewhat saltier than sea water, which is why they are so successful in the Salton Sea. However, beginning at salinities about 20% higher than sea water, growth, respiration and food consumption all take a header and the fish do not do well.

SALEMA (XENISTIUS CALIFORNIENSIS)

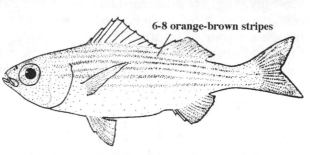

6-8 orange-brown stripes

NAMES: *Xenistius* comes from the Greek words for "strange" and "sail" or "dorsal fin" (referring to the fact that the soft dorsal fin and the anal fin are similar); *californiensis* refers to its being first recorded from San Diego, California.

IDENTIFYING CHARACTERS. A very distinctive little fish, with 6-8 orange or yellow stripes, big eyes and a small mouth.

DISTRIBUTION AND BIOLOGY: While found from Monterey Bay, central California to Peru, salemas are uncommon north of Pt. Conception. These are schooling, shallow water fishes, found from about 4-35 feet of water, typically over rocks and among kelp. The young ones may school with young black croaker and sargo.

245

Salema school during the day, then disperse and feed on their own at night.

Salema reach 11.8 inches. Females are oviparous and the eggs are pelagic. Salema feed in the water column on such prey as gammarid and caprellid amphipods, mysid shrimps, and worms.

FISHERY: Shore and vessel anglers catch this one occasionally, particularly off Orange and San Diego counties.

Croakers and Drums - Family Sciaenidae

WHITE SEABASS (ATRACTOSCION NOBILIS)

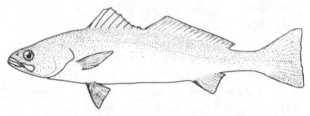

NAME: Seatrout (small ones), Weakfish, King Croaker, Curvina (Mexico). *Nobilis* means "noble" in Latin.

IDENTIFYING CHARACTERS: Very young seabass up to a few inches long are usually brown or golden, but can be silvery. Juveniles, to about 24 inches, are silvery-gray or silvery-dusky, with a series of dark bars on their sides. Adults are gray-blue, bronze or almost yellow. Juveniles are often mistaken for white croakers. Hey, wise up out there. White croakers *don't* have bars on their sides and *do* have a tiny barbel on their chins.

DISTRIBUTION AND BIOLOGY: White seabass have been taken from Juneau, Alaska to southern Baja California and in the northern Gulf of California. At the turn of the century, they were abundant as far north as San Francisco, and the fishery was centered there. The late 19th Century was probably a warm water period off California, and it looks like the seabass followed the water from the south into central California. Currently, these fish are most common from about Pt. Conception south, with an occasional fish taken in central California. (An informant tells me that they are common in the warm water discharge at the power plant at Diablo Cove, near Avila.) They live in different habitats at different life stages. Very young seabass, say around 2–4 inches, live in drift algae just behind the surf line. Older juveniles occupy bays and shallow coastal waters, often near rocks or kelp. Adults are usually found near reefs or kelp beds. While juveniles usually school up, adults may be found either singly or in schools. These fish seem to move about, but their migrations are unclear. At least some whites, particularly large adults, move into deep water (120–350 feet) during winter.

These big fish reach 5 feet and some live at least 20 years. A 36-incher is 8–9 years old. Half of males are mature at 24 inches, half of females at about 28 inches. Seabass spawn from April through August, peaking in May and June. Based on some video footage taken by Terry Maas, it appears quite possible that adult females develop dark vertical bars during spawning season. Terry has some quite remarkable footage of a number of bar-less adults chasing after a barred individual. They eat a variety of mobile prey, including sardines, mackerels, anchovies and squids.

FISHERY: White seabass are prized in both sport and commercial catches. Most of the fishery is south of Pt. Conception, though a few fish are taken north of Pt. Conception (particularly in the Morro Bay and Monterey Bay regions) by salmon trollers and gilnetters. While many recreation-caught seabass are taken in summer and fall, there is now a sizeable fishery for these guys during the winter and early spring when they feed on spawning squid. At this time, Santa Catalina Island is particularly favored by anglers. Other hotspots include Pt. Conception; Santa Rosa, Santa Cruz and San Clemente Islands; Carpinteria; Pt. Dume; Palos Verdes; Laguna Beach and the Coronado Islands. The average ocean temperature for taking seabass is about 65° F. Almost all of the sport catch comes from party and private vessels, but a surprising number of fish are taken from piers and jetties. This was particularly true 40 or 50 years ago when these fish were much more abundant off southern California. I remember a ferocious run of seabass off the Santa Monica Pier when I was a kid during the El Niño of 1957. At sunrise and sunset, anglers would catch sardines with snaglines and transfer them to live bait rigs, then stand back and await developments. For several weeks, a number of pretty big fish, some in the 30–40 pound class, were dragged off that pier. (I didn't catch one and wound up frustrated out of my mind.) Large numbers of immature seabass, called "seatrout," are taken by anglers, particularly from Long Beach south. Throw these fish back, people. It's illegal to keep them and they grow up to be big fish.

Commercial catches are made almost entirely by drift and set gillnets. Most seabass are marketed fresh or frozen, as fillets or steaks. They have a fresh shelf life of 5 days at 40° F and a frozen life of 9 months at 0° F.

Both commercial and recreational seabass catches have really declined over the last 60 years (though catches have rebounded somewhat in the 1990's), and it's popular (and I suppose fun) for sport and commercial anglers to blame each other. Quite honestly,

I think there is enough blame to go around. Everyone probably catches too many. In addition, various other factors, including pollution and habitat destruction, may be involved. Why don't all of you folks get together and try to work cooperatively (as they tried to teach you in kindergarten)?

REMARKS: As of this writing, there is a seabass hatchery operating at Hubbs-Sea World in Mission Bay, and a number of organizations are releasing little ones all along the coast. Whether releasing small seabass into the ocean is going to markedly affect the seabass catch off southern California is anyone's guess. This kind of operation has not been particularly effective in other situations (salmon aside), but I guess time will tell.

Here's an interesting observation. While scuba divers rarely see seabass underwater, my free-diver friends (those who dive without tanks) report seeing these fish all the time. Perhaps seabass, which may have very good hearing, are frightened off by the noise a regulator makes when divers breathe.

In the late 1940s, there was a commercial white seabass fishery off Pismo Beach involving war-surplus landing craft. Spotter planes would locate seabass schools just behind the breakers and report it to fishermen on the beach. The fishermen would drive down the beach, enter the water and drop a beach seine net behind the fish. The landing craft was then driven to shore and the net was pulled in by horses. Pretty substantial numbers were taken before beach seines were declared illegal.

Remains of white seabass have been found in fossil beds about 20,000 years old.

White seabass are not "bass," are not "seabass" and are not "white," so go figure.

BLACK CROAKER (CHEILOTREMA SATURNUM)

NAME: China Croaker, Chinese Croaker. *Cheilotrema* is Greek for "lip pores," *saturnum* means "dusky" in Latin.

jet-black edging on gill cover

IDENTIFYING CHARACTERS:
These are perch-shaped croakers with back colors of dusky, purplish, bluish, brownish or coppery hues and silvery bellies. The

rear part of the gill cover is black and there is a pale bar at midbody. DISTRIBUTION AND BIOLOGY: Black croakers live from Pt. Conception to northern Baja California, and there is also an isolated population in the upper Gulf of California. They are one of the few croakers that prefer rocky reefs and kelp beds, and, in fact, are often found in crevices and caves. Black croakers are most abundant in 10–50 feet, with a maximum depth range of 150 feet. Juveniles are usually found in large schools and adults may either school up (often with salemas and sargos) or goof around by themselves.

Black croakers grow to about 28 inches. Really. This mutant was measured by investigators at the Hubbs-Sea World Research Institute. And they live at least 20 years. These fish mature at about 10 inches and spawn in late spring and early summer. Very small ones settle behind the surf line from August–October over sandy bottoms. Black croakers eat small crustaceans such as shrimps and crabs.

FISHERY: This is an occasional species in pier and sport boat catches taken from Santa Barbara southward.

WHITE CROAKER (GENYONEMUS LINEATUS)

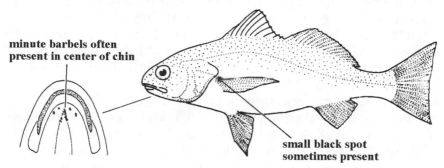

minute barbels often present in center of chin

small black spot sometimes present

NAMES: This fish has been given about as many names as any on the coast–most of them uncomplimentary. "Sewer Trout" is one of the few I can mention in a family book. In southern California, from San Diego to perhaps Ventura, the most common name is "Tomcod," whereas in the Santa Barbara area, "Ronkie" or "Roncador" is usual. In central California, and in most fish markets, "Kingfish" is most often used. *Genyonemus* is formed from 2 Greek words meaning "lower jaw barbel"; *lineatus* means "striped" in Latin.

IDENTIFYING CHARACTERS: These are small, silvery fish, some with slightly yellow-bronze backs. The fins are yellow or white and usually there is a small black spot where the pectoral fin meets the body.

DISTRIBUTION AND BIOLOGY: White croakers are found from the

surf zone to 780 feet and from Barkley Sound (British Columbia) to southern Baja California. They are most abundant from southern California northward to about Monterey in perhaps 20–240 feet. These fish seem to move inshore during summer months and offshore in winter. While white croakers are usually found in schools, often over sand or mud bottoms, I have occasionally seen them chasing anchovies near the surface.

The largest white croaker on record was 17 inches, but fish larger than 14 inches are real honkers. This is a relatively short-lived species; the oldest one I have aged was 13 years. The fish mature between 1 and 4 years of age; half spawn after one year. Females are oviparous and although some spawning takes place throughout the year, most occurs between November and August. Eggs hatch in about 2 days at 68° F. Larvae have been found from about San Francisco southward to Punta Eugenia, central Baja California. Highest concentrations are in southern and central California. While a few larvae have been taken as much as 150 miles offshore, this is a nearshore spawner; almost all larvae reside within 20 miles of the coast. Young ones settle out of the plankton just behind the surf line, usually in 10-30 feet. Both juveniles and adults favor cloudy water, probably because it hides them from predators and because their prey live in fine sand and mud. Small croakers feed on plankton, while ones larger than about 4 inches eat such animals are worms, gammarid amphipods, shrimps and small fishes. There is some evidence that these fish feed mostly at night. Almost any large fish in the vicinity (e.g. California halibut, spiny dogfish or barred sandbass), marine mammal (harbor seal, California sea lion) and sea bird (Brandt's and double-crested cormorants, least tern, western gull) eat them.

FISHERY: White croakers are easy to catch and for this reason they are the mainstay of pier, small vessel and barge fishermen. Without this species (along with topsmelt and shiner perch), young children on many piers would catch almost nothing. They are also common in the party vessel fishery, from San Francisco southward, usually taken by anglers targeting such species as California halibut and barred sandbass. Catches tend to be highest during the summer months.

There is also a pretty sizable commercial fishery for these puppies. Most of the fish are taken with gillnets and hook and line, but I hear that some guys are experimenting with midwater trawls. Much of this catch heads to Asian markets.

REMARKS: There is no question that white croakers suffer from really bad press. Many fishermen believe they are inedible, worm–infested pests. While they are soft-fleshed, white croakers are edible and in fact are eaten in large quantities, particularly by various minority groups. As for having worms, though some white croakers are infected, other more popular species (such as California halibut) actually contain more worms. For information on the Wonderful World of Parasitic Worms, see the "Parasite" section near the end of this book.

White croakers were a major food fish of Native Americans along the California coast. Their ear bones have been found in Pliocene deposits (over one million years old) in Long Beach, California.

CALIFORNIA CORBINA (MENTICIRRHUS UNDULATUS)

NAME: Berrugata (Mexico). *Menticirrhus* is formed from 2 Latin words, meaning "chin barbel"; *undulatus* means "waved" in

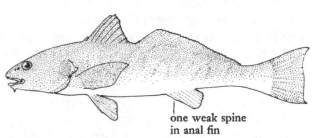

one weak spine in anal fin

Latin, a reference to the undulating lines on the sides of the body.
IDENTIFYING CHARACTERS: These are long, thin croakers with a short chin barbel. Corbina are usually gray or bluish (occasionally brown) on back and white below.
DISTRIBUTION AND BIOLOGY: Corbina range from Pt. Conception to the Gulf of California, almost always over sandy bottoms, usually where there is extensive wave action. They are found from water so shallow their backs are exposed (the pier at the Scripps Institution of Oceanography is a great place to see this) down to 150 feet. While most fish are found in shallow waters, my friend Ken Neilsen reports catching large numbers of them off southern California in waters as deep as 80 feet. Usually found in groups of 2-5 individuals, they occasionally school up in aggregations of hundreds. Tagging studes show relatively little along-coast movement.

Corbina have been taken to 32.6 inches. A 12-incher is about 3 years old and a 20-incher is about 8. Males mature at 2 years and about 10 inches, females at 3 years and about 13 inches. These are summer spawners, reproducing from June–September, primarily in July–August. Juveniles eat small crustaceans such as amphipods and mysid shrimps, as well as clam siphons. Fish larger than 8 inches prey almost entirely on sand crabs, occasionally going for clams, worms, grunion eggs and small fishes.
FISHERY: It is illegal to catch this fish commercially. Corbina are very important sport fish for both surf and pier anglers from about Santa Barbara southward.

SPOTFIN CROAKER (RONCADOR STEARNSI)

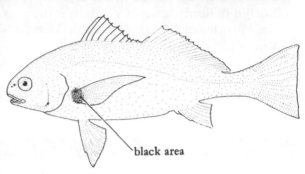

black area

NAMES: *Roncador* is the Spanish name (meaning grunt) that is given to many croaker species; *stearnsi* honors Robert E. C. Stearns, a well-known shell expert who lived in San Francisco in the late 19th Century.

IDENTIFYING CHARACTERS: Spotfins have very obvious black spots at the bases of their pectoral fins. They are bluish-gray or gray on backs, brassy on flanks and white on bellies. Males may be completely brassy or golden during breeding season, while females develop blackish streaks on their bellies.

DISTRIBUTION AND BIOLOGY: Spotfins are found from Pt. Conception, California to southern Baja California, most commonly from about Los Angeles Harbor southward. These are inshore fish, which live over soft bottoms from the intertidal zone to depths of 60 feet. However, most fish seem to hug the shoreline in 30 feet or less. Little is known of the species' movements. While some are caught year-round in southern California, the largest catches are in shallow water in late summer. Where the bulk of the population lives the rest of the year is something of a mystery. I have always had the hunch that this species (and perhaps the yellowfin croaker) heads south in the fall and north in the spring, but I have no data to back this up.

Spotfins as large as 27 inches have been taken. A 26.5 inches long fish was at least 15 years old. Most males mature at 2 years and about 9 inches, most females at 3 years and 12.5 inches. All are mature at 4 years and 15 inches long. Spawning takes place during the summer, but where is unknown. Young-of-the-year settle into the surf zone in fall. Spotfins eat bottom-dwelling organisms, primarily worms and clams. And this meager assemblage of facts is really all that is known about these fish.

FISHERY: Spotfins are a very popular sport fish, taken in shallow water by shore, pier and small vessel anglers mostly from Orange County southward. It has been illegal to catch them commercially since 1915.

REMARKS: Spotfin ear bones have been found in Pliocene deposits over one million years old.

QUEENFISH (SERIPHUS POLITUS)

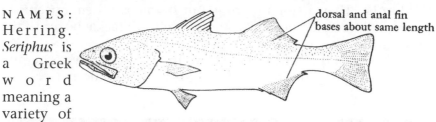

dorsal and anal fin
bases about same length

NAMES: Herring. *Seriphus* is a Greek word meaning a variety of things, including an island near Greece, a small winged insect and a kind of wormwood (Dr. Ayres in 1861 did not specify why he used this name); *politus* means "polished" in Latin, referring to the silvery body color.

IDENTIFYING CHARACTERS: This is a large-mouthed, very thin croaker, sort of bluish or tan on its back and silvery on sides and belly. The fins are yellow, sometimes with a sort of greenish tinge.

DISTRIBUTION AND BIOLOGY: While queenfish have been taken from Yaquina Bay, Oregon to south-central Baja California, they are only abundant from southern California southward. A schooling fish, they are found over sandy bottoms from the surf line to 600 feet, often co-occurring with white croaker. Most live from just behind the surf line to about 75 feet. Some adults make day-night migrations, often from a day-light depth of 15–30 feet offshore to about 75 feet at night. The fish school by day, dispersing at night when they feed actively. Queenfish withdraw from shallow water during winter and early spring.

Previously, queenies were thought to reach a length of one foot. However, Mike Shane, at Hubbs-Sea World Research Institute, tells me that he got one that was 20.8 inches long. They mature at 5 inches, during their first spring or second summer. Females are oviparous, and spawning occurs at night, from February-September, peaking May-July. Most spawning occurs during the first quarter of the moon. The largest females spawn earliest in the season. Queenfish spawn very close to shore, and the majority of the larvae are found within 20 miles of the coast. While some larvae have been noted off central California and northern Baja California, most occur in the southern California Bight. An average-sized female produces 300,000 eggs per season. These are midwater feeders, preying mostly on such zooplankton as copepods, mysid shrimps, crustacean larvae and gammarid amphipods. Lots of predators nail them, including California sea lions, least terns and double-crested cormorants.

FISHERY: Queenfish are one of the most commonly taken fish from piers in southern California. They are a minor part of the California commercial croaker catch.

REMARKS: Gee, these are boring fish – sort of the Wonder Bread of the fish world. Queenfish are called "herring" in southern California. They aren't a herring, but if you call them queenfish, people will look at you funny and move their tackle boxes to the other side of the pier.

Ear bones of queenfish were found in a Pliocene (over one-million-year old) deposit in Long Beach, southern California.

YELLOWFIN CROAKER (UMBRINA RONCADOR)

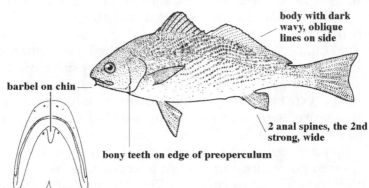

body with dark wavy, oblique lines on side

barbel on chin

2 anal spines, the 2nd strong, wide

bony teeth on edge of preoperculum

NAMES: *Umbrina* comes from the Greek word *umbra,* meaning "shade" (ancient writers called various croaker species "umbra"); *roncador* is Spanish and was a generalized term for many croakers.

IDENTIFYING CHARACTERS: Yellowfins have shiny gray, green or bluish backs, with white bellies and a series of diagonal yellow-brown stripes on backs. There is a pronounced barbel on their chins.

DISTRIBUTION AND BIOLOGY: Although they are reported as far north as San Francisco, yellowfins are rarely taken north of about Ventura, in southern California and southward they range into the Gulf of California. These are shallow water, schooling fish, found to a depth of about 25 feet, most commonly in the surf or just behind the surf zone. Found both on open coasts and in quiet embayments, these fish are most abundant off southern California in summer months, from July–September. They are scarce the rest of the year, and some have speculated they migrate into deep water. Personally, I doubt this, because no yellowfins have been taken in deeper water by scientific otter trawl collections, despite years of extensive sampling throughout southern California. I think it is more likely that the fish move south during fall and winter, spending the cold water period off Baja California. Based on observations off Santa Catalina Island, yellowfins school close to shore during the day, then disperse and move a bit off the beach at night.

Yellowfins reach 21.6 inches. A 15-incher I aged was 10-years old, a 10-incher was 4 years. They are said to mature at 9 inches. Spawning occurs during the summer. Yellowfin are primarily nighttime feeders, eating small fishes, such as anchovies, along with sand crabs, worms, clams and small crustaceans.

FISHERY: Yellowfins are a popular fish with surf, pier and small vessel anglers. It is illegal to catch them for sale.

Sea Chubs – Family Kyphosidae

OPALEYE (GIRELLA NIGRICANS)

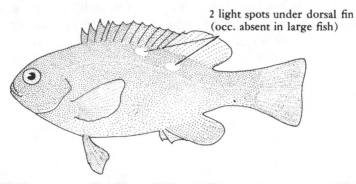

2 light spots under dorsal fin
(occ. absent in large fish)

NAME: Button Bass, Opaleye Perch. *Girella* comes from the French "girelle," which is a derivative of "julis," a very old name given to a number of small wrasses in Europe; *nigricans* means "blackish."

IDENTIFYING CHARACTERS: Opaleye are oval, perch-shaped fish, with gray-green or olive-green bodies and really cute blue eyes. Very young ones, found in open water, have blue backs and silvery bellies. Opaleyes have between 1 and 3 white or yellowish spots on their backs. Fishes off Baja California tend to have more spots than those off southern California.

DISTRIBUTION AND BIOLOGY: Though opaleye are found from Otter Rock, Oregon to southern Baja California, they are common from Pt. Conception southward. During warm water years, larvae drift north and small populations establish themselves in central California, at least as far north as Monterey Bay. Young-of-the-year live in tide pools, the smallest fish in the highest pools. Juveniles are able to breathe air. While they don't leave the water, little opaleyes need that ability, since shallow pools sometimes lose oxygen at night. Fish remain there 1–2 years, then move onto subtidal reefs and into kelp beds. While they have been found down to at least 100 feet, adults are more abundant from 5–65 foot depths. Adults are found either as solitary individuals or in small groups near the bottom, and the adults occasionally swim into midwater or even up into the kelp canopy. Tide pool opaleye tend to return to favorite pools at each low tide.

Opaleye reach 26 inches. Females are oviparous. They spawn from April–June, shedding eggs into the water column. Young ones usually enter tidepools from June to early winter. This is one of the few species off California that eats algae. The inside of a typical opaleye gut looks like the Zen Special at a New Age vegetarian eatery. Occasionally, they eat small invertebrates, such as shrimps, amphipods etc., and have been seen feeding on jellyfish. It is not clear whether these fish are actually digesting the algae or only feeding on the small animals which encrust it. Most feeding seems to occur in the daytime. Eagles at Santa Catalina Island eat them, as do California sea lions, least terns and Brandt's cormorants.

FISHERY: Opaleye are important recreational fish from Pt. Conception southward. They are commonly taken by rocky-shore, jetty and pier anglers, and they also form a minor part of the "perch" commercial market.

REMARKS: Although they can be taken on mussels and green algae, green peas are a very effective bait for this species.

Opaleye remains have been found in a number of Native American middens.

HALFMOON (MEDIALUNA CALIFORNIENSIS)

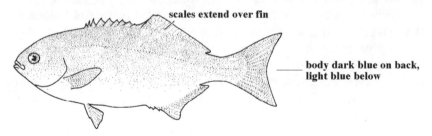

scales extend over fin

body dark blue on back, light blue below

NAMES: Catalina Perch, Catalina Blue Perch. *Medialuna* is a Spanish word for "halfmoon," reflecting on the halfmoon shape to the tail fin; *californiensis* describes the area where the fish was first found.

IDENTIFYING CHARACTERS: These are attractive, perch-shaped fish, with slate-blue or blue backs, silvery bellies and halfmoon-shaped curved tails.

DISTRIBUTION AND BIOLOGY: Abundant from Pt. Conception south, halfmoons live from Vancouver Island to the Gulf of California. While these schooling fish favor high relief areas such as rocky reefs, kelp beds and oil platforms, they are also common around drifting kelp mats. Found from the surface down to 130 feet, they are most abundant in depths of 10–65 feet.

Halfmoon reach 19 inches and mature at about 7.5 inches. Females are oviparous and they spawn from April to October. For an inshore species, halfmoon larvae are found an amazing distance from shore. Larvae are routinely found 150 miles off the beach, a few as far offshore as 300 miles. Heaviest larval concentrations are off northern Baja California. This species seems to eat a wide variety of organisms. Many fish are packed with algae, but sponges, small invertebrates and even club anemones are on their menu. Most feeding probably takes place during daylight hours. California sea lions, northern fur seals, arctic loons, rhinoceros auklets, least terns, Brandt's cormorants and bald eagles (at Santa Catalina Island) all eat them.

FISHERY: There is a fair-sized sport fishery for halfmoons, much of it from party and private vessels, particularly from Santa Monica Bay south. These fish have saved a number of party vessel fishing trips from complete failure. There is also a small halfmoon commercial fishery, with this species taken and sold along with perch.

REMARKS: Halfmoons can be a major problem to algae farmers off southern California. In some experimental offshore farms, they devastated large amounts of giant kelp.

Surfperches - Family Embiotocidae

BARRED SURFPERCH (AMPHISTICHUS ARGENTEUS)

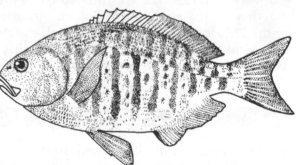

NAMES: *Amphistichus* comes from 2 Greek words meaning "double series," referring to the 2 rows of teeth in each jaw; *argenteus* is Latin for "silvery."

IDENTIFYING CHARACTERS: Barreds are silvery or brassy fish, with 8–10 yellow or rust-colored bars on their sides. Usually there are spots between the bars. They resemble redtail surfperch, but redtails have (are you ready?) red fins. Another closely related species, the calico surfperch has a series of stipples on the sides rather than distinct bars.

DISTRIBUTION AND BIOLOGY: Barreds are found from northern Washington to north-central Baja California, commonly from Santa Cruz southward. Though they have been taken down to 240 feet, these are really surf fishes, found most commonly on open, sandy coasts in less than 20 foot depths. I have routinely seen these guys in less than 4 inches of water. They also can be found around piers, in bays and over the small sandy beaches which interrupt rocky shores. These are schooling animals, and they probably live along the same stretch of coast for long periods, though some barreds move into slightly deeper water during the winter.

Barreds reach 17 inches; females live to at least 9 years, males to 6. Females grow faster than males–an 8 inch female is 2 years old, a male will be 4. Males mature in their first year, but females are 2 before they spawn. Breeding has been noted in November and spawning occurs off southern California from February–July. Like other surfperches, females are viviparous and spawning probably begins later in central California. As many as 113 young have been found in a female. These perch feed almost exclusively on sand crabs, occasionally eating clams, mussels and fish eggs (from grunion and topsmelt, for example). I imagine they have a number of predators, but only least terns are known to eat them.

FISHERY: While occasionally taken in northern California, this is a major recreational fish of sandy shore, pier and jetty fishermen, from Santa Cruz southward. It is probably the most commonly taken fish by surf fishermen in central and southern California.

There is a hook and line commercial surf fishery for barreds that is mainly in central California, between about Surf and Cayucos. In southern California, it is illegal to take them for commercial purposes, and any that are shipped there must carry a tag certifying they were caught north of Pt. Arguello. Barreds comprise about 25% of the commercial perch catch. Between 1980-91, annual average California landings of this species averaged 5.7 metric tons per year.

CALICO SURFPERCH (AMPHISTICHUS KOELZI)

NAMES: *Amphistichus* is formed from 2 Greek words meaning "double series," referring to the 2 rows of teeth in each jaw; *koelzi* is after Walter Koelz, U. S. ichthyologist.

IDENTIFYING CHARACTERS: I'll admit it, this one looks a lot like its close relatives, the barred and redtail surfperch. Here's how to tell them apart. Calicos are dotted with a series of redbrown speckles on their sides, forming rather indistinct bars. The fins are reddish and the caudal fin is dark. Barred surfperch have quite distinct vertical bars (with dots in between), and their fins are not reddish. Redtails have more distinct bars and a high spiny dorsal fin, high

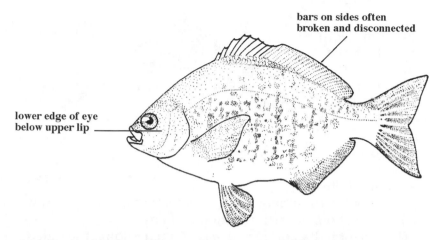

bars on sides often
broken and disconnected

lower edge of eye
below upper lip

er than the soft rays. This does not occur in calicos.

DISTRIBUTION AND BIOLOGY: Calico surfperch live from Cape Flattery, Washington to northern Baja California, almost always over sandy bottoms and in bay mouths. They are more common from Pt. Conception, central California, northward. Calicos are usually found in aggregations, from the surf zone to about 30 feet of water.

This species reaches about 1 foot in length. Not much research has been done with this one. Ed DeMartini, now at the National Marine Fisheries Service in Hawaii, looked at 10 of them and found that they ate gammarid amphipods, sand crabs and various shrimps. Harbor seals eat them.

FISHERY: Calicos are commonly taken by shore anglers, particularly those fishing the sandy surf, mostly from the Santa Barbara area northward. There is a small commercial fishery for this species; calicos are taken by hook and line and seine. Calico surfperch may not be taken commercially south of Pt. Arguello.

REDTAIL SURFPERCH (AMPHISTICHUS RHODOTERUS)

NAMES: Redtail. *Amphistichus* is formed from 2 Greek words meaning "double series," referring to the 2 rows of teeth in each jaw; *rhodoterus* is Greek for "rosy."

IDENTIFYING CHARACTERS: Redtails are silvery or occasionally brassy fish, with 8–11 red or brown bars on their sides. All fins are reddish. They resemble barred surfperch, which have yellowish fins and brassy or yellow bars.

DISTRIBUTION AND BIOLOGY: Found from Vancouver Island southward to Avila Beach, Central California, redtails are common from Washington to San Francisco. These are shallow water, schooling fish,

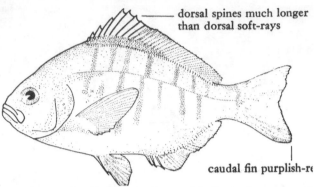

dorsal spines much longer
than dorsal soft-rays

caudal fin purplish-re

taken to a maximum depth of 24 feet. Although they are primarily found on sandy beaches along open coasts, redtails also inhabit rocky shores, jetties and enter bays to spawn from about April–September. Little is known of their along-shore migration patterns, if any.

The largest redtail on record was 16 inches long; the oldest fish sampled lived to 9 years. An 11-incher is 6 years old. Females grow faster than males. Females mature at 3–4 years (9–10 inches); most males are mature by the end of their second years (8–9 inches). Females are viviparous and as many as 39 young have been recorded from a single individual. Off Oregon (where all this research has been conducted), the fish breed in winter and spawn in estuaries and harbors from July–September, peaking from late August–early September. Redtails eat crabs, worms, fishes and such crustaceans such as amphipods and isopods.

FISHERY: Redtails are a very important recreational species from about San Francisco to Washington, particularly from Del Norte County, northern California, northward. In these areas, redtails may comprise 10-30% of the total marine recreational catch. Ocean catches peak in May and July-September; bay and estuary catches peak in January-March. A report by the California Department of Fish and Game notes a general decline in redtail catches (77%) between 1980 and 1986.

There is also a sizeable hook and line and seine commercial fishery in estuaries, bays and along the open coast. Redtails form about 73% of the commercial surfperch catch in California. Between 1980-91, California commercial landings averaged 17.8 metric tons. All surfperches have fresh shelf lives of about 5 days at 40° F. Frozen at 0° F, they are palatable for 9-12 months.

Redtails may not be taken commercially in southern California. Of course, they don't live in southern California, allowing us to speculate about the kind of information given to the Legislature.

KELP SURFPERCH (BRACHYISTIUS FRENATUS)

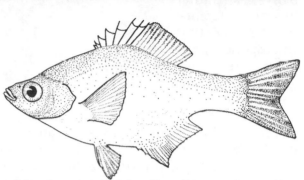

NAMES: *Brachyistius* is formed from 2 Greek words meaning "short-sailed," referring to the species' short dorsal fin; *frenatus* is Latin for "bridled."

IDENTIFYING CHARACTERS: These perch are small, brassy or golden brown with a sharply upturned snout and mouth.

DISTRIBUTION AND BIOLOGY: Found from northern British Columbia southward to central Baja California, kelp perch are abundant throughout much of their range in groups of hundreds or as single individuals. This species may make forays into open water at night. Kelp seems particularly important for newly recruiting fish and juveniles. While kelp surfperch have been taken down to depths of about 138 feet, they are most common in shallow water, among kelp and other algae.

These peanuts don't grow very large. They reach 13.5 inches and that one was unusually large. Eight inches is the norm. Females are viviparous. They breed in fall and early winter and spawn in the spring, beginning in April. Small males go after both large and small females, preferentially courting the bigger ones. On the other hand, large males usually seek out larger females. Working off Monterey, Molly Cummings, of UCSB, has noted that large schools of 50-100 adults sometimes leave kelp beds for shallow surf grass, probably for courting and mating. Small kelp perch, less than about 4 inches long, feed on zooplankton; larger ones broaden their diet to include the small invertebrates that live on algae. While most feeding occurs during daylight, occasionally a fish will get the night–time munchies. Brandt's and double-crested cormorants eat them.

FISHERY: There is no fishery for this small species.

REMARKS: Some kelp perch clean other reef fishes, particularly blacksmith, of external parasites.

SHINER SURFPERCH (CYMATOGASTER AGGREGATA)

NAMES: Leven Perch, Pogie, Seven–Eleven, Yellow Shiner, Shiner, Bay Perch, Sparada. *Cymatogaster* was formed from 2 Greek words

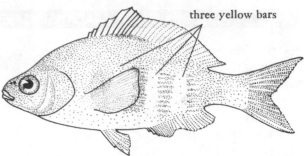

three yellow bars

meaning "fetus belly," a rather bizarre reference to the fact that this species gives birth to live young; *aggregata* is Latin for "crowded together," referring to the schooling behavior of these animals.

IDENTIFYING CHARACTERS: These are small silvery fish, with dark spots on scales which form a vague series of black stripes on the sides. Also, there are usually 3 yellow vertical bars on the mid-body. There is often a dark spot on the lip below the nostril. Courting males are blackish or have a horizontal black bar.

DISTRIBUTION AND BIOLOGY: Shiners are found from southeast Alaska to central Baja California, including Guadalupe Island, and are abundant from British Columbia southward. They inhabit a number of habitats, including quiet bays and backwaters, eelgrass and kelp beds, oil platforms, piers and jetties and occasionally the tidal zone of coastal streams. Some will even ascend into freshwater. Shiners are reported to live in waters ranging from 39-70° F. This species shows slight seasonal movement in some parts of its range, cruising into shallow waters in the spring, then departing for slightly deeper climes in the fall. They are most likely to be found in depths of 50 feet or less (into the surf zone), though they are common to 200 feet and have been taken down to 690 feet. While shiners school by day, they may disperse at night.

Shiners don't grow very large; the biggest one on record was 7 inches. They live to 8 years; females grow faster than males and reach larger sizes. A typical 4-incher is 3 years old. Females are viviparous, mature after one year and may produce as many 36 embryos. Males mature soon after birth. Displaying what I consider to be a significant lack of the Spirit of Adventure, courting males seek out only females of their own size. The males attack each other at this time, but Ed Demartini found that only similar-sized males duked it out. Here's another fun fact: While mating takes place in June or July (at least in southern California) females store the sperm until winter. Off southern California, spawning occurs in April and particularly in May, while off British Columbia it is June-August. Shiners feed primarily during daylight hours, though some night feeding has been noted. They eat such plank-tonic items as copepods, arrow worms, amphipods and fish eggs and also search for food over sand and rock bottoms. Kelp bass

and barred sand bass, California halibut, harbor seals, California sea lions, great blue herons, western gulls, bald eagles, least terns, Brandt's and double-crested cormorants just love these tasty morsels.
FISHERY: Without shiner perch, little kids fishing on some piers from southern California northward would have tough days indeed. I probably caught two billion of them before I was 8. Most are taken in bays and estuaries, particularly in San Francisco Bay, where they make up 3-5% of the total marine recreational catch. Recreational catches peak in July.

There is also a limited commercial catch in California, averaging a mighty 600 pounds per year. In southern California, shiners are taken incidentally for live bait; they are popular with anglers seeking California halibut, barred sand bass and the like.
REMARKS: Fossil shiner ear bones have been taken from Pliocene (over one-million-year old) deposits in Long Beach, California.

PILE SURFPERCH (DAMALICHTHYS VACCA)

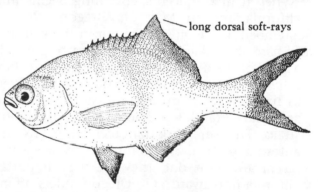

long dorsal soft-rays

NAME: Pile Perch, Piler. *Damalichthys* is a fusion of 2 Greek words meaning "calf fish," yet another strange allusion to the species' birthing live young; *vacca* is Latin for "cow." Also known as *Rhacochilus*.
IDENTIFYING CHARACTERS: Pilers are usually colored gray, occasionally brown or dusky, usually with a dark mid-body bar on the sides. They have a deeply forked caudal fin, and the soft rays of the second dorsal fin are long. Some individuals closely resemble rubberlip surfperches, which have thick lips and a caudal fin which is not deeply forked.
DISTRIBUTION AND BIOLOGY: Pilers occur from southeastern Alaska to north-central Baja California, commonly from British Columbia southward. They have been taken from shallow subtidal waters to 690 feet depths, but are most common in perhaps 10–60 feet. Off Redondo Beach, southern California, they tend to move into shallow waters during winter and spring, retiring a bit when waters warm. While you can find them as solitary individuals, they are as likely to be in small groups or even in dense schools of 100 or

more. These guys are very common in kelp beds, over rock reefs, around piers and oil platforms. Active during the day, pilers shut down at night.

Pilers are big perch, reaching 17.5 inches; some live at least 9 years. They become sexually mature in about their second year, at around 7 inches. Males mature slightly earlier than females and females grow faster than males. Females are viviparous and give birth to a whole slew (how big is half a slew?) of babies, up to 50 young ones. This next is from the ever-vigilant Molly Cummings, reporting from the kelp beds of Monterey. During courtship, male pilers turn very dark, almost black, and leave the protection of the kelp for the adjacent midwater. There they hang head down in the middle of the water column. This apparently tells the female, "Hey baby, look at me. I need you so much that I'm willing to risk being eaten by a harbor seal!" Molly has also seen males fight each other during mating season. They face off, erect their fins and bite each other. During the same period, she has also noted groups of females being escorted about by a single male. Ah, love.

When it finally occurs, spawning begins in April off southern California and in May off Oregon, where it runs through September. Little pilers hide out in thick algal cover. Brittle stars and hard-shelled animals, such as crabs, mussels and snails, make up most of the diet. It's not surprising that they have molar teeth in their throats for crunching hard shells. Even newly-born ones can handle tiny clams and mussels. Harbor seals, northern elephant seals, Brandt's and double-crested cormorants all eat them.

FISHERY: These are important recreational fish from Washington to California, particularly from piers (divers spear a lot of them, too). Year in and year out, they are very important from northern California northward. Off Oregon, pilers often comprise 3-8% of all fishes caught in the marine recreational fishery. Pile perch catches peak in February off Oregon and California. Ninety percent of all pilers taken in these two states were caught in San Francisco Bay, according to a study written by the California Department of Fish and Game.

Throughout their range, there is a small commercial fishery for pilers; the fish are taken by hook and line and nets. In California, it averages only about 200 pounds per year.

REMARKS: Occasionally you will see pilers with bright purple mouths, which comes from their eating wentletraps, a marine snail. During breeding season, they develop light yellow pelvic and anal fins and the males have black spots (they look like freckles) on their snouts.

When I was a kid in Santa Monica, some pier fishermen specialized in catching pilers. They wrapped mussel clumps in wire and connected about 6 leaders and hooks to this wrapping. Small whole mussels were attached to the hooks and the entire mass was then lowered over the side on a rope. A wire clothes hanger held the rope and its bouncing signaled a bite. Not very sporting, but it sure caught a lot of pilers.

Historically, this species, along with every other fish they could catch, was widely used by coastal Native Americans for food.

BLACK PERCH (EMBIOTOCA JACKSONI)

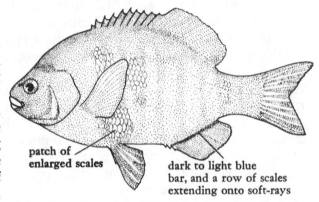

patch of enlarged scales

dark to light blue bar, and a row of scales extending onto soft-rays

NAME: Buttermouth Perch. *Embiotoca* is based on two Greek words meaning "living within" and "offspring," a reference to the live bearing behavior of the perches; *jacksoni* refers to A. C. Jackson, a resident of San Francisco who, in the mid-19th Century, first alerted scientists that seaperches give birth to live young.

IDENTIFYING CHARACTERS: These are variably colored fish, actually never black, most often various shades of brown or red, orange, gray and green (Plate 26). Sometimes they have a very tasteful blue flecking on scales and blue and gold markings on anal fins. Lips run from orange or yellow to reddish-brown, and there is a patch of large scales between the pectoral and pelvic fins.

DISTRIBUTION AND BIOLOGY: Black perch are found from Fort Bragg, northern California to central Baja California, mostly from San Francisco south. These typically rock reef fishes are most abundant in kelp forests, but they can also be found over sand, around piers and occasionally in estuaries, particularly near algae. Usually living either solitary lives or in small groups (they may occasionally school in numbers of 100-200), black perch tend to stay within about 3 feet of the bottom. "Teenagers" often school with females in the winter. While they have been taken from tide pools to 165 feet, they are abundant from just barely subtidal waters to about 80 feet.

Black perch reach 15.5 inches. They mature at about 6 inches (1-2 years old) and live at least 9 years. Males and females mature at the same age and have similar growth and survival rates.

Females are viviparous and produce as many as 31 young. Spawning time varies; it is mainly in the spring in southern California and late summer-early fall in central California. In southern California, there is some evidence for limited year-round spawning. Like many other reef perches, little black perch seek shelter in the fronds of bottom algae. These perches feed during daylight hours on a wide range of bottom organisms, including amphipods, crabs, brittle stars and worms. Even though most feeding is over hard bottoms, such as rocks or pilings, they will occasionally grub around in the sand. Like rubberlip seaperch, after sucking in a mouthful of algae, hydroids, amphipods, snails, rocks etc., black perch can actually winnow small prey from non-nutritious material using special muscles in their throats. They separate the goodies and spit out the "chaff." Harbor seals, Brandt's and double-crested cormorants, among other predators, eat them with great abandon.

FISHERY: These are very important sport fish in central and southern California, commonly taken by pier, jetty and rocky shore fishermen. They are also targeted by divers, and there is a small commercial fishery for them (averaging 400 pounds per year).

REMARKS: Black perch seem to be able to change color depending on their environment; they are light colored in sand environments and darker in algae.

Small individuals sometimes clean parasites from other fish.

STRIPED SEAPERCH (EMBIOTOCA LATERALIS)

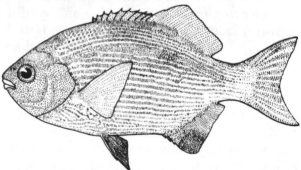

NAMES: Blue Perch, Stripes, Blue Surfperch. *Embiotoca* is formed from 2 Greek words, meaning "living within" and "offspring," referring to the species producing live young; *lateralis* is Latin and means "side," referring to the species' stripes.

IDENTIFYING CHARACTERS: Stripes are handsome perches which have alternating orange and blue stripes on the sides and neon blue mottling on heads. Shaped like black surfperch, stripes are much more colorful and do not have the large scales between the pectoral and pelvic fins. Rainbow seaperch, which have similar coloration, are more elongated and have black bars on their backs.

DISTRIBUTION AND BIOLOGY: Stripes are cold water animals, found from southeastern Alaska southward to central Baja California. On the mainland coast they are rarely seen between Santa Barbara and Punta Banda, Baja California. They are present around the islands of San Miguel, Santa Rosa and part of Santa Cruz, where cool waters exist, and in the cold, upwelled waters around several of the rocky points off Baja California. Stripes are found in estuaries (usually in eelgrass beds) and in the ocean from intertidal waters to 150 feet. On rocky reefs, they prefer areas with lots of bushy algae in 10–70 feet. Look for them to be near the bottom or in midwater, either as solitary individuals or in small groups. In spring and summer, stripes form pretty dense schools.

Stripes reach 15 inches and live at least 8 years. A 6-incher is about 2 years old and a one-footer is around 8 years. A few males and females mature when 2 years old and most mature in their third year (at 9 and 10 inches). Males and females mature at about the same age, and their growth rates are probably similar though males may grow slightly faster. Females are viviparous and spawning occurs from May into early summer off Oregon and Washington. Females produce between 11 and 92 young. Newly-spawned young live among the algae of shallow water reefs. Shrimps, crabs, gammarid amphipods, worms and other small bottom-dwelling invertebrates make up much of their diet. Unlike black perch, stripes don't winnow through debris for food. Rather they pick and browse for their prey. Brandt's cormorants eat them.

FISHERY: Stripes are major fishes in mud flat, rocky shore, pier, jetty and diver catches from southern California (Santa Barbara Channel) northward. North of San Francisco, they may form as much as 5-10% of the total recreational catch. In the Oregon/California fishery, the area from Mendocino to Del Norte Counties accounts for about 70% of all stripes taken. Catches peak in March and May.

A small number of stripes are taken commercially, with hook and line and seines.

REMARKS: Striped seaperch remains are commonly found in the middens of Puget Sound Native Americans.

WALLEYE SURFPERCH (HYPERPROSOPON ARGENTEUM)

NAMES: Walleye. *Hyperprosopon* is formed from 2 Greek words meaning "above the face," referring to the upward slanting mouth; *argenteum* is Latin for silvery.

IDENTIFYING CHARACTERS: Walleyes are distinguished by just what

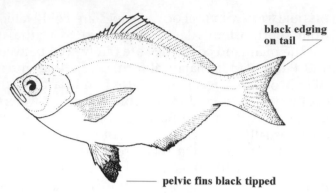

black edging on tail

pelvic fins black tipped

their com-mon name implies— a very large pair of eyes. They are sil-very perch, with purple or bluish backs and large up-turned mouths. During court-ship, males develop dark, vertical bars, and yellow pelvic, pectoral and anal fins.

DISTRIBUTION AND BIOLOGY: Found from Vancouver Island to central Baja California, walleyes are common from Washington southward and are particularly abundant off California. Occurring from very shallow waters to 600 feet, they are most often seen in 30 feet or less. By day, walleyes aggregate in dense schools (often several thousand individuals) along sandy beaches and sand-rock margins. At night, they move onto reefs, disperse to 3–10 feet above the bottom and feed on zooplankton. They are one of the few species on our coast that is active at night, and during this period they can be the most abundant midwater fishes in kelp beds.

Walleyes reach 1 foot and live about 6 years. Your typical 7-incher is 4 years old. Males mature earlier than females. On the other hand, females grow faster and live longer than males. Most fish mature during their first year, by 4.5 inches. Females are viviparous. Mating occurs in November, and the fish spawn from April–June; a female produces up to 19 young. Walleyes eat krill, amphipods, isopods and small fishes. The ubiquitous harbor seal, which apparently eats any fish around, also eats walleyes. They are also consumed by least terns and Brandt's and double-crested cormorants.

FISHERY: This is one of the mainstays of the pier fishery. It is also taken in some numbers by jetty and shore fishermen. Highest catches occur from San Francisco Bay northward. In a central California study, walleyes were even an important species for small vessel fishermen. There is a small commercial fishery for these fish.

REMARKS: Like many other near shore surfperches, walleyes were frequently eaten by coastal Native Americans; walleye fossils have been found in deposits over one million years old.

SPOTFIN SURFPERCH (HYPERPROSOPON ANALE)

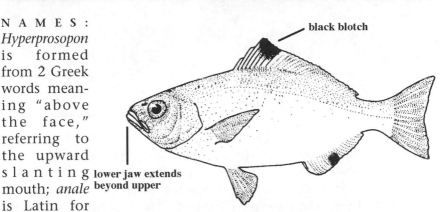

NAMES: *Hyperprosopon* is formed from 2 Greek words meaning "above the face," referring to the upward slanting mouth; *anale* is Latin for anal area (referring to the dark blotch on the anal fin).

IDENTIFYING CHARACTERS: They are small, sort of silvery with a dark spot on the dorsal and anal fins. And now you know the rest of the story.

DISTRIBUTION AND BIOLOGY: Found over sandy bottoms from Seal Rock, Oregon to central Baja California, spotfin surfperch are quite abundant in shallow water, though they have been taken down to 300 feet. These are aggregating fish, where you find one, you're likely to have a bunch. There is some evidence that females move into very shallow water during the summer and release their young.

They reach 8 inches in length and live to at least 3 years. It is possible that females may live longer and grow faster than males. Females are viviparous and produce between 4-20 young. The young ones are born between June and August. Small fishes and zooplankton make up their diets.

FISHERY: Once in a while, a shore fishermen takes one of these little perch.

REMARKS: Spotfins were occasionally eaten by Native Americans.

SILVER SURFPERCH (HYPERPROSOPON ELLIPTICUM)

NAMES: *Hyperprosopon* is formed from 2 Greek words meaning "above the face," referring to the upward slanting mouth; *ellipticum* is Latin for "elliptical."

IDENTIFYING CHARACTERS: A very distinctive fish is the silver surfperch, not easily mistaken for many other species. Its body is quite oval, and on the back it is silvery-gray or sort of olive. It has large eyes and a pinkish caudal fin. If you are not right on top of it, you might mistake this one for a walleye, but walleyes have black-

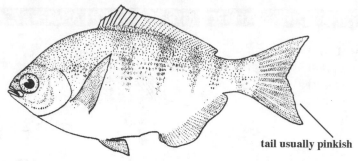

tail usually pinkish

tipped pelvic fins, so never fear.

DISTRIBUTION AND BIOLOGY: Brooks Peninsula, British Columbia to northern Baja California is where you will find this one. For a sort of flimsy-looking species, silvers are found in pretty hairy surf. They have been taken down to 360 feet. They spend most of their time over sandy bottoms.

A small species, silvers reach 10.5 inches and live about 7 years. Some males are mature at 1 year and 6 inches; all are mature at 3 years and 7 inches. Some females are mature at 2 years (7 inches), all at 3 years (8 inches). Males mature at a smaller size than females and grow more slowly. Females are viviparous, mating has been noted in late September and October. Off Oregon, the young are born from late June to early August. Females produce 4 to 16 young per season. Gammarid amphipods, sand crabs, small fishes and small clams are major parts of their diet.

FISHERY: This is an important recreational species, caught in some numbers from piers, docks and the shore. Though occasionally taken in southern California, most of the catch is from Pt. Arguello northward. In California and Oregon, most fish are caught in the open ocean, and catches peak in April; the summer bay catch peaks in May. Humboldt and San Francisco Bays contribute the most to the overall California-Oregon bay catch, while open ocean anglers catch most silvers in San Luis Obispo County.

RAINBOW SEAPERCH (HYPSURUS CARYI)

NAMES: *Hypsurus* is formed from 2 Greek words meaning "high tail"; *caryi* refers to Thomas G. Cary, this species' discoverer.

IDENTIFYING CHARACTERS: Rainbows are really quite lovely fish. They have blue and orange stripes along their bodies, with orange bars on their backs. There are also a number of blue spots, streaks and blotches on the heads. Look, too, for the long belly and the dark blotches on the anal and soft dorsal fins.

DISTRIBUTION AND BIOLOGY: Cape Mendocino, northern California

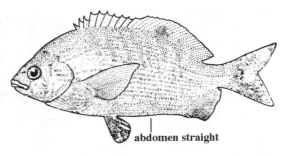

abdomen straight

to northern Baja California, from inshore waters to 132 feet, is home to this species. They may be seen as solitary individuals, in small groups or in very large schools. Molly Cummings, at UCSB, has noted that large numbers of females enter very shallow surfgrass areas in May. In general, she has found that rainbows off Monterey move into shallow water in the spring and depart in the fall. In King Harbor, southern California, they come into shallow waters during winter and spring.

Rainbows reach 1 foot in length. Females are viviparous, mature at about 5 inches long and produce 5-22 young per season. Courtship occurs in September and October, over shallow sand bottoms with some drift algae. In Halfmoon Bay, central California, spawning occurs from mid-August to mid-September. There is some evidence that the young may be born either head- or tail-first. The young, a little over 2 inches at birth, are found in shallow waters, among algae. Rainbows go for gammarid amphipods in a big way, but they will also suck down isopods and other crustaceans, as well as snails and brittle stars.

FISHERY: Rainbows are occasionally taken by boat, pier and shore anglers, particularly in central and northern California. There is a small commercial fishery for them, averaging about 400 pounds per year.

REMARKS: Rainbow remains are only rarely found in Native American middens.

Divers have seen them clean ocean sunfish in Monterey Bay.

REEF PERCH (MICROMETRUS AURORA)

NAMES: *Micrometrus* comes from two Greek words for "small measure"; *aurora* is Latin for "sunrise," a rather pretty reference to the orange glow on the species' lower sides.

IDENTIFYING CHARACTERS: A very cute little fish, reefs have a black triangular patch at the base of their pectoral fins and, the big tipoff, a bunch of black-tipped scales between the pectoral and anal fins. There is also a yellow or yellow-orange stripe on the lower side.

DISTRIBUTION AND BIOLOGY: Reef perch are found from Tomales Bay, northern California to north-central Baja California. These are schooling fishes, found among vegetation in the intertidal and very shallow (usually 6 feet or less) subtidal. Mostly, you find them over surfgrass

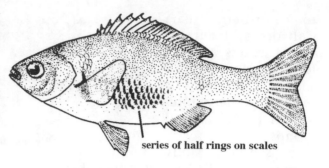

series of half rings on scales

and red and green algae. They are quite abundant in the tidepools of central and northern California. Carl Hubbs, late of Scripps Institution of Oceanography, noted that they occasionally leap out of the water.

One of the smallest marine perches, reefs reach 7 inches in length and may live to 6 years. Females grow faster than males, grow larger and live longer. Courtship takes place during July and August in Monterey Bay. Males are born mature. Females store sperm and retain it until winter when they mature and fertilize their eggs. Females are viviparous, spawn in the late spring and early summer and produce 5-30 young. Reefs feed primarily on algae.

REMARKS: Reefs may have been occasionally eaten by Native Americans. This species' ear bones are rarely found in middens.

DWARF PERCH (MICROMETRUS MINIMUS)

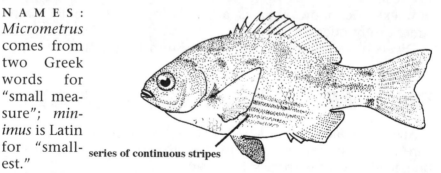

series of continuous stripes

NAMES: *Micrometrus* comes from two Greek words for "small measure"; *minimus* is Latin for "smallest."

IDENTIFYING CHARACTERS: Dwarfs are blue or green on the backs, with a black triangle, like reef surfperch, at the base of the pectoral fin. Unlike reefs, dwarfs are covered with dark blotches. Males have a half-moon shaped depression at the base of their anal fins and a large gland on the anal fin itself.

DISTRIBUTION AND BIOLOGY: Found from Bodega Bay, northern California to central Baja California, dwarf perch are schooling, shallow water fish living between the intertidal zone and depths of about 30 feet. They prefer shallow eelgrass and surfgrass beds as well as rocky areas, generally in waters less than about 6 feet deep. Juveniles are most abundant in the intertidal zone.

True to their name, dwarfs only reach 9.4 inches, and as a species they live to 6 years. However, females grow faster and larger than males and live longer. In fact, a lot of males croak in their first year, and relatively few squeak past Year 2. Making up for the time Nature has denied them, male reef perch are sexually mature at birth and quickly mate with newborn females. Interestingly, the newborn females are not mature; rather they store sperm for more than 6 months, until their eggs are ready in the winter and early spring. Females are viviparous and produce 2-25 young. In southern California, females give birth from April to July. There is a certain symmetry in who breeds with whom in this species. During breeding season, large males maintain territories of about 20 feet by 20 feet, chasing out other large male dwarfs. Small males are ignored by both large males and large females. Small males are attracted to small females and follow and court them, even defending them against other small males. Small females occasionally chase after large males, but are invariably ignored by these stud muffins.

Here is a stirring description of male courtship from Warner and Harlan (Evolution, 1982, p. 44-55). "Courtship consists of a male swimming toward a female from the rear at about a 45° horizontal angle, terminating with a bite to the area just posterior of the operculum [cheek]. This is followed by the male positioning himself in front of and at a right angle to the female, head slightly downward. His median fins [dorsal, anal] are erected, and he rapidly lowers and raises his pelvic fins." And so on and so on. There is a bit more about everybody vibrating wildly and some talk about copulation, but you don't really want to know about that, do you? Females often mate with males within 5 minutes of giving birth, and they may mate with more than one male during the breeding season. Males spend an inordinate amount of time courting, about 45 minutes a day over the 4 month season. And what is the return on the money? Pretty low. Larger males court an average of 28 minutes for each mating, smaller ones about 12.5 minutes per. Males tend to court females that are about to give birth (Is it hot in here, or is it just me? I think my Power Mac is starting to melt). Dwarfs eat various crustaceans, such as gammarid amphipods and isopods, as well as worms, snails and algae.

FISHERY: They are very occasionally taken by pier anglers.

REMARKS: Regarding male dwarf perch being mature at birth: Without putting too fine a point on it, this is obviously a case of

American ingenuity at its finest. I doubt if fishes from other economic systems could do as well.

SHARPNOSE SEAPERCH (PHANERODON ATRIPES)

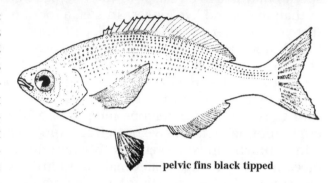

pelvic fins black tipped

NAMES: *Phanerodon* was formed from 2 Greek words meaning "evident tooth," yet another puzzling, one might say bizarre, allusion for a species without particularly evident teeth; *atripes* is at least marginally better, coming from 2 Latin words for "black foot," for its dark gray or black-tipped pelvic fins.

IDENTIFYING CHARACTERS: These are sort of silvery or reddish fish, with black or dusky-tipped pelvic fins.

DISTRIBUTION AND BIOLOGY: Yaquina Bay, Oregon to central Baja California is where the sharpnose call home. They have been taken from inshore waters to depths of 750 feet. From various diver surveys along the Pacific Coast, it is apparant that, while they are spotted from time to time in kelp beds and over reefs, sharpnoses are just not that abundant in the nearshore environment. Most diver sightings are in relatively deep water, perhaps 60 feet or more. They are common, sometimes very common, on offshore oil platforms. Both juveniles and adults occasionally form larger aggregations. In one study off La Jolla, these fish (particularly the juveniles) moved inshore on flows of water below 66° F.

They grow to 13.7 inches and live to at least 7 years. Relatively little is known about this one. Like all embiotocids, sharpnose females are viviparous, and based on examination of only a few females, they produce as many as 11 young per season. It is likely that that these are summer spawners. Sharpnoses commonly eat gammarid and caprellid amphipods, isopods, bryozoans, limpets, chitons, copepods and kelp.

FISHERY: A very occasional catch by recreational anglers. There is no commercial fishery for this one.

REMARKS: These are occasionally found in Native American middens.

Sharpnoses will, on occasion, clean other fishes of some exterior parasites and probably of some damaged flesh as well. Blacksmith, rockfishes and perhaps ocean sunfish have all been recipients of this largesse.

WHITE SEAPERCH (PHANERODON FURCATUS)

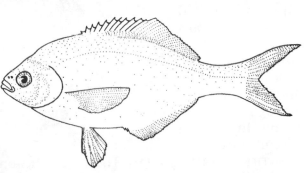

NAMES: *Phanerodon* was formed from 2 Greek words meaning "evident tooth" – a pretty obscure allusion, because this species does not have particularly evident teeth; *furcatus* is Latin for forked, referring to the species' deeply forked tail.

IDENTIFYING CHARACTERS: These are boring, nondescript silvery fish, with a black line at the base of the dorsal fin.

DISTRIBUTION AND BIOLOGY: White seaperch are found from Vancouver Island southward to northern Baja California, from the surf line to 231 feet, most commonly from about 10–100 feet depths, usually in loose schools. Inhabiting a wide range of habitats, they can be found over both sandy and rocky bottoms (often around oil platforms), in both quiet waters and fairly heavy surf. Whites are midwater fish by day and midwater or bottom ones at night.

Twelve and one-half inches is the size record for these fish. They live to 7 years and females grow faster than males. Females are viviparous. As many as 33 young have been found per female. Spawning occurs April–July in southern California and May–August in northern California. White seaperch eat bottom organisms such as crabs, worms and amphipods and they feed during the day. These are opportunistic fish and among the first to arrive around any kind of disturbance to see if anything edible has been routed out. As with most perches, harbor seals and California sea lions are known to prey on these guys. Least terns, California gulls, and Brandt's and double-crested cormorants also nab them.

FISHERY: White seaperch are a commonly-taken species from piers and jetties from southern California northward. Catches in the ocean peak in January and May and are highest in bays and estuaries in February-March. The number of white seaperch caught along California and Oregon decreased by 61% between 1980 and 1986, according to a study by the California Department of Fish and Game.

In the California of the 1930s and 1940s, white seaperch were an important commercial species. Today, they form a minor part of that fishery. I do see them fairly frequently in Vietnamese markets.

NAMES: Rubberlips, bigmouth. *Rhacochilus* means "rag lip" in Greek; *toxotes* is a Greek word for an East Indian archer fish, though no one seems to see the resemblance.

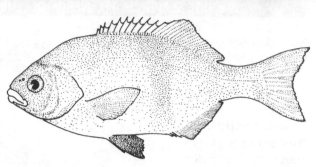

IDENTIFYING CHARACTERS: These are the only perch with very thick, white or pale pink lips. Black perch have prominent, but thinner, lips that come in yellow, orange, or reddish-brown. Rubberlip body color ranges from silvery-green to brassy and they occasionally come in black.

DISTRIBUTION AND BIOLOGY: Found from Mendocino County (northern California) to central Baja California, rubberlips are common from central California southward. They are abundant near hard structures such as kelp beds, rocky reefs, pilings and oil platforms and sometimes in quiet backwaters (rarely in the surf). Although they have been taken from shallow subtidal to 156 foot depths, 10–100 feet is their usual haunt. This is often a schooling fish (found in groups of up to about 50 individuals), usually swimming near the bottom or in midwater in the lower kelp canopy.

Rubberlips are large perch, the largest of the family, reaching 18.5 inches. Not much is known about them. A 17-incher I aged was 9 years old and a 13-inch one was 4 years old. Like pile seaperch, rubberlip males turn very dark during courtship and attract females by drifting about with their heads down, out away from the kelp. Also like pilers, during this time groups of females may be escorted by a single male. Young ones live in shallow waters, among algae. Rubberlips eat small, bottom-dwelling invertebrates such as gammarid amphipods and shrimps. Harbor seals and Brandt's cormorants are known to eat them.

FISHERY: Pier and jetty fishermen take a fair number of these large perch. They are also a favorite target of divers. I have seen small numbers in coastal commercial fish markets. Commercial fishermen catch them with seines and hook and line.

REMARKS: Rubberlips use their large, flexible lips as suction devices when feeding, clamping them onto invertebrate-covered rocks and pulling their food into their mouths. What is really cool about these fish is their ability to separate small invertebrates from all the mung they suck in, without having a tongue to help. (Surprise! Fish don't have tongues. The structure that looks like one is actually a support for their gill arches.) This trick is equivalent to your putting a bunch of miniature marshmallows, broken glass, fingernail clippings and cubic zirconiums in your mouth, then separating and swallowing only the marshmallows, all without using your tongue or fingernails. Good trick, yes?

Their habit of slowly gliding around pier pilings, blithely ignoring all baits, has driven any number of 10-year-old anglers into frenzies of frustration.

These are often found in native American middens.

PINK SEAPERCH (ZALEMBIUS ROSACEUS)

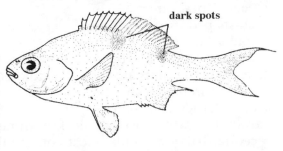

dark spots

NAMES: *Zalembius* is a particularly poetic name, formed from 2 Greek words meaning "surges of the sea" and "life within"; *rosaceus* is Latin for "rosy." I wonder if it's too late to rename my daughter *Zalembius*. I think there's time, she's only 17.

IDENTIFYING CHARACTERS: This one's easy. Really quite an elegant little species, it's the only surfperch that is pink and it has 2 chocolate spots below the dorsal fin. The upper lobe of the male caudal fin trails off in a merry little streamer.

DISTRIBUTION AND BIOLOGY: Pinks are found from Pt. Delgada, northern California, to central Baja California, in 26 to 780 feet of water, most often between about 150 and 500 feet. An isolated population lives in the Gulf of California. They are the deepest dwelling of the perches. From our underwater observations, they usually live over sand, but occasionally you can find them over low rocks. We have never seen big schools; mostly it's small groups.

Pinkies grow to 8 inches. Females are viviparous and, off southern California, mating occurs primarily from March-June. Females give birth during the winter and produce between 2 and 6 young. Pinks feed on a wide range of benthic or near-bottom creatures, including various gammarid amphipods, polychaete worms, ostracods, brittlestars and snails. They are eaten by harbor seals and glaucous-winged gulls.

Damselfishes and Anemonefishes - Family Pomacentridae

BLACKSMITH (CHROMIS PUNCTIPINNIS)

NAMES: *Chromis* is a very old Greek word which probably referred to some sort of croaker; *punctipinnis* comes from 2 Latin words meaning "spot fin."

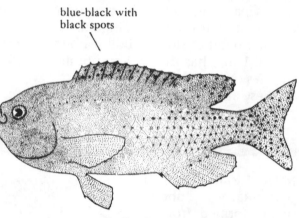

blue-black with black spots

IDENTIFYING CHARACTERS: These are perch-shaped fish, gray-blue or gray on sides with black spots on the rear of their bodies (Plate 25). Males guarding nests are very light colored – almost white–with a dark bar through each eye. Young ones, to about 2 inches, are bicolored; they have blue-gray fronts and brassy-orange rears.

DISTRIBUTION AND BIOLOGY: Blacksmith range from Monterey Bay to central Baja California, most commonly from Pt. Conception southward. However, during some periods (as in the late 1980s), they are present at least as far north as Cannery Row in Monterey Bay. These are very abundant midwater fish over structures (such as rocky reefs and oil platforms) in nearshore waters from the surface to 150 feet. During the day, large schools with hundreds of individuals can be found over most reefs. Adults tend to hang out at the incurrent side of these reefs, waiting for zooplankton to drift in, while young ones are usually found near the bottom, close to refuge. At night, most blacksmith shelter in crevices or on sand near crevices. These are really gregarious fish – you can find caves just packed with resting fish. During breeding season, males clean nest sites (overhangs or small caves in rocky reefs) and guard eggs until they hatch.

Blacksmith reach one foot in length. They probably mature at around 5.5 inches and 2 years of age. Females are oviparous. Spawning occurs in summer and perhaps fall. Larvae have been captured from central California to southern Baja California. Peak concentrations occur from the U.S.-Mexican border to Punta Baja, northern Baja California. Most larvae stay near the coast (within 100 miles); a few have been taken as much as 300 miles from shore. During most years, newly-recruited juveniles first appear in late summer or early fall. Schools of these very young fish are semi-pelagic, occasionally entering kelp beds. Blacksmith feed on zooplankton, such as copepods, crustacean larvae and eggs. In turn, they are eaten by larger fishes (including kelp bass, moray eels and lingcod), marine mammals (harbor seals and California sea lions) and birds (least terns, Brandt's and double-crested cormorants). Bald eagles at Santa Catalina Island get fair numbers.

Harbor seals observed at Santa Catalina Island feed on blacksmith at night. They probe the crevices for sheltering fish, perhaps finding them by touch. Fish are swallowed under water, and one animal was seen to eat 20 or more blacksmith in 45 minutes.
FISHERY: There is a small sport fishery for blacksmith, particularly by divers, but the fish's small mouth prevents many hookups. They are also a minor commercial species, occasionally appearing in perch catches.
REMARKS: If you dive at Santa Catalina Island during late spring or early summer, you may see hundreds of dead blacksmith on the bottom, all with sores on their sides. The sores and subsequent deaths are caused by *Vibrio damsella*, a bacterium my friends and I discovered in 1980. Blacksmith in various locations along the coast succumb to this germ from about April–June. Among fishes, only blacksmith seem to become ill, although some humans who cut themselves in warm seas (such as on coral reefs) become infected.

GARIBALDI (HYPSYPOPS RUBICUNDA)

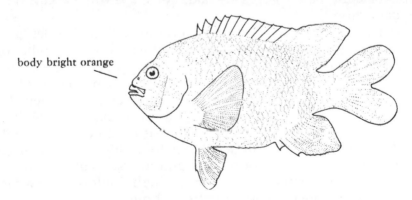

body bright orange

NAMES: *Hypsypops* comes from 3 Greek words which means "high below the eye," referring to the wide distance from the front of the head to the eye; *rubicunda* is Latin for "red."

IDENTIFYING CHARACTERS: Garibaldi are perch-shaped and bright orange; the juveniles (to about 6 inches) have intense blue markings. That's all you need to know.

DISTRIBUTION AND BIOLOGY: Found from Monterey Bay to southern Baja California and Isla Guadalupe, garibaldi are abundant from about Santa Barbara southward. These are strictly rocky bottom fish, found from intertidal waters to about 95 feet. The adults are remarkably territorial; both males and females defend large expanses of reefs against each other and almost any other intruder. Even larger fish-eating fishes, from which you would expect garibaldi to flee, are often chased away. When pursuing intruders, these fish make a clacking sound, produced by rubbing their throat teeth together. One of the few animals not attacked is the harbor seal, which probably views such behavior as before-dinner entertainment.

Garibaldi reach 14 inches in length and 17 years of age. A 6-incher is 3 years old and a 12-incher is at least 10. They begin to reproduce at about 6 years and 8–9 inches long. Spawning takes place from March–October, beginning when water temperatures reach around 59° F. Females are oviparous, producing 15,000–88,000 eggs. While both males and females are territorial, only males guard nests. Beginning in spring, males begin to tend the nests, removing everything except red algae – other algae, rocks, seastars etc. are all carried away (Plates 27-29). (Hours of simple enjoyment can be yours by putting something heavy in a nest, such as a dive knife, and watching a little gangster try to remove it.) During courtship, female garibaldi swim about the reef, checking out the local guys. She may come and go from her territory a number of times before making a choice. The lucky gentleman having been selected, the female enters the male's territory and lays her eggs in the nest. Females often return to the same male until all her eggs are laid. Most spawning occurs during daylight.

When spawning begins, males go through "brood cycles." In a brood cycle, a male receives clutches of eggs from a number of females for 5-10 (rarely to 20) days. If a typical garibaldi is pretty defensive about its territory, a male is positively psychotic about defending eggs. He guards these until they all hatch, then the cycle begins again. The eggs take 2-3 weeks to hatch, depending on temperatures. Eggs hatch at night, within 2 hours of sunset. Newly hatched larvae are attracted to light. While they have been taken from southern California to southern Baja California, heaviest larval concentrations occur off southern California. Few larvae are taken more than 30 miles from shore.

Young garibaldi first appear in shallow water (less than 15 feet) from July–November. Garibaldi feed during daylight hours on attached animals such as sponges, bryozoans and small anemones and occasionally dine on worms, nudibranchs and crabs. One researcher saw them eating a *Pelagia*, the purple-striped jellyfish. Bald eagles at Santa Catalina Island eat them.

FISHERY: It is illegal to take garibaldis, and considering how easy they are for novice divers to spear, this is the reason there are any left. An acquaintance claims that as a child she caught garibaldi on green peas off the Newport Jetty (southern California), took these protected fish home and ate them. She says they were pretty good.

REMARKS: Young, immature garibaldi are rarely harassed by their elders. Apparently their blue markings, which disappear when they mature, give them some protection from adults.

Wrasses - Family Labridae

ROCK WRASSE (HALICHOERES SEMICINCTUS)

lateral line with an abrupt arch

male has deep blue bar behind pectoral fin

12 anal soft-rays

NAMES: *Halichoeres* is formed from 2 Greek words meaning "sea young pig," *semicinctus* is Latin for "half-banded."

IDENTIFYING CHARACTERS: Rock wrasse are multicolored, cigar-shaped fish, with large scales and prominent, forward-pointing teeth. Small juveniles are green, becoming orangish-brown with one white stripe on their backs, one on the sides and 2 black spots on the dorsal fins. Mature fish are green or green-orange on backs and sides, and yellow below. Males have a black bar behind the base of their yellow pectoral fins; all other fins are orange. Females may have a number of faint bars.

DISTRIBUTION AND BIOLOGY: Found from Pt. Conception to Isla Guadalupe and into the Gulf of California, rock wrasses are most often seen from Palos Verdes south (including Santa Catalina Island). However, during El Niño periods larvae are carried further north, and young-of-the-year show up as far north as Santa Barbara. Rock wrasses have been seen from tide pools to 132 feet; most are found from 10–50 feet, often hanging out in sand or gravel patches near algae-covered rocks. Most often you will spot these fish as solitary individuals, but occasionally they come in pairs and small ones may school-up. These are diurnal animals, active during daylight hours and asleep during the night. They take shelter in bottom algae about 20 minutes after sunset and reappear about 20 minutes before sunrise. There are some reports that they also bury themselves in the sand at night, with their heads exposed.

Rock wrasses reach 15 inches and live to 14 years. An 8-incher is 10 years old. Most fish mature at 2 years, at 5-6 inches. About 5% of the fish off southern California change sex, with females becoming males. Spawning occurs from June-September, peaking in July. One-inch fish come into shallow water in fall. They eat bottom organisms including crabs, amphipods, snails, algae and bryozoans.

FISHERY: What can you say? Their small mouths make them an unusual sport catch, although rocky reef fishermen take a few. They are also remarkably difficult for divers to approach and only a few are speared.

REMARKS: Rock wrasse may occasionally clean other fish, picking off dead bits of tissue and external parasites. Actually, this statement is based on a report of perhaps one individual which apparently cleaned other fish periodically over a number of months.

SENORITA (OXYJULIS CALIFORNICA)

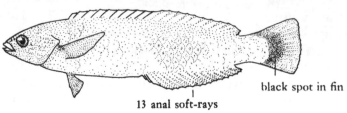

13 anal soft-rays

black spot in fin

NAMES: *Oxyjulis* is a combination of a Greek word for "sharp" and "julis," an ancient name for small wrasses; *californica* refers to the location of the first fish taken.

IDENTIFYING CHARACTERS: A little cigar-shaped fish, senoritas have large scales and cute buck teeth that stick out of their mouths and simply cry out for a competent orthodontist. Most senoritas are orangish or brownish; a few are sort of pink or yellow. All have a large black blotch at the base of their caudal fins.

DISTRIBUTION AND BIOLOGY: Senoritas are found from Salt Point (northern California) to south-central Baja California and during some years are common from northern California southward. During relatively cold water periods, their range contracts and they are found primarily south of Pt. Conception. Juveniles occasionally range into intertidal waters; adults have been seen by research submarines down to at least 320 feet. Most fish are found between 5 and 240 feet. The fish hang out anywhere from the bottom to near the surface. Senoritas always hang out over reefs or among algae with the young ones tending to shelter close to cover and bigger ones ranging away from structure. While they usually form small aggregations, solitary individuals or pairs are common. These are strictly diurnal fish; they are active during the day and sleep at night. Actually, it's sort of neat watching their bedtime routine. About 15 minutes after sunset the fish search out a coarse sand bed adjacent to the reef and, almost faster than you can see, they barrel headfirst into the bottom, burying themselves for the night. Some senoritas may also produce a mucous net around themselves. About 15 minutes before sunrise, they shake themselves loose, comb the sand from their gill slits and head for the office, ready to trade plankton futures for yet another day.

Senoritas reach 11.7 inches and live for about 7 years. Most mature at 3 inches and one year. Females are oviparous. Spawning occurs from March to about October, peaking June-September. The eggs are pelagic. While spawning has been noted from central California to southern Baja California, heaviest larval concentrations are found off southern California. Larvae often occur 150 miles offshore, occasionally as much as 300 miles off the coast. Young-of-the-year appear in inshore waters from June-November. Small ones eat a lot of plankton (copepods, ostracods, etc.), while larger ones pick food off algae such as hydroids, bryozoans and amphipods. They also eat parasitic copepods and isopods from the skins of other fishes (see Remarks). Brandt's cormorants and California sea lions eat them.

FISHERY: Considered a nuisance by some anglers because they are accomplished bait stealers, senoritas have small mouths and are taken only occasionally from piers and boats. My son likes to eat them and since he has shown no ill effects, I guess they are okay.

REMARKS: Senoritas are cleaners, picking external parasites and dead tissues from the bodies of other fishes (Plate 25). Many kinds of fishes are cleaned by this species, including bat rays, giant sea bass, garibaldi, molas, kelpfish, blacksmith, etc. are cleaned by this species. However, while some tropical cleaners are full-timers, senoritas are sort of dilettantes in the field, cleaning only when they are in the mood, and the mood strikes only an occasional fish, only once in a while. However, when the "cleaning thing" does begin, it causes quite a commotion. For instance, a senorita might begin by casually inspecting a blacksmith's skin, looking for parasites. When the blacksmith notices this, it often stops swimming, holds its fins erect and motionless and drifts (frequently in a head down position). Other fish see what is going on and quickly move in, often forming a ball of activity around the cleaner. The senorita soon moves away, perhaps to inspect and pick at other fishes, which are busily throwing themselves in its path. After a relatively short time, the cleaner loses all interest in the matter and swims off, leaving in its wake a trail of disappointment and despair.

CALIFORNIA SHEEPHEAD (SEMICOSSYPHUS PULCHER)

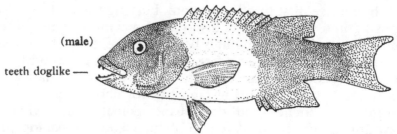

(male)

teeth doglike ——

NAMES: Sheepie, Billygoat, Redfish, Humpy, Vieja (Mexico). *Pulcher* is Latin for "beautiful."

IDENTIFYING CHARACTERS: Color and body shape give these fish away. Young ones are really cute, colored gold or salmon, with at least one white stripe along the side, 2 black spots on the dorsal fin, one on the anal fin and one on the caudal peduncle (Plate 14). This juvenile coloration lasts to about 4 inches. Females are pink all over with a white chin; an occasional fish will be brown or almost black (Plate 15). Males are a bit more imposing, with black heads (white chins) and tail regions, and a red or pink midriff (Plate 16). They also have a prominent bump on their foreheads. Both sexes have large, thick canine teeth.

DISTRIBUTION AND BIOLOGY: Sheephead are found from Monterey Bay (central California) to Isla Guadalupe and into the Gulf of California, over reefs and in kelp. The fish are common along much of their range, particularly from Pt. Conception southward. North of Pt. Conception, one area of concentration is in the warm water discharge at the Diablo Canyon Nuclear Power Plant, near Avila Beach. Young-of-the-year do not recruit to the northern part of their range (from Pt. Conception northward) unless carried north by strong, warm, southerly currents, as in El Niño years. Some of these northern reefs contain only one size of sheephead, all of them settled on the reef during the same year. While these are usually solitary fish, you might see them in small aggregations. Sheephead have been reported from shallow subtidal waters to depths of at least 281 feet, with juveniles reported from 10 to over 100 feet and adults common from about 10 to over 200 feet. Sheephead are active only during the day; they sleep in caves and crevices at night and some surround themselves with a mucous envelope while they sleep. (How do you keep the stamp from falling off a mucous envelope?) Juveniles have been seen sleeping in gorgonians (sea fans).

Sheephead reach 3 feet and males have been aged to 53 years, females to 30. These are relatively slow-growing fish, reaching 5 inches after one year and 18 inches after 10–20 years. Fish from Guadalupe Island grow even slower and don't get as large as mainland ones. Females mature at 4 years, and they change sex at around 8 years (12-14 inches). Rapidly growing fish become males sooner, and very slow growers may not change sex at all. The sex change comes between spawning seasons. At Catalina Island, spawning occurs from July–September, and each fish probably spawns several times. Sheephead eat lots of hard-shelled or encrusting animals, smashing them with their strong teeth and jaws. Crabs, barnacles, clams, mussels, snails, octopi and various worms are all favored tidbits. On an artificial reef made of wooden street cars, sheephead bit off chunks of the wooden frame to get at the ship worms, then spit out the splinters. Large adults have been seen hanging onto mussels in midair after waves have receded. (I just report 'em folks.) Giant sea bass, as well as various sea mammals, eat sheephead. I have seen harbor seals hold and eat them like ears of corn. California sea lions, bald eagles and Brandt's cormorants also go for them.

FISHERY: For many years, sheephead were disdained by anglers, even though they were often taken by fishermen. As more popular species have declined in abundance, sheephead have become an acceptable quarry. Sport divers also take many of these slow, lumbering fish. Most are taken from Pt. Conception southward, although I notice that they are often taken in spear fishing tournaments as far north as Carmel (central California). In some areas of southern California, they may comprise 1-3% of the total marine catch. Though they are taken throughout the year, recreational vessel catches tend to peak from August to October.

There has been a small, steady commercial market for sheephead, with the fish taken incidentally in gillnets, lobster traps and by hook and line. Around 1880, Chinese fishermen caught and dried large quantities. Recently, a very lucrative live fish market has developed, and hook and line commercial fishermen are targeting this species. Most sheephead are now sold live, to Asian markets and restaurants. Large individuals are marketed fresh or, occasionally, frozen. Sheepie fillets have a refrigerated life span of

5-7 days at 40° F. They can be frozen at 0° F for about 9 months.
REMARKS: As I suggested previously, almost all California sheephead change sex from female to male. The changeover occurs when they are about 8 years old and takes less than a year to complete. Many members of the wrasse family change sex, always from female to male. In fact, sex change is fairly common among fishes, and while usually from female to male, a few species (particularly some basses) go the other way. Personally, I think it's neat to contemplate the effect on our society if we changed sex. Consider, for a moment, if most humans changed sex when they were say, 30 years old. Sexism would be less common, as all of us would understand what both sexes experience.

Fossil teeth and jaws have been found in deposits as old as the Miocene (6-23 million years ago).

Sheephead remains are common in Native American middens. In fact, they are the dominant fish species in the middens at San Clemente Island.

Juvenile sheepheads may occasionally clean other fishes.

Yet more doggerel, this time about fishes that change sex.

REPRODUCTIO AD ABSURDUM

There are fishes, we scarcely dare mention,
With behavior that merits attention.
   At ages quite tender
   They blithely change gender
Disdaining the normal convention.

There's *Labroides*, a wrasse quite compact,
Where polygamy, in harems, is fact.
   If the male succumbs
   A female becomes
The male in appearance and act.

Some basses now fight for their rights,
After lifetimes of onerous slights.
   When all's said and done
   They're both sexes in one -
Power to oppressed hermaphrodites!

These fishes go others one more:
"To us, one sex is a bore.
   It may not be great
   But if we can't find a date
On ourselves we surely can score."
These are, all you fathers and mothers,

The wrasses and basses and others.
  If we followed their lead
  Henceforth, then, our creed:
"All humans are *sisters* and brothers."

Clinids and Klipfishes - Family Clinidae

GIANT KELPFISH (HETEROSTICHUS ROSTRATUS)

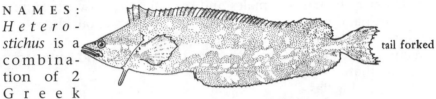
tail forked

NAMES: *Hetero-stichus* is a combination of 2 Greek words meaning "different rank," referring to differing widths between the dorsal spines; *rostratus* means "longnosed."

IDENTIFYING CHARACTERS: These are charming little fish, shaped like kelp blades, which come in 3 flavors (red, brown and green) along with a whole series of silvery patterns. Their forked tails and pointed snouts easily separate them from other kelpfishes.

DISTRIBUTION AND ABUNDANCE: Reported from British Columbia to southern Baja California, giant kelpfish are abundant from about Pt. Conception southward. These fish are found only among marine plants, most often red and brown algae. They spend most of their time trying to look like their surroundings, with their bodies angled in the same direction as the algae, swaying in the same way. Although newly recruited juveniles school up, when they reach 2–3 inches (2–4 months) they develop adult colors and begin a solitary life.

A giant kelpfish has been reported to 2 feet, but that one must have had a pituitary problem, as fish over 15 inches are rare. A 16.5-incher was 5 years old. Females seem to live slightly longer and to grow slightly faster. A 7 inch fish is about 1 year old, a 12 incher is 2.5–3 years. These puppies mature at 7–8 inches. Females are oviparous. While they have been reported to spawn year round, spawning peaks from January–May off Santa Catalina. The eggs have entangling threads which hold onto mats of red or brown algae. Males guard the eggs until they hatch (12–17 days). Each nest contains the eggs of one female (usually 400–1,200 eggs). Larvae drift in the plankton for a relatively short 2 weeks, and most young ones recruit in spring and summer in 5–30 feet of water among marine plants. Before they settle, the larvae tend to school with transparent mysid shrimp along the bottom. Giant kelpfish feed primarily in the daytime, eating such small crustaceans as shrimps, mysids and amphipods, as well as small fishes such as clingfish, kelp perch and senorita. Brandt's cormorants and least terns eat them.

FISHERY: While kelpfish are occasionally taken by pier, jetty and boat anglers, these catches are relatively rare. I have read that they are okay to eat.

REMARKS: Kelpfish can alter their colors. Juveniles switch fairly quickly from green to brown, responding to changes in background color. The picture is more complicated in adults. Females are better at it than are males and over time can switch among red, green and brown. Males are sort of hapless about the whole thing. They can't change to red and really can't make a true green; some can make it to a sort of olive-brown and some can't even do that.

Pretty sad, fellas.

SARCASTIC FRINGEHEAD (NEOCLINUS BLANCHARDI) AND ONESPOT FRINGEHEAD (NEOCLINUS UNINOTATUS)

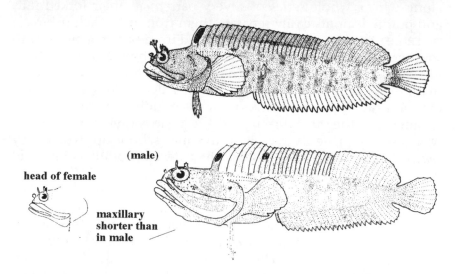

(male)

head of female

maxillary
shorter than
in male

NAMES: *Neoclinus* is formed from 2 Greek words meaning "new Clinus"; *blanchardi* honors S. B. Blanchard, who discovered the species at San Diego and passed it on to Girard, its describer; *uninotatus* means "one mark," referring to the one spot on the species' dorsal fin.

These 2 species are pretty similar, and do sort of the same things, so I threw them together.

IDENTIFYING CHARACTERS: Both fringeheads have enormous mouths (larger in males), which extend way behind the eyes (Plate 31). Most sarcastics are brown or gray; males can be almost black and have greenish or pale blotches. The rear part of the jaw is yellow in males. There are 2 spots (ocelli) on the dorsal fin which are metallic blue, surrounded by yellow. Onespots are brown with black flecks and mottling, and they do have one spot on the dorsal fin.

DISTRIBUTION AND BIOLOGY: Sarcastics are found from San Francisco to central Baja California, in depths of 10–240 feet. They live in various kinds of shelters, such as empty clam shells, abandoned invertebrate burrows and cracks in clay or rock outcroppings. Onespots have been observed from Bodega Bay (northern California) to northern Baja California, most commonly from about Monterey southward, from 10– 90 feet down. This species also occupies empty shells, cracks and crevices, etc. Both species, but particularly onespots, have a great fondness for empty bottles and cans; the bigger the container opening, the bigger the occupant. In some areas, such as the beer bottle field at the head of Redondo Canyon, southern California, nearly every bottle will house a fringehead. A fish usually lies in its home (which it considers its territory) with just part of its head exposed. Fringeheads are extremely aggressive, and they will lunge at intruders (even divers) with jaws snapping.

Sarcastics reach 1 foot, and onespots get all the way to 9.75 inches. I have aged sarcastics to 6 years and onespots to 7. Onespots mature when they are about one year old and 3.5 inches long. Both sarcastics and onespots have very long spawning seasons; sarcastics from January to August and onespots from January to at least October. The females of both species lay eggs in abandoned boring clam holes, under rocks, in beer containers, etc., and the males guard them until they hatch. I have found that female onespots produce between 600 and 7,700 eggs.

FISHERY: Fringeheads, particularly sarcastic fringeheads, are occasionally taken by both sport and commercial fishermen, and when this happens, no one is completely comfortable. The fish tend to be cranky and the fishermen tend to be nervous. I have seen very rugged commercial fishermen, men who laugh in the face of danger, doing fairly amusing little dances while 6-inch-long fish clamp sharp teeth around their thumbs.

REMARKS: Here is what Jordan and Evermann (*The Fishes of North and Middle America*,1898) say about the sarcastic fringehead: "A remarkable fish." Okay, it's not Percy Shelley or Oscar Wilde, but remember, J. and E. were a couple of pretty uptight guys. "A remarkable fish" was florid prose for a scientific paper in 1898.

There is no question that fringeheads are pretty remarkable and that sarcastics are positively cool. With their funky coloring, little doodily whoppers above the eyes, strange body shapes and great, toothy mouths, these fishes closely resemble descriptions of the aliens that apparently sucked Elvis into their saucer. (By the way, a slim, trim Elvis is appearing nightly at Squaggy Zornak's famous Captive Earthling Club on the fifth planet surrounding Betelgeuse. It's a limited engagement, but try to catch the King's show if you can.)

Family Blenniidae - Combtooth Blennies

ROCKPOOL BLENNY (HYPSOBLENNIUS GILBERTI)

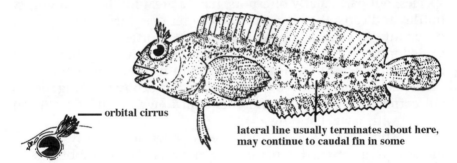

orbital cirrus

lateral line usually terminates about here, may continue to caudal fin in some

NAMES: *Hypsoblennius* is formed from the Greek words for "high blennius," the ancient Greek name for this group, "blennius" alludes to "slime"; *gilberti* refers to the prominent 19th Century ichthyologist Charles H. Gilbert.

IDENTIFYING CHARACTERS: A round-headed little fish is our rockpool blenny. They are gray or olive-brown and they have multi-stranded cirri above each eye. If you look at them from the side, you will see a little notch behind the eye. During spawning season, females turn golden and males become a sort of velvety black.

DISTRIBUTION AND BIOLOGY: Pt. Conception, California to southern Baja California is home to this little cutie. These are shallow water (intertidal to 60 feet) rock dwellers, usually found along cobble shore and in rocky tide pools, from the low intertidal to depths of about 15 feet. Pools in the lower part of the intertidal, particularly ones with lots of crevices and algae, seem to be preferred. When removed, many rockpools are able to return to their favorite pools.

The biggest one on record was 6.75 inches long. Rockpools live for at least 6 years, and males and females grow at the same rate.

At least some individuals mature by the end of their first year; the smallest mature female was 2.5 inches long. Females are oviparous, spawn 3-4 times in spring and summer and produce about 600-3,200 eggs per spawning. Prior to a female's spawning, a male prepares a nest by cleaning rock surfaces of debris. The female lays purplish-pink eggs in these nests, the male fertilizes them, drives the female out of the area and then guards them until they hatch (4-18 days, depending on temperature). During their stint as homemakers, guarding males rub the eggs, deposit mucous on them (perhaps to retard infections) and remove dead ones. The larvae probably stay in the water column for as long as 3 months, and young ones first recruit to inshore waters in August. These little go-hards eat a wide range of prey, including algae, limpets, urchins and bryozoa. While they are probably eaten by lots of predators, only kelp bass and wooly sculpins have been identified for sure.

Pricklebacks - Family Stichaeidae

HIGH COCKSCOMB (ANOPLARCHUS PURPURESCENS)

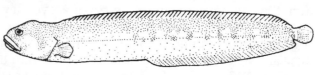

NAMES: Crested Blenny, Cockscomb Prickleback. *Anoplarchus* is formed from 2 Greek words meaning "Unarmed anus", referring either to the anal fin that lacks spines or (I sincerely hope) the name of the best punk band to ever hit Needles, California; *purpurescens* is Latin for "purple."

IDENTIFYING CHARACTERS: These fish are long and snake-like, with a fleshy crest on top of their heads. Males have larger, more prominent cockscombs than females. This species is occasionally mistaken for young monkeyface pricklebacks, but high cockscomb dorsal fins are composed entirely of spines, while monkeyfaces have soft rays in the rear half. Males are brown or black, with intense red-orange pectoral and anal fins and a bit of red on the dorsal. Females are brown with purplish hues and appear speckled. An occasional female has orange pectorals.

DISTRIBUTION AND BIOLOGY: High cockscombs are found in rocks and algae from the Bering Sea to Santa Rosa Island, southern California, commonly as far south as central California. These slippery little devils have been taken from the intertidal zone to

663 feet, but they are by far most abundant from intertidal depths to perhaps 20 feet. They seem particularly fond of cobblestone beaches, where the cobbles sit on gravel and/or crushed shells; they are not usually found on cobbles over mud. In some areas, they are most common in the lower intertidal zone, but a British Columbia study found them quite common in holdfasts of bull kelp and other understory algae.

This is a small species, reaching 7.75 inches. Females grow slightly faster than males and grow to a somewhat larger size. They reach about 4.5 inches in 3 years, maturing at 2-3 years. Females are oviparous and spawn from January to March. Prior to spawning, males start picking fights with other males; there are two kinds of agonistic displays. In "lateral displays," a male comes up alongside another male, raises the front part of its body off the bottom and erects its fins and crest. This may be followed by the rather jolly "spasm" display, where the male jerks its entire body in a single spasm. Spasms may occur 1-3 times, with 1-2 seconds in between. Sometimes the males apparently just say, "The hell with it," and bite each other. Females lay their eggs underneath rocks in shallow waters, producing all of them at the same time. Females guard the eggs, curling around them until they hatch, in about 3-4 weeks. Males do not provide care for the eggs and may spawn with more than one female. Eggs are white when first laid, turning yellow soon after, then greenish when the embryonic eyes develop. Females produce about 1,000-3,000 eggs per season. High cockscombs eat lots of gammarid amphipods, crabs, worms and plants, including green algae and eelgrass. Yoshiyama and Darling (Environmental Biology of Fishes, 1982, p. 39-45) note that high cockscombs are somehow able to eat a worm that is distasteful to other local fishes. Amazingly enough, terrestrial gopher snakes go into the intertidal waters and chow down on these guys.

REMARKS: Jeff Cross (Structure of a Rocky Intertidal Fish Assemblage, University of Washington, PhD Dissertation, 1981) reports that newly-settled high cockscombs closely resemble fir needles, which often fall into Washington State tidepools.

MONKEYFACE PRICKLEBACK (CEBIDICHTHYS VIOLACEUS)

NAMES:
Monkey-
face Eel.
Cebidichthys
comes from
2 Greek words meaning "Sapajou" (a kind of monkey) and "fish"

humps on head

one lateral line

(hence, "monkey fish"); *violaceus* is Latin for violet (don't say it, I know the fish is not colored violet). If you look at this fish head on and sort of squint, you will see a vague resemblance to a monkey. Actually, the fish looks remarkably like Joseph Stalin (minus the mustache), circa 1926. Obviously, the logical and appropriate action is to change the name of this species to the Stalinface Prickleback (maybe the "Uncle Joe Eel" for short).

IDENTIFYING CHARACTERS: There are a slug of eel-shaped fishes along our coast, and here is how to tell a monkeyface from the others. First, these fish are a uniform black, gray or olive and have black lines radiating from their eyes. A few monkeyfaces have orange spots on their sides and orange-tipped fins. Adults have a lumpy ridge on top of their heads, one lateral line and (this is important, so stop playing with your oatmeal and pay attention) the first half of their dorsal fins are spines and the second half are soft rays. Most other pricklebacks have dorsal fins composed entirely of rays and/or have more than one lateral line.

DISTRIBUTION AND BIOLOGY: Monkeyfaces are found from southern Oregon to northern Baja California, but they are very rare south of Pt. Conception. These are very common fish in crevices and caves or under rocks in the upper intertidal zone, but they also live in shallow subtidal rocky areas and have been taken down to 80 feet. In central California, they are most abundant from 1.5-2 feet above mean low water level. This is one of the fishes that you will see rapidly slithering away if you roll rocks over in the intertidal zone at low tide. If you turn rocks over, put them back the way you found them. If you don't, very, very, very bad things will happen to you. [One of which is having to appear on the *New Dating Game* after going out with 1) Margaret Thatcher, 2) Idi Amin or 3) the entire governing board of the American Bar Association. Remember, you have been warned.] Monkeyfaces probably do not move much from their rock shelters; one study showed movement of less than 15 feet. When they do leave their homes, they often return to the same place time after time. Most monkeyfaces are active on flood tides, when they go out and look for stuff to eat. These fish are able to breathe air and remain out of water for long periods. Some large ones can do it for more than 35 hours.

Monkeyfaces reach 2.5 feet in length (they are the largest fish in the intertidal zone of the eastern Pacific). Some live at least 18 years. Males and females grow at about the same rate for their first 8 years, then males outstrip females. However, males and females probably have the same life spans. A 12-incher is 3 years old and a 2-footer is around 15 years old. A few fish mature at 14 inches and 4 years; all are mature at 18 inches and 7 years. These pricklebacks spawn from January–April. A 16 inch female contained about 18,000 eggs and one 2 feet long had 46,000 eggs. Small monkeyfaces eat a mixture of animals (amphipods, worms, clam siphons) and algae. At somewhere between 2 and 3 inches in length, they shift their diets and eat almost nothing but algae, preferring reds and greens. In a very nice study in Bodega Bay, northern California, Roger Helm of UC Davis showed that a number of fish-eating birds, such as great egrets and great blue herons, eat large quantities of juveniles.

FISHERY: From central California northward, monkeyfaces, along with other eel-shaped fishes, are commonly caught by rocky shore sport fishermen. Many (perhaps most) are taken by "poke poling." This is the perfect activity for someone who has a bamboo pole or broom stick, a short piece of wire, a hook and the driving need to use all of them at the same time on a rocky beach. (You would be surprised at the number of people who seem to have this compulsion.) Well, what these good folks do is attach the wire (about one foot long) to the pole and connect the hook to the wire. They bait the hook (maybe with mussels or squid) and clamber onto a rocky promontory at low tide. Now, you might think that most folks would be content to just stand there, poke pole in hand, savoring a job well done. But some people go even farther; they insert the baited hook into various crevices and holes in tide pools and surge channels. Pricklebacks, along with rockfishes, lingcod and cabezon, are frequently taken in this mildly bizarre manner. Monkeyfaces occasionally are seen in fish markets, but there is no directed fishery for them. They, and all the pricklebacks, are pretty good to eat.

REMARKS: Monkeyfaces are frequently found in Native American middens.

BLACK PRICKLEBACK (XIPHISTER ATROPURPUREUS)

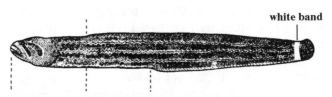

white band

dorsal fin origin about 1/2 distance from
snout to opposite anal origin

NAMES: *Xiphister* is Greek for "swordbelt"; *atropurpureus* comes from 2 Latin words "black, purple."

IDENTIFYING CHARACTERS: Check the characters for the rock prickleback below. The big difference is that this species has dark bars, edged with white, radiating backwards from the eyes.

DISTRIBUTION AND BIOLOGY: Black pricklebacks are found from Kodiak Island, Alaska to northern Baja California, in intertidal waters and down to 25 feet. They are common as far south as central California. These are fish of rocky areas with algae cover, mostly in the lower intertidal and shallow subtidal zones. Small ones seem to be more common in tidepools, while larger ones favor living under rocks.

One foot long, that's as big as they get. They are about 4 inches at 2 years, 8 inches at 6 years and over 10 inches at around 12 years. Black pricklebacks live to at least 12-13 years. They mature at 2-3 years. Spawning takes place from February to April in central California and in late April-May off British Columbia. Females are oviparous and lay eggs in a nest underneath lower intertidal boulders. Apparently, they are a bit particular about the boulder; rumor has it that it has to be sitting on pebbles or small rocks. Spawning seems to be limited to areas of some wave action. Females produce 738-4,070 eggs per season, and all eggs are laid in one batch. The eggs are deposited one by one, fertilized and shaped into a sphere-like mass by both parents. After the male fertilizes them, he guards the eggs until they hatch. Males may fertilize eggs from more than one female and guard multiple clusters. Males don't seem to be particularly territorial; as many as four have been seen under one boulder, all curled around egg clusters. What do they eat? Oh, crabs, gammarid amphipods, worms, plus some algae. Like high cockscombs, black pricklebacks are eaten by gopher snakes (*Thamnophis sirtalis*), at least on San Juan Island, in Puget Sound.

REMARKS: Black prickleback remains have been found in middens of Native Americans from the Puget Sound region.

ROCK PRICKLEBACK (XIPHISTER MUCOSUS)

NAMES: Rock - Blenny. *Xiphister* is Greek for "sword-belt"; *mucosus* is Latin for "slimy."

pectoral fin shorter than eye diameter

1 anal spine

dorsal origin about 1/3 distance from snout to opposite anal origin

IDENTIFYING CHARACTERS: Let's see here. They are eel-shaped and have no pelvic fins and little bitty pectorals. The color is basically greenish-black, and the small ones have white blotches on the rear end. The big giveaway are the light bars radiating backwards from the eyes, they are bordered in black; in black pricklebacks the bands are dark and bordered with white.

DISTRIBUTION AND BIOLOGY: Port San Juan, southeastern Alaska to Pt. Arguello, Central California is where they live. This is an inshore species, found from the intertidal zone down to 60 feet. These fish like the lower rocky intertidal, particularly areas with algae cover.

Rock pricklebacks reach a respectable 23 inches. They are about 10 inches at 3 years, 17 inches at 7 years and 20 inches at 11 years. They live to at least 11 years and mature at 4-5. Females are oviparous and produce adhesive eggs that they glom onto the substrate, under rocks in the intertidal and (reported off central California) shallow subtidal. Spawning season is October to December in central California and late winter and spring in British Columbia. Females produce 5,500-9,500 eggs per season. Males guard nests. Larger rock pricklebacks are primarily herbivores; in a central California study they ate mostly red and green algae. Smaller ones in Washington State ate crustaceans, then switched to algae as they grew larger.

FISHERY: Most of the recreational catch is made in northern California, by the inimitable, rocky intertidal poke polers. See monkeyface pricklebacks for a diatribe on this bizarre behavior.

Gunnels - Family Pholidae

PENPOINT GUNNEL (APODICHTHYS FLAVIDUS)

NAMES: *Apodichthys* is formed from 2 Greek words meaning "without feet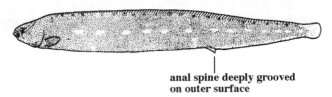

anal spine deeply grooved
on outer surface

fish," a reference to its lack of pelvic fins; *flavidus* is Latin for "yellowish."

IDENTIFYING CHARACTERS: Penpoints are long, thin, eel-like fishes, distinguished by a spine at the front of the anal fin, a line extending downwards through the eyes and an absence of pelvic fins. They are highly variable in color, coming in orange, red, magenta, bright green, olive or bronze. Occasionally, you find a mottled one and sometimes there are spots on the sides.

DISTRIBUTION AND BIOLOGY: Penpoints are found from Kodiak Island, Alaska to Santa Barbara Island, southern California, and are common as far south at least as northern California. Intertidal, they are found in tidepools and beneath rock. Smaller individuals are more likely to be in tidepools, bigger ones under rocks. Penpoints are particularly abundant around algae and surfgrass.

Penpoints reach 1.5 feet. A 9-incher is about 2 years old and they live to at least 6 years. Spawning occurs from January to March. Gammarid amphipods, isopods, harpacticoid copepods, juvenile crabs and shrimps have all been taken from penpoint stomachs.

ROCKWEED GUNNEL (XERERPES FUCORUM)

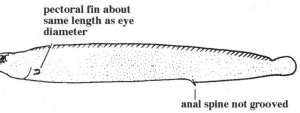

NAMES: *Xererpes* comes from two Greek words for "dry" and "creeper," referring to this species' habit of living part-time in the drier intertidal; *fucorum* is from *Fucus*, a type of seaweed rockweed live in.

IDENTIFYING CHARACTERS: Another of the patented eel-shaped gunnels, this one is characterized by tiny pectoral fins and no pelvic fins. They come in various colors, dark red and bright green in the intertidal zone, light brown or tan in kelp areas.

DISTRIBUTION AND BIOLOGY: You can find them from Banks Island, British Columbia to north-central Baja California, commonly as far south as northern or central California. They are found in both the intertidal and subtidal zones. Rockweeds are very common in seaweeds well above the waterline at low tide. In a study from central California, rockweeds were much more abundant in the intertidal in late spring and summer, probably taking advantage of the relatively mild summer surf and the greater amount of intertidal algae. Among the favorite algae to nestle in were two reds, *Gigartina* and *Rhodoglossum,* and a brown, *Pelvetia.* In almost all situations, red ones are found among red algae, green ones among green, etc. In a laboratory experiment, red ones could slowly change color to green, but most green ones were pretty inept. They are capable of breathing air for extended periods.

Rockweeds grow to 9 inches, and because no one gives a fig about them, we don't know much regarding their life history. They are probably winter spawners. Rockweeds dine mainly on crustaceans, including gammarid amphipods, isopods and copepods.

Wolffishes - Family Anarhichadidae

WOLF-EEL (ANARRHICHTHYS OCELLATUS)

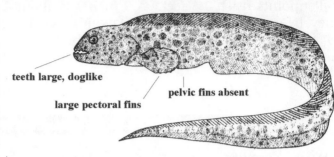

teeth large, doglike

large pectoral fins

pelvic fins absent

NAMES: Ribonookami (Japanese). *Anarrhichthys* comes from the Greek word *Anarhichas*, a fish which resembles this species; *ocellatus* is Latin for "eye-like spots."

IDENTIFYING CHARACTERS: Wolf-eels are really easy to identify. We are talking about an eel-shaped fish, colored gray or occasionally brown or greenish, with dark eye spots on its body and fins (Plate 30). Combine this with big canine teeth and massive molars and you can't miss. Oh, yes, the adult males have white, lumpy, sort of misshapen heads and look like the title characters in *Chainsaw Flesh Eaters from the Planet of Mutant Savings and Loan Executives*. On the other hand, the juveniles are exquisite fish, often orange in color with beautiful dark spots.

DISTRIBUTION AND BIOLOGY: Wolf-eels are found from the Sea of Japan and the Aleutian Islands southward to Imperial Beach, southern California. These are cold water fish, abundant from central California northward. Wolf-eels live from barely subtidal waters to at least 740 feet. Juveniles are pelagic at first, living in the upper part of the water column (some for at least 2 years). Eventually, these juveniles settle out on the ocean floor and maintain an active lifestyle over open bottom. After a time (the period seems to vary), these fish find a rock shelter and settle down to become couch potatoes. A male and female will occupy the same cave for years, apparently mating for life. You will often see these fish lying with their heads together near their den opening. When disturbed, or if food is presented, the male is more likely to come out and the female will usually withdraw. Occasionally, a pair is forced out of a den by other wolf-eels or by very large octopi.

Wolf-eels reach at least 6.7 feet. In aquaria, males and females form pairs at about 4 years of age (3 feet long) and produce eggs at 7 years old, with spawning occurring from October into late winter. During courtship, a male butts his head against the female's abdomen, then wraps himself around her and hopes for the best. He probably fertilizes the eggs as they are laid, and at least 10,000 eggs have been seen in a single mass. Both parents wrap themselves around the egg mass, and only one at a time leaves to feed. Females periodically rotate the egg masses until they hatch in 13–16 weeks. Benthic rockfishes and kelp greenlings, among other predators, eat the eggs when they can get to them. Wolf-eels eat various invertebrates, such as crabs, sand dollars and snails. After eating, these fish often rub themselves against the bottom.

FISHERY: Wolf-eels are an accidental catch of both sport and commercial fishermen. In northern waters, they are occasionally trawled up, and many are also taken in crab traps. They are good to eat and some northwest Native American tribes reserved this species for tribal healers.

REMARKS: Jeff Marliave, at the Vancouver Aquarium, raises baby wolf-eels by the bushel. I believe you can buy them for home aquariums.

Sand Lances - Family Ammodytidae

PACIFIC SAND LANCE (AMMODYTES HEXAPTERUS)

NAMES: Kitaikanago (Japanese). *Ammodytes* comes from 2

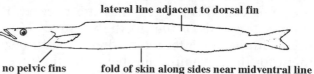

lateral line adjacent to dorsal fin

no pelvic fins

fold of skin along sides near midventral line

Greek words translated as "sand diver"; *hexapterus* is formed from 2 Greek words meaning "six fins or wings."

IDENTIFYING CHARACTERS: It's long, with a projecting lower jaw, forked caudal fin and a curious fold of skin along each side of its belly. Add to that a blue or green back and silvery belly and, *voila*, the Pacific sand lance.

DISTRIBUTION AND BIOLOGY: A very wide ranging, schooling species, this sand lance inhabits waters from the Sea of Japan to the Bering Sea and southward to Balboa, southern California. They are common from Tomales Bay, northern California, northwards. Pacific sand lances have been reported from the intertidal zone to depths of at least 330 feet and probably down to 908 feet. While primarily a marine species, they are also found near freshwater inputs. Most live in waters less than 300 feet deep, over sand or sand-gravel bottoms. These fish spend much of their time burrowed in the substrate; underwater observations imply that this species buries itself throughout the night. While they are commonly encountered in spring and summer, they seem to disappear in fall and winter; probably, the little dears are dug in during this time of cold water.

How big do they get? Oh, about 10.5 inches. And they live to at least 8 years. Based on studies off Japan, this species matures at 1-3 years and at lengths greater than 5 inches. Female Pacific sand lances are oviparous and probably spawn once per year. Sand lance spawning season may be variable and depend on location, ranging from as early as October to as late as May, perhaps peaking from January to March. Around Kodiak Island, Alaska, sand lances spawn on October high tides in the intertidal zone. Sand lance eggs are adhesive, sticking to the bottom, and take about 3-4 weeks to hatch. Larvae are generally found in shallow surface waters (less than about 90 feet), descending at night into slightly deeper waters (to about 260 feet). In a study off Auke Bay, Alaska, sandlance larvae were most abundant just before the spring phytoplankton bloom. Larvae metamorphose into juveniles in anywhere from 100 to 131 days. Juveniles are often found with adults, particularly in shallow waters; they may also school with other fishes, such as Pacific herring. Zooplankton are always on the menu for both juveniles and adults, particularly calanoid copepods, but also including such items as mysid shrimps, crustacean larvae, gammarid amphipods and chaetognaths. Everyone and their dog eats this species; they are chewed by just about everything that swims or flies in the vicinity. Much of the predation occurs in the late afternoon, when the fish begin to seek out sediment for their evening slumber. Among the eager eaters are various fishes (such as Pacific cod, Pacific halibut, Pacific whiting, various soles, rockfishes, salmons), seabirds (pigeon guillemots, puffins, auklets, murres, kittiwakes, cormorants) and marine mammals (fur seals, harbor seals, Steller sea lions, spotted seals, minke whales, sei whales, humpback whales).

FISHERY: There is no recreational fishery for these skinnies, though rumor has it that they are yummy.   And, except for a small bait fishery in Washington and British Columbia, there is no commercial fishery either, at least on this side of the Pacific. The Japanese fishery takes about 100,000 tons per year, using a variety of nets.

Gobies - Family Gobiidae

BLACKEYE GOBY (CORYPHOPTERUS NICHOLSI)

NAMES: Blackspot Goby, Bluespot Goby, Onespot Goby. *Coryphopterus* is formed from 2 Greek words meaning "head fin," *nicholsi* honors Henry E. Nichols, the discoverer of this species.

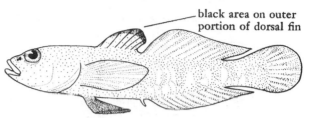

black area on outer
portion of dorsal fin

IDENTIFYING CHAR-ACTERS: This is a small fish, tan or almost white, with a large black eye, a black tip at the front of its dorsal fin and a small blue spot under the eyes. The pelvic fins are fused into a disc and those of males turn dark during breeding season.

DISTRIBUTION AND BIOLOGY: Blackeyes live from northern British Columbia, near the Alaskan border, to central Baja California. They are a common part of the shallow reef community from southern British Columbia south. These are territorial little squirts, living on the bottom, usually at a sand-rock interface. Within their little territories, they will have a crevice or burrow into which they can retreat if facing off an intruder doesn't work. They have been taken from tide pools down to 450 feet and seem to be abundant from perhaps 10 feet down to who knows where. Juveniles have been found far out to sea, near the surface and in albacore stomachs. They range perhaps 3–5 feet from their bur-rows out onto sand or into the water column, chasing after food, intruders or (for males) mates. These gobies are active during the day, and take shelter at night.

The world record, all-tackle blackeye was 6 inches long, a true giant. These gobies mature at about 2 years of age and 1.5-2 inches and they live for about 5 years. Females are oviparous and produce about 3,300-4,800 eggs. They may be multiple spawners. Spawning seasons are long and have been reported from February–October, probably peaking in late spring and early sum-mer. During breeding season, males hollow out a depression underneath a rock and scrape clean a nest site on the underside of a ledge. To attract females, they rise up into the water, spread their blackened fins, descend and try to look sensitive yet in control. After spawning, males guard circular egg masses until the eggs hatch and the young enter the plankton. All blackeyes start life as females and at about 2.5-3 inches change to males – Nature's way of supporting equal rights. Crustaceans, such as copepods and amphipods, and mollusks, such as limpets and snails, make up most of their diet. Pelagic, Brandt's and double-crested cormorants eat them.

TIDEWATER GOBY (EUCYCLOGOBIUS NEWBERRYI)

NAMES: *Eucyclogobius* is formed from three Greek words, "well, circle,

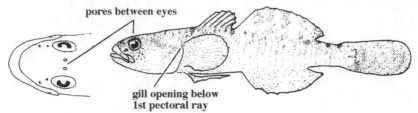

pores between eyes

gill opening below
1st pectoral ray

gobius," gobius is the ancient Greek word for this group; *newberryi* refers to Dr. John S. Newberry of the U. S. Geological Survey.

IDENTIFYING CHARACTERS: Non-breeding fish tend to be brown or gray, with darker dorsal mottling. Breeding individuals are fishes of a different color, as described by Cam Swift, et al. (Natural History Museum of Los Angeles County, Contributions in Science, 1989, number 404). Females are tan or reddish-brown with gold-brown or dark brown sides. Females change color when fighting, becoming blue-black on their sides. Breeding males are blackish, with small white spots on backs and sides.

DISTRIBUTION AND BIOLOGY: Most of the following data comes from the very nice paper by Swift, et al. (noted above) and the work of Ramona Swenson at UC Berkeley.

Tidewater gobies are found from Del Norte County, northern California, southward to Del Mar, southern California. These are coastal lagoon animals, restricted to the shallow, usually brackish waters near the sea. While these gobies are able to tolerate full sea water, they seem to be most common in waters with salinities ranging from fresh to about one-third sea water. Most fish are found very close to the coast, though a few have been recorded as much as about 5 miles inland. Tidewater populations may fluctuate seasonally. In Aliso Creek Lagoon, southern California, the winter-early spring population was estimated at 1,000-1,500 fish; after the summer-fall spawning, the population rose to 10,000-15,000 individuals. You can find tidewater gobies in small groups or in aggregations of hundreds.

Tidewaters reach 2.5 inches. They seem to live for only one year and females mature at about 1.25 inches. Females are oviparous and produce between about 180 and 600 eggs. While it is possible that there is some low-level spawning throughout the year, virtually all of it takes places from late April-early May through the fall. The breeding behavior of tidewaters is so cool and so sweet I thought we would discuss it in some detail. Beginning in late April or early May, males laboriously excavate more-or-less vertical burrows in coarse sand (occasionally mud), hauling out the grains mouthful by mouthful. Mucous from the male's body helps cement together the sand grains. Inside the burrows, the male often closes the entrance by spitting a sand-mucous plug into the opening.

Okay, it's time to spawn and the ready-to-mate females become very aggressive. Frequently, they attack each other over a male. This involves a lot of posturing, with fins erect, tail slapping and some biting (reminiscent of some military reunions). A female finds males by selecting a sandy area and either settling on the bottom with her lower jaw on the sand or hopping about in a circle. Usually, this causes a male to create an opening in his burrow and stick his head out of the sand. Once the male comes into sight, the female kicks into high gear, erecting her dorsal and anal fins and really putting the hurt to a whole repertoire of hops and short dashes. She will often bump the male's head with her caudal fin or anal vent area or lay her vent over the burrow opening. Amazingly enough, despite what we all would call a very direct approach, a large number of these female come-ons are unsuccessful. Swift, et al. report that "Of 23 courtships...only one led to a female successfully entering a male's burrow....On 17 occasions the male either: (1) opened the entrance, poked his head out briefly, and then retreated and remained quiet; or 2) resealed the entrance." Hey, no wonder these fish may soon be considered endangered. Fellas, fellas, it's time to get a life. If you guys don't get your acts together, some studly male mosquitofish is going to take over your responsibilities. I mean, this is just one more indication of the decline in the American Spirit, a decline I attribute to the invention of jockey shorts.

Once a female manages to convince one of these rather reticent males, she lays her eggs on the roof and sides of the burrow, suspending them one at a time. In aquarium observations, this process may take around 2 hours. Males guard the eggs until they hatch in 9-10 days. These little wheezers feed on a range of animal prey, including insect larvae, snails, ostracods and amphipods. REMARKS: A lot of tidewater goby habitat has been destroyed by human activities, and there is just tons of evidence that some populations have disappeared.

LONGJAW MUDSUCKER (GILLICHTHYS MIRABILIS)

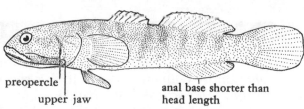

preopercle

upper jaw

anal base shorter than head length

NAMES: *Gillichthys* honors Theodore Gill, a prominent ichthyologist of the 19th Century; *mirabilis* means "wonderful" in Latin.

IDENTIFYING CHARACTERS: Mudsuckers are small brown or dark brown fish with very large upper jaws, which reach almost to the gill openings. Young ones often have 8 bars on their bodies and a dark blotch on the rear part of their dorsal fins.

DISTRIBUTION AND BIOLOGY: Mudsuckers are one of the most common fishes in bays and estuaries and are found from Tomales Bay, northern California into the Gulf of California, commonly from San Francisco Bay southward. They were planted in the Salton Sea in 1950. They are abundant in shallow muddy backwaters and on tidal flats. At low tide, you can often find them hiding in holes (sometimes in crab burrows) in the mud. These are pretty tough hombres. They can tolerate water ranging from almost fresh to 2.5 times saltier than sea water and temperatures as high as 95° F, which is very hot indeed for a fish (they prefer 48° to 73°). If stranded on mudflats by retreating tides, mudsuckers can wriggle their way across the mud to find water.

Mudsuckers as large as 8.25 inches have been reported. In the Salton Sea, mudsuckers live about 2 years, and they mature in the first year, at 2–3 inches. Spawning occurs from December–July, peaking in spring. Males build nests in mud banks and defend their territories against other males. When defending territories, males raise their fins, which turn black, open their jaws wide and push each other, mouth to mouth. It's fairly tiresome after a while, but what with the poor cable reception there is just not much to do down there in the mud. Females lay between 4,000–9,000 club-shaped eggs and attach them to the burrow by adhesive threads. The males guard for them about 12 days until they hatch. Ghost shrimps and crabs form most of their diet. Least terns eat them.

FISHERY: Mudsuckers are fished commercially for use as bait in freshwater sport fisheries.

REMARKS: If the oxygen content of the water drops too low, these fish can breathe air, coming to the surface, gulping and returning to the bottom. The air is held in their throats, which contain lots of blood vessels and act like lungs, transferring the oxygen to the blood. After the oxygen is used up, the fish release the gas and swim to the surface again.

BLUEBANDED GOBY (LYTHRYPNUS DALLI)

NAME: Catalina Goby. *Lythrypnus* is Greek for "blood [red] sleeper"; *dalli* honors William Healy Dall, this species' discoverer.

IDENTIFYING CHARACTERS: Bluebandeds are very distinctive little fish, red or red-orange with 4–9 intense blue bands (no great sur-

prise there).
DISTRIBUTION AND BIOLOGY: Found from Morro Bay (central California) to central Baja California and in the Gulf of 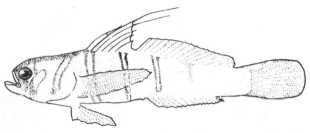 California, bluebandeds are abundant from Pt. Conception southward. These fish are often one of the most common fish on reefs. You can usually find them sitting horizontally on reef crests and sides near a conveniently located crevice. They are territorial and actively defend their property, ducking into the crevice only as a last resort. While found from the intertidal to 250 foot depths, they are most abundant from about 10–60 feet.

Bluebandeds reach a mighty 2.5 inches, and a few live as long as 19 months. Bluebandeds can be hermaphrodites. You can find them as pure females, pure males, female-biased hermaphrodites and occasionally male-biased ones. Females can become males fairly rapidly. Females are oviparous. These little fish have an extended spawning season, from at least February to September and perhaps longer. Peak spawning is reported to be from May-September. A female produces anywhere from 60-2,200 eggs and usually lays them in crevices or empty shells (such as those of rock scallops). The male guards them until they hatch. Larvae stay in the plankton for 2+ months and the juveniles settle onto reefs at slightly less than half an inch. Setttlement occurs from June-January, peaking in July-August. Bluebandeds mainly eat zooplankton, particularly copepods, amphipods and ostracods. Occasionally, they also go for bryozoans, sponges and the like.

REMARKS: These are extremely short-lived fish, one of the shortest in the northeast Pacific. Their populations go through remarkable boom and bust cycles. Some years they are everywhere, littering the bottom, while in others they are scarce or even absent from the same reef.

ZEBRA GOBY (LYTHRYPNUS ZEBRA)

NAMES: *Lythrypnus* is Greek for "blood [red] sleeper"; *zebra* refers to its stripes.

IDENTIFYING CHARACTERS: This really pert little fish is sort of coral colored, with lots of narrow, vertical blue bands running along its body (Plate 33).

DISTRIBUTION AND BIOLOGY: Tolerant of a wide range of water temperatures, zebra gobies are found from Carmel Bay, central

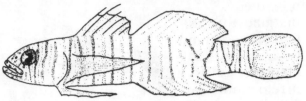

California, south-
ward to the tropi-
cal waters of
Clarion Island,
Mexico, most com-
monly south of Pt.
Conception. Zebra gobies usually occur in lower densities than
bluebanded gobies, perhaps 10 fish per square meter, compared to
30+ for bluebandeds in the same area. Zebras are also more retiring than their louder relatives. They tend to prefer the sides or
underhangs of reefs, usually orienting themselves either upside-
down or vertically.

They aren't big-2.25 inches is the record. And they don't live
long, maybe 2 years at the most. Zebras are simultaneous hermaphrodites. Some individuals are female-biased (they contain
mostly ovarian, but some testicular tissue), some male-biased
(mostly testes, but some ovary) and some are pure female. In the
one study that examines this really fun phenomenon, no pure
males were found. More-or-less females are oviparous, laying eggs
in empty shells, worm tubes or crevices from May to October
(peaking during the summer). Females produce about 170-800
eggs. Most males and females die soon after spawning and nest
guarding, though a few make it into their second year and spawn
again. Larvae drift about for 2-5 months, and young ones recruit
to the reefs from August to February. Zebras tend to feed on sub-
strate-oriented prey, such as benthic copepods, isopods and gammarid and caprellid amphipods.

Barracudas - Family Sphyraenidae

PACIFIC BARRACUDA (SPHYRAENA ARGENTEA)

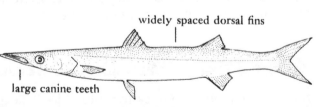

widely spaced dorsal fins

large canine teeth

NAMES: Barries,
Snakes, Califor-
nia Barracuda,
Scoot, Scooter.
Sphyraena is an
ancient Greek
name meaning "hammer fish"; *argentea* is Latin for "silvery."
IDENTIFYING CHARACTERS: It would be difficult to confuse barracuda with anything else (Plate 34). These guys are long, skinny, have
bluish or brownish backs, silvery sides and a mouth full of pointed teeth. Paul Nakatsuka states that the anal fin of males are tan or
grayish; those of females are black.

DISTRIBUTION AND BIOLOGY: Barries live from Kodiak Island to southern Baja California. Except during warm water years, when they are commonly taken in central California, these fish are found from Pt. Conception southward to Punta Canoas, Baja California. These are schooling, more-or-less pelagic fish; adults and near-adults are found near reefs or kelp, almost always close to the coast. While they usually swim close to the surface, I have seen them taken as deep as 120 feet. Young ones are found near shore, sometimes in protected or semi-protected areas such as coastal lagoons and marinas, and often right in the surf. Young-of-the-year appear in very shallow water in fall and are abundant as far north as Santa Barbara during warm water years. Barracuda make well-defined annual northward migrations, moving from Baja California into southern California in late spring and early summer, probably in concert with increasing sea temperatures. Southward migrations are less ritualized, and some fish winter over in southern California. For instance, there are usually a number of large barracuda off Pt. Conception during the winter.

Although they have been taken to 48 inches, fish anywhere near that large are now rare indeed. In fact, fish larger than 35 inches are seldom seen. These are rapidly growing fish– a 14-incher is 1 year old, a 28-incher is 4–5 years old and a 41-incher is 11. They probably live to somewhat over 12 years. All males are mature in their second year; all females spawn by the third and females probably grow larger than males (almost all fish heavier than 10 pounds are females). Spawning occurs from April to perhaps November, peaking from May–July. Barracuda larvae have been taken from southern California to southern Baja California, with highest concentrations between Punta Eugenia and Cabo San Lazaro, southern Baja California. These are near-shore spawners; few larvae are found more than about 30 miles from the coast. A female 6–7 years old produces 300,000–400,000 eggs per season. Barries eat mostly small fishes such as anchovies, sardines, young Pacific mackerels and jackmackerels, grunions and squids. Least terns and bald eagles (at Catalina Island) eat them.

FISHERY: These popular sport fish are taken primarily from party and private vessels, but also by pier and jetty fishermen and occasionally from the shore. Pier fishermen take mainly small fish, as larger ones tend to stay a bit offshore. While most catches occur in southern California and Baja California (they are the most commonly taken species in the Ensenada party vessel catch), some years see a decent snap as far north as Morro Bay, central California. During 1982, a few were taken in the recreational fishery off Del Norte County, northern California. Over the years, most of the recreational catch has been made during spring and summer, peaking in June and July, in water temperatures averaging about 64.5° F. During the El Niño of 1957–58, barracuda were so plentiful in southern California that it was difficult to catch anything else. A number of anglers, overjoyed to have seen barracuda a few months before, started saying bad words when they couldn't get their lines through to the bass and halibut because of all the "%#@* barracuda." Such is human nature.

The %#@* barracuda are also taken by commercial fishermen by gillnet, trolling and hook and line. Once a very popular food fish, barries were the target of a bustling commercial fishery. Demand has dropped over the last 40 years, and today the fishery is relatively small. Barracuda are usually sold fresh or, occasionally, frozen, often as steaks. These puppies are still tasty when stored up to 5 days at 40° F. Frozen at 0° F, they are good for about 12 months.

REMARKS: Unlike the very large barracuda of tropical waters, California barracuda do not attack humans.

Fossil earbones of California barracuda are known from strata over one million years old near San Diego.

Barracuda soften and spoil quickly unless kept cool. You have been warned. Many people like barracuda eggs, comparing them favorably to shad roe.

Mackerels, Tunas and Bonitos - Family Scombridae

SKIPJACK TUNA (KATSUWONUS PELAMIS)

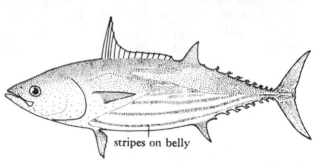
stripes on belly

NAMES: Oceanic Bonito, Lesser Tuna, Aku, Striped Tuna, Arctic Bonito, Watermelon, Skipjack, Skippy, Barrilete (Mexico), Katsuo (Japanese), Ga-da-raeng-i (Korean) and (in what is probably the most implausible name ever given to a fish) Victor Fish. *Pelamis* means tuna in Greek.

IDENTIFYING CHARACTERS: Skipjack are readily identified by the 4–6 stripes on the lower sides of their bodies. A typical fish is colored blue or blue-purple on back with a silvery belly.

DISTRIBUTION AND BIOLOGY: Skipjack are found worldwide in the Pacific, Atlantic and Indian Oceans and occasionally in the

Mediterranean Sea, primarily in subtropical and tropical waters. While they live in waters as cold as 68° F, they prefer 77°+. Primarily a surface dweller, they have been taken as deep as 330 feet. In the eastern Pacific, they have been taken from Vancouver Island to Peru, and they are sporadically present off southern California, most often during warm water years. Generally, they migrate north from Baja in late summer and fall, often associating with yellowfin tuna. Even in the extremely warm water of the 1983–84 El Niño, they were only abundant as far north as Santa Cruz Island; more often they stop at about the Mexican border (primarily because they don't have green cards). Fish found off southern California spawn in the central equatorial Pacific. As juveniles migrate east from this area, they probably split into two groups: one heads to Panama and southward, the other to Baja and northward.

Skipjack are relatively small tuna, reaching 40 inches in length. As with so many other tunas, it is difficult to age these fish; perhaps they live 8–12 years. They mature at about 20 inches and after about one year. Spawning takes place year round, and a female probably spawns every day. Females are oviparous and produce about 400,000-1,000,000 eggs. During spawning or feeding, fish often display dark bars on their sides; during spawning they seem to become darker overall. Skipjack eat fish, squid, krill, pelagic red crabs, etc. In a study off southern California, skippies were found along upwelling fronts, where cool, nutrient-rich water came to the surface and concentrated prey animals. Skipjack are eaten by various tunas, billfishes, sharks and the little ones are picked off by sea birds. People report seeing these fish hiding behind basking or whale sharks when marlin are in the vicinity.

FISHERY: Party vessel sport fishermen nail these guys when they get near southern California in late summer and fall. They are usually taken with albacore or yellowfin tuna, but also occur in their own schools. Their relatively small size makes them a less-prized catch than the larger tunas. In fact, when you have a boatload of anglers who have paid $150 a pop to catch yellowfin but catch skipjack instead, you do not have a lot of happy campers.

Worldwide, skipjack are the subject of a major fishery and are taken by purse seine, gillnet, longline and hook and line. Most skippies are canned, though some are sold fresh. Refrigerated shelf life is 5-7 days at 40° F; frozen shelf life is 6-9 months at 0° F. Please check the comments regarding scombroid poisoning in the "Remarks" section under albacore.

REMARKS: Like the yellowfin tuna, skipjack are fond of hanging around floating objects such as logs, kelp mats or other debris.

Except for one village site on Santa Catalina Island, skippies are only occasionally found in Native American middens.

PACIFIC BONITO (SARDA CHILIENSIS)

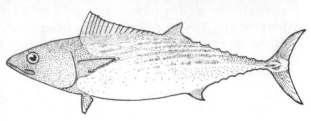

NAMES: Bone-heads, Bonies, California Bonito, Skipjack (they aren't, you know), Laguna Tuna, Magneto, Striped Tuna, Ocean Bonito. *Sarda* is the ancient Greek name for a European bonito; *chiliensis* means "living in Chile," where this species was recognized first.

IDENTIFYING CHARACTERS: Bonito are typical tuna-shaped fish and are easily identified by the dark, slanting stripes on their greenish-blue backs. Just to confuse you, a rare individual will not develop striping. When they are feeding or hooked, bonito develop a series of black bars on their sides. Charles F. Holder (*The Game Fishes of the World*, 1913, Stoddard and Houghton) sums them up thusly: "I should call it the humming-bird of the sea, so radiant is it, so bathed in myriads of color and tints...its silvery skin blazing and flashing with ten thousand tints and coruscations". "Coruscations," eh? Nice going, Chuck.

DISTRIBUTION AND BIOLOGY: The Pacific bonito has an interesting geographic range. In the north Pacific, it is found from Alaska to southern Baja California, while in the south Pacific it ranges off Peru and Chile. This is a temperate-subtropical species, and the warm equatorial waters between the two populations are inhabited by a different bonito species. Bonito are usually found in large schools, usually at or near the surface, anywhere from just behind the surf to several hundreds of miles out. They are most abundant within about 15 miles of the coast. While occasionally common off central and northern California, usually they are encountered from Pt. Conception southward to Bahia Magdalena, Baja California. These are active, migratory fish; individuals tagged off Baja have been recorded off Santa Barbara, and vice versa. Many (though not all) move south in the winter.

Pacific bonito have been measured reliably to 40 inches, though fish over 36 inches are rare. These are fast-growing and short-lived fish; the oldest one ever found was 6 years old. A 20-incher is 1 year old and a 27 inch fish is 3. A few females mature at 2 years and about 25 inches (fork length); many males mature at 1 year and about 20 inches (also fork length). Females are oviparous and may spawn more than once per season. Some spawning takes place off southern California, apparantly from January-May. However, based on where the larvae are concentrated, most spawning occurs off central Baja California. Including Baja California, larvae are found from January to September. Fishes (particularly anchovies) and squids are their major foods, though they will eat krill if other prey are not available. Always eager eaters, this species consumes about 6% of its body weight per day. FISHERY: During some years, the Pacific bonito is a very important recreational and commercial species off southern California. Similarly, it is often one of the key species in the Ensenada, northern Baja California, party vessel catch. Party and private vessels take the bulk of the catch, but pier and even jetty anglers nail a good number. Most of the recreational catch is made in summer and fall, particularly July-October, from Santa Monica Bay southward. However, during the 1983-84 El Niño, a good number were taken as far north as Del Norte County, northern California. During some years, in some areas, they comprise as much as 21% of the total southern California marine recreational catch. While the average sea surface temperature for catching bonito off California is about 65° F, they can sometimes be found off southern California throughout the year, even in the dead of winter. They are attracted to warm water, and the hot water outfall of the Southern California Edison Facility in King Harbor, Redondo Beach, is often a spot to find them.

Commercial fishermen take bonito by purse seine, gillnet and trolling, with occasional landings as far north as Eureka. Bonito are sold fresh and frozen, as fillet and steaks. The flesh is brownish red, turning sort of tan when cooked. Shelf life for fresh fish is 5 days at 40° F; frozen ones stay acceptable for 9-12 months. If not stored at low enough temperatures, bonito may develop scombroid poisoning. See the "Remarks" section under albacore for details.

REMARKS: There is no pleasing some people. From the late 1930s until 1957, bonito were relatively scarce in southern California, and everyone got excited at the thought of catching one. The 1957–58 El Niño brought gobs of these fish to the area. They were everywhere, with folks catching them on virtually every bait, even in the surf. Well, everyone was happy, for about 2 months. Then the grumbling began. People started complaining that they were catching bonito and barracuda while fishing for bass, yellowtail or even halibut. Suddenly these fish became trash, fit only to be cursed at and heaved into the sea. Aren't you folks ever satisfied?

By the way, bonito are excellent food fish, but only if bled soon after capture and kept really damp and cool. If you let them warm up, sitting in the sun in a dry bag, you get what you deserve.

Bonito bones are common in Native American middens. See the quote under "Remarks" in the yellowtail section.

PACIFIC MACKEREL (SCOMBER JAPONICUS)

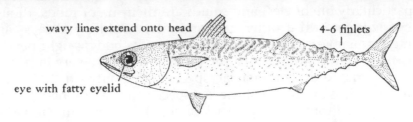

wavy lines extend onto head   4-6 finlets

eye with fatty eyelid

NAMES: Blue Mackerel, Chub Mackerel, Striped Mackerel, American Mackerel, Greenback Jack, Japanese Mackerel, Macarela (Mexico).   *Scomber* is the ancient Greek name for the common mackerel of the Mediterranean; *japonicus* refers to Japan, where the species was first recognized.

IDENTIFYING CHARACTERS: Pacifics are sleek little fish, easily identified by the series of slightly wavy, dark bars on their green or blue backs.

DISTRIBUTION AND BIOLOGY: Pacific mackerel range from Alaska to the Gulf of California in the northeast Pacific, and worldwide in temperate and tropical seas.   On this coast, they are most abundant from about Pt. Conception southward, but during some periods they are commonly found as far north as Oregon.   These are schooling fish, usually found at or near the surface, but occasionally retreating to waters as deep as 990 feet.   Compared to many other tuna-like fishes, Pacifics aren't too finicky about where they are.   Adults tolerate temperatures ranging at least from 50-72° F. Subadults and adults move northward with warming summer waters.   Pac macs can be found both offshore and in nearshore waters, occasionally coming into kelp beds.   Mackerel are most abundant inshore from July-November and offshore from March-May.   They are attracted to lights and are often found around illuminated oil platforms and piers.   Tagging studies show that, as is typical with fast and continuous swimmers, Pac macs move about between California and Baja California.

The species seems to go through boom-and-bust cycles of abundance, mostly due to changes in survival of young ones, with warm northward flowing water perhaps favoring the survival of juveniles.   Pacifics were abundant off southern California during the late 50s and early 60s, after the 1957 El Niño.   During the 60s and early 70s, the population went down the tubes, then resurged in the warmer waters of the late 70s and 80s.   However, a 1994 study shows that the population has again taken a header and is down substantially.

Pacific mackerel reach 25 inches.   They have been aged to over 11 years.   Like other tunas, these are fast growing fish; a 2-year-old is 12 inches long, and an 8-year veteran is 18 inches. Almost 90% of males are mature at age 1; all reproduce at age 3. On the other hand, only 25% of females are mature at age 1 and about 67% reproduce at age 2. While these fish may spawn from January–October, most spawning occurs from April–August. Spawning takes place from central California to the Gulf of California, concentrated between Punta Baja, northern Baja California to at least southern Baja California. In tropical waters, this species may spawn year round, with a December-March peak. Females are oviparous and spawn 8 or more times per season. Most spawning occurs within 200 miles of the coast in depths anywhere from the surface to 300 feet. Mackerel eggs float near the surface, hatching in 4-5 days. Pacific mackerel eat anything they can get their teeth around, particularly small fishes, squids and large zooplankton, such as copepods and krill. California sea lions, northern fur seals, bald eagles and least terns all eat them.

FISHERY: Pacific mackerel are a very important part of the recreational fishery off southern California and, occasionally, central California. During years when their populations are high, large numbers are taken by fishermen from party and private vessels, barges and piers. During the 1983-84 El Niño, they were frequently taken in the recreational catch at least as far north as northern Oregon. Pacific mackerel also form a significant part of the fishery off Ensenada, Baja California. In some areas of southern California, pac macs may form 40% or more of all the marine recreational fishes taken during a year. In most years, catches peak betwen May and September. Some party vessels actively avoid schools. One study showed that about 40% of all mackerels caught were released.

Mackerel are also taken in large numbers by commercial fishermen, particularly by purse seine and lampara, but also by scoop (dip) nets and occasionally gillnets. Previously, they were taken by longline and hook and line. While some of the catch goes to human or pet food, some is used as bait for lobsters, crabs, etc. Some Pacific mackerel are canned, some sold fresh and frozen, usually as whole fish. Like many other species, this one has a fresh shelf life of about 5 days at 40° F and can be frozen for 9-12 months at 0° F. Improperly stored mackerel may cause scombroid poisoning. See remarks under "albacore" for details.

REMARKS: Huge schools of Pacific mackerel have recently invaded British Columbia waters. Busily eating baby salmon, they may be partially responsible for the decline in B. C. salmon stocks.

ALBACORE (THUNNUS ALALUNGA)

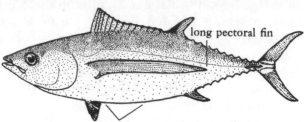

long pectoral fin

body depth greatest in this area

NAMES: Longfin, Albie, Pigfish, German, Germon (French), Albecor, Longfinned Tuna. *Thunnus* is an ancient Greek word for "tuna"; *alalunga* is a name used in Sardinia meaning "long wing."

IDENTIFYING CHARACTERS: Albacore are readily identified by their very long pectoral fins, which (except in very small fish) reach beyond the front of the anal fin. These elegant, streamlined fish have dark blue, almost black backs and silvery bellies.

DISTRIBUTION AND BIOLOGY: Albacore are found throughout the world in temperate and subtropical waters. Based on longline catches, they may live as deep as 1,254 feet. There are two populations in the Pacific, one north of the equator and one south. In the northeastern Pacific, these pelagic, schooling fish have been taken from Alaska to the Revillagigedo Islands, Mexico, usually in oceanic waters from 59–68° F. These fish are supreme migrators, and here's the latest theory I can find about their travels. The ones that appear in the northeastern Pacific are spawned in an area from the northern Philippines to about Hawaii. As you might expect, the youngest fish (1–2 years old) live in the western Pacific, near and west of Japan. (Very occasionally, a 1-year-old appears off Baja California.) Three-year-olds move eastward, most travelling into the California Current region, along North America. Typically, these arrive offshore beginning in June. Four-year-olds are common across the North Pacific, implying that some of the 3-year-olds are beginning to leave North American waters. Almost all 5-year-olds are back near Japan. The 3-, 4- and 5-year-olds that appear off North America in summer and fall return to the central Pacific for the winter and spring. Spawning adults make smaller movements and rarely appear off North America. Some researchers believe there are 2 populations north of the Equator. One would travel east to Oregon, Washington and British Columbia; the other would hit North America off California and Baja California.

Albacore tend to concentrate on the warm sides of upwelling fronts, most often in the clear, blue oceanic waters on the seaward edge. Most of the fish usually stay one hundred, two hundred or more miles offshore. In some years, albacore come inshore, within 10 or 15 miles of the coast in southern California and even closer central California northward. An even more notable migration occurred during the 1983 El Niño, when a horde of albacore moved to within a mile or so of Palos Verdes, near Long Beach, California.

The largest albacore on record was 4.5 feet long. Although we aren't sure how accurate aging techniques are for this species, albacore probably live at least 10 years. A 2-footer is about 2 years old, a 3-footer is about 5, with fish beginning to mature at about 5 years. Estimates of size at first maturity vary, but they tend to fall in the range of 2.8-3.3 feet. Females are oviparous and spawn more than once per season. Spawning takes place during summer and females produce 800,000–2,600,000 eggs. Albacore feed on whatever animals come by, both day and night. Fishes, krill, squids, etc., are all fair game and, in turn, large billfish and sharks chow down on unwary albacore.

FISHERY: For many, this is the most popular and emotional sport fishery that ocean anglers encounter off southern and central California. Perhaps it's the real gamble involved. Albacore move about so much that it is difficult to know from day to day where they will be and if any will be taken. On many trips, if no albacore are taken, nothing is caught. So when that first hookup occurs, after 5 minutes or 5 hours of mind-numbing trolling, the passengers sometimes go a bit haywire. As the boat slows to a stop, lines are cast out, fish are hooked and then lost in tangles. At that point, it is amazing how a group of ordinary, fairly civilized folk can become so unpleasant. There are among us people of a more sensitive nature who would rather suffer gangrene of a limb than board another albacore boat. On the other hand, a remarkable number seem to thrive on the turmoil, for they keep coming back, making albacore fishing the big time sport fishing that it is.

In the worldwide commercial fishery, albacore are taken primarily by longlines, trolling and by pole and line. Only rarely do they school up in large enough numbers to make them the target of a purse seine. These are the "white meat" tunas that you pay more for in the can. In season, off the Pacific Coast, albacore are usually sold fresh, as steaks or fillets and occasionally as a smoked product. Fresh albacore has a shelf life of 7-10 days at 40° F and 6-9 months when frozen and kept at 0° F. The best fish and chips I have ever had was made from fresh albacore in a fish market/restaurant in Fort Bragg Harbor.

Very occasionally, albacore and other tuna and tuna-like fishes may develop scombroid poisoning if improperly stored. When this occurs, bacteria in the flesh produce histamines that upon ingestion can cause nausea, vomitng and diarrhea among other symptoms. For a brief description of treatment, see B. W. Halstead, et al., *A Color Atlas of Dangerous Marine Animals*, 1990, CRC Press.

REMARKS: See page 22 for a stimulating discussion of the red muscle found along the sides of albacore.

Along with swordfish, sea lions and other pelagic (open water) animals, you will occasionally see albacore with neat, round holes in their sides. These wounds are caused by the cookie-cutter shark, *Isistius brasiliensis*, a most delightful little predator. Cookie-cutters are small sharks, with wicked, tooth-filled little mouths. They feed by quickly swimming at a larger animal and cutting out a meaty plug from its side. Though cookie-cutters are known only from tropical and subtropical waters, it is quite possible that they move into California waters during El Niños.

YELLOWFIN TUNA (THUNNUS ALBACARES)

NAMES: Ahi, Allison   Tuna, Pacific Yellowfin. *Thunnus* is the ancient   Greek name for tuna.

IDENTIFYING CHARACTERS: True to its name, yellowfins have, well, yellow fins. The finlets, behind the dorsal and anal fins, are light yellow, edged in black. Their pectoral fins are long but do not extend back to the anal fins. In adults, the dorsal and anal fins are very long and sort of sickle-shaped. These beautiful fish have blue backs and silvery bellies and may have white spots or stripes on bellies (Plate 37). In contrast to bigeye tuna (*T. obesus*) and bluefin tuna, the livers of yellowfins are not striated.

DISTRIBUTION AND BIOLOGY: Found worldwide in tropical and temperate seas, in the Western Hemisphere yellowfins have been taken from Morro Bay (central California) southward to Peru. While they are primarily near-surface fish, they have been captured down to 924 feet. Yellowfins move into California waters from Baja California in late summer and fall, returning south as the waters cool. Since the fish prefer waters between 68–86° F, strong El Niños, which smother southern California in warm water, may bring in substantial numbers. In the 1983–84 El Niño, yellowfins were abundant as far north as Santa Cruz Island, while during most years they routinely come up as far as the Coronado Islands and off San Diego. These tunas are mostly surface-dwelling, schooling fish, often found a bit away from the coast. It is likely that most of the fish found off California were spawned in the equatorial waters off Central America. Like yellowtail, albacore and dolphinfish, these puppies like to hang around drifting kelp mats.

The good folks at the National Marine Fisheries Service and the University of Hawaii in Honolulu have come up with some tasty tidbits regarding yellowfins and the anchored fish-aggregating devices (FADs) off the Islands. Yellowfins were caught near the FADs and tagged with transmitter tags; these relayed each fish's position and depth. The research showed that the tunas very accurately navigated between FADs, even those that were at least 10 nautical miles apart. The tuna tended to swim close to the surface at night. They also hung out near FADs or reef dropoffs during the day, swam away at night (excursions averaging 5 nautical miles), then returned with daylight.

Yellowfins reach 6.5 feet. No one seems to have figured out a good way to age these folks, though we know they live more than 5 years. Males reach a larger size and may live longer. In the eastern Pacific, most females seem to die after about 3.5 years. Coastal populations mature at 20-24 inches, but in the central Pacific it seems more like 3 feet. In both areas, they mature in 2-3 years. In many parts of their range, yellowfins spawn more or less throughout the year, though the season varies a bit with location. Females are oviparous and produce 1,000,000-5,000,000 eggs per year. Yellowfins eat fishes, krill, pelagic red crabs, squids and the like. Bigger yellowfins, marlin and spearfishes eat them. A 157-pound yellowfin was found inside a 1,500-pound black marlin.

FISHERY: The southern California sport fishery is sporadic, usually occurring in late summer and fall, near or below the Mexican border. In some years, yellowfin, usually mixed in with skipjack, are taken in considerable numbers. A fish weighing 50–100 pounds, taken on medium ocean tackle, can reduce an inexperienced angler to jelly.

Worldwide, purse seine, long line, gillnet and pole fishermen take lots of yellowfin. The Central American purse seine fishery, heavily dependent on setting nets around schools of porpoise, may be on the decline (at least as far as American fishermen or those who sell to American canneries are concerned). It is thought that yellowfin school with certain porpoises in the eastern tropical Pacific because of happenstance. Both just happen to be about the same size, both are streamlined, and so they swim at about the same speed. Mammal and fish happen to feed on the same prey, which occurs in the same patches in the upper layer of the ocean.

Beaucoup yellowfins are canned, though a bunch are marketed fresh, particularly for sushi bars. Yellowfins are good fresh for 5-7 days if kept at 40° F. Frozen at 0° F, they poop out in 6-9 months. Like other tunas, see "Remarks" under the albacore section for details, improperly stored yellowfins may develop scombroid poisoning.

Fishermen off Senegal have recently developed a novel and effective way to catch yellowfin, skipjack and bigeye (*Thunnus obesus*) tuna with hook and line (Aquatic Living Resources, 1994, vol. 7, p. 139-151). The fishermen take advantage of these tunas' tendency to hang around drifting material. A fishing vessel will find a tuna school and try to associate itself with the fish—not fishing the school, just keeping up with it. Gradually, more and more tuna are drawn to the vessel, which then begins hook and line operations. The vessel stays with the tuna day and night, until its holds are full, then trades position with a second vessel, which assumes the duties of the first.

BLUEFIN TUNA (THUNNUS THYNNUS)

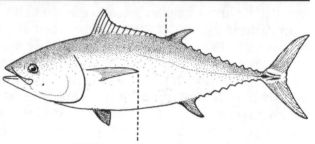

NAMES: Tunny, Giant Bluefin, Football, Shortfin Tuna, Great Albacore, Northern Bluefin, Thon Rouge. *Thunnus* is

pectoral fin not reaching origin of 2nd dorsal fin

an ancient Greek name for "tuna."

IDENTIFYING CHARACTERS: Bluefins are dark blue or black on backs and silvery below, with short pectoral fins. The first dorsal is yellowish or bluish, the second sort of red-brown. In contrast to yellowfins, bluefin livers are striated.

DISTRIBUTION AND BIOLOGY: Bluefins are found worldwide, across the north Pacific from the Philippines, South China Sea and Japan to North America. On our coast, they have been taken from the Shelikof Strait, Alaska, to southern Baja California, commonly from around Santa Barbara, southwards. These are generally pelagic, schooling fish, found near or at the surface. Of all the tunas off California, they are the most willing to come inshore. For instance, I have seen them just behind the surf line off Santa Barbara and in Santa Monica Bay. Schools may be of immense size. There is one report of 200,000 pounds of bluefins taken from a single school off Isla San Benito, Baja California. Bluefins often school with albacore, yellowfin tuna, bigeye tuna, Pacific bonito, skipjack tuna and yellowtail.

Bluefins spawn from the Philippines and Japan eastward, perhaps as far west as Hawaii. The larvae drift towards Japan, where some young ones may remain. Others migrate across the Pacific, arriving off Baja in April and May. Some of these move north into southern California, generally in May and June. By October or November, bluefin have returned southward into Mexican waters where they winter until the following spring. Bluefin usually remain off North America until they are 3–6 years old, migrating back west across the Pacific to spawn. Rarely, very large, mature fish return for short visits to North America. In the fall of 1989, schools of truly humongous fish (as large as 1,008 pounds) took up residence off the back side of Santa Rosa Island, near San Nicolas Island and Tanner and Cortes banks, the first time in memory that fish this large were taken off southern California. All the large fish that were examined were males.

Bluefins reach 6.5 feet. It is difficult to figure out a bluefin's age, but these fish probably live more than 9 years; on the Atlantic coast they apparently live for at least 30 years. Bluefins are about 23 inches long and 10 pounds at 1 year, 43 inches and 60 pounds at 3 years and 63 inches and 180 pounds at 5 years. They mature at about 5-6 years. Females are oviparous and may produce as many as ten million eggs per year. Spawning season is April-August, later in the year the further north you go. Young-of-the-year live off Japan. Some young fish migrate eastward and may or may not remain there for a few years. Most fish taken off the west coast of the U. S. are 2-3 years old. Fishes (such as anchovies, sauries, hake), squids and pelagic red crabs seem to be major food items off North America. Bluefins caught in very shallow waters off California ate sanddabs, white croakers, perches and even a starfish or two. Orcas have been seen munching on these guys.

FISHERY: Bluefins are a very popular sport fish, but notoriously hard to hook. They seem to be able to sense that something just is not right with an anchovy impaled on the curved piece of metal. Large schools of bluefins will often flog some poor school of anchovies, happily ignoring everything an angler sends out. They are most apt to bite when found in schools mixed with other species, such as albacore or yellowfin tuna. There is a large commercial fishery for this tuna worldwide, mostly by purse seine, but also with long line and gillnets. Purse seines are the primary technique in southern California. Shelf life of bluefins is similar to that of yellowfins. Like other tunas, bluefins may develop scombroid poisoning if improperly stored. See the "Remarks" under albacore.

REMARKS: The concentration of very large bluefins occurring in fall and winter 1989 and 1990 off southern California was really quite an event. The fish were so large that in a number of cases they simply plowed through surrounding purse seines and gillnets, leaving massive holes in their wakes. Most of the fish were sold to Japanese buyers for the Japanese sushi trade. Prices to fishermen who sold their catches outright reached $12 per pound, while a few who opted to sell their fish in Japan received a share of profits ranging from $16 to $35 per pound. Several home mortgages and numerous boat loans were paid off over a few frenetic weeks.

A bluefin swimming at normal speeds can travel 50–156 miles per day and at maximum speeds can move out at about 50 miles per hour. Like other tunas, bluefins have circulatory systems which serve as "heat exchangers," allowing the fish to be "warm blooded." They can metabolize more quickly than most other fish and therefore can keep swimming at a faster clip.

Swordfishes - Family Xiphiidae

SWORDFISH (XIPHIAS GLADIUS)

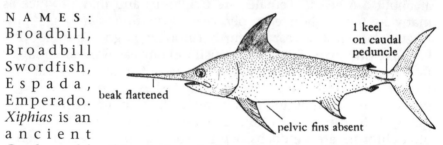

NAMES: Broadbill, Broadbill Swordfish, Espada, Emperado. *Xiphias* is an ancient Greek word for this species; *gladius* means "sword" in Latin.

IDENTIFYING CHARACTERS: Dead swordfish are black or brown-black; live ones (this from Ken Neilsen) are purple. Swordfish do not have pelvic fins. The sword is a flattened extension of the upper jaw. Other billfishes, such as the sailfish and various marlins, have rounded bills and do have pelvic fins.

DISTRIBUTION AND BIOLOGY: Swordfish are found worldwide in temperate and tropical seas. In the eastern Pacific, they have been taken from just below Vancouver Island, southward. Swordfish appear to migrate northward from Baja California in summer and fall, probably returning south in winter. While they are most common in our waters from Pt. Conception southward, fishermen occasionally encounter slugs of them farther north. For instance, in the fall of 1989 a large concentration developed about 100 miles offshore of San Francisco. These are usually solitary fish, occasionally seen in pairs. Swordfish generally hang out between the surface and perhaps 400 feet, though they have been sighted in depths of 2,000 feet. The behavior of these fish was monitored off the tip of Baja California using sonic tags which allow the tagged fish to be followed, often for days. The fish usually spent daylight hours close to the bottom, over a bank 300 feet deep. As the sun set, they headed offshore, swimming up to the surface for the night. At daybreak, they returned to the same inshore spot. It is likely the fish were feeding on pelagic fish or squids at night over deep water and on bottom species during the day. Curiously, in southern California swordfish often bask at the surface during the day, a rare occurrence in the tropics. These sunning fish rarely feed, and it is likely they have come up during the day to the warm surface waters to digest their night meals. This may explain why generations of sport fishermen have thrown everything in their tackle boxes and bait tanks at sunning swordfish with rarely a hookup.

Swordfish reach 15 feet in length. They live at least 9 years and probably more, but no hard numbers are available. Females grow larger than males, but we don't know if that is because they grow faster, live longer, or both. No one seems quite sure at what length they mature; the most recent estimate is at about 3.5 feet, measured from eye to tail fork. In the Pacific, spawning occurs in the central, western and southern portions. Off Hawaii, spawning takes place from April–July. A female produces up to 6,000,000 eggs per season. Larvae are usually found in waters between 75–84° F. Swordfish feed on just about anything. Off California, sardines, anchovies, sauries and squids seem popular. At least occasionally, these fish use their swords when feeding. Prey are often found with slash or stab marks in swordfish stomachs. Swordfish have been seen with impaled dolphinfish on their bills, and pieces of bills have been found in blue and fin whales and in other swordfish. These guys also jab at the occasional boat. Small swordfish are eaten by tunas, billfishes, blue and mako sharks and probably other large fishes.

FISHERY: Very few swordfish are taken by sport anglers, perhaps because most of these fish feed at night, while most anglers are drinking lite beer and watching reruns of *Three's Company*.

Worldwide, swordfish are a major commercial species, taken by long line, gillnet and harpoon. Off the Pacific Coast, the harpoon was the primary means of capture until drifting gillnets became popular in the 1970s. Lesser numbers are taken on longlines. Today, the commercial fishery stretches northward into Oregon. Swordfish are sold fresh or frozen. In the commercial trade, different size fish have different names. Those less than 25 pounds are "rats," 25-49 pounds are "pups," 50-99 pounds are "mediums" and "markers" are 100 pounds and up. Fresh swordfish has a very long shelf life (10-15 days) when stored at 40° F. Like most fish, it's okay for 9-12 months when frozen at 0° F.

Billfishes and Marlins - Family Istiophoridae

STRIPED MARLIN (TETRAPTURUS AUDAX)

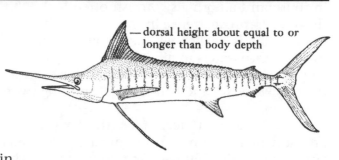
— dorsal height about equal to or longer than body depth

NAMES: *Tetrapturus* comes from 3 Greek words meaning "4 wing tails," referring to the winglike keels on the caudal fin.

IDENTIFYING CHARACTERS: These fish are colored dark blue on backs and silvery on bellies, with 15–25 light blue bars or vertical rows of spots on sides. Characteristically, the first part of the dorsal fin is quite high.

DISTRIBUTION AND BIOLOGY: Striped marlin are found in the temperate and tropical waters of the Pacific and Indian Oceans and occasionally in the Atlantic off the Cape of Good Hope. Off North America, they have been taken from near Winchester Bay, Oregon, southward, though they are rare north of about Santa Barbara Island. In the Pacific, the highest concentrations occur in a roughly semi-circular piece of water, extending from eastern Australia to central America and Mexico, then running westward though the Hawaiian Islands to Japan. While fish from throughout the Pacific probably travel around considerably, recent genetic research shows that such movements may be somewhat limited. Normally found in the top 50 or 60 feet of water, striped marlin have been taken at depths down to about 953 feet. Marlin catches off southern California are highly seasonal. Fish migrate into our waters in summer, probably from Baja California and return south in late fall. Maximum catches are from mid-August to mid-September, at temperatures of 68-70° F. Most fish are sighted and caught in a band from San Clemente Island on the west to the mainland and running south to below the Coronado Islands.

Striped marlin reach about 13.5 feet. They mature at 4.5-5 feet, eye to tailfork length. Females produce between 11 million and 29 million eggs, and the spawning season off Mexico appears to be in July and possibly August. Fish found off California have already spawned off Mexico. Tagging studies off Cabo San Lucas, Baja California, suggest that marlin make spawning migrations toward Socorro, Clarion and Revillagigedo Islands. Tunas, jacks, sardines, anchovies, sauries and squids are all part of the wide variety of animals these fish eat.

FISHERY: These popular recreational fish off California are taken primarily by private vessels, but are caught occasionally aboard party boats, particularly on albacore trips. Off southern California, most fish are taken from Santa Barbara Island, southwards, including San Clemente and Santa Catalina Islands. In California waters, only recreational fishermen may legally take striped marlin. Worldwide, striped marlin are a major commercial species, taken by long line and gillnet throughout much of the Pacific and Indian Oceans. From 1980-1990, worldwide catches fluctuated between 12,600 and 18,300 metric tons annually.

Butterfishes - Family Stromateidae

PACIFIC BUTTERFISH (PEPRILUS SIMILLIMUS)

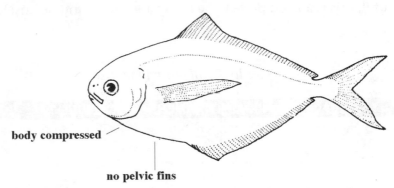

body compressed

no pelvic fins

NAME: Pompano, California Pompano. *Peprilus* is Greek for *Peprilos* (an unknown Greek fish); *simillimus* is Latin for "similar," referring to its resemblance to the butterfish (*Peprilus triacanthus*) of the Atlantic coast.

IDENTIFYING CHARACTERS: Butterfish have round, compressed bodies, silvery-green or blue coloration on backs and are silvery below. They have small mouths, blunt heads and forked tails.

DISTRIBUTION AND BIOLOGY: Found from Queen Charlotte Sound, British Columbia to central (probably southern) Baja California and the Gulf of California, at 8-600 foot depths, butterfish are abundant from central California, southward. These are schooling, midwater fish that move about considerably. Butterfish reach

323

11 inches. Little is known of their growth rates; a 7-incher I aged was 4 years old. From my quick study, they seem to mature at about 5.5 inches. Females are oviparous. On the Pacific Coast, a few fish may spawn throughout the year, though most larvae are found from May to July. Larvae are found from central California southward to at least southern Baja California. Peak concentrations occur between Punta Baja and Punta Eugenia, central Baja California. Larvae are found as far out to sea as 200 miles, but most reside from nearshore to around 100 miles offshore. Butterfish are eaten by a variety of predators, including kelp bass, barracuda, California halibut, California sea lions, Dall's porpoise, common murres, tufted puffins, least terns, rhinoceros auklets and Brandt's cormorants.

FISHERY: Anglers, particularly those fishing from piers and jetties, take moderate numbers of butterfish, from central California southward. These are valuable commercial fish, and there is a small fishery for this species; most of the catches are made by lampara net fishermen targeting other species, such as northern anchovies.

REMARKS: Young butterfish are often found swimming around and through the tentacles of jellyfish. They are not immune to the stinging cells, just really agile. Throughout the world, it is common for juvenile fishes to hang around jellyfish and, if you think about it, this is a good place to be if you are young and defenseless.

Family Paralichthyidae

PACIFIC SANDDAB (CITHARICHTHYS SORDIDUS)

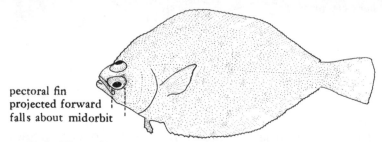

pectoral fin
projected forward
falls about midorbit

NAME: Soft Flounder, Sole, Mottled Sanddab, Catalina Sanddab, Megrim. The most common market name is "sanddab." *Citharichthys* is a combination of 2 Greek words and means "fish which lies on its ribs"; *sordidus* is Latin for "sordid" (dull).

IDENTIFYING CHARACTERS: Pacifics are brown, left-eyed flatfish, often with yellow, orange or reddish-brown spots. They closely resemble speckled sanddabs, but that species is lighter-colored and profusely dotted with tiny black spots.

DISTRIBUTION AND BIOLOGY: Found from the Bering Sea southward to Cabo San Lucas, southern Baja California, these flatfish are abundant at least from the Gulf of Alaska to central Baja California. Pacifics have been reported from intertidal waters to depths of 1,800 feet. Though small ones are found inshore, even in brackish waters, most of the population lives between 150 and 450 feet. These are primarily soft-bottom dwellers, living over sand or occasionally mud, but they have also been reported from hard, flat substrate. We don't know if these fish make along-coast movements, but there does seem to be a general inshore migration during summer. Pacifics are unusual for flatfishes in that they will swim well above the bottom in search of food, particularly at night. From a research submarine, I have seen lots of these fish hovering 3-6 feet above the bottom.

Pacific sanddabs reach lengths of at least 16 inches. The oldest one aged was about 11 years, but it is likely they live a bit longer. Females grow slightly larger, slightly faster and may live slightly longer than males. Over half of females are mature at 7.5 inches, almost all by 9 inches, generally at 2-3 years. Females are oviparous and may spawn twice per season. Off California and Baja California, based on larval surveys, some spawning may occur throughout the year. Greatest concentrations occur from about June-October. In Puget Sound, spawning has been noted from March-May. Larvae may drift about for 9 months or more before settling out at .75-1.5 inches. Pacifics are opportunistic feeders, likely to chomp on almost anything they can find, such as copepods, krill, shrimps, squids, small fishes and worms. They seem to feed both on and above the bottom, during both day and night. Northern fur seals, California sea lions, Pacific white-sided dolphins, Dall's porpoises, common murres, pigeon guillemots, western gulls, arctic loons, rhinoceros auklets and pelagic, Brandt's and double-crested cormorants eat them.

FISHERY: Despite their relatively small size, this is a popular fish with some anglers. It is commonly taken aboard party and private vessels (some anglers target this species), and in some years it is a major part of the pier catch, particularly from central California northward.

This is also a fairly important commercial species, taken by trawl and long line from southern California northward. Virtually all of the fish are sold fresh and whole (a bit is frozen) to local markets and restuarants. Large sanddabs may be filleted. This species is sometimes called "Catalina sanddab" in these establishments (despite the fact that only part of the catch is taken from around the island). Sanddabs have a short shelf life.

REMARKS: You may find Pacific sanddabs with a rather peculiar parasite sticking out of their eyes. This is the parasitic copepod, *Phrixocephalus concinatus*, which lives almost exclusively in the eyes of this flatfish (occasionally in eyes of other species). Although the parasite likely blinds the inhabited eye, the partially sighted sanddabs seem to be able to function pretty well. In fact, once in a while you may find a fish with both eyes infected.

Otoliths from Pacific sanddabs have been found in Pliocene (over one-million-year old) deposits in Long Beach, California.

SPECKLED SANDDAB (CITHARICHTHYS STIGMAEUS)

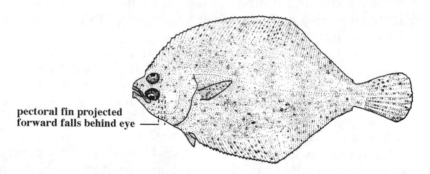

pectoral fin projected
forward falls behind eye

NAMES: Sanddab. *Citharichthys* is a combination of 2 Greek words and means "fish which lies on its ribs"; *stigmaeus* means "speckled" in Greek.

IDENTIFYING CHARACTERS: Hey, like it says above, they are speckled with lots of black dots.

DISTRIBUTION AND BIOLOGY: Speckleds are found from Prince William Sound, Alaska to Bahia Magdalena, southern Baja California. While this sandy-bottom dweller has been found from nearshore water to 2,004 feet, they are basically a shallow-water species.

They are little, 6.75 inches max. It's been estimated that they live to about 3.5 years and mature at about 2.75 inches. Females are oviparous, produce pelagic eggs, and in southern California, spawn from March-October. While larvae are found throughout the year, they are found in greatest numbers from about August to December. Studies along the California and Baja California coast show that spawning is particularly heavy in central Baja California, between Punta Baja and Punta Eugenia. Most larvae are found within about 150 miles of the shore, but some have been taken as much as 200 miles off the beach. The larvae stay out at sea a considerable period of time, sometimes more than 10 months. At about 1.0-1.5 inches, young juveniles settle out on the open coast and in bays at an average depth (in southern California) of 35 feet. Speckleds nail a wide variety of prey, including mysid shrimps, gammarid amphipods, shrimps, worms, squids and occasionally fishes. They are eaten by various piscivores, including harbor seals, Brandt's cormorants and pigeon guillemots.

FISHERY: Considering how small their mouths are, an amazing number of these fish are taken in the recreational fishery. Most of the catch is made in central and northern California. There is no commercial fishery to speak of.

REMARKS: Pliocene fossil ear bones from speckleds have been found.

BIGMOUTH SOLE (HIPPOGLOSSINA STOMATA)

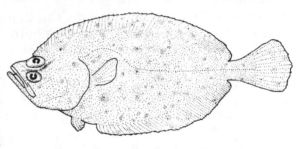

NAMES: Basically, *Hippoglossina* means "little *Hippoglossus*", and *Hippoglossus* refers to the very large flatfishes that live in the North Atlantic and Pacific; *stomata* is Greek for "large mouthed."

IDENTIFYING CHARACTERS: This is an easy flatfish to I.D. The things to look for are a large mouth and a highly arched lateral line. The eyed side is brown, with a profusion of blue spots and dark blotches.

DISTRIBUTION AND BIOLOGY: Found over soft substrate from Monterey Bay, central California to the Gulf of California, bigmouths are very abundant from southern California to southern Baja California. They have been taken from 24-834 feet.

A moderately small species, bigmouths reach 15.75 inches. Females mature at about 7.0 inches and are oviparous. Off California and Baja California, some larvae are found throughout the year; based on larval abundances, peak spawning seems to occur from July to October. Larvae tend to be found near the coast; while a few have been taken as far offshore as 200 miles, most are within 100 miles of the beach. Heaviest larval concentrations are found south of Punta Eugenia, central Baja California. Bigmouths eat a lot of mysid shrimps and amphipods; fishes, squids and crabs are also on the bill of fare.

FISHERY: They are occasionally taken by pier and boat anglers from Santa Barbara southward. There is no commercial fishery.

CALIFORNIA HALIBUT (PARALICHTHYS CALIFORNICUS)

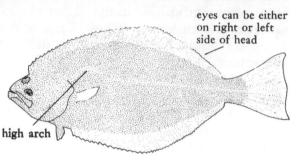

eyes can be either on right or left side of head

high arch

NAMES: Bastard Halibut (I know this is a family book, but that is what they are called), Monterey Halibut, Flyswaters (little ones), Barndoors (big ones), Chicken Halibut, Southern Halibut. Anglers often call these fish "flatties," not a particularly stunning example of originality. *Paralichthys* is a combination of 2 Greek words meaning "parallel fish"; *californicus* means "Californian."

IDENTIFYING CHARACTERS: Perhaps the best way to identify this flatfish is to stick your finger in its mouth. If your finger starts bleeding in a relatively short time (don't keep it in there for hours), you probably have a halibut there; few other flatfish on our coast have much in the way of teeth. These fish are usually brown or blackish with various blotches on eyed sides and white on the blind sides. I've seen them come in green or wildly splotched with white or orange. Other distinguishing features are a highly-arched lateral line and a caudal fin which is indented near the upper and lower lobes. Bigmouth sole have a round caudal fin and no teeth to speak of (or with). Pacific halibut have a tail indented in the middle.

DISTRIBUTION AND BIOLOGY: California halibut are found from off the Quillayute River, Washington to southern Baja California, most commonly from about Bodega Bay southward. While these fish live on soft bottoms (often with only their eyes and mouth unburied), they really seem to like hunkering down near structure. You will usually find them near rocks, artificial reefs, kelp holdfasts, etc. Even slight irregularities in the bottom will be enough to aggregate them. There is some evidence that sand dollar beds are also attractive, as are mouths of streams or rivers. In the latter case, they are probably not attracted to the fresh water, but rather to the rocks and debris that are often found near these features. Flatties live between the shore and 600 feet, most commonly from about 5 to 180 feet. Very young ones are found in the shallowest water; they tend to move out as they grow older and larger. While the species can be found in estuaries, adults usually live in the open ocean.

Contrary to popular belief, California halibut are pretty active fish. For instance, many move around with schools of anchovies, white croakers, and other preyfish. I have been on anchored sport fishing vessels as anchovy schools came by periodically. Only at these times would passengers catch halibut; the fish were traveling with the anchovy schools. During a study of halibut reproduction, I noted that most of the fish we trawled up were taken when the trawls were towed through schools of these same small, midwater species. Again the halibut seemed to be keeping up with these meandering schools.

Halibut tend to make seasonal inshore-offshore movements, moving inshore and aggregating in late winter and early spring to spawn and feed, staying through summer and fall then dispersing offshore in late fall and winter. Having said this, I note that there are exceptions. For instance, during January of 1986, anglers took large quantities of halibut right along the kelp line near Gaviota, southern California. It is still a bit uncertain as to whether and how much halibut move along the coast. Many of the fish do seem to move northward during warm water years, as halibut fishing improves in central California and declines in southern California. Moreover, in a tagging study my associates and I conducted, California halibut tagged in southern California tended to move north, even in non-El Niño years. Perhaps the most interesting results of that study were the recoveries at the northern Channel Islands (Santa Cruz and Santa Rosa) of halibut tagged at the mainland. There are very few small halibut around these islands, and I theorize that few young-of-the-year settle out there. Rather, I believe that most of those fish come from the mainland, swimming over ocean bottoms of at least 600 feet deep to get there. Tag returns tend to confirm my ideas.

California halibut reach 5 feet in length and probably about 72 pounds in weight. Females live as long as 30 years and grow faster and much larger than males. A 1-year-old fish is about 7 inches long; a 22-incher is 4–5 years old. Half of all males are mature at 9 inches (2 years), all are mature at 13 inches (3 years). Females mature later: half at 19 inches, all at 23 inches. Most females are mature at 4–5 years, all by 7 years. Females are oviparous. While California halibut spawn throughout the year, most spawning occurs from February–June and the spawning peak varies annually. For instance, in southern California in 1983, spawning peaked in February, while it peaked in April in 1984. Spawning occurs in inshore waters, and most larvae are found over water shallower than 250 feet. Off northern Baja California, larvae have been taken as far as 150 miles offshore. While larvae are found from around San Francisco southward, highest concentrations occur from Pt. Conception to Punta Eugenia, central Baja California. In laboratory studies, eggs hatched at 54, 61, and 68° F, but not at 46 and 75°. As the larvae develop, they move inshore. The larvae settle out of the water column in less than 30 days after hatching, at around .5 inches.

Fish settle out over a period of months. As an example, in 1988, they settled out from January - September. There is some confusion about where the settlement takes place. It appears that larvae settle out in very shallow water, often only a few feet deep. Both protected and semiprotected embayments, such as Mission Bay, Agua Hedionda Lagoon and Alamitos Bay, are good nursery grounds. In some years, the fish also settle out along the open coast. When this happens, the young fish appear to swim into protected areas when they reach about 1.5 inches long. At around 2 years old, most halibut living in lagoons or estuaries move into the ocean. Very small ones eat bottom-dwelling invertebrates such as amphipods and copepods; slightly larger fish (to about 10 inches) concentrate on mysid shrimps. Larger halibut eat fishes, squids and octopi, concentrating mainly on fishes and squids. Almost any fish that comes by (but particularly anchovies) is fair game. I have found anchovies, white croakers, sardines, walleye perch and queenfish, to name a few, in their stomachs. Halibut have been seen leaping out of the water while dashing after anchovies and during grunion runs have beached themselves chasing after those little sex maniacs. This is one of the few fish species on our coast that may be active during both day and night. In fact, otter trawlers report that fewer halibut are taken during the night, implying that the fish are more alert and/or are off the bottom during those hours. Sea lions, angel sharks, electric rays and other larger predators eat these guys.

FISHERY: This is a major sport fish from Bodega Bay southward, with anglers seeking halibut from sport and private vessels, piers, jetties and shore. During most years, party vessel catches peak between spring and early summer. A lot of anglers aboard private vessels tend to concentrate their efforts in water that is too shallow. While the fish are numerous in 5-60 feet, my studies indicate that probably more good-sized fish are in 100–150 feet. Try trolling near the bottom out there and see what happens.

Commercial fishermen take large numbers of fish with gillnets and otter trawls, and a few fish are taken by bottom trolling. Most California halibut are sold fresh, as fillets and steaks, but some are frozen. Shelf life is about 5 days at 40° F and 9 months if they are frozen and kept at 0° F. Relatively recently, a fishery developed for halibut that are kept alive for sale. Fishermen sell live fish for twice as much as dead ones.

Recreational and commercial catches of California halibut have declined markedly since the 1920s, probably the result of nursery ground destruction and over-fishing by both commercial and recreational fishermen.

REMARKS: An albino halibut has been reported, as well as numerous ambicolored individuals pigmented on both sides. Completely ambicolored fish always have a "hook" (a large depression) behind the eye, near the dorsal fin. What seems to have caused this color anomaly is a botched-up eye migration. As a larvae begins to settle out of the water column, one of the eyes begins to migrate from one side of the fish to the other. (In most species, it is always the same eye, either left or right, that migrates. In the California halibut, it can be either eye.) The fish then flops over on its side, eyes upward, and lives from then on as a "flatfish." Only the up (eyed) side develops pigment; the downside, which is against the sand, is white. If the eye does not migrate properly (that hook is a symptom), the fish's brain seems to get confused and does not turn off pigment production to one side, and both sides are colored.

Fossil halibut ear bones, extending back to at least one million years, have been found in southern California.

Halibut bones are commonly found in Native American middens.

FANTAIL SOLE (XYSTREURYS LIOLEPIS)

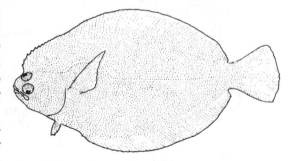

NAMES: *Xystreurys* is Greek for "raker" and "wide," referring to this species' wide gill rakers; *liolepis* is also Greek, this time for "smooth scales."

IDENTIFYING CHARACTERS: These are fairly oval fish, with a highly arched lateral line. The mouth is small, and the pectoral fin is longer than the head. While the eyed side is basically brown, there can be some blue in there somewhere. Often you will find a couple of dark spots, one near the pectoral fin, the other further back.

DISTRIBUTION AND BIOLOGY: Fantails are found from Monterey Bay, central California to the Gulf of California, over soft bottom. In general, these are relatively shallow water fish; they have been taken between 15-348 feet.

Fantails reach 21 inches and mature at about 6.25 inches. Females are oviparous. Most fantails are summer-fall spawners, though larval studies off California and Baja California imply that there may be some small spawning activity throughout most of the year. Most spawning takes place off central and southern Baja California, from about Punta Baja to Cabo San Lazaro. Fantail larvae are almost limited to the nearshore environment; few are found more than 100 miles from the coast, most are within 40 miles. Juveniles settle out at about .75 inches on the open coast in water averaging 20 feet. Fantails eat mainly invertebrates, primarily crabs, shrimps, amphipods and squids.

FISHERY: Fantails are only occasionally taken by pier and boat recreational anglers, from Santa Barbara southward. There is no commercial fishery.

Righteye Flounders - Family Pleuronectidae

ARROWTOOTH FLOUNDER (ATHERESTHES STOMIAS)

NAMES: Long-Jaw Flounder, Arasukaaburagarei and Aburagarei (Japanese). *Atheresthes* is a combination of 2 Greek words "spike, eat"; *stomias* means "mouth" in Greek.

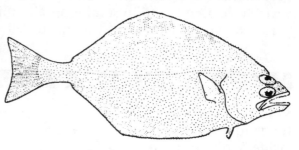

IDENTIFYING CHARACTERS: This is a large-mouthed, prominent-toothed, right-eyed species. A major giveaway is that the upper eye sits right at the animal's midline; in other words, it's right in line with the dorsal fin. It bears some resemblance to the Greenland halibut, but Greenlands are not white on their blind side (they are dusky, dontcha know).

DISTRIBUTION AND BIOLOGY: While they have been found from the Bering Sea (perhaps the Chukchi Sea) to San Simeon, central California, the big numbers are in the Bering Sea and the Gulf of Alaska. They are occasional as far south as San Francisco, northern California, and abundant from central Oregon northward. While they have been found from 60-2,970 feet, they are most common in perhaps 600-1,200 feet. Like many other northern flatfishes, arrowtooths spend the winters in the deeper part of their depth range, moving into the shallower areas during the spring and summer. Work by Russian scientists in the eastern Bering Sea found that arrowtooths were able to live over a wide temperature range (32-48° F), but were most abundant in waters of 37-39° F.

Arrowtooths reach 2.75 feet and live to 20 years. Males mature at 1.0-1.4 feet (3-7 years), females 1.2-1.4 feet (4-8 years). Females are oviparous, and both eggs and larvae are mesopelagic. Spawning occurs from December to March in the Bering Sea and March to at least August in the Gulf of Alaska. In the Gulf, spawning individuals have been taken from depths ranging from 350 to about 1,200 feet, most often between 350 and 660 feet. Arrowtooths eat a wide range of prey, including various fishes (even each other), shrimps, worms and krill. One study in the Bering Sea found that walleye pollock were numero uno in the lunch bucket.

FISHERY: These are occasionally taken by recreational anglers, particularly off Alaska. There is a moderate-sized trawl fishery for this one.

SLENDER SOLE (EOPSETTA EXILIS)

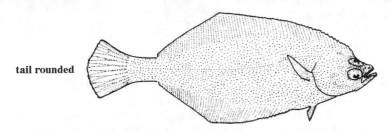

tail rounded

NAMES: *Eopsetta* is from the Greek words for "morning flounder"; *exilis* means "slender" in Greek. Formerly *Lyopsetta exilis*.

IDENTIFYING CHARACTERS: It's right-eyed, that's a start. And it is real slender, so you're on your way to identifying it. And when you add the large, easily dislodged scales and the brown coloration, you pretty much have it aced.

DISTRIBUTION AND BIOLOGY: Southeastern Alaska to central Baja California is where slenders hang up their shingle. They have a wide depth range, from 48-3,294 feet. They seem most abundant in 300-1,000 feet of water.

Slenders reach 13.75 inches. Males mature at 2-3 years, females at 3-5 years. Females are oviparous and produce pelagic eggs. Spawning season is late winter and early spring. In larval studies off California and Baja California, most larvae are captured from February to July. Along this stretch of coast, highest concentrations occur between about San Francisco and Pt. Conception and again between Punta Baja and Punta Eugenia (central Baja California). While most slender sole larvae live relatively close to shore, a few have been taken out to 250 miles. Slenders eat a wide variety of organisms, with shrimps, amphipods, salps, mysid shrimps, worms, fishes and krill among the hot prey. What are perhaps slender sole remains have been found in northern elephant seals.

FISHERY: Slenders are almost never taken in the recreational catch, ditto the commercial.

REMARKS: The late John Fitch of the California Department of Fish and Game found fossil ear bones of this species from the Pliocene deposits (older than a million years) in Palos Verdes, southern California.

PETRALE SOLE (EOPSETTA JORDANI)

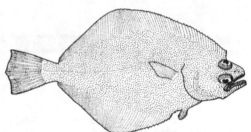

NAMES: California Sole, Brill, Roundnosed Sole, Jordan's Flounder, Petoraru Nameta (Japanese), Tsubame Garei (Japanese). *Eopsetta* is formed from 2 Greek words meaning "morning flounder"; *jordani* honors the remarkable 19th Century ichthyologist, David Starr Jordan, a man of prodigious talents and an ego to match.

IDENTIFYING CHARACTERS: This is a right-eyed, large-mouthed flatfish, whose jaw reaches to below the middle of the eye. The upper jaw has 2 rows of teeth.

DISTRIBUTION AND BIOLOGY: Petrales are found over sandy bottoms from the Bering Sea southward to northern Baja California, and they are abundant from southern California northward. While they have been taken from intertidal waters to 1,815 feet, they are most frequent from about 300–900 feet in depth. The fish make extensive inshore-offshore migrations; off British Columbia they summer in 240–420 feet, then migrate to 1,020–1,500 feet to spawn in winter. Some individuals also move along the coast. Fish tagged off Eureka, northern California, have been recovered off British Columbia.

Petrale reach 29.5 inches. A 25.25-inch female was aged at 25 years, a 19.75 inch male at 19 years. Half of females mature at about 17 inches (8 years), while half of males reproduce at 15 inches (7 years). All males are mature by 16 inches, and all females are mature by 18 inches Females are oviparous and produce between 400,000 and 1,200,000 eggs. Off British Columbia, the fish spawn from January–April, while off Oregon everyone goes to it from November–March, peaking in December and

January. However, just to confuse the issue, an occasional ripe female is found off Oregon during the summer. The pelagic eggs hatch in about 8 days. Petrale are active predators, feeding on fishes, large crustaceans, octopi and squids. Harbor seals eat them. FISHERY: Petrales are popular recreational fish, taken aboard party and private vessels. They are usually taken during deep water rockfish trips when the boat drifts off the rockpile onto the adjacent sand. While they enter the recreational catch from southern California north to at least Oregon, nowhere do they comprise a high percentage of the total catch.

Commercial trawlers working from California to the Gulf of Alaska take substantial numbers. Most are taken from 300-900 feet. Petrales are sold fresh and frozen, often as fillets. Shelf life is 5 days when stored at 40° F. Feel free to freeze them for 9-12 months at 0° F.

REX SOLE (ERREX ZACHIRUS)

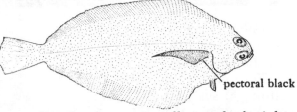

pectoral black

NAMES: Longfin Sole, Witch, Hirenaganameta (Japanese); *zachirus* is also Greek and refers to the species' long pectoral fin.

IDENTIFYING CHARACTERS: Rex are brown, small mouthed, right-eyed flatfish characterized by a long pectoral fin on the eyed side.
DISTRIBUTION AND BIOLOGY: Found from the western Bering Sea southward to Isla Cedros, Baja California, rex are abundant on mud and mud-boulder habitat along much of their range. They have been taken from intertidal waters to 2,850 foot depths. These guys move inshore in summer and make offshore spawning movements in winter. Studies off British Columbia show that they like water temperatures around 45° F.

Rex reach 23.5 inches and live to at least 24 years. Females grow faster and larger and live longer than the hapless males. A 12-inch female is 10 years old and a similar-sized male is 12. Off Oregon, half of males mature at 6.5 inches and 3 years, 100% at 8.5 inches and 5 years. Half of females are mature at 9.5 inches and 5 years; all reproduce at 12 inches and 9 years. Females are oviparous and produce 3,900-238,000 eggs. Spawning season appears to be extremely variable, so I will just list what the various studies show: Bering Sea–September; Gulf of Alaska–February to at least August; Oregon–January to June (peaking March-April);

California–January to September. In the Gulf of Alaska, spawning fish were taken in depths of 350-1,000 feet, most commonly 660-1,000 feet. While a few larvae have been found as far south as southern California, most are taken further north. Larvae take about a year to metamorphose into bottom-dwelling juveniles, and depths of 490-660 feet have been reported as nursery grounds. Small rex eat small crustaceans, such as gammarid amphipods; big ones dine primarily on worms, gammarid amphipods, shrimps and crabs. Fishes (sharks, skates, lingcod, rockfishes), marine mammals (harbor seals and California sea lions) and birds (western gulls, pelagic and Brandt's cormorants) like to eat them.

FISHERY: Although they are only rarely taken by recreational fishermen, rex sole are a major part of the flatfish trawl fishery from California northward to the Bering Sea. Most catches are made in 300-1,200 feet. Rex are marketed filleted or whole, fresh and frozen. Fresh shelf life, like most other flatfishes, is about 5 days at 40° F; frozen, it's 9-12 months at 0° F.

FLATHEAD SOLE (HIPPOGLOSSOIDES ELASSODON)

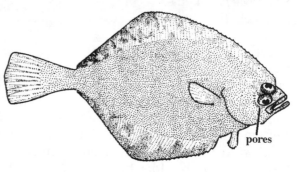
pores

NAMES: Umagarei and Shirogarei (Japanese). *Hippoglossoides* is formed from "Hippoglossus" (an old name for a halibut) and the Greek words for "similar to"; *elassodon* comes from 2 Greek words "small" and "tooth."

IDENTIFYING CHARACTERS: Flathead soles are very thin, right-eyed flatfish. I don't know, to me this looks like every nondescript flatfish rolled into one. However, here is what J. L. Hart, *Pacific Fishes of Canada*, has to say: "The following combination of characters serve to identify this flatfish: mouth nearly symmetrical, extending as far as the pupil of the eye but not beyond, caudal fin nearly straight or slightly rounded, an exposed spine at the base of the anal fin, no dorsal branch to the lateral line canal, teeth on the upper jaw in one row."

DISTRIBUTION AND BIOLOGY: Flatheads are found from Japan to the Okhotsk and Bering Seas and southward to Pt. Reyes, northern California. While they have been taken from 20-1,800 feet, adults usually live in water less than about 600 feet. The eastern Bering

Sea contains the greatest concentration of flatheads. Adults migrate from deep waters in the winter to shallow waters in the spring and early summer. Flatheads off British Columbia and in the Gulf of Alaska are reported to occur mostly at 900-1,200 feet during the winter and 600-900 feet during the rest of the year. Juveniles and adults have a pretty hefty temperature tolerance, from waters below 32° to about 54° F. They seem to prefer it on the cool side, between about 36-39° F.

Flatheads reach 1.5 feet and live about 21 years. They mature after 6 years in the Bering Sea (about 1 foot) and 1-2 years (8 inches) in Puget Sound, Washington. Females are oviparous and produce pelagic eggs. Spawning season is at least February to August, perhaps peaking around April-May. In the Gulf of Alaska, fish in spawning condition have been taken in waters between 350 and 1,000 feet, most often between 350 and 660 feet. Summarizing several studies, fecundity ranges from 52,000-600,000 eggs. In a study in Auke Bay, southeast Alaska, maximum larval production occurred at the same time as maximum copepod numbers. Eggs are found most commonly in the surface layer, say 0-50 feet, and most larvae hang out between 0-150 feet. Eggs hatch between about 9 and 21 days, depending on water temperature. Larvae do some vertical migration over 24 hours, descending slightly during the night. Small flatheads eat mainly krill; as they grow larger, they eat lots of things, including fishes, worms, krill, shrimps, brittle stars and clams. There is some evidence that these fish do not feed as heavily during spawning season.

FISHERY: Rarely taken by recreational anglers and not a terribly important commercial species. Flatheads are taken as a "bycatch," a species fishermen catch while pursuing other fishes. This flatfish is taken by trawlers targeting more valuable species.

PACIFIC HALIBUT (HIPPOGLOSSUS STENOLEPIS)

NAMES: Ohyo (Japanese), Tcal (Native American-Tlingat). *Hippoglossus* is the ancient Greek name for the halibut and it means "horse tongue" (Dang, weren't those Greeks a wild and crazy bunch of folks? Can you imagine going into a market today, striding up to the fish counter and saying "A pound of horse tongue, please"); *stenolepis* is formed from 2 Greek words meaning "narrow scale."

IDENTIFYING CHARACTERS: These are the largest flatfish you will even see (Plate 32). They are brown to black on the eyed side, usually with lighter markings. A good identifying character is their slightly indented tails, found only on Pacifics, Greenland halibut and

337

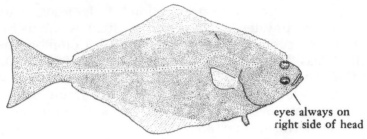

eyes always on
right side of head

arrowtooth flounders. Pacifics also have a high arch to their lateral lines, not present in the other 2 species.

DISTRIBUTION AND BIOLOGY: Pacifics are cold water fish (preferring 37-50° F), found from the Sea of Japan eastward to the Bering Sea and southward to Punta Camolu, Baja California; they are rare south of about San Francisco and are common from Oregon northward. Unlike many other flatfishes, Pacifics will lie right on rocky bottoms, along with sand or gravel. They have been taken from depths of 20–3,600 feet, and most spend their time in waters shallower then 600 feet. It appears there are at least 2 fairly distinct populations, one stretching from Japan to the Bering Sea, the other in the Gulf of Alaska and probably points south. The Bering Sea population seems to make considerable inshore-offshore movements, migrating to shallow water in summer, then moving deeper to spawn in winter. Pacifics in other areas may not make such distinct seasonal movements. Younger halibut, to about 10 years of age, are highly migratory and in the Gulf of Alaska generally move in a southeast (clockwise) direction. The longest individual movement was 2,500 miles from the Aleutian Islands to Oregon.

Pacifics reach truly horrific sizes, with an authenticated length of 8.75 feet–a fish that, as my 13-year-old would say, "You wouldn't want to meet in a dark alley." Females grow larger and live longer; the longest male known was about 4.5 feet long. The oldest female was 42 years and the oldest male, 27. In the Bering Sea, they grow to 6 inches in 2 years, 2 feet in 8–11 years, and 3 feet in 11–15 years. Size and age at maturity varies, with females mature at 8–16 years (3–4.5 feet.) and males at 5–13 years (2.5–3.5 feet). Spawning along the Pacific coast is from December–March and in the Bering Sea from October–March. Most spawning occurs off the edge of the continental shelf, in depths of 600–1,800 feet. Some researchers believe mature females may not spawn every year. Fecundity ranges from 100,000–2,800,000 eggs per season, and females spawn repeatedly over a season. Eggs remain in deep water until they hatch in 11-23 days, depending on temperature. In a laboratory study, hatching occurred at 43-46° F; 37 and 50° were fatal. Eggs and larvae drift in the water column for up to 7 months. As the larvae develop, they move into shallower waters and young ones recruit to about 20-120 feet. As the fish mature, they tend to move somewhat offshore. Pacifics eat fishes (such as Pacific sand lances and walleye pollock), crabs, octopi and the like. Northern fur seals eat them.

FISHERY: This is a very important sport and commercial species. Sport fishermen commonly take Pacifics from Oregon northward, mostly from party and private vessels. While the sport fishery off Alaska and British Columbia has been active for many years, sport fishing for Pacifics off Oregon really has just started.

The Pacific halibut commercial fishery is a very large, very highly regulated endeavor. Every year, a catch quota is set by an international commission, and when this quota is met the fishery is shut down. In recent years, this "fishing season" has lasted just a few days. A new system, one giving specific quotas to each fisherman has just been set in place. Commercial fishermen catch Pacifics with long lines. A major problem in the Pacific halibut fishery is overfishing, particularly by trawlers fishing for other species. This is a particular problem in fisheries which accidentally catch large quantities of juvenile halibut. Most halibut in the commercial fishery are 8-15 years old, and most fishing takes place in 100-750 feet of water.

REMARKS: This is from M. Boelscher, *The Curtain Within, Haida Social and Mythical Discourse* (UBC Press, 1988). The Haida, of southeastern Alaska and British Columbia separated food into "high-class" and "low-class." High class food came from large animals and could serve lots of guests. Pacific halibut were certainly in the high-class category.

Here is a very spiff fishing custom of the Tlingit tribe of Alaska (from J. R. Swanton, *Social Condition, Beliefs, and Linguistic Relationship of the Tlingit Indians*): "The Tlingit always talked to their halibut lines, halibut hooks, and buoys, addressing them as 'brother-in-law,' 'father-in-law,' etc. If one did not do so, these would become ashamed and refuse to let the fish bite. While baiting the hook a person spit upon it and said, 'Go right to the fireplace. Hit the rich man's daughter' then the hook did not become ashamed."

DIAMOND TURBOT (HYPSOPSETTA GUTTULATA)

NAMES: *Hypsopsetta* is formed from 2 Greek words meaning "deep flounder," a reference to this species' oval body; *guttulata* is from the Latin for "with small spots."

IDENTIFYING CHARACTERS: Diamonds are right-eyed flatfish, colored

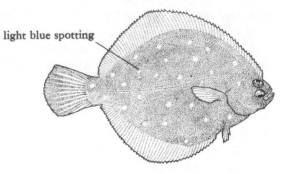

light blue spotting

dark green, brown or greenish on the eyed sides, usually with light blue spots. The white, blind side has a yellow rim near the mouth.

DISTRIBUTION AND BIOLOGY: Diamonds are found from nearly intertidal waters to 270 feet, from Cape Mendocino (northern California) to southern Baja California and into the Gulf of California. They are most abundant from Tomales Bay southward, in perhaps 5-30 feet. These small fish are common in estuaries, bays and backwaters and just behind the surf on open-coast beaches. There is some evidence that these flatfish move out of estuaries to the open coast to spawn. Diamonds can tolerate salinities about twice that of ocean levels.

These fish reach 1.5 feet and have been aged to about 8 years. A 5-incher is 1 year old, a 7- incher is 2. Females mature at 2-3 years, both sexes are mature at about 6.5 inches. Females are oviparous and, near Anaheim Bay, southern California, they spawn from September-February, peaking during November-January. In San Francisco Bay, the season is June-October. Both eggs and larvae are usually found within one mile of shore. Larvae drift about for 5-6 weeks before metamorphosing. From about January-March, when they are about .5 inches long, little diamonds settle out at an average depth of 3 feet. Clam siphons, worms, fishes and small crustaceans make up most of their diet.

FISHERY: Diamonds are a minor part of the sport catch, taken primarily by anglers fishing from shore, piers or small vessels in shallow bays and estuaries. Diamonds are occasionally sold in markets, though their shallow habitat prevents large catches.

REMARKS: What do you suppose is the function of the bright yellow splotch around their mouths? Does it camouflage them in beehives, banana plantations and lemon groves?

YELLOWFIN SOLE (LIMANDA ASPERA)

NAMES: Koganegarei and Rosukegarei (Japanese). *Limanda* comes from a Latin word meaning "old man," which was the name for a European flatfish; *aspera* is derived from the Latin for "rough."

IDENTIFYING CHARACTERS: This is another in the seemingly endless

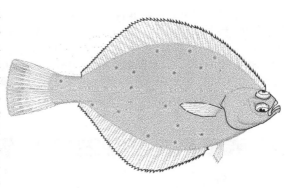

array of right-eyed flatfishes. Yellowfins are distinguished by a highly arched lateral line that is not branched (butter soles and rock soles have branched lateral lines). Another good character is the dorsal and anal fins covered with scales.

DISTRIBUTION AND BIOLOGY: Yellowfins are found from South Korea (Sea of Japan) eastward to the Bering and Chukchi Seas and southward to British Columbia, from shallow waters down to about 1,190 feet. These are soft-bottom dwellers (sandy-silt or sand bottoms), and they are particularly abundant in the eastern Bering Sea, where their biomass is estimated to be 1.9-2.6 million metric tons or more. In the eastern Bering Sea, yellowfins make seasonal migrations. During the winter, the fish hunker down in deeper waters, about 300-890 feet. In April or May, they move inshore to spawn and feed. Spawning grounds are in very shallow waters (around 100 feet); feeding grounds are slightly deeper. Generally, the fish stay in waters less than 300 feet throughout the summer.

Yellowfins grow to about 17.5 inches, and some live more than 25 years. As they mature, females begin to grow more rapidly than males. Generally, males mature at about 4-5 years, females at 6-9. Studies have given various estimates of size at first maturity, with males ranging from 5-8 inches, females from 10-13 inches. Females are oviparous, fertilization is external and the spawning season is quite variable, from late May through August. In the eastern Bering Sea, spawning occurs in relatively shallow water, down to about 160 feet. Females produce anywhere from about 1,300,000-3,300,000 eggs. At 55° F, larvae hatch out in 4 days. Juveniles tend to stay in shallow waters (less than about 180 feet) throughout the year. Yellowfins are opportunistic feeders, eating a wide range of prey, including clam siphons, worms, gammarid amphipods, krill and fishes. Most yellowfins do not feed in the winter; they begin to chow down during the spring feeding and spawning migration. Pacific cod, walleye pollock, Pacific halibut, various sculpins, some sea birds and marine mammals eat them.

FISHERY: Yellowfins form a major trawl fishery in the eastern Bering Sea, off the Kamchatka Peninsula, around Sakhalin Island

and in Peter the Great Bay (Sea of Japan). In the 1950s, they were initially fished by the Japanese and Russians and turned into fish meal. Catches rose sharply, then declined in the early 1960s due to overfishing. Currently, populations are again fairly high and catches have increased. Yellowfin sole are now mainly used for human consumption.

DOVER SOLE (MICROSTOMUS PACIFICUS)

NAME: Slime Sole, Namet-agarei (Japanese), Babagareirui (Japanese), Amerikanameta (Japanese).

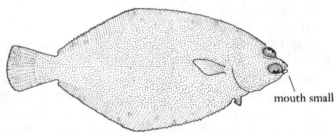

mouth small

Microstomus is formed from 2 Greek words meaning "small mouth"; *pacificus* refers to the area in which it is found.

IDENTIFYING CHARACTERS: One of the slimiest, softest fish on the coast, they are slender and small mouthed, brown on the eyed side and gray on the blind side. They can be mistaken for the rex sole, which has a much longer pectoral fin.

DISTRIBUTION AND BIOLOGY: Dovers have been taken from the Bering Sea and Aleutian Islands southward to San Critobal Bay, central Baja California. They are common from the Bering Sea to at least southern California over sand and mud bottoms. I usually see them just lying on the mud, sometimes near rocks or boulders, usually covered or semi-covered by sediment. These fish are found from depths of 30-4,800 feet; juveniles are found in relatively shallow water, adults are deeper. As an example, off central California, young ones live in waters less than about 650 feet. At about 9 inches, they abruptly move into 1,000-1,300 feet of water. Off Oregon, the first downwards migration occurs at about 15 inches and by 16 inches, many Dovers are in 2,600-3,300 feet. Females tend to inhabit deeper waters than males. One study showed that 96% of the fish living deeper than 4,000 feet were females. Some Dovers move into the "oxygen minimum zone," waters where there is relatively little oxygen. And some Dovers, primarily young ones, make inshore-offshore spawning migrations, moving inshore during the summer and offshore to spawn in winter. Older adults may not move inshore at all.

Dovers as long as 2.5 feet have been taken. Females live at least 53 years and some males live to 58 years. Females grow faster and reach a larger size than males. An average 1-footer is 3–4 years old, an 18-incher is 11+ years. In a study conducted in the 1950s, males were found to mature earlier than females; some males matured at 1 foot, half at 13 inches and almost all by 16 inches. A few females matured at 13 inches, half at 14 and all at 18 inches. More recent research came up with different results, indicating that the average female matures at around 13 inches and about 7 years of age. It is unclear whether the original data was incorrect or if the species is starting to mature at a smaller size. Females are oviparous, produce 52,000-256,000 eggs per season and may spawn them in as many as 9 egg batches. Spawning season appears to vary with area. A recent study off central California found it to be December-May, while one off Oregon yielded February-July (peaking in April). Eggs hatch in 10-38 days. While some larvae are found south of Pt. Conception, most spawning seems to take place further north. Larvae have been taken as far offshore as 280 miles. Larvae stay aloft a long time, in some cases up to about a year and maybe more. They are positively chunky (1-2+ inches) when they settle onto the bottom in 150-1,000 feet. Off Oregon, larvae settle out from January to perhaps April. Small clams, worms, brittle stars, snails and shrimps all form part of their diet. California sea lions, harbor seals, western gulls, common murres and Brandt's cormorants eat them.

FISHERY: Their small mouths make Dovers a rare item in the sport catch. On the commercial side, Dovers are a major and we might say massive, part of the flatfish trawl fishery from central California to British Columbia. Dovers are the most important flatfish in the Oregon commercial fishery. Much of the Dover sole catch is made in 1,200-1,800 feet.

REMARKS: You wouldn't think it, but a live Dover in an aquarium is about the most endearing animal you can imagine. A few years back, I visited a refrigerated tank full of Dovers at a National Marine Fisheries Service lab in California. Instead of lying inert on the bottom like other flatfishes, when these fish saw someone coming they swam over, stood up on their tails and stuck their faces against the glass. They looked for all the world like pop-eyed flying squirrels.

As Dovers age and migrate deeper, the water content of their bodies increases and they develop what commercial fishermen refer to as a "jellied" condition. The relatively high water content makes their muscle tissue very flaccid and gelatinous.

The name "Dover" sole is a recent one. Before they were intensively fished, they were called "slime soles" or "slippery soles." To no one's intense surprise, marketers felt there would be a fairly limited appeal for "Fillet of Slime Sole," so the name was changed in honor of Jedidiah Dover, the first person to slip on one of these fish and break his neck (just a joke, just a joke).

Here is a very good line from Waldo Wakefield's notorious PhD dissertation, *Pattern in the Distribution of Demersal Fishes on the Upper Continental Slope off Central California with Studies on the Role of Ontogenetic Vertical Migration in Particle Flux* (UCSD, 1990 - soon to be a major motion picture). "Along the 400-m transect during March, there were three instances when the asteroid [seastar] *Rathbunaster californicus*, had extended one of its arms along the body surface of *Microstomus pacificus*. One can only speculate about the functions of this observed behavior and I choose not to." Ah, Waldo, discretion is the better part of valor.

The Dover's very soft flesh firms up after freezing.

STARRY FLOUNDER (PLATICHTHYS STELLATUS)

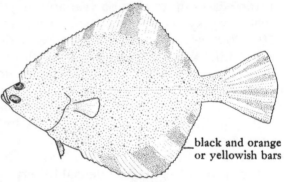

black and orange or yellowish bars

NAME: Diamond Flounder, Grindstone, Roughjacket, Swamp Flounder, Numagarei (Japanese). *Platichthys* is formed from 2 Greek words meaning "flat fish" (no great surprise here); *stellatus* is Latin for "starry."

IDENTIFYING CHARACTERS: Starries are instantly recognizable by their alternating yellow or orange and black bars on their dorsal, caudal and anal fins. If that doesn't give it away, the skin on their eyed side is extremely rough, caused by starshaped scales.

DISTRIBUTION AND BIOLOGY: Starries range from Korea, Japan, the Chukchi and Bering Seas and the Aleutians all the way down to Los Angeles Harbor. They are occasional south of Pt. Conception and common from Central California northward. These fish (particularly the juveniles) are quite freshwater-tolerant. Young ones have been taken 75 miles up the Columbia River and well into the San Joaquin, Sacramento and Mokelumne River systems; and youngsters up to about 6 inches may be found in fresh water. While they have been taken from intertidal waters to depths of 1,238 feet, most are found between about 5 and 150 feet. Tagging studies show that, in general, starries are sedentary fish, moving little during their adult lives. There are a few exceptions, such as the fish that moved 130 miles from the Columbia River near

Cape Flattery, Washington. There is some evidence that adults move inshore in winter and spring and offshore come summer. Starries occasionally must boogie around well off the bottom. A commercial fishermen tells me he caught one 18 feet below the surface, in water 240 feet deep.

Starries reach lengths of 3 feet and have been aged to 24 years. Females grow faster, larger and live longer than males. A 12-incher is about 4 years old. Most males mature at 2 or 3 years (about 14.5 inches), females at 3-4 (16 inches). Females are oviparous and produce 900,000-11,000,000 eggs per season. Off California, spawning takes place from October to February, peaking in December and January; off British Columbia and Washington, it's February-April. Off British Columbia, spawning occurs in 60-270 feet. Some spawning may also occur in estuaries. Once spawned, the eggs stay near the surface and hatch in 2-15 days, depending on temperature. Larvae metamorphose into bottom-living juveniles in 39-75 days. Young starries first settle out in shallow water, most commonly in estuaries, but also in the sandy intertidal zone and in freshwater. The youngest fish are generally found the furthest upstream. Clams, brittle stars, fishes and crabs are major parts of their diets. Harbor seals, herons and cormorants eat them.

FISHERY: Starries are important fish in the shore, pier and boat fisheries from central California northward. They are particularly important in the pier and shore fisheries that are located in bays. Smaller fish predominate in the shore and pier catches, while larger adults are taken by offshore anglers. Though starries have never approached the commercial popularity of some other flatfish, such as petrale sole, there is a moderate, steady market for the species. Starries are fairly important in the flatfish trawl fisheries in the Strait of Georgia and in some parts of Alaska.

REMARKS: Confused, infatuated or kinky starries may occasionally mate with English sole and produce a hybrid, often called *Inopsetta ischyra*.

Here's some interesting information. Off California, Oregon and Washington, half of starries are right-eyed and half (naturally) are left-eyed. Off Alaska, it's 70% left-eyed and around Japan, almost all are left-eyed.

Starry remains are quite common in Native American middens.

ROCK SOLE (PLEURONECTES BILINEATUS)

NAMES: *Pleuronectes* means "side swimmer" in Greek; *bilineatus*

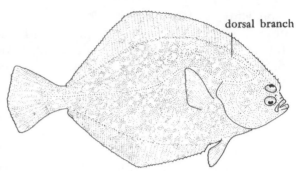

dorsal branch

means "two lined" in Latin and was inspired by the species' forked lateral line.

IDENTIFYING CHARACTERS: Rock soles are right-eyed flatfish, easily identified by the high arching lateral line over the pectoral fin and the small extension of that line near the dorsal fin. The fish range in color from brown to gray and have darker (sometimes yellow or red) mottling.

DISTRIBUTION AND BIOLOGY: These fish range from the Sea of Japan, Korea and the Sea of Okhotsk eastward across the Bering Sea and southward to Tanner Bank (southern California). Moderately common in central California, they are more abundant in the north, with major populations from the Kamchatka Peninsula to British Columbia. While they have been taken from intertidal waters to 1,898 feet depths, they are most common down to about 300 feet, often over pebbly or semi-rocky bottom. In at least some areas, rock sole migrate into shallow water in summer. In the Gulf of Alaska, spawning individuals are noted at bottom depths of 400-700 feet, mostly at 500-660 feet. However, they do not appear to make long journeys along the coast. Off British Columbia, rock soles are found at temperatures between 45-50° F. They tolerate temperatures from below 32° F to 54° F.

These soles reach 23.5 inches in length. Males live to 22 years, females to 15 years. Growth seems to be faster off British Columbia than in the Bering Sea. In the Bering Sea, it takes 9-11 years to grow to 1 foot, while British Columbia go-hards get there in only 4-5 years. Females grow faster and mature at a greater size than males. All males are mature by 14.5 inches, females by 17. Fish off British Columbia are reported to mature at about 4 years; in the Bering Sea, it's 5-7 years. Females are oviparous and spawn 400,000-1,300,000 eggs. Spawning season varies between areas. Off Kamchatka, it's February-April; in the Bering Sea, from March-June and off North America, in February and March. Rock soles are unusual for flatfish in having adhesive eggs that stick to the bottom until the young hatch. Eggs hatch in 6-25 days, depending on temperature. During the day larvae tend to be from near the surface to about 100 feet down; some descend to about 200 feet at night. A study off of Auke Bay, southeast Alaska, showed that larvae were most abundant just before the spring phytoplankton bloom. Larval fish transform into juveniles when they reach about 1 inch. What do they eat? I'm glad you asked. These puppies have a fairly wide range of favorite items, including worms, shrimps, clams, brittle stars (full of roughage, no doubt) and the occasional fish.

FISHERY: From central California northward, rock sole are commonly taken by anglers from shore, pier and boat. They form a major part of the flatfish trawl fishery around British Columbia, in the Gulf of Alaska and in the Bering Sea and are a less important part of the catch from Washington to California.

BUTTER SOLE (PLEURONECTES ISOLEPIS)

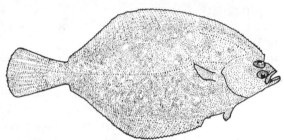

NAMES: *Pleuronectes* is formed from the Greek words for "side swimmer"; *isolepis* is also derived from Greek, and means "equal scales". Formerly called *Isopsetta isolepis*.

IDENTIFYING CHARACTERS: Butter sole are right-eyed. A good character is their dorsal and anal fins, which are edged with yellow.

DISTRIBUTION AND BIOLOGY: Butter sole are found from the Bering Sea to Ventura, southern California in depths ranging from 54 to 1,404 feet, most commonly from perhaps 150-350 feet. Mature fish move inshore to spawn.

A medium-size flatfish, butters reach 21.75 inches. The oldest known males are 10 years old, the oldest females 11. Off British Columbia, male butters mature at 2 years and 4 inches and females at 3 years and 10 inches. Females are oviparous and the eggs tend to be found near the bottom (they are not adhesive, however). While it has been stated that spawning occurs between February and April, off Oregon larvae have been found in almost every month (though with spring peaks). Females produce between at least 350,000-1,000,000 eggs. Off Oregon, most larvae are found within about 10 miles of shore, with about a 30 mile maximum and a peak at around 4 miles from shore. Larvae have also been found in the Columbia River and in Yaquina Bay, Oregon. Newly-settled butter sole live in near-shore areas–in bays and estuaries, and in open waters down to at least 180 feet. Young ones eat benthic prey, such as worms, clam siphons, harpacticoid copepods and amphipods. Older ones eat worms, crabs, small clams and occasionally fishes.

FISHERY: Butters are taken by trawlers in some numbers, but rarely by recreational fisherman.

ENGLISH SOLE (PLEURONECTES VETULUS)

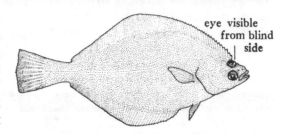

eye visible
from blind
side

NAMES: Common Sole, California Sole, Lemon Sole, Igirisu Garei (Japanese). *Pleuronectes* means "side swimmer" in Greek; *vetulus* is Latin for "old man." I cannot imagine why Girard in 1854 ever came up with that name. Could he have been hitting the lab alcohol again?

IDENTIFYING CHARACTERS: English are right-eyed flatfish, with distinctively pointed heads. The eyed side is invariably flat brown in color, and the blind side is white or pale yellow.

DISTRIBUTION AND BIOLOGY: Found from Agattus Island (Aleutian Islands) and Nunivak Island in the eastern Bering Sea southward to Bahia San Cristobal, southern Baja California, English are abundant from the Gulf of Alaska to southern California. These fish have a wide depth range, from intertidal waters to 1,800 feet. In spring, young, .75 inch fish recruit primarily to estuaries and bays (and to a certain extent the shallow open coast). The fish leave these nursery areas in late summer and fall and slowly migrate into deeper water as they mature. Adults are most abundant in 150–900 feet over soft bottom. English make annual spawning migrations into deep water, but with only a few exceptions seem to stay in the same general geographic area. A few tagged fish have shown significant movements, travelling as far as from British Columbia to California. They seem to like 45-46° F water off British Columbia.

English reach 22.5 inches and have been aged to 22 years (this was a 20.5 incher). Females grow larger and mature later than males. All males are mature by 11.5 inches (2–3 years); all females by 14 inches (3–5 years). Females are oviparous, probably spawn more than once per season and produce between 150,000 and 2,100,000 eggs. The spawning season is often quite variable, depending on bottom temperature and upwelling intensity. From British Columbia to Oregon, it runs from early fall to spring. Off California and Baja California, larvae can be found in every month, with a January to April peak. These are near-shore spawners. Most larvae are found within 30 miles of shore, though a few have been taken as much as 250 miles off the beach. English sole eggs hatch in 4-12 days. The larvae transform into the "flatfish" shape, with eyes on one side, at 6-10 weeks. This is a fish with a very diverse diet. Worms, amphipods, clams, brittle stars and small fishes have all been found in their stomachs. They often feed by digging their sharp snouts into the sand and pulling out goodies. Arrowtooth flounder, California sea lions and pelagic, double-crested and Brandt's cormorants eat them.

FISHERY: Once in a while, particularly in the northern part of their range, an English is taken from a pier or boat, but their small mouths make this a comparative rarity in the recreational catch. On the other hand, they are a major part of the flatfish trawl fishery from California to British Columbia and a minor contituent in the Gulf of Alaska. Along much of the coast, English are second only to Dover sole in total pounds landed. They are the most important flatfish in the Puget Sound fishery. Most English are taken at depths of 120-900 feet and are sold fresh and frozen, whole and filleted. Shelf life is the same as for most other flatfishes; see rex soles.

REMARKS: Fossil English sole ear bones have been found in Pliocene deposits over one million years old in Long Beach, California.

English occasionally hybridize with starry flounder, producing the hybrid or forkline sole.

C-O TURBOT (PLEURONICHTHYS COENOSUS)

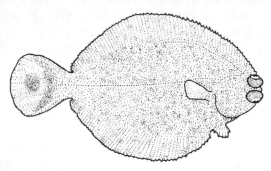

NAMES: *Pleuronichthys* is formed from 2 Greek words meaning "side" and "fish"; *coenosus* is Latin for "muddy."

IDENTIFYING CHARACTERS: This is a nice, oval, right-eyed flatfish. The eyed side tends to be dark brown and there is usually a dark blotch on the midline. The big characters are a dark spot and crescent on the tail (read upside down, this is the "C-O").

DISTRIBUTION AND BIOLOGY: C-Os have been taken from Sitka, Alaska to northern Baja California, from inshore waters to depths of 1,150 feet. These are sandy bottom dwellers, though often you will find them in the vicinity of rocks and algae.

Not a big fish, C-Os reach 14 inches. Not much is known about them. The spawning season is about March - August. Females are oviparous and produce pelagic eggs. C-Os eat sediment dwellers, digging prey out of the sand. Worms are very high on the hit list, though small crustaceans and small fishes are occasionally taken. FISHERY: Like many other small flatfishes, C-Os are occasionally taken by recreational anglers, from piers, jetties and boats. Like spotted turbots and curlfins, they are often sold in Asian markets.

CURLFIN TURBOT (PLEURONICHTHYS DECURRENS)

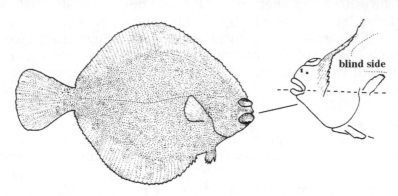

NAMES: *Pleuronichthys* is formed from 2 Greek words meaning "side" and "fish"; *decurrens* comes from the Latin "running down," perhaps a reference to the dorsal fin starting on this species' blind side.

IDENTIFYING CHARACTERS: A right-eyed, rather oval species, usually brown or blackish. Let's cut to the chase here. The fast, easy, effective way to tell this one apart is to turn one over. If there are 9-12 dorsal rays creeping over onto the blind side, you have found your species.

DISTRIBUTION AND BIOLOGY: Curlfins have a wide geographic range, from the Bering Sea to north-central Baja California, and a wide depth range, from 25-1,746 feet.

Curlfins reach a mighty 14.5 inches. Females are oviparous and produce pelagic eggs. Curlfins tend to dig around the bottom for their food; worms, gammarid amphipods and worm-like peanut worms are favorite curlfin prey. A study from Monterey Bay, central California, showed that small market squid were also on the menu. They are perhaps eaten by harbor seals.

FISHERY: Fishermen of various stripes catch them once in a while. Asian markets carry them more often than you might think.

SPOTTED TURBOT (PLEURONICHTHYS RITTERI)

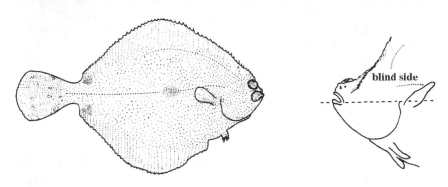

NAMES: *Pleuronichthys* is formed from 2 Greek words meaning "side" and "fish."

IDENTIFYING CHARACTERS: A very round, right-eyed species, with one dark spot in the middle and 2 other spots at the rear part of the body near the anal and dorsal fins.

DISTRIBUTION AND BIOLOGY: This is a southern species, and while it has been found from Morro Bay, central California to at least Bahia Magdalena, southern Baja California, it is not common north of Santa Barbara, southern California. Spotteds are shallow water fish, living from the almost intertidal zone to 285 feet.

Spotteds are compact little devils, reaching 11.5 inches. They mature at about 6 inches. Females are oviparous. Based on when larvae are found, there may be some spawning throughout the year, but the peak period appears to be from about July-October. Basically, spotted turbot are southern, subtropical fishes and their larvae distribution shows this very nicely. While a few larvae occur as far north as central California, the big concentrations are from Punta Baja, central Baja California to Cabo San Lazaro, southern Baja California. While a few larvae have been taken as much as 100 miles from the coast, most occur within about 40 miles of the shore. Newly-recruited juveniles settle out at about 1.5 inches, on the open coast, at an average depth of 30 feet. At least one study found that anemones attached to worm tubes were the important spotted turbot prey.

FISHERY: These are an occasional catch by recreational fishermen. I have seen good numbers of these, as well as other turbots, in the Vietnamese markets of southern California.

HORNYHEAD TURBOT (PLEURONICHTHYS VERTICALIS)

NAMES: *Pleuronichthys* is formed from 2 Greek words for "side fish";

verticalis is Latin for "vertex," the top of the head where the spines are situated.

IDENTIFYING CHARACTERS: These are round, right-eyed flatfish with one or 2 sharp spines between the eyes. They are usually brown or yellow-brown and have various blotches or vermiculations, often with irregular white spots.

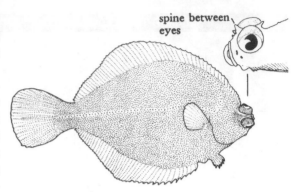

spine between eyes

DISTRIBUTION AND BIOLOGY: These folks are found from south of Trinidad Head, northern California, southward to southern Baja California, with an isolated population in the northern Gulf of California. They are common from about Pt. Conception southward, on soft mud or sand bottoms. While they have been taken from depths of 20–660 feet, most inhabit waters of 30–300 feet.

Horneyheads reach 14.5 inches and fish larger than about 12 inches are rare. Males mature at 4 inches, females at about 6.5 inches. In southern California, these flatfish spawn year round, which is unusual for any California marine fish; off Monterey Bay, central California, the season runs from March-August. Females are oviparous and batch spawners. Based on patterns of larval occurrences, spawning occurs from central California to southern Baja California. Highest concentrations are found between Punta Baja and Punta Eugenia, central Baja California. These are nearshore fish; few larvae drift more than 50 miles from shore. Little ones settle out at about .75 inches, on the open coast, at an average depth of about 30 feet. Daytime feeders, they eat worms and clam sipons. Tubeworms seem a particular favorite. When a tubeworm is detected, hornies lift off the bottom, bring their mouths down vertically and pull worm and tube out of the sediment. After some gustatory pyrotechnics, the tube is spit out and the worm swallowed.

FISHERY: The small mouths of these turbots make them difficult to catch, and only occasionally are they taken by sport anglers. Taken by trawl fishermen pursuing other species, they make up a small part of the commercial flatfish catch in southern California.

SAND SOLE (PSETTICHTHYS MELANOSTICTUS)

NAMES: Karei-Rui (Japanese), *Psettichthys* is formed from 2 Greek

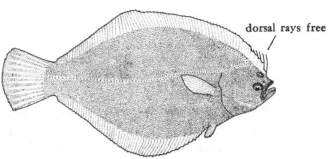

dorsal rays free

words meaning "turbot fish"; *melanostictus* is also Greek for "black spotted."

IDENTIFYING CHARACTERS: This one is easy to identify. The rays on the front of the dorsal fin are very thin and are not connected by a membrane to one another. See, I told you it was easy.

DISTRIBUTION AND BIOLOGY: Found on sandy bottoms from the Bering Sea southward to Redondo Beach, southern California, sand soles are common from central California northward. They are basically an inshore species, and though found from depths of 3 to 1,073 feet, most live in water shallower than 300 feet.

Sand soles reach 24.5 inches. A 12-incher is about 5 years old. Males mature at around 2 years, females at 2-3 years. Females are oviparous. Spawning time varies, but it usually begins in January and may extend into July. Young ones recruit out of the plankton at about 1 inch, seeking shallow water. Most settle out in estuaries, but some hit bottom on open coasts. Sand soles eat fishes, shrimps, worms and clams.

FISHERY: While commonly taken by shore, pier and boat fishermen, sand soles are particularly common in shore and jetty catches. Most of the recreational catch is made from Monterey, central California, northward. They form a minor part of the commercial flatfish catch.

GREENLAND HALIBUT (REINHARDTIUS HIPPOGLOSSOIDES)

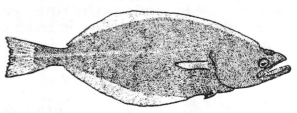

NAMES: Greenland Turbot, Karasugarei (Japanese). *Reinhardtius* honors Professor J. Reinhardt, a researcher on Greenland fishes from the University of Copenhagen; *hippoglossoides* is Greek for "resembles Hippoglossus," the old name for halibut.

IDENTIFYING CHARACTERS: The key thing here is that the blindside of Greenlands is dusky, not white like other flatfishes. Another good character is that the left eye is situated along the dorsal midline and is visible from the blind side. These are right-eyed flatfish, meaning that the left eye is the one that migrated. The eyed side is black or dark brown.

DISTRIBUTION AND BIOLOGY: Greenlands have an unusual geographic distribution. They are amphiboreal, a two-dollar word meaning they occur in both the North Pacific and North Atlantic though not in the Arctic Ocean in-between. In the North Pacific, they are found from the Sea of Japan northward to the Bering Sea and southward to northern Baja California, with a center of abundance in the eastern Bering Sea. Greenlands live in waters between 46-6,600 feet. In the eastern Bering Sea, young fish, which live on the continental shelf move into relatively shallow water starting in spring and into the summer. By fall, the fish have returned to deeper waters. Adults, on the continental slope, make a similar movement, though not into waters as shallow. There is no evidence for long-distance migrations.

Greenlands grow to about 4 feet and live longer than 23 years. In one eastern Bering Sea study, fish matured at 5-10 years old. In the Sea of Okhotsk, females mature between 1.6-2.6 feet, males 1.3-2.3 feet–here, 75% of females were mature at 13. Females are oviparous and produce pelagic eggs. In the eastern Bering Sea, spawning takes place from September to March, apparently peaking November to February. In the western Bering Sea, spawning season is probably October-December. Bering Sea fish produce between about 24,000 and at least 149,000 eggs. Eggs and larvae stay relatively deep in the water column, and the young do not settle out for 6 or more months. Juveniles live in waters less than 600 feet for the first few years, then, at age 4 or 5, begin to move off the continental shelf onto the continental slope. Immature fish can tolerate temperatures below 30° F. Fishes are a major part of the diet, particularly walleye pollock, with squids of some importance and krill and shrimps also in the mix. They are eaten by northern fur seals.

FISHERY: These fish are only very rarely taken in the recreational fishery. They are taken by trawlers and occasionally long-liners, primarily in the Bering Sea.

Tonguefishes - Family Cynoglossidae

CALIFORNIA TONGUEFISH (SYMPHURUS ATRICAUDA)

NAME: Tongue Sole. *Symphurus* is formed from 3 Greek words – put them together and they form "together, to grow, tail" which is shorthand for describing the way the fins are united at the tail;

atricauda is formed from 2 Latin words meaning "black tail."

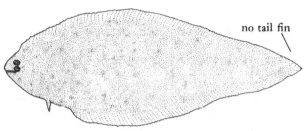

no tail fin

IDENTIFYING CHARACTERS: Tonguefish are easily recognized by their slim bodies, tiny eyes and mouth and the fact that they are so slimy you won't be able to pick them off the deck. Any little slimy flatfish that you eventually stop trying to pick up is likely to be a tonguefish. Really, my son, Elan, describes it as trying to pick up a fish from the deck with velcro for a belly.

DISTRIBUTION AND BIOLOGY: Found from Puget Sound, Washington, to Panama, these little fish are abundant from about Pt. Conception southward. Found over sand and mud, they have been taken from depths of 5-660 feet and are most abundant from nearshore waters to about 300 feet. You'll occasionally see them in estuaries. They are active at night, burying themselves during the day.

Tonguers reach 8.25 inches, they mature at around 5 inches. Females are oviparous, producing pelagic eggs. Spawning occurs from May to October, peaking in July and August. Larvae transform at about 1-2 inches and settle out on the open coast in late fall and winter. Young ones recruit to bays and open coast, at a depth of around 30 feet. A variety of bottom-dwelling organisms, such as amphipods, crabs and worms, make up their diet. Arctic loons, pelagic, Brandt's and double-crested cormorants eat them.

FISHERY: There is no sport or commercial fishery for this species. Trawlers catch considerable numbers when the fish get stuck in net meshwork.

REMARKS: Even though this fish is usually left-sided (the eyes are on the left side), a right-sided individual has been reported.

Molas or Ocean Sunfishes - Family Molidae

OCEAN SUNFISH (MOLA MOLA)

NAMES: Headfish, Mola, Môle Commun (French). *Mola* is Latin for millstone, the round stone used in crushing grain for flour. Why Linnaeus repeated the word in his original description is a mystery to me. Perhaps he was late for a hot date and just wrote it down twice.
IDENTIFYING CHARACTERS: Look at the drawing, people. What

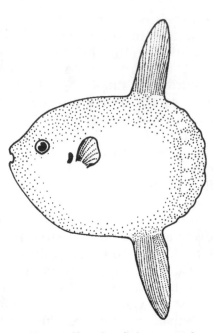

more need I say? These cuties are gray, gray-brown or silvery and resemble a frisbee designed by Salvador Dali (Plates 35-36).

DISTRIBUTION AND BIOLOGY: Found worldwide in tropical and temperate waters, ocean sunfish occur on our side of the world from British Columbia southward to South America. Off western North America, these fish are usually summer or fall visitors, spotted at or near the surface, either singly or often in small groups. Though they can be seen many miles from the coast, they may be attracted to structure because they are often found near kelp beds, drifting kelp mats and around oil platforms. Typically, the fish are either seen upright with their dorsal fins out of the water or lying on their sides at the surface, pectoral fins waving in the breeze. Very little is known of their movements or migrations.

Ocean sunfish reach truly respectable sizes, at least to 10 feet and 3,000 pounds, perhaps larger. Off our coast, most fish are small, probably 100 pounds or less, though I have seen a few that would scale out around 500 pounds at least. Females are oviparous and spawn in spring and summer. A 4.5 footer contained 300 million eggs. Sunfish eat soft midwater dwellers, such as jellyfishes and salps, as well as bottom-dwelling crustaceans, brittlestars and an occasional fish.

FISHERY: There is no sport or commercial fishery for ocean sunfish, although they are occasionally hooked, snagged, netted or gaffed.

REMARKS: Why these fish "bask" at the surface is unknown, but there are several interesting possibilities. These fish could be sick and/or dying and are incapable of normal behavior. It is certainly easy to capture many of these basking fish; I have even reached over the side of a boat and picked them up in my hands. Another possibility is that the fish are signaling to sea gulls to clean them. Ocean sunfish have lots of parasites, both inside and on the outside of their bodies. On two occasions, I have seen sunfish come to the surface, flop on their sides and wave their exposed pectoral fins about. On both of these occasions, a sea gull paddled over and pecked at the fish for a little while. When the bird finished, it moved away and the fish turned over and went through the same motions. The gull returned and pecked for a few moments more. Perhaps heavily parasitized fish come to the surface to elicit cleaning. Certainly, many divers have seen sunfish near kelp beds being cleaned by a variety of small fish.

Two dieoffs of sunfish have occurred in Monterey Bay one in 1960, the other in 1965. No reason for the many deaths was found.

Remoras, the small fish that attach themselves by their heads to sharks, rays, boats, etc., have been also found clinging to the inside of the mouths of molas.

Don't you just love them; they are just so appealingly bizarre. The Monterey Bay Aquarium has kept some in a back tank for a while and found out just how neat they are. When they were first captured, they were fed on jellyfish. Someone got the idea of trying bits of fish, which the sunfish liked so well they then refused to eat the jellies. In what can only be described as a moment of profound mental weakness, prawns were substituted for fish. The molas quickly figured out they were onto a good (and really expensive) thing and from then on would only eat prawns. One of these fish also grew very quickly–nearly 100 pounds in eight months, at which point it outgrew its tank and had to be released.

Molas suck and spit when they feed. They suck in prey and water, hold the food in their long, claw-like throat teeth, then spit the water out. Molas also spit water to tear prey apart. Of course, spitting has other uses. After a visitor tapped on its tank, one sunfish at the Monterey Bay Aquarium rose to the surface and, perhaps signaling its disapproval, spit right into the gentleman's face.

Tierney Thys, who probably knows more about ocean sunfish than anyone, reports on the carnage that ensues when these fish enter Monterey Bay in the summer. As the unsuspecting fish arrive in the Bay, they are massacred by hordes of sea lions, often very close to shore. Interestingly (from our point of view, if not the fish's), sea lions do different things to different individuals. Sometimes they pull the fins off and swing the body around, then abandon it. Or, they may pull the fins off and take one bite out of the gut, or just go for the gusto and eat most of the body. It's actually quite disquieting to watch the ferocity with which sea lions attack these animals, as these predators slam the bodies vigorously against the water in an attempt to tear through the very thick skin.

Here's a really, really weird story, related to me by Shane Anderson, at UC Santa Barbara. Shane says that on 3 occasions, he has seen octopi hanging onto sunfish in the Santa Barbara Channel. In each case, he spotted gulls pecking on molas and went over to check it out. How could a bottom-dwelling octopus wind up clinging to a surface-living sunfish? One possible transfer point is the drifting kelp mats. Octopi are often found among them, and molas often swim around and through them.

L E T ' S   T A L K   P A R A S I T E S

Really, when you get down to it, what is more fun in life than horrifying your friends and loved ones? One of the quickest, easiest and most amusing ways to do that is to talk about parasites (if you can bring one out of your pocket, so much the better).

Basically, a parasite is an organism that lives on or in another species (the host) and obtains its nourishment from that species. If you look carefully at almost any fish on the Pacific Coast, you will find one or more species of parasites somewhere on or in that host. Generally, larger and older hosts carry more kinds of parasites and more individuals of each kind. Parasites can be found on the external surface of the fish (that's where most people see them), or in any internal area. Most parasites cause little or no damage to their hosts. (This also applies to human hosts. For instance, many of us have an amoeba, *Entamoeba gingivalis*, living in our mouths. This microscopic sucker hangs around our gum lines, waiting for the occasional white blood cell to pop out, but does not appear to cause us any harm.)

I took much of the following information from a pamphlet Mike Moser and I put together for the California Department of Fish and Game (*Common Parasites of California Marine Fish*), in 1978. The illustrations are by Dave Crouch.

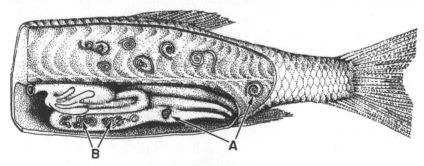

Larval Roundworms
While most fish parasites do not harm humans, there are exceptions and larval roundworms (nematodes) are the big exceptions.

Larval roundworms are found in many marine fishes–in their flesh, on the surface of intestines and livers and in body cavities. These worms are .5-.75 inches long and often resemble (A) a watch spring or (B) a ball of yarn. Collectively known as "anisakids," many live as adults in the intestines of such marine mammals as seals, porpoises, whales and dolphins. The eggs of these worms leave the mammals through their feces. In the water, the worm eggs are eaten by small crustaceans such as krill or copepods, which in turn are eaten by fishes or squids. If this infected host is consumed by the proper marine mammal, the larvae will mature into adults and everyone is more or less contented (the hosts do not seem to be harmed). Unfortunately, if humans eat seafood which contain live larvae, the worms can become active and suddenly no one is particularly enthused. The worm can become nonplussed, finding itself in an environment quite different from that of a marine mammal, and it often responds in a tacky way, burrowing into the stomach lining. This creates lesions or growths on the stomach wall, and someone has to go in and pull the little guys out, yet another event that no one is happy about. This process used to require major surgery; now it can be done with fiber optics. The surgeon puts a little camera down your throat, finds the offender and takes it out orally. Still that's the kind of thing you probably don't want done on a Saturday morning. This disease is called "anisakiasis," or "codworm" or "herringworm" disease. Anisakiasis is fairly common in countries where eating raw or only slightly pickled fish is prevalent (Japan and some northern European countries come to mind). Cases in Japan run to about 1,000 per year.

However, with only a minimal amount of care, these worms will not be a problem. Thorough cooking will kill the larvae. If you want to eat raw fish (and it's a free country, you know), carefully examine the flesh before consuming. These worms are quite obvious and can be easily seen. Just a friendly word of warning. If you are checking your fish in a sushi bar, be subtle. Sushi chefs tend to be armed with cleavers and it is uncool to hold up each piece to the light, while loudly noting, "Don't worry, Margaret, no worms in this piece!" Another approach is to freeze the fish at -4° F for 24–60 hours. Getting people to freeze fish before consumption has proven very effective in the Netherlands, where lightly-pickled herring was responsible for about 300 cases per year. After the "Green Herring Law" was passed, requiring that all herring be frozen at -4° F for 24 hours, anisakiasis cases nearly ceased.

Some fish recipes, such as ceviche, call for an acidic or brine-based marinade. These marinades are not strong enough to kill the larvae. Similarly, the preparation of various popular

Scandinavian salmon dishes, in which the fish are lightly salted and sugared for a couple of days, will not kill the larvae. Basically, it comes down to this: 1) examine and remove all the larvae from the flesh, if it is to be eaten raw, or freeze it for 24-60 hours at 40° F; 2) cook or smoke the fish thoroughly; 3) don't depend on pickling, curing or home refrigeration to kill the larvae. They are tough little dudes.

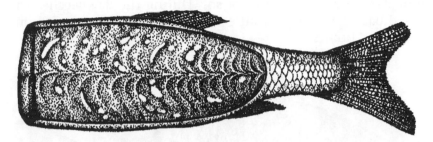

Protozoa

These microscopic organisms are found in a majority of fish species on the Pacific Coast. Most are unnoticeable to the naked eye and only when they form small cysts are they readily apparent. The cysts are most likely to be noted by the casual observer in the flesh of such forms as rockfishes (bocaccio seem a particular target), flatfishes, herrings and salmons. The structures in rockfish are usually white or yellow and are about the size of rice grains. Each cyst contains millions of protozoa and these are harmless, even if consumed raw. I have heard deck hands on sport fishing vessels call these little structures "flavor buds."

I love that.

Leeches

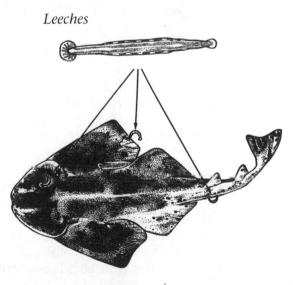

Leeches are found on the body surfaces of a number of species, including sharks, skates, flatfishes, salmons and cabezon. Generally, leeches are elongated, flattened worm-like creatures, with suckers on each end. The smaller sucker surrounds the mouth. Often they can be seen inching their way across the host's body surface. On rough-skinned fishes such as skates and sharks, leeches are found most often on the host's soft stomach or in the spiracle (the holes on the upper part of the fishes' bodies). Typically, leeches feed by making a series of small cuts on the fish's skin and then ingesting the blood. An anticoagulant in the parasite's mouth prevents the blood from clotting. Some species feed as often as once per week, while others only chow down every 6 months or so. During the day, leeches with slicked-back hair sleep in little water-tight coffins strapped onto their hosts' bodies.

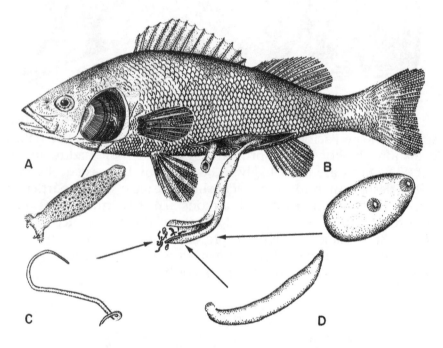

Flukes and Roundworms

These are small, wormlike organisms, usually unnoticed by most folks. They can inhabit any part of a fish's body and most fish on our coast are infected with at least one species: A) monogenetic fluke, B) digenetic fluke, C) adult roundworm (nematode), D) thornyheaded worm.

Tapeworms

Adult tapeworms are found in the intestines of a variety of marine fishes, including the rockfishes, rays, sharks, basses, surfperches, salmons and tunas. Adult tapeworms range in size from an inch to more than a foot in length. They are most often seen crawling from a fish's anus or when the gut is accidentally cut while the fish is being cleaned. Tapeworms attach themselves to

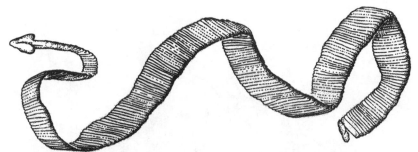

digestive system walls with a "scolex" or head. Tapeworms have no mouths and absorb all their nutrients through their body walls. The parasite's body grows by producing small, reproductive segments (called proglottids). Fortunately for these parasites, tapeworms can fertilize themselves and by the time the proglottid reaches the end of the worm it is full of ripe eggs. The eggs leave the fish through the feces and some are eaten by planktonic animals such as copepods. Inside this host, the larval tapeworm undergoes development in the hopes that its host will be eaten by a fish. If this occurs, further development takes place and the larvae remain there unless or until this second host is eaten by the proper final host. If this does not occur, the tapeworm will never develop into an adult and will probably have to seek some sort of career counseling. Many fish carry larval tapeworms, which often resemble grains of rice and are located on the outside of the stomach or intestines.

Copepods

Copepods (commonly called "fish lice") are extremely common on marine fishes on the exterior surfaces, in mouths, on gills and occasionally inside body cavities. Most people first spot these critters when they notice small organisms scuttling along a fish's skin. Copepods vary dramatically in size, shape and position on or in fishes. Generally, there are 1) those that crawl freely over their hosts and move from fish to fish, 2) those that are less motile and 3) those that are permanently attached to a host. Copepods that crawl around on their hosts are usually flattened and sort of shieldshaped. Many copepods attach themselves to the lining of the mouth and gill cavities and to gill filaments. These rarely move about and some can cause severe gill damage. A number of copepods burrow into the flesh of their hosts. The younger stages make a hole in the skin, insert their head and when the skin heals over, the copepod is permanently attached. Some species will actually penetrate into the host's heart. The most extreme modification of any copepod on our coast is that of *Sarcotaces*, a parasite which lives in the body cavity of rockfish. The male and

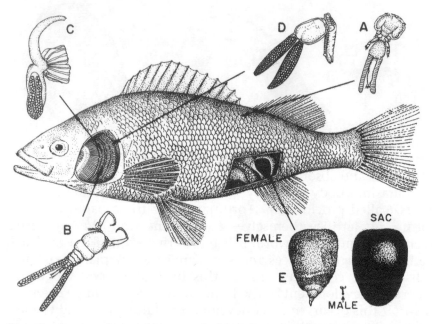

female copepods are surrounded by a sac, which has been formed from intestinal tissue. When the sac is opened, the large female appears to be little more than a pearshaped bag covered with wart-like growths. Males are much smaller than females and shaped like an arrow. Most people come across this parasite when they accidentally cut open the sac while filleting a rockfish, releasing a mass of black, inky fluid (the remains of host blood).

Isopods

Clambering from gill chambers of rockfish, sea perch and various other bottom fishes is this fairly unpleasant customer. Isopods are gill and mouth parasites, and they may eat the gill filaments of their hosts. Distantly related to the com-

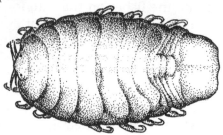

mon garden sowbug or pillbug, isopods are whitish and their bodies are divided into 7 segments, each bearing a sickletipped leg. All of the parasitic isopods on our coast have scientific names which are anagrams of the word "Carolina"; including *Nerocila*, *Rocinela* and *Lironeca*. As the story goes, these organisms were named by Stimpson in the mid-19th Century after his wife, Carolina. Soon after, he developed cholera in Italy and died.

Let that be a lesson to you all.

Incidental Infections

Once in a while, parasites get into humans in unusual ways. Here, from the steamy pages of *Fish Parasites and Human Health* (J. A. Sakanari, M. Moser and T. L. Deardorff, 1995, California Sea Grant College Publication) are two such stories.

"In one case..., a 40-year-old Japanese patient complained of pharyngeal pain, which began about 3 hours after he had eaten raw squid (*Ommastrephes solani pacificus*). During examination, a larval tapeworm (*Nybelinia surmenicola*) was found firmly anchored by its tentacles to one of his tonsils. This was a highly unusual infection since the hooked tentacles of this parasite are not normally extruded in the larval stage."

Whoa, I hate when that happens.

"There have also been reports of cases which resulted from handling infected seafood. In one, involving the fluke *Nanophyetus salminicola*, human transmission occurred during the handling of freshly killed coho salmon. It is likely that the patient ingested the larval parasite when he simultaneously cleaned fish and smoked cigarettes."

In there a moral here, or what?

INDEX TO THE FISHES

YOU SAY YOU WANT MAPS?
OKAY, WE'VE GOT MAPS.

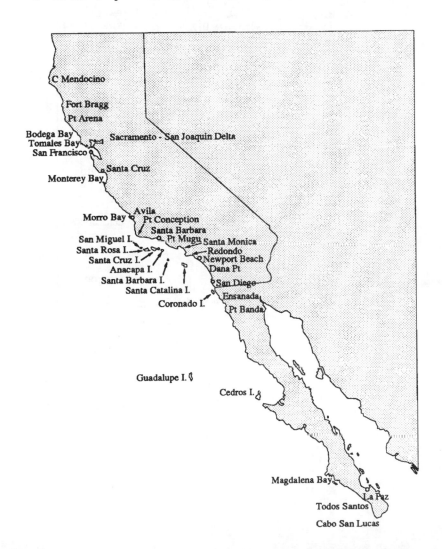

C Mendocino

Fort Bragg

Pt Arena

Bodega Bay
Tomales Bay
San Francisco

Sacramento - San Joaquin Delta

Santa Cruz

Monterey Bay

Avila
Morro Bay
Pt Conception

Santa Barbara

San Miguel I.
Pt Mugu
Santa Monica
Santa Rosa I.
Redondo
Santa Cruz I.
Newport Beach
Anacapa I.
Dana Pt
Santa Barbara I.

Santa Catalina I.
San Diego
Coronado I.
Ensanada
Pt Banda

Guadalupe I.

Cedros I.

Magdalena Bay
La Paz
Todos Santos
Cabo San Lucas

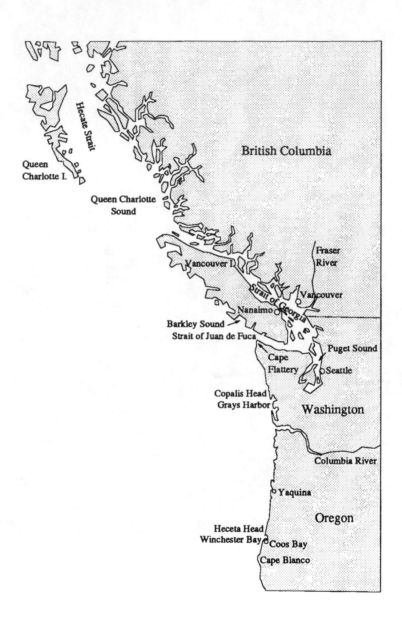

British Columbia

Hecate Strait

Queen
Charlotte I.

Queen Charlotte
Sound

Vancouver I.

Fraser
River

Strait of Georgia

Vancouver

Nanaimo

Barkley Sound
Strait of Juan de Fuca

Puget Sound

Cape
Flattery

Seattle

Copalis Head
Grays Harbor

Washington

Columbia River

Yaquina

Oregon

Heceta Head
Winchester Bay

Coos Bay

Cape Blanco

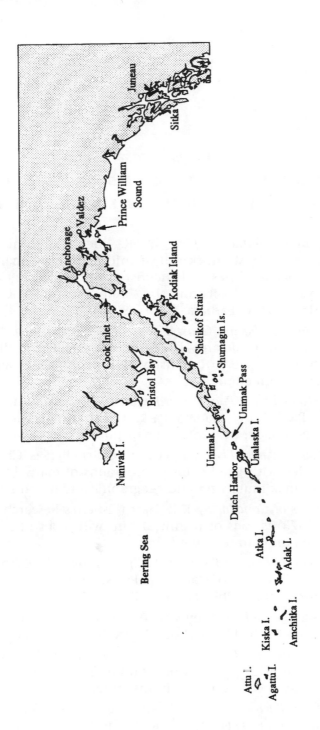

Bering Sea

Nunivak I.

Anchorage
Valdez
Prince William
Sound

Juneau

Sitka

Cook Inlet

Kodiak Island

Bristol Bay

Shelikof Strait

Shumagin Is.

Unimak I.
Unimak Pass
Unalaska I.
Dutch Harbor

Atka I.
Adak I.

Kiska I.
Amchitka I.

Attu I.
Agattu I.

YUMMY FISH
PUBLICATIONS I JUST
KNOW YOU WILL LIKE

A Guide to California Seafood, by R. Price (California Seafood Council, 1994). Just chock full of information on many of the major commercial fishes and shellfishes of the Pacific Coast. It's $40 and you can order it from the California Seafood Council, P. O. Box 91540, Santa Barbara, CA 93190.

A Field Guide to Pacific Coast Fishes of North America, by W. N. Eschmeyer, E. S. Herald and H. Hamman (Houghton Miflin, 1983), is a really fine guide to our fishes, with nice plates and pretty up–to–date information.

Coastal Fishes of the Pacific Northwest, by A. Lamb and P. Edgell (Harbour Publishing, Madera Park, British Columbia, 1986), is another good book, with lots of color photographs.

Pacific Coast Inshore Fishes, by D. W. Gotshall (Sea Challengers, 1989) is filled with good color photographs of many local fishes, along with maximum sizes and geographic and depth ranges.

Pacific Fishes of Canada, by J. L. Hart (Fisheries Research Board of Canada, 1973) is tons of technical fun, with gobs of life history information on many marine fishes.

Marine Food and Game Fishes of California, by J. E. Fitch and R.J. Lavenberg (University of California Press, 1971), is a little treasure trove of interesting tidbits about California fishes.

Inland Fishes of California, by P. B. Moyle (University of California Press, 1976) is the best book about the freshwater fishes of that state.

Fish: An Enthusiasts's Guide, by P. B. Moyle (University of California Press, 1993). A nice, peppy introduction to fishes, in all their piscine glory. A really good first book on this rather complex subject.

Fishes of the Pacific Coast: Alaska to Baja, including the Gulf of California and the Galapagos Islands, by G. Goodson (Stanford University Press), contains a fair amount of information and, of just as much importance, lots of color illustrations.

ABOUT THE AUTHOR

Dr. Robin Milton Love is a moderately well-respected marine biologist at the Marine Science Institute, University of California, Santa Barbara. He has written quite a few scientific papers on the marine fishes of the Pacific Coast and he thinks he knows more about these animals than just about anyone. No one knows if this is really true or if he just has an ego the size of Mount Kilimanjaro.

Dr. Love claims he is a channel for Zoxxar, 230th ruler of the Kwarkarkians, a race of space aliens which once occupied 837 planets. Even as you read these words, Dr. Love states that the last remnants of this great race are on a single spaceship, heading for Earth. Unfortunately, on their way here, Zoxxar and the Kwarkarkians stopped off at Xandar 9, home planet of the Xandarians, the official bookies of the Lesser Magellenic Cloud. There they placed what, in retrospect, was an unfortunate bet on Quagtster's Lil' Toaster Cozy in the 812th race at Blorgrett. Finding themselves without sufficient funds to cover the resulting loss, they had to depart from Xandar in somewhat unseemly haste. Pursued by a number of irritated Xandarians (Plate 41), Zoxxar reports that both his ship and life support system were damaged. Zoxxar has made Dr. Love promise that he will prepare an emergency landing site that, as fate would have it, lies directly atop Rodeo Drive, in Beverly Hills. Dr. Love estimates he will need about $100 million to buy up enough of that area for the landing pad. Fortunately, Dr. Love is a man of honor and he pledges that some of the profits from each book sold will go toward purchasing Rodeo Drive.

WHEN ONE BOOK IS NOT ENOUGH!

That's right. In this possession-obsessed society, where your very worth as a human being is measured in the sheer tonnage of items clasped to bosom, one of anything is not enough. This is particularly true of *Probably More Than You Want to Know About the Fishes of the Pacific Coast*, the standard by which all other things material is measured. In the name of John Maynard Keynes, don't be found wanting! Here's your chance to order way more copies than you can use, thus propelling yourself into the Pantheon of Immortal Consumers and, parenthetically, helping to pad my SEPP-IRA account.

Name _____

Address _____

            Street   Apt. #

            _____

            City   State   Zip Code

Cost: $19.95, plus handling and mailing.
          TOTAL: $22.45
          California Residents, please add sales tax.
          TOTAL: $24.00

For your safety and our peace of mind, please send checks only. Cash has a peculiar way of disappearing without a trace.

    ❐   Yes. *Probably More Than You Want to Know About the Fishes of the Pacific Coast* has changed my life for the better. I have more energy, have lost 27 lbs. (mostly around my hips and thighs) and am now sorry for insinuating all those terrible things about Adriana G. in the eighth grade.

    ❐   No. *Probably More Than You Want to Know About the Fishes of the Pacific Coast* has not changed my life in the least. I am still that repellent reptile everyone despised in high school.

Really Big Press
P.O. Box 60123
Santa Barbara, CA 93160